Spain

Spain

A Unique History

Stanley G. Payne

THE UNIVERSITY OF WISCONSIN PRESS

Publication of this volume has been made possible, in part,
through support from
**the Program for Cultural Cooperation
between Spain's Ministry of Culture and
United States Universities.**

The University of Wisconsin Press
1930 Monroe Street, 3rd Floor
Madison, Wisconsin 53711-2059
uwpress.wisc.edu

3 Henrietta Street
London WCE 8LU, England
eurospanbookstore.com

Originally published in Spain as *España: Una historia única*,
copyright © 2008 by Stanley G. Payne, Jésus Cuéllar (trans.),
Ediciones Temas de Hoy, S.A. (T.H.)
English edition copyright © 2011
The Board of Regents of the University of Wisconsin System

1   3   5   4   2

Printed in the United States of America

Library of Congress Cataloging-in-Publication Data
Payne, Stanley G.
[España. English]
Spain: a unique history / Stanley G. Payne.
p.   cm.
Includes bibliographical references and index.
Originally published in Spain as España: una historia única, c2008.
ISBN 978-0-299-25024-9 (pbk.: alk. paper)
ISBN 978-0-299-24933-5 (e-book)
1. Spain—History. 2. Spain—Historiography. I. Title.
DP63.P1913   2011
946—dc22
2010015039

To the memory of

Francisco Javier de Lizarza Inda

(1928–2007),

most loyal of friends

Contents

Contents

Maps

Abbreviations

ARMH	Asociación para la Recuperación de la Memoria Histórica (Association for the Recovery of Historical Memory)
BOC	Bloque Obrero y Campesino (Workers and Peasants Bloc)
CEDA	Confederación Española de Derechas Autónomas (Spanish Confederation of Autonomous Rightist Groups)
CNT	Confederación Nacional del Trabajo (National Confederation of Labor)
ETA	Euskadi Ta Askatasuna (Basque Homeland and Freedom)
FAI	Federación Anarquista Ibérica (Iberian Anarchist Federation)
FET	Falange Española Tradicionalista (later Movimiento Nacional)
ICGP	International Conference Group on Portugal
INI	Instituto Nacional de Industria (National Institute of Industry)
JSU	Juventudes Socialistas Unificadas (United Socialist Youth)
NDH	Independent State of Croatia
ORGA	Organización Regional Gallega Autónoma (Autonomous Regional Organization of Galicia)
PCE	Partido Comunista de España (Communist Party of Spain)
PNV	Partido Nacionalista Vasco (Basque Nationalist Party)
POUM	Partido Obrero de Unificación Marxista (Workers' Party of Marxist Unification)
PSOE	Partido Socialista Obrero Español (Spanish Socialist Workers' Party)
PSUC	Partit Socialist Unificat de Catalunya (United Socialist Party of Catalonia)
SSPHS	Society for Spanish and Portuguese Historical Studies
UCD	Unión de Centro Democrático (Union of Democratic Center)

Spain

Introduction

The Image of Spain

All history is specific and singular, and therefore in key respects unique. Though certain similarities may be observed, all history is also in some sense "different," just as all human beings have many things in common yet in every case remain different individuals. At a certain level of comparison and abstraction many common factors and characteristics may be identified in the histories of diverse countries, yet the history of every land also remains individual and in important ways different from all others.

Some histories have seemed more singular, more different from the supposed norm, than others, and in western Europe the history of Spain has for several centuries been considered the most unique. What has often been called "the problem of Spain" first emerged in the seventeenth century with the decline in military and economic power, accompanied by an early failure in "modernization," even though issues of unity and stability were resolved in terms of maintaining the status quo. After the great work of Juan de Mariana was published in 1602, Spaniards virtually ceased to write general histories of Spain, an activity that became increasingly the work of French and British authors during the eighteenth century.

Foreign historians tended to see Spain's history as different from the supposed western European norm and also as problematic. Although the nationalist historiography of the nineteenth and twentieth centuries claimed to resolve the problems, many have not agreed. Claudio Sánchez Albornoz, for example, was one of the greatest Spanish medievalists during the twentieth century. He lived half his life as a Republican émigré in Buenos Aires, but he was also a practicing Catholic and ardent Spanish patriot. When he published a massive two-volume interpretation of his nation's history in 1956, he titled it *España, un enigma histórico*.

Attitudes toward major aspects of Spanish history have generally been more negative and critical than to any other west European country. This begins with the evaluation of the Visigoths, often seen as divided, inept, and quickly decadent. The medieval kingdoms have been viewed as peripheral and backward, the Reconquest as dubious, conflictive, and long delayed. While the relative tolerance of a large and thriving Jewish community in the Middle Ages might have earned Spain good marks, the Inquisition and the subsequent expulsion brought opprobrium. The use of Habsburg military power and the terms of the conquest of America generated widespread criticism, while the seventeenth-century decline was soon seen as the most classic case of "decadence" since the fall of Rome. From that time on Spain has been viewed in varying ways as a special "problem," defined in varying terms—and sometimes with regard to quite different issues—from the seventeenth century to the present.

This was less the case during the Middle Ages when Spain was perceived as a normal and regular, if geographically peripheral, part of Latin Christendom. The popularity of the pilgrimage to Santiago de Compostela rivaled that of Rome, while the struggle against the Muslims sometimes took an international character, as foreign crusaders and adventurers intermittently flocked to the peninsula. In the later Middle Ages Italian merchants increasingly found commerce and finance in Spain to be lucrative, while the crowns of Aragon and Castile played normal roles in the west Mediterranean and west European international systems.

The sixteenth century was characterized by a growth in Spanish prestige, somewhat counterbalanced by the steep rise in criticism and denunciation that Julián Juderías would baptize four centuries later as the Black Legend. Diplomatic and military prestige was very high, soon to be accompanied by cultural influence. Castilian became an international language, and by the beginning of the seventeenth century Spanish literature was widely read abroad, either in Castilian or in translation. Spain was a religious leader as well, along with Italy playing one of the dominant roles in the Counter-Reformation. Classic Spanish religious writings in theology and philosophy, such as those of Francisco Suárez or Luis de Granada, would sometimes be read extensively, even in Protestant countries, into the eighteenth century.

During the late sixteenth century, a dual image of Spain developed. On the one hand was respect for the empire and for the monarchy's military power (strongly tinged with fear), accompanied by respect for its literary and intellectual culture, all the while coexisting with the Black Legend stereotype of cruelty, fanaticism, and lust for power and destruction. As military power declined, negative stereotypes increased, though their content began to change.

To be sure, west Europeans had found Spain an exotic place even in the fifteenth century, with an oriental touch in so far as it was the only western land where sizable numbers of Jews and Muslims might be found. As travel increased during the sixteenth and seventeenth centuries, visitors, especially those from France, left an increasing number of accounts. They could not get used to smaller portions of food, the absence of beer and butter, the heavy use of garlic, olive oil, and saffron. Xenophobia was common throughout Europe, but the Spanish seemed more xenophobic than most. Arrogance was the quality most commented on about Spaniards both at home and abroad, while visitors were also taken aback by the egalitarian manners of the lower classes, finding that beggars insisted on being addressed as "señor" and requested almsgivers to remove their hats when providing charity.[1]

The most positive evaluation seems to have been made from the opposite end of Europe. The elite of Catholic Poland, on the extreme eastern frontier of Western civilization, facing Muscovy and also sometimes the Turkish empire, developed some sense of affinity with a Catholic Spain on the borderlands of Christendom far to the west and south. Polish leaders who intervened in Russia during its early seventeenth-century "Time of Troubles" likened themselves to Spanish conquistadores extending the frontiers of Catholicism and European civilization.[2] Later, in a manner partially parallel with the decline of Spain, the large Polish-Lithuanian empire in eastern Europe would falter, then eventually disappear from the map altogether. By the early nineteenth century the historian Jan Lelewel would develop a broad comparative and parallel history of Poland and of Spain from the sixteenth through the eighteenth centuries.[3] Even in the twenty-first century, Polish commentators are the least likely to engage in "politically correct" criticism and commentary on developments in Spain.

Broadly speaking, the content of foreign images and stereotypes of Spain has changed its terms and emphases in different historical eras.[4] These may be roughly categorized as (1) the classic Black Legend stereotype of the sixteenth and seventeenth centuries; (2) "enlightened" criticism of the second half of the seventeenth and eighteenth centuries; (3) the "romantic Spain" myth of the nineteenth century; and (4) the composite stereotypes of the late nineteenth and twentieth centuries, which revived aspects of each of the foregoing versions, sometimes adding to them contemporary political content that often created new myths and stereotypes.

What they all have in common is the penchant for stereotyping, simplification, and Manicheanism, with little or no concern for the diversity of Spain, not merely in term of its regions but also with regard to varying political values or projects, cultural attitudes, and practices, and even differences in religious emphasis. At the same time, we should recognize that much of the content in these images and stereotypes was first developed by the Spanish themselves, beginning with Fray Bartolomé de las Casas in the sixteenth century. In more recent times, particularly, nearly all the most absurd and exaggerated statements about Spanish culture and history have been made by Spaniards themselves.

The Black Legend viewed the Spanish as cruel, bloodthirsty, sadistic, power-hungry, and monstrously destructive, while "enlightened" attitudes from the late seventeenth century on described a militarily weakened Spain as no longer cruel or dangerously destructive, but as a land inhabited by proud, lazy, ignorant, and unproductive people, dominated by hollow vanity and spiritual benightedness.[5] Spaniards were no longer to be hated and feared, but rather to be pitied and scorned.

The early nineteenth century became a time of "paradigm shift," with a new emphasis placed on the romantic and the picturesque, increasingly interpreted in terms more favorable to the Spanish. Foreigner travelers had often found elements of the exotic and picturesque in the country, but in earlier times evaluated such aspects in a negative manner as typical features of a strange and rather hostile land. The French, British, and American travelers and writers, who forged the "romantic Spain" myth in the first half of the nineteenth century, focused on certain stereotypes that they interpreted as the enchanting reflection of a distinct pre-modern, pre-industrial culture possessing positive features, which, if not superior (or even equal) to those of their own countries, were at least worthy of esteem. The formerly fanatical Spanish were now seen as people of faith and ardent commitment who spurned the crass materialism of northern countries. What was once called ignorance was now viewed as a sense of honor disappearing from the commercial society of other lands. Behavior once denounced as violent now betokened courage and the capacity for self-sacrifice. The rudeness and egalitarianism of the lower classes was no longer evaluated as a Spanish grotesquerie of the uncouth but as the survival of a sense of authentic and individual personality no longer found in the humdrum world of London and Paris.[6]

"Romantic Spain" was no more real than the Black Legend, to which it was related, and was not by any means uniformly positive in its evaluation but gave a new twist to the old stereotypes. From the early nineteenth century the two visions often coexisted in the images of Spain held in other western lands, being vaguely combined in modified forms by many observers and commentators. The comparatively slow rate of modernization during the nineteenth century served only to perpetuate these stereotypes, as did the political and military failures of the period. The romantic Spain motif was so firmly established as late as the mid-twentieth century that the tourist program of the Franco regime even co-opted certain aspects of it in the commercially successful "Spain is Different" tourist promotions of the 1950s.[7]

All this did nothing, however, to incorporate the history of Spain into the broader history of Europe, for it meant that Spain continued to be seen as an exception, a kind of Other. Aside from its success in occupying much of the Western Hemisphere, the place of Spain within broader European and Western history from the fifteenth century on continued to be viewed as either negative and destructive or passive, relatively nonparticipatory, and irrelevant. The partial exception was medieval Spanish history, which was seen to play a certain role in Europe's development. A deeper, more comprehensive and objective treatment of Spanish history by scholars abroad would emerge with the great expansion of historical studies in the 1960s and afterwards. Even then, progress at first would be limited, for some of the foreign scholars writing about contemporary Spain in the second half of the twentieth century had only a limited grasp of Spanish history as a whole, and so in their comments on earlier periods would either consciously or unconsciously repeat certain standard tropes drawn from the myths of romantic Spain or the Black Legend, or both.[8]

Only the completion of socioeconomic and educational modernization during the later years of Franco, followed by the success of the democratic Transition, would finally put an end to most of these stereotypes, at least with regard to contemporary Spain. There, by the end of the century, the old myths would, as J. N. Hillgarth puts it, "be replaced by an even more misleading generalization, that Spain is a European country with a historical trajectory exactly like any other."[9] The work of the historian is never done.

Part I

The Formation of a Hispanist

The study of Spain is rather unique among scholarly enterprises in having become an "ism"—"Hispanism." Scholarly activity is normally recognized as an "ism" only when it pertains to a very broad field of study, as in "classicism" and "orientalism," not with regard to a single country. Foreign scholars who study Germany or Russia are sometimes described as Germanists or Russianists, but the term "Germanism" or "Russianism" is not normally applied. The word "hispanista" was originally used in Spain during the late nineteenth century in two different senses, one of them being equivalent to panhispanista or hispanoamericanista, applied to those who sought closer ties among all Spanish-speaking countries, the second referring to foreign scholars who dedicated themselves to studying Spanish themes. During the first half of the twentieth century, the second sense of the term came to predominate.

Hispanism originated during the nineteenth century, parallel to the estheticism of the "romantic Spain" concept developed primarily by the writers and artists of France and England. As distinct from the latter, however, scholarly Hispanism developed at the same time as the expansion of the universities, even though it was vitally assisted by independent scholars and philanthropists. Although individual Hispanists might be found throughout western Europe, their work appeared especially in French and English, and to a lesser degree in German, during the course of the nineteenth century, developing rapidly in the United States. By 1909 Martin Hume, perhaps the leading British Hispanist of his generation, would declare that the North American academic world "now stands absolutely pre-eminent in this branch of learning." Three years later, in a lecture in Salamanca, Miguel de Unamuno expressed much the same judgment.[1]

The origins of Hispanism in the United States are complex.[2] Hume referred to what he termed an "instinctive mutual attraction" between Spain and the United States, but that is probably an exaggeration. The remote origins of the United States lie in Elizabethan England, for whom Spain was the major enemy and which sedulously cultivated what more than three centuries later would be termed the "Black Legend," certainly not a promising beginning. Moreover, during the eighteenth century, the government of Spain was generally aligned with France, the principal enemy of Great Britain, and the attitudes of the Black Legend continued to inform American attitudes during the nineteenth century, and to some extent during the first half of the twentieth century as well.

Spain was much more important for the United States during the early years of the American republic than it would be later. The empire reached its all-time greatest geographical extent just as the United States was being born in the 1770s, and the revival of the Spanish navy meant that it continued to be a European power of some significance. The intervention of Spain on behalf of the thirteen colonies in their war of independence against Great Britain was of some importance in the American victory, while imperial Spain would continue to be the southern neighbor of the United States throughout the first generation of its existence.[3] The fledgling American republic initially established only three full-scale embassies (as distinct from more modest legations) abroad, in London, Paris, and Madrid, relations with Spain being surpassed in importance only by those with Britain and France. Even after most of America was lost to the Spanish crown, two of the three territories closest to the United States—Cuba and Puerto Rico—were retained, so that Spain would remain an important neighbor throughout the nineteenth century, a relationship that reached a violent climax in 1898. After that, connections with Spain dwindled, though they became more important again during the Second World War and the Cold War.

Interest in Spain among American scholars seems to have stemmed from three sources: (1) the importance of classical Spanish literature, which always enjoyed respect in the English-speaking world, facilitated by the fact that Spanish is not a difficult language for English-speaking people to learn to read; (2) the importance of relations with Spain during the nineteenth century; and (3) the sense of Spain and of Spanish culture as fundamental to the greater Western Hemisphere, and therefore of greater importance to the United States than these would be to most European countries.

Its scholarly origins stem from the second quarter of the nineteenth century. George Erving, chargé d'affaires of the Madrid embassy during the 1820s, may be considered the first American Hispanist scholar, publishing the first book to appear in English on the language and culture of the Basques. American writers of the same generation also helped to develop the myth of romantic Spain. Washington Irving (in this regard the earliest ancestor of Ernest Hemingway) published the longest-lived of all American books on Spain, *Tales from the Alhambra* (1831), which remains in print after nearly two centuries. A considerable number of travel books and historical works published by Americans during the nineteenth century continued in this vein. The first major work of erudite Hispanism was George Ticknor's *History of Spanish Literature* (1849), followed by the widely read works of the historian William Hickling Prescott.[4] Prescott was, in fact, the first major American historian of any European country; thus, at least in serious American historiography, Hispanism initially led the way. Not for another half century would subsequent American historians of Europe rise to Prescott's level in terms of primary research and interpretative synthesis, and his achievement was all the more notable in that he was nearly blind.

It may have been Prescott, even more than Irving, who set the tone. He was the greatest Hispanist historian of his era in any country, but Prescott provided a sort of canonical statement of the Black Legend during the nineteenth century, defining what Richard Kagan has termed the "Prescott paradigm," which would long dominate attitudes toward Spain. This interpretation made of Spain the very opposite of the United States, its intrinsic antithesis. "America was the future—republican, entrepreneurial, rational; while Spain—monarchist, indolent, fanatical—represented the past."[5] This vision—vision more than analysis—would be repeated in a series of books on Spain, the American Southwest, and Latin America during the nineteenth century, and would resonate on a broader, more popular level during the Spanish-American War of 1898.

There was, however, from the mid-nineteenth century on a minority current within American writing about Spain that was less negative and rather more objective toward the country's problems. Its first major exponent was the Baltimore lawyer and sometime diplomat Severn T. Wallis, who published two judicious and well-balanced books between 1849 and 1853 about contemporary Spanish problems.[6] Wallis did not find Spain to be hopelessly deformed by history, culture, or national character, but to be suffering from a series of problems and flawed policies, which were amenable to reform and need not permanently handicap the country.[7] This minority current, however, would not completely come to the fore until the beginning of the full flowering of a later Anglo-North American Hispanism in the field of history during the 1960s.

Somewhat ironically, the Spanish-American War more or less coincided with the initial flourishing of American Hispanism at a high scholarly level, the product of the expansion of American universities during the latter part of the nineteenth century. The next century would bring the opening of the privately funded Hispanic Society of America in New York, and then completion of the classic study of the Inquisition by Henry Charles Lea. Despite the major work of historians such as Prescott and Lea (and later Robert B. Merriman), American Hispanism would focus heavily on the esthetic, with the proliferation of "Spanish departments" in American colleges and universities, departments dedicated almost exclusively to the study and teaching of language and literature.[8] During the first half of the twentieth century, Spanish history (by comparison, at least) probably received less attention than it had earlier, and more often than not was entirely missing from history curricula, although the study of Latin American history slowly and steadily expanded. As it was, the study of Spanish history was nearly nonexistent when I entered graduate school in 1955.

Moreover, arguably the only book in English at that time that had attempted a searching analysis of the problems of contemporary Spain was Gerald Brenan's *The Spanish Labyrinth* (1944). Based on Brenan's experience of more than a decade in Spain and his research in secondary literature in the British Museum, it probed many of the key political and social issues, often with a depth and originality not to be found elsewhere. Nonetheless, despite Brenan's lengthy personal experience in the country, he often got lost in his labyrinth and sometimes fell far short of objectivity. As William Phillips has pointed out, in his broader judgments and conclusions Brenan often fell back on his own reworking of the stereotypes of both the Black Legend and "romantic Spain." He insisted on the existence of a national character dominated by spontaneity and by "faith," a "religious ideal" that did not stem from Christianity (since Brenan was not a Christian) but instead "is doubtless due fundamentally to the influence of Moorish ideas in Christian communities. The deepest strata of Spanish thought and political sentiment are oriental."[9] Only in the final years of his life did Brenan retract such stereotypes in an article published in the Madrid daily *El País*.

The question most frequently asked me, especially in Spain, was what led me to become a Hispanist in the first place. This was never part of any careful plan but simply developed as a consequence of a series of events and experiences, some of them perfectly fortuitous. I was born in 1934 in north Texas in Denton, just to the north of Dallas, then a small town of around 12,000 inhabitants. My parents were "northerners" who had moved to Texas from Colorado in the hope of encountering better economic conditions during the Great Depression, a hope that was completely disappointed. Denton was not part of Hispanic south or southwest Texas, but was almost entirely Anglo-American (with a small segregated black population) and culturally more part of the southern "Bible Belt." There were very few Mexicans, though a slight influence of Mexican food was noticeable. During my four years in elementary school in Denton, I only very briefly had one classmate who was bilingual in Spanish.

During World War II, however, the Texas Board of Education decided that the new global context made it desirable that all Texas schoolchildren, from at least the fifth year of elementary education, should study a foreign language. This was done in a very simple and rudimentary way, having the homeroom teacher simply insert two hours of language study per week into the existing curriculum. Few, if any, of the teachers were particularly expert in a foreign language, but the language almost universally chosen was Spanish, which had already become the one most widely studied in the country. There was one Mexican girl in my class, named Carmen, who happened to be relatively bilingual, and it quickly became apparent to me that Carmen possessed a fluency and precision of pronunciation that quite surpassed our teacher, so that I tried to pattern my pronunciation on that of Carmen. The amount of Spanish that I learned in this way was nonetheless minimal. In June 1944 my family became part of the great wartime migration to California, where language instruction in the elementary schools was not practiced, but nonetheless my brief exposure to Spanish during 1943–44 had, in retrospect, set a precedent.

The standard curriculum in American secondary schools at that time offered (indeed, required) foreign language study only during the final two years. In the larger schools the choice lay between Spanish, French, and German, and it seemed natural that I chose Spanish. When I entered university-level studies at Pacific Union College in the Napa Valley in 1951, I found that the curriculum required both a major and a minor field of concentration. It was a foregone conclusion that for me the former would be history. I had been strongly attracted to history since my early childhood, though my reading had been informed much more by stories of Indian fighting and historical novels than by scholarly studies. Yet approaching history through the imagination was almost undoubtedly the best way for a boy to do so, and it gave me a certain empathy with the past that I could then apply in a more systematic and scholarly fashion later on.

For my minor field of concentration I chose Spanish, without the slightest hesitation, simply because I found studying the language interesting and congenial. At the age of seventeen or eighteen I had little if any thought of using it in a serious way. Moreover, studies in Spanish or about Spanish-speaking countries in the United States had come to focus primarily on Latin America, not Spain. Thus as an undergraduate I learned something about Spanish literature but almost nothing about the history of Spain, nor, for that matter, did the latter then interest me in the slightest. For me, serious historical study revolved around the United States, England, Germany, and Russia. I did learn to read Spanish reasonably well and began to develop a modest conversational ability in the language, but I still had not a thought of using it for more advanced work. My principal research paper dealt with the Colombian poet José Asunción Silva, not with a Spanish writer, and when my Spanish instructor suggested that I might want to learn Portuguese as well, I shrugged the suggestion off, having at that point no particular interest in the Iberian Peninsula. (I could not have imagined that within less than twenty years I would become, so far as I know, the only American historian ever to write a history of Portugal.)

My most absorbing interest in history and culture, during the last two of my four years as an undergraduate, was focused on Russia. At that time, immediately after the death of Stalin, the Soviet Union seemed at the height of its power, but I was more attracted by the literature and culture of Russia, and by its history prior to Communism. This seemed to me the most singular and fascinating of European histories, because of the uniqueness of the culture and the character of its development. The Russian language was not taught at my small college, however, so I was not prepared to enter a doctoral program as a candidate in Russian history. I made application to the Russian Institute at Columbia University, then the leading center of Russian studies, but the institute asked for further letters of recommendation, a response that was held up for some three months in the mail. By the time that it arrived, the deadline had long since passed, together with my principal opportunity to become a Russianist. But "no hay mal que por bien no venga" (there is no ill that doesn't lead to good)—this breakdown in mail delivery proved a blessing in disguise. Temperamentally I would have been unsuited to research in the Soviet Union, which would have been a source of endless irritation and frustration. Undoubtedly I would have accomplished much less in that field, but I never abandoned altogether my interest in Russia. Even after beginning research on Spanish history, I took six weeks during the summer of 1956 to enroll at the University of California–Berkeley in order to begin the study of the Russian language. In retrospect, however, I never necessarily curse inefficient mail service, because in 1955 it had possibly changed the course of my life for the better. I received only one good offer of a fellowship to begin graduate study in 1955. It came from the Claremont Graduate School (now Claremont University), one of the cluster of colleges in Claremont, at the eastern end of Los Angeles County in Southern California. Claremont provided the encouragement to begin work on Spanish history and also an attractive and supportive environment for me to gain the experience needed to make the transition from a small college in a rural setting in northern California to a much more complex and sophisticated scholarly environment in Columbia University and the city of New York two years later.

It was during the summer of 1955 that I first developed an interest in Spain as a possible area of research, stemming from two books that I read at that time. One was a treatment of Spanish society and culture, *The Spanish Temper* (1954), by the noted British literary critic (and avocational Hispanist) V. S. Pritchett; the other was a book on Spanish art history, focusing especially on the Middle Ages, whose title and author I have long since forgotten. These two works were in fact the first that I had ever selected to read on Spain (aside from the minimal reading required in literature courses) and both fired my imagination, for the very first time giving me the idea that Spain might be a genuinely interesting—and original—area of study. Since at Claremont I had been accepted in modern European history but was obviously not going to be specializing in Russia—a field not then offered at Claremont—I had to find a focus for my initial research.

The faculty at Claremont were completely receptive to the idea of working on Spain, which seemed to them both valid and original. I had two different faculty advisors, the first being Henry Cord Meyer in German history, who served as my Europeanist advisor. I also worked for him as a research assistant and learned a great deal from him about becoming a professional scholar and about European history more generally.

There was no one at Claremont who specialized in the modern history of Spain, as indeed no such field was offered in any other graduate school, though a very few American scholars, such as C. J. Bishko at Virginia, worked in earlier Spanish history. Gabriel Jackson at that time was teaching at Wellesley College, but this was a women's institution with no doctoral program. At Claremont I was therefore referred to the only professor who taught Latin American history, Hubert Herring.

This was a fortunate encounter, for at that time Herring was one of the few Latin Americanists in the United States with an interest in Spain. Herring had been at one time a Protestant missionary in Latin America, but later turned to an academic career and was best known for a popular textbook on general Latin American history, *Good Neighbors*, published in 1955. He had visited Spain three times and at least had some sense of the country.

Herring encouraged my interest and also suggested a very fruitful research topic. I myself had few ideas about that, for the notion of working on Spain had just entered my mind, and I had had neither time nor opportunity for the preliminary reading needed to select a topic. I believe that I first suggested Manuel Azaña as a topic; besides Franco, he was one of the few figures in contemporary Spanish history that I had even heard of. Little did I suspect that he would later become a sort of bête noire of mine.

Herring, to his credit, wanted me to do something different and rather more original. He suggested the figure of José Antonio Primo de Rivera, whom I had never heard of, but I responded instinctively to Herring's guidance and to what seemed to me an interesting project. This became my master's thesis, a two-hundred-page study titled "José Antonio Primo de Rivera and the Beginning of Falange Española" (Claremont Graduate School, 1957), which focused on the movement during the years 1933–36.

This was a mere start, and I assumed that I would have to switch to a completely different theme for my doctoral dissertation. Consequently I had no idea that this was only the first step in what would become a fifty-year involvement with the history of Falangism and Franquismo, and later with the comparative history of fascism in general. I had no personal research "agenda" and at that time had no more interest in fascism and/or the radical Right than in a dozen other themes. Moreover, at that time there was no such field as "fascist studies," and those would begin to emerge only in the following decade of the 1960s.

I wrote to José María de Areilza, then ambassador in Washington, asking for any materials that he might be able to provide, and he sent to me copies of the *Obras completas* and the *Biografía apasionada* by Felipe Ximénez de Sandoval. The only primary data that I had to consult was the complete collection of *El Sol* for the years of the Republic, then held in the library of UCLA, not far away. This gave me a relatively accurate and objective account of the first street violence between Falangists and the Left in 1933–34.

It is important to understand that none of my professors, not even Herring, knew anything in detail about contemporary Spanish history, so I had the total personal responsibility of the autodidact. I never complained about this, because I have a good deal of intellectual independence and felt perfectly capable of learning Spanish history on my own.

During this first phase, the only professor with whom I talked who had extensive personal knowledge of contemporary Spanish affairs was the Catalan Socialist and former Republican diplomat, Luis Monguió, then at Mills College in Oakland. Like Francisco García Lorca and a number of other professional diplomats who had supported the Republic, after the Civil War Monguió became a professor of Spanish and Latin American literature, and soon joined the Spanish Department at the University of California–Berkeley. Perhaps his major work was a volume of criticism that appeared during these years on *La poesía posmodernista peruana*; this caught my eye because I have always considered Peruvian postmodernism the most interesting school of poetry in Latin America during the twentieth century.

Time and distance had not moderated nor added any complexity to Monguió's understanding of contemporary Spanish politics, which he assured me was simply a class struggle between "exploiters" and "exploited." When I pointed out to him that my preliminary research indicated that under the Republic lethal violence was first used in Madrid by the Left and not by Falangists, he simply dismissed the data out of hand as erroneous. This was my first experience of the extraordinary imperviousness of the Spanish Left to any critical research findings, and to their persistent use of a mythified treatment of history. At that time, however, I merely attributed this to the personal idiosyncrasy of Monguió, for I was then strongly sympathetic to the Left.

Since Claremont did not at that time offer the doctorate in European history, after two years I had to move on for my doctoral studies. Only in 1956–57 did I come firmly to abandon any further consideration of working in Russian history. I had a brief chat with Nicholas Riazanovsky in the summer of 1956 at Berkeley, where I studied the Russian language intensively for six weeks, and he told me that he judged that the field of Russian history was becoming adequately developed and no longer in such need of young scholars as had been the case a few years earlier. My last Russianist application, to study with Donald Treadgold at the University of Washington in 1956, had produced only the meager offer of an alternate teaching assistantship, and I then put that offer firmly behind me.

In 1957 I applied for admission to the doctoral programs at Harvard, Columbia, and Chicago. All three admitted me and offered a fellowship, though only in the case of Chicago was the fellowship large enough to pay my full expenses for a year. I decided to accept the fellowship at Columbia not because that university was any more prestigious than the other two, but because I calculated that a university in a city like New York would be more likely to have the resources to foster research in a new field such as the contemporary history of Spain. This was not something that I knew for a fact but more an intuitive hunch or wager, which, in fact, turned out to be exactly correct.

Columbia proved to be the best choice for three different reasons. First, it had adopted an accelerated doctoral program, which required of students already possessing a master's degree scarcely more than two semesters of class work (most of which could be taken simply as "registration credit"), as well as a written qualifying examination and a two-hour oral examination for the doctorate, before moving on to dissertation research. Thus, given the powers of concentration that I possessed at that time, I had only to spend one academic year meeting requirements at Columbia, whereas at Harvard and Chicago two full years or more would have been required. This enabled me to move much more rapidly and greatly eased the potential financial strain, since I was otherwise hard put to finance graduate study.

Second, I had the good fortune to have Shepard Clough as my adviser at Columbia, although I had not been aware of this ahead of time, and it formed no part of the reasoning behind my selection of that university. It turned out that Clough had served on the admissions and fellowship committee of the History Department the year before and had urged that a fellowship be offered to the potential young candidate in Spanish history. Clough was a former student of Carlton J. H. Hayes, who had been ambassador in Madrid during 1942–45; Clough was a specialist in modern French and Italian economic history. About that time, his *Economic History of Modern Italy* was awarded a prize by the Italian government. Clough had no knowledge of Spanish history but thought it useful and even important that others study the topic. Thus I became the first of several students to carry out research on Spain under Clough (the next would be Edward Malefakis). He strongly supported my work, helping me to obtain a fulsome research fellowship from the Social Science Research Council (SSRC), which would in fact provide more money than I could spend in the very inexpensive Spain of 1958–59.

The third advantage that I derived from Columbia was key contacts with the Spanish émigré community, which worked out even better than I had hoped. The first Republican exile I met was Emilio González López, who had been one of the two key leaders of the Organización Regional Gallega Autónoma (ORGA), the main party of the Galicianist Left Republicans (its other principal leader being Casares Quiroga). In exile Don Emilio was for many years professor of Spanish literature at Hunter College (City University of New York), and I had several fruitful conversations with him about contemporary Spanish history and historiography, in addition to the politics of the Second Republic, in which he had played such an active role. Though González López had been a man of the Left, he was not sectarian like Monguió but objective and insightful. He was, in a totally informal way, the only instructor in Spanish history I had had to that point.

In addition to my discussions with Don Emilio, I made a series of other contacts, such as those with Eloy Vaquero, a veteran politician of the Radical Party who had been a cabinet minister under Lerroux, and with the Confederación Nacional del Trabajo (CNT—National Confederation of Labor) leader and journalist, Jesús González Malo, who was married to the literature professor Carmen Aldecoa. Through González Malo I was introduced to the biweekly *España Libre*, founded originally by Left-leaning Republicans (if I recall correctly) but supported by other sectors of the Spanish Left in New York. Later the first book review that I ever wrote for publication, on Víctor Alba's *Historia del Frente Popular*, appeared in *España Libre*.[10]

By far the most significant for me of the émigré Spaniards whom I met in New York was Joaquín Maurín, cofounder of the famous Partido Obrero de Unificación Marxista (POUM—Workers' Party of Marxist Unification). He would become an important friend, with whom I maintained frequent contact up to the time of his death in 1973. In some sense Maurín "adopted" me almost as a kind of American stepson. He was a remarkable man and a very good friend, retaining the vigorous personality and rather striking physical appearance that had made him a key leader among the revolutionary Left during the early 1930s. His Franco-Russian wife, Jeanne Lifschitz, was rather puzzled by the special relationship that developed between us, for, though by 1958 Maurín was largely social democratic in his political outlook, she knew that I did not at all share the revolutionary Marxist orientation that characterized his active career in Spain. I can only say that there quickly developed a special elective affinity between us on the basis of certain shared interests and a mutual liking and esteem. Maurín appreciated the seriousness of my scholarly interest and the willingness to work hard at it—things that he had never encountered before in American attitudes toward Spain during what was already his decade-long exile in New York. Soon his concerns became almost paternal, unfailingly solicitous of my best interests and well-being. Much more sophisticated than most of his revolutionary counterparts of the 1930s, Maurín had also preserved much of the puritanism of his Aragonese origins and sternly warned me of the dangers of "Caribbean corruption" when I went to Havana in June 1960 to inspect Castro's revolution. I will never forget our last farewell in 1973, when he was already stricken with what was a fatal illness. Since it was raining, he insisted on accompanying me with his umbrella as I hailed a taxi in front of his apartment building in New York.[11]

I was originally introduced to Maurín by Francisco García Lorca, a brother of the poet, whose career as a diplomat had been cut short by the Civil War. He developed a second career as Spanish literature professor at Columbia, where he was one of the editors of the *Revista Hispánica Moderna*. García Lorca was a member of the tribunal of my oral doctoral examination, which took place late in April 1958. During the course of that examination Frank Tannenbaum, then the senior professor of Latin American history at Columbia, queried me about the character of the contribution of Spain to Latin American civilization. I knew that Tannen-baum was a proponent of the Black Legend, was interested primarily in the Indian and black populations of Latin America, and always tended to denigrate the role of the Spanish. There were obviously severe limits to the extent that any humble student could question the opinions of a professor who formed part of the tri-bunal, but I have always had an independent streak that rebelled against forms of political correctness. I chose very carefully the terms of my response and indicated that the positive contributions of Spain to Latin American civilization should not be dismissed out of hand.

My response was carefully noted by García Lorca, who was pleased and later recounted it to Maurín. The latter in turn then wrote it up in slightly exaggerated form as a stirring defense of Spanish civilization, publishing it in *España Libre* and elsewhere. This points up the extent to which the Republican exiles, despite their critique of current Spanish institutions, maintained a strong and defensive Span-ish identity abroad, almost to the point of a cultural nationalism.

The most important thing that Maurín did for me was to open the route to the oral history research that I would soon undertake in Spain. He put me in touch with his veteran POUMist colleague Julián Gorkín (one of the POUM leaders prosecuted in Barcelona by the Negrín government in 1938). Gorkín was active in Paris with the exiled opposition and was also a vigorous anti-Soviet publicist. He maintained contact with Dionisio Ridruejo, who by that point had joined the ac-tive opposition to the Franco regime and had formed a small clandestine social democratic group with Enrique Tierno Galván and a few others. Gorkín's letter of presentation to Ridruejo would be fundamental in initiating the long series of contacts that I would develop for my research with current and ex-Falangists.

I embarked for Spain in September 1958 on the *Queen Mary*. The era of trans-atlantic jet travel would begin just one year later, so that I participated in the final phase of ocean voyages just before they would be rendered technologically obso-lete. My first stop was in Paris, where I was able to meet a variety of émigré politi-cal personalities, ranging from Gorkín to José Antonio de Aguirre. Julio Just, a former leader of Izquierda Republicana from the Levante, even invited me on a short bus trip to the Paris suburbs to meet the elderly Diego Martínez Barrio, then president of the Republican government-in-exile. At that point the former Radical and Unión Republicana leader was old and feeble, and our conversation lacked substance, but it was very generous of Just to take me to meet him.

The most interesting Republican political figure in Paris at that time was José Antonio de Aguirre, head of the Basque government-in-exile, which inhabited its own separate building in the "Délégation d'Euzkadi" on the Right Bank of the Seine. The position of lecturer had been arranged for Aguirre at Columbia during World War II as a sort of wartime "cover," and thus I came from the university with a strong letter of introduction to him. On the personal level Aguirre was most engaging and likeable, very friendly and agreeable to talk with. He gave me a great deal of time, and we had a very interesting and lengthy conversation about Spanish and, especially, Basque affairs, which was repeated nine months later when I came back through Paris. My interest in Basque nationalism was awakened by these conversations, though prior to them I had read almost nothing about the Basque Country.

Only many years later would I learn that Aguirre's lectureship at Columbia had been largely artificial, a political arrangement. Nor did I understand altogether that Aguirre had so much time to spend with an American doctoral student because at that point Basque nationalism was in the doldrums, a state of weakness and inactivity that would lead to the emergence of Euskadi Ta Askatasuna (ETA—Basque Homeland and Freedom) only a few years later.

From Paris I traveled by rail to Spain by way of Toulouse. I wanted to make contact with the Spanish Socialist leadership there, which had possession of the mediation proposal of José Antonio Primo de Rivera of August 1936, confiscated by Indalecio Prieto and eventually deposited with the party leadership. Rodolfo Llopis, the party secretary, received me promptly and brusquely, and within twenty-four hours provided me with a photocopy of the document.

I entered Spain by way of Port Bou and Barcelona, where my main goal was to meet the great historian Jaume Vicens Vives, who already ranked in my eyes— limited though my vision was—as the outstanding historian then practicing in Spain. Vicens invited me to his home and then to dinner the following night in a restaurant in the old Plaza Real. This was the beginning of my friendship, and also discipleship, with Vicens, a striking personality whom I still consider the most dynamic historian that I have ever known. I cannot precisely explain why he took such an interest in me, since I had no work to show him except for a seminar paper written at Columbia the preceding spring, based on very little in the way of primary research but incorporating much material from the extraordinary holdings of the New York Public Library. Altogether I saw Vicens on five different occasions that year—three times in Barcelona (September and December 1958, April 1959) and twice in Madrid (February and May 1959). We talked about the history of Spain and of Catalonia, and also the domestic political situation.

I spoke at length with Juan Linz, who was beginning work on an SSRC postdoctoral fellowship at the same time that I started my predoctoral research. He had spotted my name on the SSRC list and had written to me before I had left home. Linz had convinced me that there was not likely to be any change prior to the death of Franco, but early in 1959 Vicens was engaged in negotiations with monarchist dissidents and still hoping that enough pressure might be exerted to effect a change of regime, a hope that he had abandoned by the spring of that year.

Our final meeting in May 1959 consisted of a dinner with Vicens and his wife at a sidewalk café not far from the Plaza de España.

Vicens made a more powerful impression on me than any other historian I have known. His example was one of extraordinary dedication, energy, analytical ability, concern for opening new fields, and also of a rigorous self-control and objectivity—the latter to an extent rare even among professional scholars. It was Vicens who pointed out to me the importance of a study of the politics of the military, which would be the subject of my second major book. When I learned of his death from lung cancer in June 1960 I could scarcely believe it, for he had always seemed so vital, lively, and full of energy. He accomplished a great deal in what turned out to be a relatively short career. When I published the book on the Falange the year after his death, it seemed most appropriate and fitting to dedicate it to the memory of Vicens.

As I began research in Spain at the beginning of October 1958, I had no clear idea what to expect, but enjoyed the carefree self-confidence of youth, which in this case proved appropriate. I appreciated that the regime had become somewhat more moderate and, though still a police state, was not totalitarian, which hopefully would allow me some freedom for research. As a precaution, the announcement of my research award from the Social Science Research Council had been camouflaged, listing my topic simply as research on "corporatist ideology" in Spain. As it turned out, the timing was ideal: with the passage of twenty years since the Civil War and the frustration of the Falangist revolution, a good many veteran *camisas viejas* (lit. "old shirts") were willing to serve as oral history subjects, while my status as a North American research student also proved an advantage. The Pact of Madrid with Washington had been signed five years earlier. Though it may not have guaranteed freedom of activity for an American scholar, it certainly helped. My status as a foreigner and as a doctoral student was also useful, for the former freed me from identification with either of the two bands in the Civil War, while the latter went some distance to establishing bona fides, without ulterior political motives. Thus I think that I was accepted for what I was, by most but of course not all, of my Spanish research contacts.

Central to the project was the active assistance of Dionisio Ridruejo, without which it probably could not have been carried out. Ridruejo accepted my letter of introduction from his distant political colleague Gorkín and provided almost every kind of help that he could. This consisted primarily of two things: a lengthy series of discussions in the book-lined study in his home on the calle de Ibiza, on the far side of the Retiro Park, and an even more lengthy series of introductions to a large number of veteran Falangist militants, most of whom were willing to talk with me.

Here once more the timing was good, because Ridruejo had only recently passed from nonsupport of the regime to active opposition. His generosity and his effort to be honest, objective, and self-critical were impressive. All the later years of his life were characterized by a deep moral concern not to repeat the errors of his youth but to make amends for them and to do all he could to achieve a responsible and democratic future for Spain. I never achieved the personal friendship with Ridruejo that I did with Vicens and Maurín, but I was deeply grateful for his assistance and extremely impressed with his intellectual and moral seriousness.

At that time no archives dealing with the Falange were open, so my research was conducted in two quite different dimensions. The first was the official publications, newspapers, and secondary literature available in the Biblioteca Nacional and the Hemeroteca Municipal; the second was oral history with Falangist militants from the 1930s and with survivors of other political groups, as well. At that time the term "oral history" was scarcely used, and I had had absolutely no training in it. I simply threw myself into the water and learned to swim. If I had had appropriate methodological instruction, I would probably have done better, but interviewing is a matter partly of intuition, of asking the right questions, and of rapid adjustment, not merely formal techniques. The majority of the Falangists and others whom I interviewed sought to be helpful, though of course often not very objective, and sometimes provided important information and data. Only a minority refused to speak seriously or made elaborate efforts to deceive. The relatively good results that I obtained were partly the product of timing, because they could not have been achieved to the same extent a decade earlier.

A photocopy of the official police report on my activities that had been prepared in 1959, which I recently obtained, observes of its subject that "his appearance is innocent in the extreme though, in fact, he has possession of documents and contacts that are very interesting, having interviewed people ranging from General Aranda to Ridruejo, Suevos, and Hedilla." It goes on to detail two primary documents, copies of which had been provided by my interlocutors, some of whom, of course, were in contact with the police. The report concludes, almost plaintively, that "the work of Stanley Payne is attractive and innocent in appearance," which made it possible for me to carry out research that for someone in an official or political capacity "would be against nature, inherently more difficult, more suspicious. As it is, he can even publish a book in all tranquility there . . . , beyond the state and in any event relying on the United States, without having to deal with the Spanish government, despite the latter's authority."[12] All of which was true enough.

The first person whom I sought when I arrived in Madrid was Juan Linz, and our long talks together in the autumn of 1958 were invaluable, the beginning of a half century of friendship and scholarly collaboration that has benefited me more than my contact with anyone else. Juan was an invaluable source of information, analysis, and advice on Spanish affairs, indispensable in forming my first informed perspective on contemporary Spanish politics and history. By the early part of 1959 he was back in New York, beginning his teaching career at Columbia (later moving to Yale in 1968). Juan Linz is the most outstanding analyst of comparative modern European politics that I have encountered—probably the best in any country during the later twentieth century—combining encyclopedic empirical knowledge with a depth of analysis, comparative study, and scholarly imagination, which have been unrivaled. He helped me a great deal in each of the two main fields of inquiry that I would develop—contemporary Spanish history and the comparative history of fascism—so that it was only fitting that in the 1990s I dedicated two books to him.[13]

The other particularly close friend during the first year in Madrid was Francisco Javier de Lizarza, to whom I was introduced indirectly by Jaime del Burgo. Javier Lizarza, like Juan Linz, was a dear friend for an entire half century, and throughout ever the most reliable and true. Scion of a distinguished Navarrese Carlist family, he led in the effort to maintain the highest ideals of traditionalism in the politically correct society of the late twentieth and early twenty-first centuries. Following his death in October 2007, it is appropriate that the present book be dedicated to our half century of the warmest friendship.

In Madrid I made contact with Clay La Force, also on an SSRC fellowship, who was preparing a dissertation in economic history at UCLA on state industrialization initiatives in the reign of Carlos III, later to be published by the University of California Press. Clay and I would subsequently be colleagues between 1962 and 1968 at UCLA (he in economics, I in history), where he would go on to become the distinguished director of the Graduate School of Business Management.

In the late autumn of that first year, Juan Linz indicated that we should make the acquaintance of a young American woman "working on Antonio Maura," as current misinformation had it. This turned out to be Joan Connelly Ullman, at that time the director of the Instituto Internacional, who later completed an important dissertation and book on the Semana Trágica, as well as developing an influential career at the University of the Pacific and the University of Washington. She, Clay La Force, and I made up the trio of American dissertators in Madrid that year working on Spanish history of the two preceding centuries, something of a portent of things to come, since we would have many successors.

Two years later Edward Malefakis, who came right after me at Columbia, would begin his research in Madrid. His dissertation on the Republican agrarian reform would in fact constitute the deepest and most accomplished piece of work of all the American dissertations of those early years. I was fortunate in my fellow-researchers, for all were able scholars and have remained good friends, though in later years the only one whom I would see fairly regularly was Ed Malefakis, especially because of his home in Madrid.

It was a unique privilege to live and work in Spain before the close of the 1950s, for at that time many aspects of traditional Spanish society and culture were still alive. In those years manners and mores were in fact more formal, hierarchical, and conservative than they had been a quarter-century earlier, a result of the counter-revolution wrought by the Civil War. At that moment I could scarcely have imagined that within no more than a decade—by the late 1960s—the society and culture would have been drastically transformed by a vertiginous process of modernizing change, for good and for ill. I had arrived just in time to witness the final phase of more traditional Spanish life before it disappeared forever. Undoubtedly the new society, eventually a political democracy, would be much freer and more prosperous and also in some ways happier, but it would also lose touch with many of the values, symbols, and mores that had made Spanish society and culture distinctive. Hence in part the obsessive emphasis on fostering local and regional identities, together with the local festivals, that became so marked by the last years of the century.

A major concern during that first year in Spain was to make my own assessment of the Spanish and their culture (in the sense of ordinary society rather than high culture). The stereotypes of "romantic Spain," thanks to Ernest Hemingway and others, were by no means dead in the 1950s. Because of the Civil War and the Franco regime, Spain was viewed as an exceptional country, and the Spanish as rather exceptional people, given to violent conflict and fits of passion. Even the government had adopted the tourist slogan that "Spain is different," though its intention was not the same. My concern was to determine whether the Spanish really were "different" or rather normal people whose life had simply been marked by severe conflicts. After my first two months in Madrid I came to the conclusion that the Spanish were indeed basically normal people, not a collection of fanatics and extremists, though like all national groups they exhibited certain cultural idiosyncrasies.

I also devoted considerable time to travel that year, crisscrossing much of the country by bus, train, and plane, with special attention to several parts of the north and to Andalusia, spending more time in the south than I ever would again. In the process I met and dealt with people from every social background and all parts of the political spectrum, with the sole exception of the Communist Party. My own role was strictly that of researcher and observer. The only time that I was tempted to become involved politically was when I learned of the plight of the blind CNT leader Félix Carrasquer, once more in jail, since international publicity might improve the chances for his release. He was indeed released early in 1959, without further prompting from the outside, and I was able to visit Carrasquer within days of his regaining liberty.

Of all political sectors, the one that most impressed me on a personal level was the Pamplonese Carlists, with whom I made contact in December 1958. What most struck me about the Carlists was their spontaneity, forthrightness, and lack of affectation. Their authenticity was impressive, and initiated what would become a long-term friendship with a number of them.

The doctoral thesis on the Falange was largely written during the summer of 1959 and defended at Columbia the following spring. My first teaching took place at Columbia during 1959–60 and at Hunter College (City University of New York), after which I was offered a regular position at the beginning level at the University of Minnesota in 1960. I submitted the manuscript on the Falange to the Stanford University Press and obtained a quick acceptance, the book appearing in October 1961. A year or so later the new émigré press Ruedo Ibérico, founded by José Martínez in Paris, asked for the rights to editions in Spanish and French, which then came out in France in 1964–65.

The success of the book, generally well received on every hand, was gratifying and even surprising. It was also related to the fact that contemporary Spanish history was then a completely unworked field. Virtually all the reviews were favorable, some of them extremely so. The review that appeared in the *Revista de Estudios Políticos* was inevitably negative, standing as the more or less official response of the regime, but I understood that this would have to be the case, and in fact had the response in such an organ been favorable, it would probably have indicated that there was something seriously wrong with the book.

The original study of the Falange was no more than a doctoral thesis, based in part on oral history, an immature work some passages of which are a bit embarrassing to read in retrospect. It was in fact a training device for a fledgling historian who still had a great deal to learn, both about researching and writing history in general, and about contemporary Spanish history in particular. Although the findings about the Falange as an attempt to impose fascism in Spain were all negative, the book made some allowance for the charismatic qualities and intentions of José Antonio Primo de Rivera and some of the original Falangists—more so than would have been the case at a later stage in my career as a historian. There was an element of youthful romanticism in the style of writing that would have been impossible for me to sustain ten or twenty years later, but which probably helped to convey the human drama of the Spanish disaster of those years. At any rate, the first printing in English sold out and soon led to a second, which meant that the book remained available on the market at the Stanford University Press for thirty-five years, until 1996. Ruedo Ibérico undoubtedly sold even more copies in Spanish, but José Martínez never issued royalty reports to his authors in the manner of a normal publisher, so one never knew. Ruedo Ibérico always struggled financially as an émigré press, unable to sell directly in Spain, and depended on the sales of a few particular titles to stay afloat.[14] We generally understood this and did not complain when years sometimes passed without any payment of royalties.

The year 1961 was in fact the time of the emergence of contemporary Spanish history as a scholarly field in English, with the publication of Hugh Thomas's *The Spanish Civil War* and Burnett Bolloten's *The Grand Camouflage*, on the fate of the revolution in the Republican zone, as well as my own book. There was a kind of symmetry between them, with one history of the Civil War in general, a second on the Left, and a third on the Right. The most important of these was Thomas's book, even though its first edition carried the inevitable number of minor errors. It was a major scholarly achievement, and the product of a young autodidact abroad, Thomas being only three years older than myself.

At the time that his book appeared, I had been working for some months on a history of the Spanish Civil War of my own, but quickly concluded that at that stage I would be unable to improve on Thomas's work. I soon decided to follow up on Vicens's suggestion of the importance of a book on the politics of the military, being able to carry out a full year of research on it in Spain during 1962–63, thanks to a Guggenheim fellowship, which came as a result of the book on the Falange and especially of the good offices of my senior colleague at Minnesota, John B. Wolf, a noted specialist on the history of seventeenth-century France.

I had first returned to Spain in the summer of 1961, where my efforts were devoted to preparing a brief study on the historiography of Vicens Vives, which became my first major article.[15] Most of that summer was devoted to an extensive honeymoon with my new bride, Julia Sherman, a psychologist from Minneapolis, as we spent nearly two and a half months crisscrossing Europe on Eurail passes. Among many other adventures, we twice passed through the Berlin Wall during the first week of its construction.

The year 1962–63, dedicated to researching the politics of the military, was memorable for a number of things, but perhaps most of all because it was the last full year that I spent in Spain in which the old social and cultural order was largely intact. After May 1963 I passed the longest period of my life without returning to the country. I was busy with a new position in UCLA, developing new courses, and becoming a father, and I did not return to Spain until September 1967, a period of more than four years. The mid-1960s constituted a turning point in economic development, and when I got back to Madrid I found that things were not the same. It was not merely that the number of automobiles had greatly increased, so that I encountered the first major "modern" traffic jams that I had ever seen in Spain, but more importantly that social and cultural attitudes were also changing rapidly. The ambience was much more liberal and more hedonist, almost exaggeratedly so, much more in line with attitudes and values in contemporary western Europe.

Research on the politics of the military was in some ways more difficult than working on the Falange, the possibilities of oral history greatly reduced. I spent a considerable amount of time that year at the Servicio Histórico Militar, then on the calle de los Mártires de Alcalá, and used the same heterogeneous mix of source materials that had been employed in the Falangist study. The resulting book was published by Stanford in 1967 and soon afterward in a Spanish edition by Ruedo Ibérico. Its most important finding was that in political terms the military were not as much of an independent variable as most of us had thought. Although they had intervened, or tried to intervene, many times between 1814 and 1936, these interventions, whether successful or not, were much more dependent on general political variables than on the purely independent volition or ambitions of the military. This book was also very well received, particularly in a major review by Gerald Brenan in the *New York Times Book Review*.

It was completed after I had moved to Los Angeles, where I taught at UCLA from 1963 to 1968, passing rapidly through the ranks from assistant professor to full professor, and serving also as vice-chairman of the department (my first term in administration) in 1967–68. Though I had lived the greater share of my early life in California, and though in the mid-twentieth century Los Angeles had remained a very attractive city, that too was changing rapidly by the 1960s. The enormous expansion and crowding, the massive volume of traffic on the freeways and elsewhere, the growth of smog and other pollution, and the pervasive influence of a peculiarly Southern California/Hollywood form of hedonism and materialism— all contributed to an increasingly disagreeable ambiance. My wife and I decided in 1968 that we would be happier in a more tranquil and stable environment at the University of Wisconsin in Madison, whose environs were rather more similar to those of a major European university, such as Cambridge or Marburg, located in a small city.

During the Los Angeles years I was also involved in my first major undertaking in broader European history, being asked by my old mentor Shepard Clough to write part of a new multivolume textbook called *A History of the Western World* (but meaning essentially the history of Europe, the Mediterranean, and the ancient Near East, at least in the original version.) Together with Otto Pflanze, the noted historian of Germany, who had been my colleague at Minnesota, I wrote the third volume on nineteenth- and twentieth-century Europe, published in December 1964. This project went through two revised editions during the next eight years, in which it was broadened to become one of the first of the subsequently fashionable histories of the world. It also became more extensively illustrated, enjoying a viable commercial life of about a decade and a half, the first publishing project from which I drew any significant income in royalties.

I was also asked by the New York publishing firm Thomas Y. Crowell to write a very brief study of the contemporary situation in Spain, which became the short volume *Franco's Spain* (1967). This took little time, but was my first effort to analyze and summarize recent developments in all the major aspects of Spanish affairs, dealing with social and economic changes, cultural life, and international relations, as well as with the politics of the Franco regime.

The 1960s were a decade of greatly expanded interest in history in all the Western world. The student activists who became famous in that era were especially attracted to history, but beyond that, general cultural conditions stimulated enrollment in history courses among the enormously expanded student populations of that decade. Interest in history courses among university students generally follows a sort of cyclical pattern. The 1960s were an especial high point and enormously stimulated the zeal of publishers to bring out new history books. More than at any other time in my experience, they took the initiative in offering lucrative contracts to historians, rather than simply responding to manuscripts presented by the latter. Altogether, I accepted four publishers' initiatives during the 1960s—the aforementioned textbook, the short project on contemporary Spain, a proposal to prepare a history of the Spanish revolution of the 1930s, and also the suggestion that I develop a general history of Spain and Portugal.

The Spanish Revolution stemmed from the invitation of Jack Greene, a specialist in the era of the American Revolution of the 1770s, to write one of ten volumes in a series called Revolutions in the Modern World. That a volume on Spain was even included demonstrated considerable perspicacity by Greene, since many general and comparative treatments of modern revolutions tend to ignore the Spanish case. I was certainly aware of the presence of the revolutionary worker movements and of the revolution in the Republican zone during the Civil War, but knew little about them. My research was initially assisted by two special collections that had become available in California, the Southworth Collection at the University of California–San Diego and the Bolloten Collection in the Hoover Institution at Stanford, both particularly rich in materials from the Republican zone.[16] Data on the CNT-FAI, as well as the POUM, were also available at the Institutional Institute of Social History in Amsterdam, but I would not be able to gain access to the Civil War archive in Salamanca (then generally closed to researchers) for another five years.

Research for this book would turn out to mark a kind of watershed in my grasp of Spanish politics. I had been brought up in the standard politically correct understanding of contemporary Spanish affairs, which holds that the Right was iniquitous, reactionary and authoritarian, while the Left (despite certain regrettable excesses) was basically progressive and democratic. My investigation of the revolutionary process in Spain produced quite different findings, revealing that the Left was not necessarily progressive and certainly not democratic, but in fact during the course of the 1930s produced a regression in Spanish affairs from the relative liberal democracy achieved in 1931–32.

The Spanish Revolution was brought out in New York by W. W. Norton in 1970 and became my first book to appear inside Spain, thanks to two factors. One was the new press law introduced by Fraga Iribarne four years earlier, which finally began to loosen restrictions on publication; the other was that this book offered a critical perspective on the Left, rather than on the Right, as in the case of the two previous books, so that it might theoretically be more acceptable to the censorship that continued to exist. Even so, there was continuing resistance in official circles to permitting a book of mine to appear within Spain, a resistance only finally vanquished by a vigorous review published by Ricardo de la Cierva, strongly endorsing publication. Without this initiative by La Cierva, the book might not have appeared, despite the eagerness of Alejandro Argullós to publish it in the new series on contemporary Spain presented by Ediciones Ariel. Due to a mistake on the part of the agent in charge of the series, a completely separate Spanish edition was brought out by Argos Vergara five years later, while the Tokyo firm Heibonsha published a Japanese translation in 1974, thanks to a strong recommendation made to them by Joaquín Maurín prior to his death.

Equally or even more important was the invitation extended by Norman F. Cantor, the imaginative medievalist who served as history editor for Thomas Y. Crowell, to write a full-scale general history of Spain and Portugal. This had not been done in the English-speaking world for a very long while and presented me with a great opportunity, for it was the preparation of this book that gave me a full grasp of the history of the peninsula for the first time. It was nonetheless a daunting undertaking, which occupied me for four years and required a huge amount of reading in the secondary literature. Though it was possible to read no more than a fraction of the enormous bibliography pertaining to the subject, that bibliography had not yet undergone the exponential expansion that took place during the latter part of the century and which would make such an enterprise by a single scholar totally impossible within any finite amount of time. My goal was not merely to narrate facts but to render intelligible the peninsula's history, so that most subsections of each chapter were organized by concepts, not chronology. In general I think that I was successful in achieving an analytic focus on the subject matter that generally made sense, although some points would have to be modified as a result of the massive research by historians during the decades that followed. The most original aspect for me was coming to grips with the history of Portugal, which first gave me an understanding of that country's history and decisively broadened my perspective on the peninsula.

Crowell was soon taken over by Dun and Bradstreet, which immediately lost interest in the project, so that I managed to redirect it to the University of Wisconsin Press, thanks to an invitation from Thompson Webb, its director. This initiated my long collaboration with this university press. *A History of Spain and Portugal* came out in two volumes in 1973, remained in print for about fifteen years, and was briefly a History Book Club alternate selection. A slightly revised and expanded Spanish edition was finally published in five brief paperback volumes by Carlos Alberto Montaner's Editorial Playor in Madrid between 1985 and 1987, enabling the Portuguese chapters to be grouped together as a one-volume *Breve historia de Portugal* (1987), which for several reasons was at that time unique among publications in Spanish on Portugal. An inexpensive reprint edition was done by Editorial Grupo five years later, and a digital edition of the original first volume of the English edition was later made available by the digital publisher LIBRO in 2002.

From the time of my first visits to Barcelona and Bilbao in 1958–59, and after my initial discussions with Aguirre and Vicens Vives, I had formed considerable interest in the peripheral nationalisms. I thought that they were important in the country's contemporary history and would also be important in the future, though for some time neither I nor many others would understand how large a role they would play in the politics of a future democratic Spain. After 1970 the emergence of a radical form of Basque nationalism in ETA achieved greater prominence than the more moderate initiatives of the Catalanists, exactly the opposite of the relative salience of the two movements during the years of the Republic.

My original intention was to prepare simply a very long article on the politics of Basque nationalism under the Republic for a special issue on contemporary Spain to be published by the *Rivista Storica Italiana*.[17] During the summer of 1971 I visited the University of Nevada in Reno to spend a brief period researching the collection of the Basque Studies Program, initiated there not long before. I had known the noted Basque bibliographer Jon Bilbao for nearly fifteen years, having been introduced to him by Aguirre and having stayed at his home in Guecho briefly during an earlier visit to Bilbao. He and the anthropologist William Douglass, the long-term director of the Basque Studies Program, urged me to expand the long article into a short monograph on early Basque nationalism. I had never conceived of this as a full-length project, but at that time there was scarcely any scholarly literature on the topic, so over the next year and a half I expanded this into a brief account of the early political history of the Basque movement, up to 1937.[18]

During those final years of Franco's life, the cultural environment was becoming progressively relaxed, even as politics became more active. I developed some ambition to publish this brief book in Spain, encouraged by the reforms of Pío Cabanillas as minister of culture, with Ricardo de la Cierva as Director General de

Cultura Popular. I mailed a copy of the manuscript to La Cierva in the winter of 1974, and on the eve of an international conference convened in March of that year by the Instituto de Cultura Hispánica, I received a telegram from La Cierva telling me that he considered it "important" to publish the book in Spain. A few days later I carried a copy of the manuscript with me to Madrid and quickly reached a deal with Sebastián Auger to bring it out in Barcelona with the latter's ambitious new publishing firm Editorial Dopesa.[19] It published a Spanish edition within six months, in August, which was crucially important, for Cabanillas was dismissed by Franco little more than a month later, bringing in turn the resignation of La Cierva.[20] Had this taken place only a month earlier, publication of the book would have been prohibited. As it was, a special book fair in Bilbao, in which the book would have been one of those featured, was canceled. Dopesa provided a good advance for the book but submitted statements the next two years indicating that few copies were sold, which seems quite doubtful, according to all reports. Because of the dearth of material on Basque nationalism at that time, this gained for me altogether exaggerated credentials as a Basque specialist, which I really was not. I did no further research in the area after 1972–73, while only a few years later, after the death of Franco, work in that field would expand exponentially.

The 1960s and 1970s were the only decades in which contemporary Spanish history attracted attention abroad, due to the Civil War legacy and the reputation of Spain as an "exceptional country" under the Franco regime. With modernization and the success of the democratization after Franco, this status disappeared. On the international level, interest in contemporary Spanish history dwindled altogether during the 1980s.

Conversely, for the first and only time since the Civil War, interest in current Spanish politics grew rapidly during the 1970s, peaking with the years of the democratization but also continuing to some extent into the 1980s, before dropping away with the apparently complete stabilization of the new system. During those years I played an active role in advice and commentary on Spanish politics both on the government and academic levels, for in political science there were very few scholars with any expertise on the country, so that a historian like myself was called on to do double duty as political analyst.

Interest in and speculation about the country's political future began to build slowly after the official recognition of the succession of Juan Carlos in 1969. The two questions that loomed on the horizon concerned (1) how far the next chief of state would go to encourage the introduction of democracy, and (2) whether Spanish society had been transformed to the extent that such a process could successfully be completed. The experience of the Civil War and the official doctrines of the dictatorship had developed a certain discourse about the country's "familiar demons," according to which Spaniards were culturally and psychologically unsuited for democracy. Certainly all earlier parliamentary systems had failed sooner or later, and in all but one case (the Restoration regime) sooner rather than later. Nonetheless, when I completed my treatment of broader peninsular history for the two-volume work in 1970, I pointed out the achievements of parliamentary governments in Spain's past, which seemed to suggest that a more developed society might be able to cope with democracy and also concluded that something so anachronistic as the dictatorship, even if extensively reformed, might not be able to survive very much longer. The problem was not so much that parliamentary government could not function in Spain but that the chief political actors had simply to respect the rules of the game, which had hardly been the case in most of the earlier parliamentary regimes.

During his first year as official heir apparent, Juan Carlos was inevitably very guarded in remarks about any future plans, while Franco's health remained relatively stable as of 1970 and the opposition was entirely impotent. Therefore, when the influential American journal *Foreign Affairs* asked me early in 1970 to write an article on the current political situation in Spain and its future prospects, my prognosis, too, was guarded. The resulting article, "In the Twilight of the Franco Era," noted the extensive social and economic transformation of the country, and suggested that the present system would change and evolve under Juan Carlos, but that the immediate prospects were for "continuity more than change."[21]

That was technically the case as of mid-1970, but the situation continued to evolve rapidly, and during the next two years Juan Carlos gave clearer signals regarding his future plans, while by 1973 Franco's health was deteriorating seriously. During these years there were several conferences and seminars in Washington on Spanish affairs, including a special seminar at the Foreign Service Institute on July 12, 1972, on the "Spanish military," focused on their likely behavior following the death of Franco. In the spring of 1975 Washington upgraded the ambassadorship to Madrid by appointing the veteran Welles Stabler, a distinguished career diplomat and former assistant secretary of state for southern Europe. I participated in the orientation seminar organized for the ambassador-designate on May 1, 1975, and was hopeful about the country's political prospects, though the new ambassador was perhaps not surprisingly apprehensive about what he would soon encounter in Madrid.

The strangest meeting in Washington on the eve of Franco's death took place on June 10, 1975, when a Left-liberal pressure group, the Fund for New Politics, collaborated with representatives of the opposition Junta Democrática to sponsor a private, nongovernmental hearing in one of the congressional meeting rooms. Approximately fifteen people participated, together with various members of the junta, ranging from Opus Dei to the Communist Party. The message of this hearing was that the U.S. government should act directly to control the Spanish military after Franco's death; if it did not, any transition to democracy would be almost inevitably thwarted. This was possibly the only time that a foreign Communist entity urged American intervention in its country's affairs.

I was the only participant who challenged this viewpoint, pointing out first that the most active member of the Junta Democrática was the Communist Party of Spain, something that had been carefully ignored in the public presentation of this hearing. I held that American intervention or pressure would not be necessary and that Juan Carlos, after succeeding Franco, would introduce effective democratization that the great majority of Spanish people would support, and that the Socialist Party could play a constructive role in representing the main forces of the Left. The analysis that I advanced concluded that the Spanish military only intervened in moments of crisis, deep division, and disruption of legality. If the democratization process maintained stability and proceeded through legal channels, the military were not likely to reverse it. This analysis proved substantially correct.[22]

The summer of 1975 was a grim time in Washington, as North Vietnam violated its peace agreement to launch an all-out military offensive, which resulted in the fall of South Vietnam. Communist totalitarianism was expanding not merely in southeast Asia but also in some parts of Africa, while the Portuguese Communists seemed to be gaining dominance in Lisbon and the future of Spain was in doubt. The Department of State therefore called a special conference on the prospects of "The Left in Western Europe" in June 1975. These prospects were not encouraging, since the Revolution had not yet brought democracy to Portugal, and Helmut Sonnenfeldt, at that moment perhaps Henry Kissinger's principal subordinate as assistant secretary of state, lamented that for five hundred years the Russian empire had never ceased to expand. (In fact, it would continue to expand for five years more, Soviet influence reaching its peak worldwide by 1980 with the rise of Afro-Communism and the invasion of Afghanistan.)

In Spain, however, events moved rapidly and surprisingly smoothly from the appointment of Adolfo Suárez as prime minister in July 1976.[23] Shrewd and constructive political management helped to keep the military from interfering, and the Spanish democratization became something of a model, to lead the "third wave" of major twentieth-century democratizations during the 1970s and 1980s. Between 1975 and the 1980s the handful of Hispanists who dealt with politics and contemporary Spanish history were in considerable demand from various institutions and universities in the United States, so that we formed a sort of "traveling circus," which appeared with slightly varying membership in a variety of different settings.

By 1979 Felipe González had moderated both the Marxist doctrines and the political tactics of the Partido Socialista Obrero Español (PSOE—Spanish Socialist Worker's Party), which not only abandoned its peculiar concept of direct action it had thought compatible with the parliamentary democracy (which it now espoused) but also accepted the principles of European social democracy, as distinct from "socialism." All this was enormously helpful, indeed indispensable, to the consolidation of democracy in Spain. The major point on which the Socialists refused to change was their neutrality in the Cold War. Neutrality vis-à-vis the Soviet Union had never been the position of some of the older leaders, such as Indalecio Prieto, but the González group that had taken over the party in 1973 claimed that the Cold War had had the effect of prolonging the Franco regime (which to some extent was correct). To declare neutrality in the worldwide contest, which in Europe was now a clear-cut struggle between democracy and totalitarianism, seemed strange for a party insisting on its own democratic credentials. Nevertheless, ambiguity had been a persistent feature of the history of Spanish Socialism, and in this area drew an official statement of gratitude from the Soviet government, not the sort of congratulations that a newly democratic party would normally want to have.

The U.S. government and some of its west European counterparts became eager to have a newly democratic Spain enter NATO, the chief political obstacle to which was now the opposition of the Socialist Party. To try to overcome this, Washington and its NATO allies organized a meeting with representatives of the major Spanish parties at Ditchley Park (an old residence of the Dukes of Marlborough) not far from Oxford on the weekend of March 15–17, 1978. On the morning of the first full day, Gen. Alexander Haig, then commander of the NATO forces, arrived by helicopter on the large front lawn to address the group. These efforts were unsuccessful as far as the Socialists were concerned. I was seated throughout beside Luis Yáñez, the gynecologist from Seville who at that moment played a major role in the PSOE leadership. He was affable but noncommittal, and Socialist resistance on this issue would continue for six more years, until the decisive change in 1984 when González conducted his famous volte-face and referendum on NATO.

For me personally the major Spanish political event of 1978 was the first congress of the Unión de Centro Democrático (UCD), held in Madrid in October. The party leaders invited three American senators to attend, but the congress took place in the middle of the campaigning for the American elections, and none of the senators could be present. The UCD also invited me, and I became, in effect, the American representative. I was seated in the front row in the visitors' section, beside foreign dignitaries who in some cases had been chiefs of government or heads of state. Margaret Thatcher attended and gave a speech. Hugh Thomas came with Thatcher's entourage as advisor and introduced me to her, only six months before she was to win her first parliamentary elections.

I thoroughly enjoyed the congress, and realized that it would constitute the height of my otherwise nonexistent political career. Unión de Centro Democrático was the only Spanish political organization with which I have ever felt thoroughly identified, its role in the establishment of Spanish democracy being absolutely fundamental, given the limitations of the Right on the one hand and the confusions of the Socialists on the other. It never became a tightly structured and fully unified party and did not always enjoy the best leadership, but for five years its role was crucial, and in the twenty-first century I would dedicate my book *The Collapse of the Spanish Republic, 1933–1936* (2005) to Suárez and his colleagues in recognition of their decisive accomplishments, succeeding where the Second Republic had failed.

Since the 1970s I had progressively divided my time more and more between work on Spain and the comparative analysis of contemporary European history. This involved two dimensions: (1) continuation of the work on Portugal, and (2) the study of "generic fascism," the latter involving more activity than the former. Portuguese history had received a little more attention in the United States when a number of Hispanists, together with one or two Spanish scholars teaching in the country, formed the Society for Spanish and Portuguese Historical Studies (SSPHS) in 1969–70. The society would play a major role in stimulating and focusing research on Iberian history from that point on, and also in furthering scholarly ties between historians in Spain and the United States, but the attention that it could give to Portugal would obviously be limited.

An opportunity to develop a major focus on Portugal suddenly emerged at the University of Wisconsin in the spring of 1972, when I found that the university's West European Studies Program had a little money remaining in its budget at the end of the academic year. I proposed the immediate convening of a small conference to form a group for the study of contemporary Portugal. This was approved, and I invited the only five North American colleagues I could find who were doing work on contemporary Portugal in history and the social sciences. Thus in June 1972 in Madison we formed the International Conference Group on Portugal (ICGP), the first such entity anywhere outside Portugal, with the exception of literary studies. Douglas Wheeler of the University of New Hampshire became the secretary of the conference group and its indispensable leader for more than three decades. The ICGP would play a pioneering role, sponsoring a long series of conferences, publications, and eventually its own journal, the *Portuguese Studies Review*. Nonetheless, when it held its first full conference at the University of New Hampshire in October 1973, six months before the outbreak of the Portuguese Revolution, that event was not predicted by a single participant. So much for the capacity for prediction on the part of the social sciences.

By the 1980s it was observed that the era had passed in which foreign Hispanists might play a dominant role in the historiography dealing with contemporary Spain, given the democratization of the country and the great expansion of research and publication by Spanish historians, more interested in contemporary history than in any other period. This was obviously the case, the special role of Hispanists being most relevant amid the particular conditions of the 1950s and 1960s.

In normal circumstances, then, does the Hispanist still have any special function or fill an important role in Spanish historiography? His most significant contribution probably does not come from being a research scholar. That would have been the case only during the dictatorship, when Spanish historians themselves could not undertake and publish research in certain areas. The most important contribution probably stems from the ability to provide a broader critical and comparative perspective, something that Spanish historians themselves have been learning to do only within the past decade or so, and then only to a limited degree. Current Spanish historiography still has a profound tendency toward self-absorption though, happily, there are some notable exceptions. To that extent, it is important for all countries to have foreign scholars study, analyze, and write their histories, not primarily to add data—although that is occasionally important—but above all to provide a broader, sometimes more objective, perspective. Research monographs have been important, but the broader and more comparative dimension has probably been the more significant aspect.

It has been a rare and enjoyable privilege to labor in the field of the history of Spain for most of the past fifty years. The history of Spain is one of the greatest and most remarkable histories, exactly as Juan Negrín wrote in 1938, and it never ceases to impress or amaze. One of the most extraordinary things about working in the history of Spain is the generally positive reception of the Spanish themselves. Visitors in the sixteenth and seventeenth centuries found them markedly xenophobic. However that may have been, this was not the case in the twentieth century, with the possible exception of the first years of the Franco regime, long past by the time that I arrived in Spain. With rare exceptions, I have found the Spanish courteous and surprisingly welcoming and hospitable. Only a few months ago a journalist asked me to respond to a questionnaire concerning Spanish affairs and my experience in the country. Among the questions was one along the lines of "What has been your most disagreeable experience in Spain?" This required some thought on my part: for more than half a century I have had a certain number of disagreeable experiences, but they have all seemed so insignificant compared with the very many positive experiences that I had trouble responding to the question.

It has been observed that by the twentieth century the Spanish had to a large extent internalized the Black Legend—another Spanish "first," Spain being merely the first of the modern Western countries to undergo a ubiquitous process of massive self-criticism—and had developed a kind of national inferiority complex that often made them overly deferential to the opinions of foreigners. There is some accuracy in this observation, and the tendency developed in Spain long before the rise of political correctness and multicultural deconstruction late in the twentieth century.

The other side of the coin is what may be called the syndrome of the "hysterical Hispanist." Some of the foreign scholars who fall into this category may be characterized as strongly anti-Spanish and others as unreasonably pro-Spanish. Among the former one may find the distinguished American historian Prescott and the less well-known American literature professor John A. Crow. I myself have occasionally been criticized as being overly sympathetic to the Spanish.

As I explained at the outset, one of my principal goals when I first came to Spain in 1958 was to attempt to form an objective evaluation of Spanish society and history, avoiding the extremes of unfair criticism—so common among foreigners—or of romantic patronizing or superficial endorsement, which have also been very common. I leave it to my readers, who for the most part have been quite generous, to judge to what extent I have achieved this goal.

Part II

A Reading of
the History of Spain

The Hispanic Peninsula in 800

1

Visigoths and Asturians

"Spaniards"?

The Iberian Peninsula entered recorded history with the Roman conquest, after which it became an integral part of the empire. Language, culture, and economic structure all stemmed from Rome, as well as the name "Hispania," a geographic term for the entire peninsula (which became a distinct "diocese" of the empire after the Diocletian reforms of the fourth century).[1] Its society passed through each of the major phases and vicissitudes of the later Roman system, though some of the northern districts were less thoroughly Romanized than the south and east.

Spain emerged as a kingdom, if not exactly a state, under the Visigoths in the sixth century, though the Visigothic monarchy was slow to establish general control over the entire peninsula—and even then somewhat uncertainly in part of the north. Later generations would look back to the Visigoths as the first leaders of an independent "Spain," but in the twentieth century historians would challenge so simple and straightforward an interpretation. By that time the Visigothic kingdom was increasingly interpreted in negative terms of decline, disunity, and general weakness, an interpretative deconstruction that began historiographically well before the deconstruction of Spain in general became fashionable.

During the late twentieth century the Anglo-American historian Peter Brown introduced the concept of "Late Antiquity" as a relatively distinct period of historical transition from the ancient world to the Middle Ages. This term has been increasingly accepted as a way to periodize history between the fourth and seventh centuries. Somewhat similarly, it became fashionable during the second half of the twentieth century to reject the classic understanding of the "fall of Rome," replacing this with a new perspective that saw the Germanic kingdoms as evolutionary successor states, which formed a kind of functional symbiosis with the remains of the Roman world, not overthrowing it so much as reincorporating it in a new quasi-synthesis.[2]

There is no question that in most of the new kingdoms, Germanic rulers tried to cloak themselves in Roman authority and to maintain much of the existing structures, but there is also no doubt that a real break occurred during the fifth century.[3] The break was most complete in Roman Britain, where the old civilization almost totally disappeared, but much less extensive in the peninsulas of Spain and Italy, where at first more of the old order survived.

The "Grand Narrative" of Spanish history, as it took full form in the nineteenth century, defined a national identity and a kind of historical purpose and mission, the origins of which were purportedly laid by the Visigoths and developed more extensively by the kingdom of Asturias. Major aspects of this interpretation have varied, most notably between liberal nationalists and Catholic traditionalists during the nineteenth century, but for some time it constituted a meta-interpretation of the Spanish past. The Grand Narrative first began to be questioned in the mood of pessimism that gripped a part of the thinking of late nineteenth-century Spain, even before 1898. Thoroughly rehabilitated and restored by Franco, its last great avatar, it began to be yet more decisively rejected in the era of democratization and autonomies that followed the dictatorship. The political and ideological deconstruction of the Spanish nation that ensued provoked an intense debate that has only accelerated in recent years—the most intense ongoing debate in any Western country, equaled or exceeded only by that of Russia in the 1990s (the chief product of which in Russia has been the neo-authoritarian nationalism of Vladimir Putin).

In the 1970s, critics held that the formation of historically continuous Spanish institutions in the kingdom of Asturias during the generation immediately following the Muslim conquest involved a major paradox. The most succinct statement of this position was made by Abilio Barbero and Marcelo Vigil in the small study they published in 1974, *Sobre los orígenes sociales de la Reconquista*. This appeared on the eve of the democratization of Spain, and for that particular theme represented a climax of the deconstructive trend of interpretation, which had begun in the late nineteenth century. It posited a paradox, not to say contradiction, in the origins of the resistance nucleus of Asturias during the second quarter of the eighth century.

The paradox was supposed to be twofold. On the one hand, independent Hispano-Christian society first arose in what was heretofore the least Romanized and Christianized part of the peninsula, with the exception of the Basque region. On the other hand, the "neo-Gothic ideal," which emerged as a kind of political doctrine among the Asturian elite by the end of the ninth century, was held to have had the scantiest historical basis in Asturias itself, for the greater Asturian-Cantabrian region, as putatively one of the least Romanized districts, was said to have possessed little or no Visigothic political structure or identity. It was allegedly the home almost exclusively of semiprimitive autochthonous peoples, whose society was scarcely more than tribal in structure and who had had little to do with the Visigothic state at all, having never been effectively conquered or integrated by it.

Though some historians rejected this interpretation, or at least its most extreme version, it commanded a wide audience after the death of Franco, fitting nicely the mood of diversity and pluralism of the years of the democratization.[4] During that era the Grand Narrative of Spanish history, which had found its earliest limited expression in the Asturias of Alfonso el Casto and reached its height in nineteenth-century Spanish nationalism—both liberal and rightist—and in the doctrines of the Franco regime, was rejected politically and broadly deconstructed historiographically. Moreover, this reinterpretation could not easily be challenged by new historical research, for the sources on the last years of Visigothic history are the weakest of the entire Visigothic period, while the principal documentary sources for the history of the kingdom of Asturias consist of only three chronicles.

An examination of the roots of the kingdom of Asturias should begin with the Visigothic monarchy, which preceded it. For nearly a hundred years, the latter was viewed by most commentators as a semi-incoherent failure, whose sudden downfall merely reflected its internal social and political divisions and general decadence, so that its ruin became almost inevitable. The achievements and influence of its cultural superstar, San Isidoro of Seville, were seen as a unique exception that otherwise merely proved the rule. More recently, however, historians have viewed this attitude as originating, at least in part, in the cultural pessimism of Spain at the close of the nineteenth century.

For most of the twentieth century, the Visigothic state was given credit for establishing its sovereignty over the peninsula and for eventually adopting Catholic orthodoxy, but for little else. The Grand Narrative had lauded it for building the political and religious unity of Spain, but the tendency among twentieth-century historians was to judge it a decadent failure in social, cultural, and political terms. Disparagement of the Visigothic era was not new. It had been begun as early as the eighth century by French Carolingians, the first to propagate the myth that Roman culture had been almost totally submerged by "barbarian invasions," introducing the concept, if not quite the term, of "dark ages" overtaking western Europe after the collapse of Rome.

Research on the Visigoths enjoys a venerable tradition in Spain, and for long it centered on the history of law, on the one hand, and of church history and patristics, on the other. In 1941, two years after the Civil War, the young historian Alfonso García Gallo published a major one-hundred-page article in the first new number of the *Anuario de la Historia del Derecho Español*, which challenged traditional understanding of the origins of Visigothic law. The major figures in that field, led by Eduardo de Hinojosa and later by Claudio Sánchez Albornoz, had emphasized the centrality of Germanic law, whereas García Gallo argued on the basis of considerable evidence that what was known in western Europe as "Roman vulgar law" was more nearly the basis of Visigothic law codes.[5]

The Visigoths had long been recognized as the most Romanized of the Germanic peoples, and—unlike the Franks, Germans, Angles, Saxons, Burgundians, or Lombards—had never replaced the Latin name of their territory with their own. García Gallo's reinterpretation, however, considerably broadened understanding of the post-Roman character of certain Visigothic institutions, and which to some degree has been substantiated by subsequent research. Moreover, coming as it did during the high triumphal phase of early Francoism, it accorded nicely with the dominant political ideology, which was pleased to alter the origins of the conventional Grand Narrative in a more directly Roman-Hispanic southwest European, less Germanic, direction. The fact that the most recent research in Germany itself had underscored the persistence of Roman vulgar law in the various Germanic kingdoms only gave this greater credibility. At that stage the regime encouraged the friendliest of relations with Nazi Germany, but preferred a less Germanized version of the national Grand Narrative.

A more positive reevaluation of the Visigothic kingdom took place in the last two decades of the century, most notably among foreign scholars. The British Hispanist Roger Collins accused previous commentators of what he termed "virtually a 'slave-mentality,' induced by a priori acceptance of the necessary inferiority of Visigothic Spain."[6] A significant role has been played by the French Hispanist Jacques Fontaine, the leading living authority on San Isidoro,[7] though one of its first manifestations was the international conference on "Visigothic Spain: New Approaches," held at University College, Dublin, in 1975.[8] This reevaluation gives the Visigoths credit for "holding together for over a century the largest undivided political unit in seventh-century Europe," for having extended political organization rather more thoroughly across the peninsula's north than had earlier been thought, for building some degree of politico-administrative structure, and for having expelled Byzantine invaders.[9]

It is now increasingly recognized that Visigothic Spain maintained a higher level of learning and culture than any other large part of western Europe except for Italy, and that the Visigothic clergy was generally the best-educated to be found in continental western Europe, however relative such a qualification must be. During the seventh century the Visigothic church was generally recognized in Latin Christendom as the leader in ecclesiastical law, in church discipline, and even, to some extent, in theology. Its church law, administration, and liturgical forms were widely copied, the collection of church regulations known as *Hispana* circulating extensively in western Europe. One German scholar has recently called it the most advanced example of a church in one of the Germanic kingdoms.[10] Moreover, secular Visigothic law was well developed in comparison with neighboring kingdoms, the seventh-century legal codification of Recesvinto, known variously as *Forum Iudicum* and *Liber Iudiciorum*, and to medieval Castilians as the *Fuero Juzgo*, was the most extensive and relatively sophisticated Western law code of its time, and in various ways was followed in all the Visigothic successor states—even in Catalonia—for some six centuries.[11]

The Visigothic church and monarchy were the first to present the ideal of the "Christian monarchy," thus the true heir of Rome and equal, at least, to the Byzantine empire. By the seventh century, the ruler had become sacralized as more than a mere earthly ruler and was the first Western ruler to receive the royal unction upon coronation. The close association between church and state that existed from the late sixth century has long been emphasized, and earlier gave rise to erroneous judgments by foreign scholars about the roots of what they termed "Spanish theocracy." That relationship was in fact rather more caesaropapist than theocratic, but there is no doubt that the church came to have a major role in the late Visigothic system, in a manner distinct from that of the church in any other contemporary state. It did indeed have an important political and, later, administrative function, and the Councils of Toledo involved the church in formulating a primitive kind of constitutional law, though the latter was often honored only in the breach. In all, the Visigothic church became virtually a national church, whose connections with Rome continued to exist but were somewhat limited.

San Isidoro has long been recognized as the great Western polymath of his age, and indeed was the most influential Spanish scholar of all time. His massive *Etymologies* were still being laboriously copied out by hand seven centuries later. Though not a major theologian, he was the last great patristic figure of Late Antiquity. Isidoro played a crucial political ideological role, as well, for he was the first to define fully the terms of the new "Christian monarchy," an "empire"—meaning a totally independent state—not beholden either to old Rome or to the Eastern Roman Empire. In the Isidorean doctrine, the Visigothic monarchy represented a new kind of state and culture that sought but failed to achieve a sort of synthesis of Western Christianity and classical culture, the latter of course subordinated to the former. He spoke of the new kingdom as the "patria" of "the peoples of all Hispania," now joined in the united "patria of the Goths," and on one occasion referred to them as "a chosen people."[12] Jacques Fontaine has labeled this "the genesis of the Hispano-Gothic ideology," resulting in "a kind of cultural nationalism."[13] Isidoro's approach differed from that of his quasi-contemporary, Pope Gregory the Great, in that it was optimistic, whereas that of Gregory had been eschatological. Gregory had been relatively suspicious of profane culture, whereas Isidoro sought to incorporate it as much as possible, seeking a via media between yesterday and today. Fontaine claims, perhaps with a little exaggeration, that he achieved "an original and firm vision of universal history," in which the Christian monarchy followed Rome in a positive line of historical development.[14] This *Regnum Gothorum* was a precisely defined territory, in fact the first Christian and European state to be exactly defined geographically. None of its contemporaries had such definition, either in doctrine or in territory, while in late Visigothic times *Hispania* was sometimes shortened to *Spania*, and the rulers were sometimes called *reges Spaniae*.

One of the most contested points in interpreting late Visigothic society is the issue of ethnic integration. It was long assumed that a basic weakness lay in the continuing division between German Visigoths on the one hand, and Hispano-Romans or other native population on the other. Some non-Spanish specialists during the past generation have come to discount this, seeing instead a broad fusion of elites, and perhaps of much of the ordinary population as well, after the ban on intermarriage ended in the sixth century. The Fourth Council of Toledo in 633 referred to the population at large as part of a single *gens et patria*, just as the Seventh Council, thirteen years later, spoke of the kingdom as a whole as the *gens et patria Gothorum*.[15] After this there are no further references to a distinct "Roman" population. The Gothic language itself ceased to be used, even by the highest Visigothic elite, though the majority of children for which there is any record, even from more ordinary families, were given Gothic names.

This newer conclusion does not presume any sort of homogenization, much less any strong sense of harmony in society at large. Not only did the Visigothic high aristocracy maintain control of power, but by the late seventh century social tensions seem to have been increasing. Slavery persisted, there was more complaint than ever about the number of runaway slaves, and severe economic problems heightened pressures toward forms of enserfment for part of the free rural population. Spanish historians, especially, have been impressed by the severity of internal problems and are more skeptical about the degree of ethnic fusion. This remains an open question, difficult to resolve due to the paucity of evidence. Moreover, by the final generation of the Visigothic era, the tendency of the elite to assume settled territorial status seems to have created a growing equivalence with the native Hispanic elite, oriented toward land and wealth, and the maintenance of a patrimonial status, with less and less concern for military service, a factor in the military decline of the monarchy.

Américo Castro titled one brief section of his magnum opus "The Visigoths were not Spaniards," and in the fullest sense this is doubtless correct, but they did create the first political Spain, and at least began the process of forming a specific Spanish society, even though that process was far from complete by 700. They presided over a religious culture that was highly developed for that era, and also had begun to form a special kind of ideology and royal identity, so that at one point in the seventh century the Visigothic monarchy represented as fully developed a political and religious model as could be found in the West. Moreover, the Visigothic form of elite society—the military aristocracy—would remain the dominant elite form of Spain for the next millennium and more, until the nineteenth century.

The great failure of the Visigothic kingdom was not so much military as political; dissidence among elite aristocratic families could rarely be controlled for more than a decade or so at a time. The efforts by church leaders and a few others to "constitutionalize" succession to the crown, creating the most elaborate succession mechanism of any Christian state at that time, failed. Consequently the key to the Islamic conquest—part of which was not technically a military "conquest"—lay in the conditions of civil war, which reemerged in 710–11. A century and a half earlier, in 554, one Visigothic faction that claimed the throne had called in Byzantine military assistance, leading to the Byzantine occupation of the whole southeastern part of the peninsula for three-quarters of a century, before it was reconquered. The next reconquest would take much longer.

The Arab takeover of Spain was proportionately the fastest and most mysterious of all the extensive Islamic conquests. Major parts of less-developed North Africa resisted for decades before they finally succumbed. Later, seeing the fate of the Visigoths, the Merovingian French would resist far more vigorously. There is no doubt that peninsular society had been weakened in recent decades by drought, famine, and pestilence, but the key presumably lay in the suicidal rivalries within the Visigothic elite, one large sector of which assumed that after winning sizable booty, the Arabs would merely assist them in gaining power and then depart. Yet, once the king had been defeated and killed and much of the elite totally compromised, most of the kingdom collapsed politically without central resistance, thanks in part to the swift initiative of the Arab leadership, just as would be the case more than three centuries later within the more centralized, unified, and sophisticated Anglo-Saxon state after defeat in the Battle of Hastings in 1066. Earlier protracted North African resistance against the Muslims, like that of the inhabitants of the peninsula against the Romans centuries earlier, had been partly predicated on complete decentralization.

As indicated earlier, some historians have tended to view the only successful resistance nucleus emerging in Asturias as something of a spastic knee-jerk reaction by an early medieval remnant of "primitive rebels." This has been called the "indigenous theory" of the origins of the kingdom of Asturias. Crude tribesmen who had supposedly never bowed the knee to the Visigoths soon took up resistance against the Muslims, but the only continuity was local and rather primitive, the people of Asturias exhibiting no very sophisticated political, social, religious, or ideological features, as summarized in the work of Barbero and Vigil.

Since publication of Barbero and Vigil's book, northern Spain has been the object of the most extensive archaeological research that the region has ever known. Beginning with the first major new research project initiated in Asturias in 1980, a new golden age of archaeological investigation opened, soon yielding a rather different picture. Some of the results have been presented most cogently in the analytic synthesis published in 2001 by Luis Ramón Menéndez Bueyes, *Reflexiones críticas sobre el origen del Reino de Asturias.* Recent archaeological research reveals a greater degree of Romanization and of economic integration than had earlier been thought to be the case. Particularly in Asturias, though not so much in Cantabria proper, the structure of much of society turns out not to have differed so totally as had frequently been assumed. There is at least some evidence of political integration, as well. Asturias was one of the several Visigothic duchies, even though rather lightly populated and not fully integrated either socially or politically. The tentative new conclusion is that although the Asturias was not so heavily Romanized as the major areas of the south and east, the region revealed at least somewhat more sophisticated structure and political integration in Visigothic times than had earlier been thought.

This revisionist interpretation finds some evidence of incorporation of all the north, with the intermittent exception of the Basque territory, in the Visigothic system, involving a more complex social structure, greater (even if only partial) Christian identity and some degree of greater cultural sophistication. It concludes that there seem to have been three Visigothic duchies in the north—roughly Galicia, Asturias, and Cantabria—parts of which, at least, provided the structure for a successful struggle against the Muslims. One factor that all agree upon, of course, is the importance of geography, which made the northern mountains the most remote and difficult terrain for foreign conquerors to deal with. On the opposite side of the Islamic world, mountain ranges also turned back Arab conquerors. Six centuries later, the Spanish would face a similar problem in the opposite corner of the peninsula, where the conquest of Granada would constitute the longest, slowest, most costly phase of the Reconquest.

Thus the conundrum of the initiation of serious Christian resistance in the least Christanized part of the peninsula is scant problem for the revisionist interpretation, which finds somewhat more Christian structure there to begin with. Whatever Christian identity and practice already existed was quickly reinforced by the beginning of the first of a series of waves of emigration of Christians from the new Muslim-dominated Al Andalus (which comprised the greater part of the peninsula), a process recognized by all historians, which would continue intermittently for four centuries, add considerable density to the northern population, and probably a good deal more to its religious identity and intensity. There is even limited evidence of the immigration of North African Christians, as well. All this makes it rather less surprising that within a generation the resistance nucleus organized itself into a monarchy, that it soon developed new contacts with other parts of western Europe, and that it also developed a firm spirit, at least among the elites, of orthodox Roman Catholic religious identity and practice, as this was understood in the eighth century.

What remains quite controversial is the precise role and weight of sectors of the old Visigothic elite and of Visigoths or semi-Visigoths in this process. The old "Germanic thesis" held by historians in the late nineteenth and early twentieth centuries, which posited an unusually heavy concentration of Visigoths in part of what would later be Old Castile prior to the Arab conquest, was seriously challenged during the early twentieth century.

A different approach has been taken by Armando Besga Marroquín, who does not argue for any especial prior presence of Visigoths in the north, but rather, as is tersely indicated in one of the chronicles, that a significant number soon moved to Asturias to form a resistance nucleus, giving the early kingdom a heavily Gothic character.[16] We have no evidence of what Sánchez Albornoz called the ideology of "neogoticismo"—so fundamental for subsequent Spanish doctrine and the eventual Grand Narrative—before the ninth century, and no historian would maintain that Asturias represented direct continuity with the old Visigothic order. The kingdom of Asturias was a completely new creation, and the exact ethnic balance among its founders is something that can never be precisely determined. Nonetheless, the arguments of Besga Marroquín and others who emphasize direct Visigothic influences in political and religious affairs, as in culture, cannot be easily dismissed.

Whereas the Visigothic state, with its broad territorial domain, crumbled, the new kingdom of Asturias proved remarkably tough, resilient, and ultimately successful in almost every respect. It repeatedly fought off a much larger, more powerful, and sophisticated Muslim foe and even added new territory at the expense of the latter. Rather than wilting under the contest, it gained population, partly thanks to immigration and an astute repopulation policy. It created a new church

structure, reaffirmed its relations with the broader Latin Christian culture, produced at least one religious writer read widely in other lands, and created an original
style in art and architecture—the "Asturian Pre-Romanesque"—without precedent in the western Europe of that era.[17] Its society developed increasing cohesive-
ness and integration despite internal political conflicts, to which might be applied
as working hypothesis the influence of fuller Christianization in breaking down
the remnants of clan and tribal structures, and encouraging the role of the exo-
gamic family. Later, as the Andalusi state weakened in the great *fitna* (internal conflict) of the late ninth century, a portion of the Asturian elite espoused the goal of
complete reconquest, something that could hardly have been imagined a generation or two earlier. Rather than finding the first crystallization of such an ambition
artificial and pretentious, as was sometimes the tendency in twentieth-century
historiography, the revisionist interpretation finds this a natural consequence of
Asturian culture and institutions, and of the circumstances of that time.[18]

Whether the field of "climate history" is of any use here is difficult to determine. It has rather frequently been observed that Late Antiquity experienced a
harsh climate in much of the Mediterranean, with prolonged droughts and other
problems. What seems clear is that the rise of Asturias (and later of Castile) coincided with the five centuries of warmer and more benign climate in western
Europe and the north Atlantic between approximately 800 and 1300. This may
have made the northern mountainous regions of the peninsula more productive
and capable of sustaining a larger population.

The Spanish Grand Narrative tended to reify and exaggerate, as presumably all
grand narratives do. While recent research suggests somewhat greater precedent
within the kingdom of the Visigoths than had often thought, the Grand Narrative's emphasis, in its classic form, on Catholic mission, a chosen people, and implacable reconquest has always gone beyond what the historical evidence yields.
Though one may find roots of what might be termed a "Spanish ideology" in San
Isidoro, concepts of ideology and mission evolved only slowly and intermittently
among the elite of Asturias and León. Asturias was made the target of an official
"jihadi" assault under the Emir Hisham I in the final years of the eighth century,
but no official concept of "crusade" as "counter-jihad" developed. The struggle
against Al-Andalus was apparently viewed in the first generations as a sort of territorial war, first a struggle for survival and then a conflict against a usurper who
should be dispossessed of whatever was possible. Nearly two centuries were required, so far as we know, to generate the goal of total reconquest, at least as the official goal of the Asturian leadership, and then because of the internal weakening of
the Andalusi state. Nor could such a doctrine be sustained after the revival of Andalusi power a generation later. While Al-Andalus practiced jihad according to pris-
tine Islamic concepts (which, unlike some twenty-first-century variants, included

certain rules of war), the wars of Asturias and León could be called "religious wars" only in the sense of military conflict by a Christian state against an Islamic one. These were not a crusade in the later sense of a war officially blessed with special spiritual endorsement and spiritual rewards directly by the Church itself. They were, however, campaigns increasingly fought with a claim to "legitimacy," to the recovery of lands usurped by foreigners, based on an identity whose roots were rather deeper than some twentieth-century historians have thought.

2 | Spain and Islam

The Myth of Al-Andalus

During the late twentieth century, Western multiculturalists began to imagine utopias of cultural and ethnic
"diversity," as they liked to put it, in which distinct cultures and civilizations
would coexist harmoniously.[1] This ideal became a prominent feature of cultural
and educational institutions in western Europe and, especially, North America.

It was difficult, not to say impossible, to find an historical precedent for such
a utopia, since all known civilizations have insisted on the primacy of their own
culture, but some commentators have thought to identify such a unique society
in medieval Spain. As early as the mid-nineteenth century, historians and writers
evoked a mythical paradise in medieval Al-Andalus, which was declared to have
achieved a culture of genuine tolerance, compared with which all the rest of Spanish history might be seen as a decline. A century later Américo Castro gave this a
new spin from his American exile, in the several successive versions of his magnum
opus imagining a unique situation of what he termed "convivencia." Most recently
such an image of tolerance and cultural cross-fertilization has been eloquently
evoked in a work by the Harvard literature professor María Rosa Menocal, *The*

Ornament of the World (2002).[2] The title is taken from a comment by an eleventh-century German nun, and the product is a sort of novel, written with considerable charm, consisting of a series of pen portraits of leading cultural personalities.

In this idyll, Christians and Muslims quarrel more among themselves than they do with each other, while cooperating with Jews in creating a unique multicultural paradise. There is, of course, always a serpent in the Garden of Eden, and in Menocal's case it takes the form of the fanatical Islamists of the two successive Moroccan empires that invaded the Iberian Peninsula in the eleventh and twelfth centuries. The intolerant domination of this hostile and unenlightened Other is perceived as beginning to put an end to the Andalusi utopia, though it is presented as considerably oppressing enlightened Muslims more than anyone else. Menocal's novel, presented as cultural history, exerted a strong appeal in the contemporary academy, with its pretensions to the multicultural. This is all the more the case since she never mentions the centuries of bloody conflict between Christians and Muslims, and the word "conquest" or "reconquest" never appears.

Menocal's book is but one of the most concerted expressions of the "myth of Al-Andalus" that has been propagated for a century and a half, acquiring renewed force in recent years. The Muslim invaders of 711 are portrayed as variously entering, incorporating, or colonizing the Iberian Peninsula (as if no one lived there), replacing a decadent and dreary band of elitist Visigoths—presumably all "dead white males"—who failed to achieve multiculturalism and deserve no respect. The reexamination of Visigothic history that has been carried on during the past two generations is conveniently ignored because it might complicate the introduction of this dream world.

The Muslim eruption into the Iberian Peninsula took place near the end of the first century of massive Islamic empire-building. Subsequent phases under other Muslim empires elsewhere would continue for a full millennium, into the seventeenth century.[3] In extent the only equal in world history would be the conquests of the Mongols six hundred years later, while the duration was without parallel. Unlike the Mongols, the Arabs would soon construct a major new civilization, which would impose itself permanently on each of the many lands conquered, Islamized and in most cases Arabized, with the sole exception of Spain. Only in the Iberian Peninsula was a large territory both conquered and for the most part culturally and religiously Islamized, only to be reconquered and de-Islamized by a portion of its pre-Muslim inhabitants. This fact alone would have made Spain absolutely unique in world history, if the Spanish had never accomplished anything else.[4]

The rapidity of the Muslim conquest of 711–18, despite the limited numbers of the invaders, was due to the internal division of the Visigoths and their inability to mount a central or organized resistance, once the monarchy had been decapitated at the outset. By 718 politico-military control had been extended, albeit very tenuously, over the entire peninsula. From there the seemingly inexhaustible Muslim tide poured into France, establishing a limited control over its southwestern part, until a major defeat in 732. Even so, new raiding parties continued to cross into France during the next few years, these attacks coming to an end only because of the overextension and exhaustion of the invaders.

Military expansion has been a common feature of many different states and societies in human history. Islamic civilization was not the first to operate under a religious imperative for military conquest. What is unique, however, is that Islam is the only major world religion that categorically requires continuing military action against unbelievers, and its followers have been remarkable for the long persistence and, for centuries, the relative success, of their military conquests. In the West, North African Muslims would later conquer Sicily in the ninth century and continue assaults on western Europe into the fourteenth century. In the form of large-scale piracy and slave raiding, attacks would continue for half a millennium more, into the early nineteenth century. The assaults on eastern Europe began early in the eighth century (at approximately the time of the conquest of Spain) and would be continued by the Ottomans throughout the latter Middle Ages and beyond that until the end of the seventeenth century, becoming a major factor in east European underdevelopment.[5]

The obligation to "exertion" in jihad as military conquest of unbelievers was thus a constant feature of Islamic culture and practice for more than a thousand years, declining in modern times only as Muslim societies became categorically inferior in military terms. During the twentieth century the major Muslim power, Turkey, then turned to genocide against its Christian minorities. The numerous references in the Koran to the obligation to fight militarily and to kill on behalf of the faith constitute one of the most striking differences between Christianity and Islam. Mohammed also referred to personal spiritual struggle as the "greater jihad," and in modern times this spiritual interpretation has come more to the fore, but the military jihad was at no time forgotten and was always periodically revived by activists or political leaders, even though the great majority of ordinary Muslims have never participated in it.[6]

The new rulers of Al-Andalus would face militarily in three directions—to the north against Christian Europe (after the mid-eighth century meaning primarily the small, weak, new Spanish principalities), internally against all manner of domestic rebels, and later south and east toward the expansion of their power in North Africa and the west Mediterranean. Concern for the internal and southern fronts often provided a military respite to the new Spanish states, which they took advantage of for internal consolidation and the expansion of their own borders. When conditions permitted, the jihad was persistently invoked against these remaining Christian territories in the peninsula, though trans-Pyrenean assaults were eventually renounced as impractical. When Andalusi arms were successful, heads of slain Christians were regularly displayed on the walls of Córdoba, not the symbol of an especially tolerant society. On the other hand, after the 720s the Andalusi rulers made little effort to conquer completely the Christian resistance in the north, instead occupying new frontier positions or posting frontier garrisons. The goal of the frequent raids against the north, what was called the *sa'ifa* (Sp. "aceifa"), was rather to weaken the Christian enemy and to bring back slaves and booty.

The initial terms of the Muslims for subject populations tended to be relatively generous, a policy indeed virtually required by the limited numbers of the Muslims themselves at the beginning of their conquests. Aristocrats and other land-holders who accepted Muslim domination without resistance were generally confirmed in the control of their properties. Freedom of religion was recognized for Christians and Jews, and initially the latter enjoyed greater opportunities than under the Visigoths, who had persecuted them severely. It has been suggested— though historians do not really know—that the obligations of the peasantry were no greater, and possibly even lighter, than under the Visigoths. Serfs, for example, were often transformed into sharecroppers, which may have eased their lot. These factors made it easier to accept the initial Islamic domination; the Visigothic allies of the invaders soon had to accept complete subordination, even though most continued to hold their original lands, so long as they obeyed.[7]

During the course of the eighth century, however, as the Islamic system was consolidated, its full features were introduced into the new realm known as "Al-Andalus."[8] The taxes paid by non-Muslims were regularized as a land tax and a separate poll tax, and religious activities were restricted. No new churches were allowed to be built, some of the existing churches were converted into mosques, and bell-ringing and any form of Christian religious activity outside of churches prohibited. The proselytizing of Muslims was punishable by death, and any Muslim who converted was liable to the same penalty. By the middle of the ninth century, as the Muslim population increased, Jews and Christians had to wear special clothing to indicate their religion. They could not marry Muslim women, could ride only on donkeys, had to give up their seats whenever a Muslim wanted to sit, and were denied equality in judicial procedures. The terms of this kind of "discriminatory toleration" slowly grew more oppressive with each passing generation.

Given the restrictions on and discrimination against Jews and Christians, did any real "convivencia" take place in Al-Andalus, beyond mere physical juxtaposition? Two kinds of convivencia of a sort might be found. One was cooperation at the elite level between individual Christians, Jews, and Muslims, who to some extent worked with each other and exchanged information regarding learned texts and scholarly interests. In addition, the Andalusi state frequently employed

Christians in various capacities, just as the late medieval Spanish kingdoms employed Jews. There was also considerable economic contact, trade, and also the hiring of labor. None of this, however, in any way blurred the basic caste lines.

In the mixed population of the cities, there was a tendency to segregate neighborhoods, but this was sometimes impractical, so that there were sometimes Christian and Muslim households living side by side. We have little or no information as to how this functioned. The households were not equal, because the Christians paid much heavier taxes, might not enjoy the same standard of living, and were subject to significant discrimination, but at least they were permitted to survive. Muslim minorities—the Mudejares, as they would be called—incorporated by the advance of the Spanish kingdoms (mainly in the thirteenth century) experienced much the same kinds of conditions, once they were part of the inferior, rather than the superior, caste. Friendly relations between individuals and families certainly took place, particularly in the mixed cities, but those friendly relations on the individual level never blurred the distinct caste lines for Andalusi or Christian society as a whole. For the most part, even in areas where populations were mixed, the castes remained distinct, and there were no systematic efforts to cross caste lines either in society or culture, for, with regard to anything beyond limited gestures, such a practice would have been tabu. Cultural elites, for example, hardly ever studied each other's religion.

Some Spanish historians have wished to see the Muslim Andalusis as to a considerable degree "Hispanized," that is, heavily influenced by the Christian society and culture whose members for approximately two centuries made up the majority of the population of Al-Andalus. There is little evidence of this. Since eventually the bulk of the Muslim population would be composed of Hispanic converts (the "white Moors," whose presence would later astonish European visitors to the peninsula), not the children of Middle Eastern or African immigrants, they undoubtedly maintained certain habits or customs that were not the same as those in Egypt or Iraq. But the entire structure of culture and of society and government became heavily "orientalized," reproducing fundamentally the same structures and mores to be found in the Middle East. Al-Andalus was not a "Western" or "European" variant of Islamic society in anything other than a geographic sense, but it simply became the westernmost projection of Arabic-speaking Middle Eastern society and culture. The great Muslim historian Ibn Khaldun recognized that, at least in one sense, the Arabs were the worst overlords—compared with Romans, Greeks, or Persians—for they largely obliterated the languages and cultures of the areas that they conquered, with only a few exceptions, and to that extent did not maintain classic empires.

This was reflected not merely in religion and high culture, but at all levels of life from urban configurations and architecture to cuisine, clothing, and social and marriage arrangements. Noteworthy was the typical Muslim subjection of women, totally different from the situation in Hispano-Christian society, where women could inherit and to some extent maintain property in their own right, and eventually reign individually as monarch of an entire kingdom. In this regard Islamic civilization constituted a marked regression from the Roman civilization that it replaced in the south Mediterranean. Late Roman law permitted daughters to inherit equally with sons and present equal testimony in court, whereas Islamic law provides women with only a half a share in inheritance and assigns their testimony only half the weight of a man's.

Arab and Berber elites zealously maintained their native tribal and clan structures, based on strongly agnatic and endogamous relationships. The political structure of Al-Andalus represented the typical despotism of the Middle East, replete with the equivalent bureaucracy and slave soldiers, without any parallel in the European kingdoms of that era. Arab and other minority non-Hispanic groups always dominated the power structure, even after the breakup of the caliphate in the eleventh century. Descendants of Muslim converts formed no taifa or independent dynasties, all of whom were led by Arabs, Berbers, or Slavic slave soldiers.[9] As Anwar Chejne puts it, Al-Andalus "was always an integral part of the literary and cultural mainstream of the East and, as such, was as Islamic as Syria or Egypt."[10] Historically and culturally, Al-Andalus followed the same chronological trajectory as the Arab civilization of the Middle East, reaching a plateau of acculturation in the ninth and tenth centuries, achieving its maximum cultural sophistication during the eleventh and twelfth centuries, then experiencing major decline, accompanied by conquest from without, in the thirteenth century.

It must be remembered that during the early formative centuries of the Christian kingdoms, from the eighth to the thirteenth centuries, the great bulk of the independent Christian population did not normally live in direct contact with Muslims. The "Mozarab" Christians in Al-Andalus were much more affected, however, and by the ninth century were becoming increasingly Arabized or, if one prefers, "orientalized." Those who found this most repugnant seem to have emigrated to the north, if conditions permitted. Later, the Muslim, or Mudejar, minority incorporated into the Spanish kingdoms proved more resistant to Christian and Spanish influence, preserving its caste identity and culture to a greater extent than had the Mozarabs, though most of them eventually Hispanicized linguistically and lost the use of Arabic.

Eventually most of the native Hispanic population remaining in Al-Andalus converted to Islam. When did that take place? The only attempt to estimate this was carried out by the American historian Richard W. Bulliet, applying a technique that he had earlier used for Egypt, Syria, and Persia. Bulliet's rough calculation was that by 800 only about 8 percent of the native population had converted,

a figure that increased to only 12.5 percent fifty years later. With the full crystallization of Andalusi society and culture during the ninth century, the rate of conversion began to accelerate. By 900 about 25 percent had converted, and 50 percent
by 950. By the end of the tenth century the figure might have stood at 75 percent,
by which time the population of Al-Andalus had become overwhelmingly Muslim. Small Christian minorities nonetheless remained until at least the twelfth
century, until they were finally eliminated altogether by the Islamist empire of the
Moroccan Almohads.[11]

In theory all Muslims form part of the *umma*, or general Islamic community.
In practice, however, Muslim society has been riven by ethnic tensions, which in
Al-Andalus were profound, as much or more than in any other Islamic land. Prior
to the eleventh century, and even to some extent afterward, the elite remained
Arab and looked down on the Berbers (the other principal group of Muslims of
foreign origins) and the native converts, as well as on Christians and Jews. Other
sectors of society responded with intense resentment, leading to sporadic revolt
and great violence, as political division formed along geographic and ethnic lines.
In theory, Islam, like Christianity, rejects racial discrimination, but reality revealed
otherwise. The Arabs exhibited a powerful sense of caste and racial superiority, de-
meaning racially inferior "sons of white women," even though those same white
women were the ones most greatly desired for Arab harems. Even the *Muwalladun*
(Sp. "muladíes"), the native Spanish converts to Islam, were sometimes derided for
their white complexions, compared with the Arab elite. Muslim society featured
widespread slavery, which like the slavery of the Ancient World was multiracial,
slaves being drawn from every race and ethnic group not Muslim, but black slaves
from Africa normally occupied the lowest position. Andalusi society remained
highly segmented, not merely among the religions, but in terms of the different
categories of Muslims—the Arab elite divided by lineages, tribes, and districts
from the Berbers (and their own internal segments) and the convert majority of
native Hispani.

At its height, the high culture of the cities of Al-Andalus rivaled that of
the great Muslim centers of the Middle East. The scholarly and scientific texts of
Greece and Rome had generally been translated into Arabic by the tenth century,
but it is a mistake to think that the classic manuscripts (Latin, Greek, Syriac, Persian) were preserved, for "infidel" texts, no matter how high the quality and originality, were generally destroyed after being translated into Arabic. The high culture that soon developed in the Islamic world was a "transfer culture," for the
lands originally conquered by the Muslims—Syria, Persia, Egypt, and to some degree the Visigothic kingdom—all had active and vibrant high cultures. The rise of
learning in the Islamic world was a matter of taking over these foundations,
though, unlike the imperialism of Rome and some later Western imperialisms,

Arab imperialism in most areas steadily erased native languages and largely suppressed independent native cultures. In toto, Arab culture borrowed much more from Syria, Byzantium, and Persia than Western culture would later borrow from it, but in its first mature phase fostered a level of learning, which, prior to the thirteenth century, surpassed that of western Europe. By the tenth century Muslim scholars were doing advanced work of their own in mathematics, astronomy, botany, geography, medicine, and other sciences. For several centuries they excelled in historical writing, but there was very limited development in humanist thought.[12]

Philosophical study was limited to a comparatively brief period, for Islam is a religion of orthopraxy and correct outward conduct, and discourages broader speculation or any extended inquiry into theology or philosophy, holding that there should be no debate or dissension among believers.[13] The most famous Muslim philosophers, the Persian Avicenna and the Andalusi Averroes (Ibn Rushd), primarily wrote commentaries on Aristotle and other thinkers, failing to develop complete new systems of their own. Such commentary ultimately had its main impact on Western thought, which, unlike that of the Muslims, learned to study contrasting points of view.[14] By comparison, Averroes had no significant influence on Islamic thought, which rejected his insights. There was very little in the way of original Islamic philosophy, for that was precluded by the literalism of the Koran and the resultant character of Islamic doctrine.[15]

By the thirteenth century, the Islamic and Western worlds were headed in different directions, as the margin of freedom and tolerance in the former shrank. The new Western universities expanded their activities, while the intellectual culture of the Islamic lands declined. The rigid, intolerant and anti-intellectual tendencies in Islamic religion and culture eventually became totally dominant. By about 1100, learning and science in the West showed the first signs of approximation in range and quality with that of the Islamic world, and by 1300 were pulling ahead.[16] Subsequent cultural development in Muslim Persia and India was primarily artistic in character. The mark of a tolerant and creative civilization is to be able to deal with contrary ideas, something that the West was slowly beginning to do to a limited degree. Differences were becoming equally or more marked in economic organization and in technology, where by the fourteenth century the West was slowly becoming dominant. In later times, wherever Muslims lived side by side with other religious communities, whether as a majority or a minority, the latter would almost always show greater capacity for development and modernization.

As of the tenth century, the Andalusis excelled in high culture, in most of the practical arts, and in most aspects of esthetics. They had introduced Arabic numerals, certain advanced agricultural techniques, and a series of new fruits, vegetables, and other foods, as well as silk, paper, glass, and new kinds of ceramics. By the eleventh century, on the other hand, Spanish Christians were beginning to excel in military technology and in political development, their structures of law, rights, and civic institutions creating stronger internal solidarity than the ultimately more fragile Muslim despotisms.

The greatest failure of Al-Andalus was political. Generally speaking, there has been little political development in Islamic societies. Since Islam originated in the commercially sophisticated Middle East, commercial and property law in the *sharia* was at first more advanced than that of the West, but criminal law remained harsh and primitive, as it stands even in the twenty-first century. The sharia enshrines traditionalism and the status quo, underwriting a tribal and clan structure of Middle Eastern and Andalusi society, which precluded political evolution. The reinforcement of clan and tribal structures hardened the segmentation of Andalusi society, in which political loyalty was owed primarily to lineages, not to institutions. Classical Islamic thought had little theory of the state or of political development and representation. To a greater degree than most other systems, Islamic states rest on military and police power. The theory of Islamic society posits a kind of utopia but, as is the norm with utopias, in practice tends to foster despotisms.

Those who propose a picture of Andalusi society and institutions as "tolerant" and "convivientes" altogether fail to explain why Andalusi history was wracked by revolts of all kinds—by Berbers, by Muwalladun, sometimes even by the Arab elites. Though the Christian Mozarabs were generally, but not always, passive, the only sector of this highly divided and segmented society that did not rebel were the Jews, the smallest religious minority, totally lacking in military power. The only periods in which there were no internal revolts were the reigns of the most strongly despotic rulers, who governed with an absolutely iron hand and distracted many of their followers by their numerous attacks against the Christian principalities. Throughout the history of Al-Andalus, rebellions of all kinds were repressed vigorously, often with the utmost violence. Cordoban rulers never hesitated to carry out full-scale massacres of their subjects, without the slightest pretext of judicial procedure. This further explains why, once the central caliphal state collapsed early in the eleventh century, most of Al-Andalus found it itself increasingly defenseless, by comparison with the Christian principalities. Under the decentralized, rights-centered, partially representative institutions of the latter, nearly that entire society could be counted on for military service. The Andalusi despotism, by contrast, tried to disarm Andalusi society, which it fundamentally distrusted, relying on its own central Arab-based tribal units, stiffened by the typically Islamic "slave soldiers" and numerous mercenaries.

Spanish Christian rulers also had to quell numerous rebellions, but this was due above all to elite dissidence, not to ethnic segmentation. Their principalities were much more successful in building polities over the long run, with evolving structures of law, social rights, and a certain degree of broader participation and representation.

Slavery was a major feature of tolerant, "conviviente" Andalusi society, which maintained major international slave markets in Córdoba and other large cities. Mohammed declared that Muslims could not be held as slaves but otherwise explicitly approved slavery as an institution in Islamic society, the slave population to be made up of the many prisoners captured in Islamic military conquest and others purchased on the international market. The frequent "aceifas" launched against the Spanish principalities were designed to a considerable extent as slave raids.

Slavery in the Islamic world was multiracial, as in ancient Rome, non-Muslims from any ethnic or racial group being possible victims. A major new feature of Islamic slavery, however, was development of a large-scale black African slave trade. Black slaves had been found in Rome, but their numbers were very few, whereas the Arabs were the first to make the acquisition of sizable numbers of African slaves a major activity. The Muslims were also the first to categorize blacks as uniquely racially inferior and hence more naturally and appropriately enslaved. Arabs were thus not inhibited in seizing slaves from black Muslim tribes, as well.[17] Whereas slavery largely died out in western Europe outside Italy, the influence of the Islamic slave-raiding border helped to sustain the presence of slavery in the Spanish Christian principalities, which imbibed the Muslim attitude toward black slavery and, by the close of the fifteenth century, would position themselves to surpass the Muslims in the African slave trade.[18] Conversely, the most positive aspect of Islamic slavery was the encouragement of regular emancipation or the purchasing of freedom after conversion (even though this was not always observed in practice), so that multigenerational slave castes generally did not develop, even though slave markets thrived in the Middle East and Africa well into the twentieth century.[19]

Despite the persistence of military violence for eight centuries, relations between Spaniards and Andalusis were extremely complex. The entire period was punctuated by numerous official truces, though none lasted for more than a few years. For centuries, Islamic orthodoxy held that there could be no regular peace between the "House of Islam" and the "House of War," that is, the entire non-Islamic world, which was to remain under assault until it had been forced to submit to Islam (the word Islam itself means "submission"). It was soon deemed appropriate, however, to desist from military operations if an adjoining non-Islamic power was willing to pay some form of tribute. In the Iberian Peninsula, whenever practical reasons moved the ruler of the Islamic state (Umayyad, Almoravid, or Almohad) to a temporary truce with one or more of the Christian kingdoms, the customary bearing of minor gifts that accompanied any embassy was interpreted by means of a legal fiction as payment of "tribute," hence rendering the truce legitimate under Islamic doctrine.

The frontier between the two civilizations was hostile and violent, but also highly permeable.[20] Spanish Christians developed a kind of familiarity of both military and political relations with the Muslims unknown beyond the Pyrenees. Rules of war often thus obtained surprised, even shocked, European Christians. When the latter helped the Aragonese to seize Barbastro in 1063, they proposed to subject the Muslim inhabitants to violent extortion, rape, slavery, or even death, but were restrained by the Aragonese, who told them that was simply not the way things were done. Roughly speaking, Spanish Christians seemed to have accepted Koranic rules of warfare, which allowed for such practices only if a city refused to agree to terms.

In times of truce both Christian and Muslim rulers, as well as opposition factions on both sides, did not hesitate to enter political deals and even cross-cultural alliances. On occasion, Christian rulers sought and obtained Muslim military assistance against either internal rebels or rival princes in other kingdoms, as did dynastic or aristocratic factions who rebelled against them. Andalusi rulers employed Christian mercenaries in their semiprofessional armed forces and also made use of Christian rebels against the northern kingdoms. By the eleventh century, as the Córdoba caliphate weakened, Muslim rulers or rebel factions sought and obtained Christian military intervention on their own behalf. Although cross-cultural political and military alliance was not the norm, neither was it infrequent, but simply one feature of a long and complex relationship that was always ultimately adversarial, but part of the time was peaceful and occasionally might even be complementary, rarely even intimate.

There was nothing uniquely Spanish about all this, for such practices have existed at times in every region in which Christian and Muslim states lived in conditions of at least relative equilibrium. Even Crusader states in Syria and Palestine sometimes formed such alliances, as much later did European governments with the Ottoman empire. None of that meant that either the Crusaders or the European states ever modified their primary identity, or were involved in any marked "cultural hybridity."

To the extent that the medieval Spanish experienced any genuine convivencia, this did not take place in Al-Andalus, where Christians completely disappeared, but in the Reconquest Christian kingdoms from the late eleventh century on. The era from the mid-thirteenth to mid-fourteenth centuries has been called the "Mudejar century," for by then the incorporation of Muslim minorities had reached its height, and a certain amount of cultural diffusion took place. In the conquered southern cities, Spanish architecture introduced its distinctive style of impressive facades but retained the existing Muslim configuration of narrow, winding streets with little public space. Christian architecture was considerably superior and had little to learn from that of the Muslims, but Andalusi or Mudejar architectural decoration generally won favor and became a common Spanish motif during this era. The public baths that existed in medieval Spain were probably not so much a matter of Islamic influence as of the Roman tradition, for at that time they sometimes existed beyond the Pyrenees as well, being eliminated throughout Europe by the sixteenth century.

The general trend of the thirteenth to fifteenth centuries was a slow but increasing assimilation to Spanish Christian culture, though much more on the part of the Jewish, than the Muslim, minority. The Jewish elite began to aspire to something equivalent to aristocratic status, while even in independent Granada, the last Muslim state, the upper class sometimes donned Christian-style clothing. Conversely, Castilian elites often found it modish to adopt bright-colored Muslim garb.

Ultimately, what took place between Christians and Muslims was a form of coexistence not equivalent to Américo Castro's convivencia. There were individual conversions, primarily of Jews and Muslims to Christianity, and also a certain number of mixed marriages (commonly of a Christian man with a Muslim woman), but the kind of cultural assimilation found among much of the Jewish population did not generally extend to Muslims. Technical borrowing in esthetics, economic production, and technology took place on both sides, but the Mudejar minority showed no signs of general assimilation, even though it seems to have had a kind of hybrid culture, Islamic in its fundamentals of religion and thought, marriage and family, food and dress, though partially assimilated in its economic life. Bernard Vincent has judged that "Morisco and Christian culture clashed in nearly every respect. Their two styles of life were diametrically opposed. The inner organization of Morisco homes and the way houses were grouped in neighborhoods in no way resembled the way in which Christians did such things."[21] Christians were offended by the sounds of Muslim music and ceremonies, the scent of the perfume Muslims used, and the bright color of their clothing, whose style and tone were so different from the more austere Spanish manner. They found equally offensive such basic domestic practices as sitting on the floor to eat without tables, chairs, or benches, and sleeping on the floor in standard oriental style on mats rather than in beds. With the Moriscos, at least, the segmented culture of Al-Andalus continued into the seventeenth century.

Beginning in the fifteenth century, and even more in the years that followed, enemies of the Spanish kingdoms denounced Spanish society as racially and culturally bastardized, a mixture of Moors and Jews, hence inherently inferior to the strictly Christian societies of other parts of western Europe. By the nineteenth century, as denunciation and propaganda began to give way to more serious observation, there arose the only slightly more empirical notion of "oriental Spain," the only part of the West that was somehow also part of the East, because of the supposedly profound influence of the "Moors." (The common use of the latter term, by Spaniards and foreigners alike, would presumably have surprised and offended the Andalusis themselves. It probably reflected the fact that most foreign Muslims who entered the peninsula were Moroccan and other Berbers, not Arabs, and also stemmed from the continued massive Moroccan invasions between the eleventh and fourteenth centuries.)

This raises the question—how much and what kind of influence did the Muslims have on Spanish culture, society, and institutions? The influence is often considered to have been profound, but was it really? The issue was at the crux of the quarrel between Castro and Sánchez Albornoz, probably the most famous two-man controversy in all Spanish historiography.

To begin with, there are approximately four thousand words in Castilian and other peninsular languages that are derived from Arabic (with rather fewer in Catalan), having to do specifically with such areas as geography, economic practices, basic technology, and administration. They are almost all words for things, rather than for sentiments (although there are a few for the latter, as well), and entered the vocabulary primarily between the thirteenth and sixteenth centuries, as the Spanish occupied nearly all of Al-Andalus and incorporated a sizable Muslim minority.[22] The vocabulary of Castilian is, however, quite large, and such words—though among those frequently used—amount to a very small percentage of the total. Grammar and syntax remained totally unaffected. Obviously Arabic had some influence, but whether this could be considered a profound influence is more doubtful.

Spanish culture, on the one hand, and the country's institutional theory and practice, on the other, are all of the west European type. There is some Islamic influence in Spanish literature, but again the degree is quite limited, having to do with certain medieval poetic forms and plotlines. No influence may be found in religious culture, theology, or church organization and administration, or in philosophical thought, high culture, or political philosophy and practice. The fact that an occasional term of Arab origin may appear in the roster of administration positions is a technicality, not an oriental model. Even Spanish diet reveals only modest traces of Andalusi or Mudejar influence, rejecting the semivegetarian Andalusi cuisine and most of its favorite foods, such as couscous, which has no place in Spanish diet, which conversely always featured pork, like that of other Europeans.

Popular songs and music have no Arab meter, and in fact Spanish music, even of the earlier period, could not be played on the typically Muslim instruments. The oldest of the well-known Spanish, mainly Andalusian, dances originated no earlier than the sixteenth century. Similarly the origins of flamenco and cante jondo, the "lerele" style, are modern Andalusian, and traditional gypsy, a style that first began to emerge in the Jerez-Cádiz triangle toward the end of the eighteenth century, achieved its full form in Seville and some of the larger Andalusian cities soon after the middle of the nineteenth century, from where it soon spread to Madrid. It does have certain oriental roots, but the orient from which part of flamenco stems is the musical culture that the gypsies brought from India, not the Arab Middle East.

In the late Middle Ages, the principal influence or expression of Muslim culture in Spanish lay in certain areas of esthetics, most especially in the decorative style generally called Mudejar. This lasted for approximately two centuries as architectural and other kinds of decoration for buildings whose plan and character, however, were not those of Muslim Granada but of Christian Spain. "Mudejar style" remained a Spanish form that was revived early in the twentieth century.

Proponents of "romantic Spain" would nonetheless argue that Spanish "psychology" reveals considerable oriental influence. To what precisely would such an observation refer? Its proponents usually point to such qualities as rhetoric, emotionality, spontaneity, frequent dissidence, and lack of cooperation, or any one of a number of other things. Richard Ford, in his famous *Handbook for Travellers in Spain* (1845), tried to be more precise than most, pointing to such qualities as hospitality, gratitude, fear of contamination or of the "evil eye," of women sitting on the floor of churches, and of the "resignation" of the Spanish. Occasional individual traits might be noticed, such as a greater tendency of Spanish women to cover their faces, or a special flourish, such as the contraction "q.s.p.b." (standing for "que sus pies besa"—who kisses your feet—a rhetorical gesture not common in other Western discourse). When totaled up, however, it is rather thin stuff, since many of these characteristics might be found in other European countries in varying degrees. On the other hand, Spanish essentialists, beginning to some extent in the sixteenth century, have held that Spanish psychology is in fact a kind of racial constant since pre-Roman times. Is either contention—the "orientalist" or the "essentialist"—correct? Is either verifiable or an empirical hypothesis capable of falsification? This would seem doubtful, since each rests on vague but sweeping generalizations that cannot be empirically verified. Many of the things that seemed so "different" about the Spanish during the nineteenth and much of the twentieth centuries were the consequence not of orientalism but of the relative traditionalism of Spanish society, slower to undergo the changes experienced by the rest of western Europe. This is not to deny that Spanish society has its idiosyncrasies, as do all others, but those customs or attitudes that can be determined to have stemmed directly from the Muslims are quite limited.

Culturally, the ethnic group that at first benefited from Islamic dominion were the Spanish Jews, who enjoyed both greater tolerance and greater opportunities than under the Visigoths, so that Al-Andalus witnessed a flowering of Jewish culture. As early as the late tenth century, however, intolerance and oppression began to mount. By the late eleventh century, Jewish attitudes were changing from a preference for Muslim rule to an equidistant attitude toward Christians and Jews, and by the second half of the twelfth century had begun to swing toward a pro-Christian orientation, by that point finding greater tolerance and opportunity under Christian rule.[23] From that time stemmed the pronounced Hispanization of peninsular Jewry.

The frontier conflict with Islam did not end with the conquest of Granada in 1492. Compared with the fifteenth century, the struggles of the first seven decades of the sixteenth century were equally or sometimes even more intense. The Testament of Isabel la Católica commended the crusade and the continuation of the Reconquest into North Africa to the Castilians, something initiated nearly three centuries earlier by Fernando III el Santo. The most difficult battles of the sixteenth century were those fought with the Turks in the Mediterranean, where the Habsburg forces gained their most famous victory (Lepanto), but also suffered their worst and most costly defeats, indeed the only notable reverses suffered by Spanish arms during that period. It is calculated that during the early modern period as many as 150,000 Spaniards were taken prisoner by Muslim pirates.[24] The historical literature is full of accounts of English, Dutch, and French pirates attacking Spanish shipping in the Atlantic, but overall the most costly piracy was the continuous Muslim assaults of the sixteenth, seventeenth, and eighteenth centuries. Through the eighteenth century the Spanish crown retained not only its Moroccan plazas but also the key city of Oran as well, but the most notable defeat suffered under Carlos III, when the Spanish empire reached its greatest geographical extent overseas, was the effort to seize Algiers and put an end to its slave raiding.[25]

The long confrontation with Islam was in some ways the major formative factor, as well as the major de-formative factor, in Spanish history. The Muslim conquest of the eastern and southern Mediterranean was a world-historical disaster, removing much of the ancient Greco-Roman world from the eventual course of civilization, largely destroying the original languages and culture of these regions, and thus consigning them to an oriental civilization that after five centuries became stagnant. It destroyed the possibility of any organic evolution of the original Hispano-Visigothic culture, which was, as we have seen, as advanced as any in western Europe. Spanish society then formed itself around a new militant culture that, though remarkably open to international influences in the Middle Ages, also developed aspects of a caste culture, partially peripheral to the European core of which it formed a part. The strongly orthodox Catholicism of the medieval Spanish guaranteed their place in the new Western culture of Latin Christendom, and they would not undergo the fate of other Christian societies to the south and east. This frontier culture, however, focused on military and, later, imperial priorities, failed to develop fully all the institutions that would become common to the Western core, and the consequences helped to set Spanish society on the differential path it trod during the sixteenth and seventeenth centuries.

Spanish society has been criticized for not fully reciprocating Islamic "tolerance," but that in fact is exactly what it did. The Spanish did not respond to the fanatical intolerance of Almoravids and Almohads in equivalent terms, but throughout the twelfth and thirteenth centuries, and after, maintained the traditional system of discriminatory toleration. In that period they were more, not less, tolerant than the Muslims, and occasionally even allowed public prayers from Mudejar minarets. In Castilian law, oaths sworn by members of all three religions at one time had equal legal value, and in early Castilian law the death penalty for killing a Jew was equivalent to that for killing a Christian, even though the long-term trend was for increasing judicial discrimination. It was precisely this situation of having maintained the system of partial toleration that placed Spanish society in a historically unparalleled situation, a situation that by the fifteenth century, faced with the European drive toward unified polities combined with the continued danger from the Islamic frontier, had become a peculiar kind of predicament.

In this regard it is interesting to compare the policy of France during the early modern period. The French crown at one time formed an official alliance with the Ottoman Empire, abetting Muslim piracy against the Spanish and Italians (a policy that in fact went much further than the provision of sanctuary to ETA terrorists in the late twentieth century). Generally sheltered from Islamic assault, the French were the first Western society to develop a sort of Islamophilia among the intelligentsia, beginning as early as the seventeenth century (dissonantly co-existing with the policy of the French monarchy to consider itself a kind of heir of Spain as sword of Catholicism and leader of Europe), leading to a series of admired, uninformed, and uncritical writings during the century that followed.

Some tendency toward sentimentalization could be seen in Spanish attitudes during the later Middle Ages, particularly in literature, with expressions of "maurofilia" versus "maurofobia" (admiration *for* vs. dislike *of* Moorish culture) in the sixteenth century, but the modern tendency toward idealization originated in the eighteenth century, with the Enlightenment critique of traditional Western Christian society. Such criticism was itself absolutely unique, with no real equivalent in any prior civilization in human history. Enlightenment attitudes were themselves profoundly contradictory, a pronounced racism co-existing with a proclaimed universalism. This marked the beginning of the concept of the idealized Other in Western culture, together with that of the Noble Savage, as supposedly enlightened oriental viewpoints were invoked to criticize Western institutions, beginning with Montesquieu's *Lettres persanes*, the Spanish equivalent being Cadalso's *Cartas marruecas*, though Cadalso revealed no particular knowledge of Morocco.

"Eurabian" concepts were later formed by some Spaniards in the nineteenth and twentieth centuries. Some—not all—of the Spanish Arabists whose work began with Francisco Codera in the nineteenth century showed a tendency to idealize Muslims, preferring to call them "españoles," rather than "andalusíes." This represented an attempted "Hispanization" of a non-Western culture, motivated in part perhaps to give greater prestige to that field of study. Conversely, in the Arab world from the nineteenth century on there developed a pronounced idealization of Al-Andalus as a lost paradise, and most recently Al-Qaeda has announced its recovery as a major priority.

By the twenty-first century, Al-Andalus has become one of the parts of the historically Islamic world that has been thoroughly studied, if not indeed the most thoroughly studied of them all. Many texts have been translated, and there is a sizable volume of scholarly literature, though writing for the broader public remains deficient. Serafín Fanjul counted 822 books published in Spain between 1970 and 1990 that in whole or in part were dedicated to Al-Andalus, ranging from folletos to multivolume works, but not including an even larger number of articles.[26]

The weak Spanish imperialism in northwest Africa during the first half of the twentieth century developed its own distinctive tropes, though in this regard it is important to distinguish between what was common to many European imperialisms and what was specific to Spain. French imperialism in North Africa and the Middle East often posited a special French relationship with the Islamic world, for whom France bore a special role of protection and *mission civilisatrice*, yet earlier French contacts had been modest compared with those of Spain. The "Moroccanism" that developed among some Spanish imperialists between 1910 and 1945 was distinctive, for its most extreme proponents presented the bizarre notion that the Spanish and Moroccans were not merely historically but also socially and culturally closely related. The most categorical even insisted that they were the northern and southern branches of the same people, but the Spanish were more advanced, which gave them the right and the duty of tutelage over Morocco. Versions of this concept were part of official diplomatic discourse during 1940–41 when Sir Samuel Hoare, the new British ambassador to Madrid in June 1940, was taken aback, to say the least, when Col. Juan Beigbeder, the foreign minister, assured him that "Spaniards and Moors are the same people." A somewhat different long-winded version of this trope by Franco bored Hitler almost to tears at Hendaye.[27] Spanish claims on Morocco, and the peculiar terms in which they were often justified, represented an interesting example of the way in which romantic myths can be made reality in the imagination of political actors. Ultimately, however, the only thing particularly Spanish about this was the specific form of the myth.

The real influence of Islam on Spain was rather different from the way in which it has usually been portrayed. The most important consequence was to confer on

Spain a historical role of frontier and periphery, which was different from what the peninsula had experienced prior to the eighth century. Under Rome and its Visigothic successors, the peninsula had been part of the core of late Roman civilization. In the new Western civilization of Latin Christendom, which was just emerging at the time that the kingdom of Asturias was being formed, the Spanish principalities would at first be more marginal and would require half a millennium to assume full participation in the core. For centuries a somewhat marginal and highly militarized periphery, the Spanish principalities would for a long time be unable to achieve the full cultural, educational, and economic level of the core areas of the West, something that they approximated only after a lengthy historical evolution. This harsh history helped to form and to fertilize the great expansion of energy and creativity that took place at the end of the Middle Ages, but it was probably not unrelated to the frustrations that followed.

3

Reconquest and Crusade

A "Spanish Ideology"?

The Spanish Reconquest was a process unique in European and in world history. In no other case was the greater share of a sizable kingdom conquered by Islam or any other foreign civilization, then not merely subjected but thoroughly transformed and acculturated into the alien civilization. Only centuries later was it fully regained by the remnants of the conquered kingdom, which not merely conquered the invaders but reacculturated the entire territory, subjecting and eventually extirpating the invading civilization. In the nearest parallels, found in eastern and in southeastern Europe, the Mongol and Ottoman empires exercised military and fiscal control over the conquered Christian peoples but did not inhabit their territories to any large degree and made no attempt to replace their religion and culture. The eventual throwing off of the Mongol and Ottoman yokes was not complicated by having to confront a large alien new population and culture in the originally conquered territory.[1] In no other part of the Islamic world has a significant Muslim society been completely replaced by a portion of the previously conquered population. The nearest equivalent in western Europe was the reconquest of Sicily in the eleventh

The Hispanic Peninsula in 1300

century, but that differed in being carried out by external forces and involved a much smaller territory that had been Islamic for scarcely two centuries.[2] As stated in chapter 2, the history of Spain for this reason would have been absolutely unique even if the Spanish had never accomplished anything else.

The Reconquest as the defining feature of the history of Spain has enjoyed a place of honor in both versions of the Grand Narrative—the Catholic and the liberal—that developed during the nineteenth century but suffered severely at the hands of the critical deconstruction of the following era. The most famous comment was Ortega's observation that something that went on for eight centuries could not simply be called a "reconquest," though he failed to explain convincingly just why that should be the case. Various objections have been advanced: the absence of documentation for any "reconquest" doctrine or policy in the eighth century, the lack of continuing commitment on the part of Spanish rulers in the later Middle Ages, the willingness of the latter on various occasions to make alliances with Muslims against other Christian rulers, and so on. Specific objections are often well taken, though some have been laid open to question by the most recent research, as in the case of Barbero and Vigil's thesis concerning the lack of acculturation and Christianity in the Cantabrian north prior to the eighth century (see chap. 1). There is no evidence of a specific "reconquest" policy during the first century of Asturian resistance, other than a reflexive disposition of the initial Asturian rulers to take advantage of any opportunity or slackening of Muslim power to extend their frontiers. In its early stages the first medieval kingdom was so weak that any grand design was unrealistic. More ambition for reconquest might be found on the part of the Frankish monarchy when it intervened against the Muslims late in the eighth and early in the ninth centuries. Muslim raiding expeditions had crossed the Pyrenees on numerous occasions in earlier years, and Charlemagne was logically concerned to roll back the Islamic menace.

Existing documentation makes it clear that when the Asturian monarchy first had the opportunity for significant reconquest, it expressed such a design as its long-range goal in the reign of Alfonso III. For some years internal fragmentation within the Andalusi despotism made it seem as though the latter might collapse, but Asturian aspirations were blocked by the massive revival of Cordoban power in the tenth century. At varying times each of the Christian principalities accepted terms of submission to the caliphate—technically under Koranic and Sharia norms the only ones on which peace was possible with the non-Muslim "House of War." There were also moments in which individual Spanish princes temporarily made common cause with the Muslims against each other, but these were brief interludes. As soon as Andalusi power weakened, the Spanish expansion resumed and, after another generation, reassumed the goal of major reconquest.

This was not a static concept but was modified from generation to generation. At times it disappeared almost altogether, but always returned. The original goal had apparently been to reclaim land and win booty; later, as aims expanded, it was to regain all the territory seized by the invader and to "restore the churches of Christ." During the eleventh century, the policy was more to establish a complete hegemony, rather than to seize the entire peninsula militarily. More than a century was dedicated to fighting off the invasions of the two successive new Moroccan empires, after which the main reconquest was completed in the thirteenth century. This did not require the expulsion of all Muslims, except for most of the urban population, but accepted terms of subordination equivalent to those for Christians and Jews in Al-Andalus. Even then, Muslim assaults did not end, for there was another major Moroccan invasion in the fourteenth century. Altogether, the Spanish world was under repeated Muslim assault for more than six hundred years, from 711 to 1340. After a partial respite, Muslim attacks resumed in the sixteenth century and did not completely end until Western powers finally imposed themselves early in the nineteenth century.

With the Great Reconquest of the thirteenth century, the Spanish advance projected itself farther afield, making its first brief incursion into Morocco. The best educated Spaniards of that era were well aware that Mauritania had once constituted the sixth province of the late Roman diocese of Hispania, and that the

Visigoths had also held a small territory there. By that point, in the mid-thirteenth century, the Reconquest had become such a fundamental and widely accepted ideal of the Iberian principalities that even land-locked Navarre, which played the most limited role in the enterprise, wrote the Reconquest into the first codification of its Fuero Antiguo (law code) in 1238.

Crusade

The Reconquest was not for four centuries a "crusade," something only institutionalized in Latin Christendom at the close of the eleventh century, but it was always in part a religious war or, at the very least, as the distinguished medievalist Hispanist Joseph O'Callaghan puts it, a "war . . . of religious confrontation."[3] The earliest statements of the chroniclers declared that the restoration and expansion of the Christian religion were basic goals, though hardly the only goals. This remained such a constant factor in Spanish history that Villacañas Berlanga can accurately say that Spain "was always on the road to Jerusalem."[4] The objective was not primarily to convert the Muslims but to regain the territory they had usurped, to recover a kingdom that had been lost. The ideal of religious conversion through missionary work did not develop originally in Spain but in Rome, and also among religious orders in Italy and France at the end of the eleventh century, and was relatively slow to be adopted in Spain. It never received prominence, but as the frontier advanced, small numbers of Muslims were converted and incorporated into Spanish society.[5]

There is a sense in which nearly all wars are declared to be "holy wars"—that is, military actions for which higher goals and sacred purposes are invoked, based on a sacralization of patriotic and national causes, if not on religion itself. To some extent, this phenomenon is observable in varying degrees in all societies. The official religious and military Crusade, however, was first codified by the papacy as a formal institution toward the end of the eleventh century, whence it was received in Spain. The idea of a military crusade as a new kind of religious institution had developed over a lengthy period from the initial idea of just war to that of "religious war" or "holy war" against non-Christians as a defensive tactic to that of "missionary wars" to extend the frontiers of Christendom, finally crystallizing in the formal ideal of the Crusade for the recovery of the Holy Land, violently seized by the Muslims more than three centuries earlier.[6] Justification and goals of the Crusade were religious, its practice earning spiritual merit. The official Crusade had special features, such as a formal vow on the part of crusaders, juridical and spiritual recognition by the Church (which also provided financial support, at least in part), military struggle to roll back Muslim conquests (primarily recovery of the Holy

Land), and the promise of remission of sins. In recent years it has been falsely presented as gratuitous aggression against peaceful Muslims, but in fact the Crusade was designed for purposes of reconquest of key Christian territory that had been seized by warlike Muslims. It did not feature any plan for a general war of conquest of Muslim territory as such or against Islamic civilization as a whole, though some such danger might be implicit.[7] Broader plans would be developed by the crowns of Castile and Portugal only during the fifteenth century.

The popes actively promoted the Reconquest in Spain, tying it together with the official Crusade, employing in their documents and exhortations to the Spanish such Latin terms as *recuperare, liberare, reparare, restaurare*, and a variety of others to urge completion of reconquest. Spanish crusaders were prohibited from joining the expeditions to the Holy Land but instead exhorted to concentrate on the Reconquest (although a small number of Spanish combatants did join the Holy Land crusades). The papacy was incensed at the interruptions of the Reconquest that occurred from time to time, persistently encouraging its resumption.

From the late eleventh century on, the bulls of crusade were regularly preached in the peninsula and soon became a regular part of the Reconquest and beyond that of the war-making and finance of the peninsular principalities. Introduction of the Crusade was but one aspect of the broadening and deepening of new ideas, institutions, and techniques from France and Italy in eleventh-century Spain, ranging from new religious institutions to economic practices and to breeding stronger horses to mount new French-style heavy cavalry. The Reconquest had long been considered a "holy war" of a certain kind, but it was a military, political, and economic enterprise that did not earn specific spiritual merit authorized by the Church until the appearance of the Crusade.[8] Reception of this new doctrine was only encouraged by the long struggle that began at approximately the same time against the new Moroccan invasions, which practiced jihad with a greater intensity than had been the norm in Al-Andalus. By the twelfth century the concepts of crusade and reconquest became intertwined. Subsequently Castilian texts would regularly refer to "guerra divinal" and "guerra santa" more or less interchangeably with the Crusade. Though the Spanish had made no ideological contribution to the idea of the crusade (beside presenting the main practical example in the West of persistent warfare against Muslims), by the later Middle Ages the peninsular kingdoms (including Portugal) were the only parts of Latin Christendom that had completely institutionalized among themselves the idea and practice of crusade, and had become its principal champions.[9] The Spanish principalities founded more individual crusading orders of monk-combatants than any other land, especially the Castilian orders of Alcántara, Calatrava, and Santiago, but there were others less known. The incorporation of the institution and ethos of the Crusade did not mean that all rulers and interests were always firmly united behind this goal and that conflicts, contradictions, and distractions did not frequently develop, nor that Christian mercenaries might not still be found occasionally in Muslim ranks. The "cruzada" tax, provided by the Church, became a major source of income for Spanish rulers, and though much of the time the proceeds were not devoted to crusading activities, after the twelfth century the principal victories of crusading against the Muslims were won in the Iberian Peninsula. At the Council of Basel in 1434, Castilian representatives argued that the crown of Castile merited precedence over that of England because it regularly practiced "la guerra divinal," while the latter did not. Though the idea of the crusade declined during the fourteenth and fifteenth centuries, after completion of nearly all the peninsular Reconquest, it was revived once more by the Catholic Monarchs.

Was There a "Spanish Ideology"?

It is not unusual for human societies of all types and at all stages of development to conceive of a special role or category for themselves. Primitive tribes, for example, often have terms for their own group translated approximately as "the human beings," all outsiders automatically relegated to a lower level. Even the ancient Hebrews were probably far from the first to understand themselves as constituting a "chosen people," for various kinds of "chosen people" concepts have been common in history.[10] Sometimes such concepts are widely shared within the society, though in other cases they do not extend very far beyond the elite. The sense of the superiority and mission of the Roman empire was widely shared by its citizens. Early on, the Frankish monarchy conceived of itself as the elect of God with a divine mission, while the Mongols of Genghis Khan considered themselves the "scourge of God," destined to conquer the world. In other cases a special national destiny is thought to be revealed through suffering, as in the case of nineteenth-century Polish nationalism, which termed Poland the "Christ of the nations" for the dismemberment and suffering it experienced. Something of the same spirit informed Serbian identity under Turkish domination, conceived as that of a "heavenly people" whose aspirations were spiritual and transcendental, though independence and dominion would eventually be restored to them.[11] The most striking case in the modern world has been the persistent example of Russian messianism, beginning with the concept originating more than half a millennium ago of Muscovy as the "Third Rome," and moving on to Pan-Slavism and then Communism.[12] Nikolai Berdiaiev subsumed it under the rubric of the "Russian idea," while, with regard to Germany, Karl Marx would write of a "German ideology," in this case referring to cultural ideas.

It seems clear that historically there has been a "Spanish idea," both similar to and different from the "Russian idea," the French concept, and others, that underwent an extensive historical evolution and transformation from the sixth and seventh centuries. It was one of the longest "national ideas" in history, stretching in various forms for nearly a millennium and a half. Its last great avatar, for better or worse, was Francisco Franco, and with his death it quickly went into terminal decline.

In modern nations, national or messianic ideas simply represent a kind of common attitude, shared either more or less widely, but usually not a fully developed ideology such as those found in the major modern political movements nor a specific continuous policy shared by all elites. Nor is a national or messianic idea the same as a specific identity or a fully developed major nationalist movement, though it may help eventually to generate the latter. It reflects a persistent attitude or mentality on the part of certain elites, but may be quite discontinuous and at times altogether ignored in favor of other interests, though reappearing once more under favorable circumstances. It does not produce a unique kind of political form, but may be found in varying modes of expression in different kinds of polities from monarchies to republics to dictatorships. For purposes of historical analysis, it may be considered a sort of ideal type, an aspiration expressed in a variety of modes or degrees through history, sometimes dominant but frequently recessive.

Origins of the first Spanish idea in the age of San Isidoro have been discussed in chapter 1. It is likely that in the seventh century such concepts were shared only by very few elites. A more direct line may be traced from the late ninth century in Asturias, during the reign of Alfonso III, with the mission of reconquest and restoration of the Gothic patrimony and Christian dominion. Although this seems to have been more directly assumed as state policy than had been the earlier idea among the Visigoths, there is again no evidence that it extended beyond a narrow elite. In later centuries it would be vigorously resumed, but sometimes not as the highest priority of policy, particularly after the completion of the Great Reconquest of the thirteenth century, though at that point North Africa was first fit within the parameters of such policy.

The sense of mission advanced a step farther in the late fifteenth century. The general religious revival of that era coincided in Spain with completion of the peninsular reconquest, stimulating a new mood of messianism (which, in other forms, extended well beyond Spain). This strongly motivated Columbus, for example, as well as having a vigorous presence at the court of Manoel "O Afortunado" in Lisbon, during whose reign the full Portuguese maritime supremacy or thalassocracy began to be established. The Testament of Isabel la Católica was explicit concerning the future responsibilities of the kingdom of Castile. Historians debate and are often skeptical regarding grander motivations among the conquistadores, but mission and extension of the faith were always mentioned and certainly played a role.

Although the Spanish Habsburg empire in Europe was largely formed through a marriage alliance and dynastic inheritance, the sense of mission to defend and expand Christendom was also strongly felt, and it formed the basis of some of the most extensive and costly of the military enterprises of the sixteenth century. During that era the Castilian Cortes showed little enthusiasm for the crown's European wars, urging it to "make peace with Christian kings," but more readily accepted the struggle against the Muslims in the Mediterranean. Despite all the other obligations of the Spanish crown, it did more to combat Turkish expansion, at least down to the time of Lepanto, than did any other European power. In recent years, historians of the reign of Felipe II have tended to downplay the role of religious motivation previously imputed to Spanish policy, emphasizing more the priority of defending dynastic rights and honor and of reasons of state, "razón de Estado." This is a useful corrective, but the concept of the Spanish crown as the "Monarquía católica" par excellence had considerable importance as well. In the seventeenth century, as the burden of empire, dynastic rights, endless wars, and internal social and economic decline began to wear down Spain, some religious spokesmen referred to this as a cross that it must continue to bear as leader of the Counter-Reformation and the chief defender of the Catholic faith. Since the late fifteenth century, certain religious, political, and cultural figures had developed the concept of the Spanish as God's modern "chosen people," successor to the ancient Hebrews. In 1629 a Navarrese friar published the *Libro de las cinco excelencias del español*, which defined the Spanish vocation in terms of a sort of martyrdom (in some ways similar to the later national doctrines of Poles and Serbs). He declared that the role of the Spanish surpassed that of the Hebrews not simply because they were the new modern incarnation of the chosen people, but because they had been given a truly universal role to unify all mankind and to convert distant continents, hastening the Second Coming of Christ. If the cost of such a universal mission meant great suffering and depopulation for Spain, the wealth and population of other countries should not be envied; rather, "let them envy our depopulation, which we suffer in imitation of the work of the Apostles and the disciples of Christ."[13] Spain's mission was to be the living *imitatio Christi*. The majority of Spanish people at that time would probably not have agreed with him, but it would seem that some, at least, did.

The suffering and relative immiseration of the middle and later decades of the seventeenth century had a chastening effect on such attitudes, which subsequently became much more rare. By the eighteenth century the Spanish ideology was in decline, but far from dead. All of Spain's wars during the eighteenth century were preached from church pulpits as veritable crusades against the enemies of God.

During the era of the French Revolution, Catholic spokesmen identified Spanish Catholics with the sufferings of the faithful in France, and compared their situation to that of the ancient Jews during the age of the prophets. The explosion of popular resistance to the Napoleonic invasion expressed popular patriotism and xenophobia, in which the clergy played a major role in articulating Spain's traditional religious values and vocation.

By that time, however, the Spanish elite were turning more and more to political liberalism, which soon constructed its own Grand Narrative—one that defined Spanish history as the history of liberty, in consonance with what was becoming known as the Western tradition. This stressed the history of rights, of the rule of law, and of popular representation, at most incorporating only selected aspects of the traditional ideology. Two different versions then existed side by side, with the emergence of the "Two Spains," though conservative liberalism made a considerable effort to join together major features of the two ideas. The traditional doctrine was revived and sustained by the Carlists, and then by the Catholic revival of the second half of the nineteenth century, incomplete though that event was. These two visions continued to clash, the liberal idea moving toward radicalism and revolutionism, until the Civil War of 1936–39 seemed to decide the issue, as during the Reconquest, by force of arms. Franco's victory led to the neotraditionalist revival of the 1940s and 1950s, whose equivalent was not to be witnessed anywhere else in the Christian world, so-called national Catholicism constituting the final major phase of traditionalist Spanish Catholicism.

What was unique about Spain was not the existence of national ideology, but that it continued to exist in related form for well over a millennium, even though the emphasis changed fairly significantly over time. The traditional Spanish idea was not a constant factor, waxing and waning frequently over the centuries, but constituted probably the longest semicontinuous concept of religious identity and mission, of war and empire, to be found anywhere in Europe. The equivalent in France was both more attenuated and more discontinuous, and its traditional form largely ended with the French Revolution.

4 | Spain and the West

W̶hereas "identity" has become a matter of controversy for Spaniards only comparatively recently, the identity, character, or image of Spain has been a polemical issue outside of Spain for nearly half a millennium. The Black Legend found its earliest expression in Italy at the close of the fifteenth century and would later be cultivated with especial fervor by the Dutch and the English. Italian detractors liked to denounce the Spanish as a bastard blend of Moors and Jews, not proper Christians or even Europeans; conversely, the principal northern libelers of the Spanish postulated a hyper-Catholic identity of unique sadism and malevolence, a few echoes of which persist today.

Stereotypes concerning the Spanish shifted emphasis and content several times between the sixteenth and nineteenth centuries. When the notion of "romantic Spain" developed, it also portrayed the Spanish as extremely different, but now as a uniquely pre-modern people motivated by honor, personal courage, and an archaic style of life, as distinct from materialism and achievement, a semi-"oriental" people strongly configured by North Africa and the Middle East. Residues of this idea linger down to the present.

The only other major European people who have become the object of equivalent attitudes are the Russians, for whom identity became a very major issue again in the 1990s, just as it had become for Spaniards.[1] In Russia, however, nationalism has won out, whereas a unique aspect of modern Spanish culture is the extent to which the Black Legend has been internalized by the Spanish themselves. Since 1985 Europe has become a kind of panacea, almost what the anthropologists would call a "cargo cult" for Spaniards, and there is no denying that membership in the European Union has been economically beneficial for Spain, at least until the recession of 2008.

An underlying feature of such attitudes has had to do with what is often considered to be the non-Western or extra-European identity of the country and its culture. To what extent can this be justified by empirical analysis, as distinct from subjective political, cultural, or ideological projections?

Hispania was clearly a normal and integral part of the Roman empire—the "West" (or, more precisely, partial pre-West) of its time. The main parts of Roman Hispania, Bética (the south), and the Tarraconensis (the northeast) were among the most Romanized and Latinized parts of the empire, producing several emperors (while none came from Gaul). Indeed, Hispania played an important role in sustaining the "Latinity" of the empire, or, more precisely, of its western half, against the Greek and east Mediterranean identity of the eastern half. The Visigothic kingdom eventually took shape as the heir of Rome, at least according to its self-conception. The religious and cultural identity that it developed as a "Catholic kingdom" was by the seventh century proclaimed as the quintessence of Western Roman Catholic orthodoxy. Visigothic Spania maintained a cultural life second only to that of Italy and played a leading role in ecclesiastical development, despite the marked decline of the Roman world from the fifth century on.

That decline was not exactly "the first decline of the West," as Julián Marías puts it, since Rome was only the predecessor of Western civilization, but its decline marked a kind of cultural and civilizational catastrophe that could be only very partially averted in Visigothic Spania. Out of the ashes of the empire (whose end was never fully accepted for another half millennium) there arose "Europe," as the term eventually came to be used, in the form of the Germanic kingdoms, which began to shift the weight of affairs more and more decisively toward the north.[2]

This became fundamental for the history of the former Hispania, whose greater world for a millennium and more had consisted of the Mediterranean, an orientation toward the east (and to a minor degree toward the south) that from the late fifth century on would be replaced by an orientation increasingly toward the north. Visigothic dominion had originally been established north of the Pyrenees, and even as Leovigildo centered the new kingdom in the peninsula, Septimania in southwestern France remained part of it. Both politico-military competition and general relations with the Frankish kingdom were closer than relations with Italy and Rome.

Visigothic Spania in fact seemed by the seventh century to represent the first successful new merging of the Germanic and the Roman, which was to be the basis of "Europe" and the subsequent "West." By comparison, Italy remained too Roman and France too Germanic. Italy had perhaps a higher level of culture but was less unified politically. The Frankish kingdom achieved a higher level of political unity but was in some respects less advanced culturally and ecclesiastically. For a moment, Visigothic Spania was the first, most successful "European" or "Western" country of that era.

Despite the success of the Islamic conquest in most of the peninsula, the invasion was firmly rejected by the Christian resistance societies in the north, to the extent that J. Marías and others have seen the Spanish as not the most marginally Western of the West European peoples, but rather as the most determined of the Western societies in being Western, Christian, and European. Unlike its counterparts in France and England, early Spanish society had to make a special choice to be Christian, independent and Western, fighting for centuries to sustain and validate that choice. According to this point of view, Spain developed not as a typical "intra-European" core society and culture but as a kind of "trans-European" society and culture, rooted in Latin Catholicism and the basic Western institutions, as they developed, but living on the semiperiphery in contact with Islam, North Africa, and—later—America, developing its own national variant of the Western culture. Holland is quite different from Hungary, and every European or Western country is European or Western in its own way.[3]

The dramatic transformation that took place in the Iberian Peninsula during the eighth century seems at first glance a uniquely Spanish development, but in fact it may also be seen as the special and extreme peninsular expression of broader transformations taking place in the west European and greater Mediterranean worlds of that time. There is no absolute agreement among historians regarding exactly when Late Antiquity ended and early Western civilization began, but a certain consensus that the key early formative period was the eighth and ninth centuries. Edward Gibbon contended that what he called "modern history" began with the formation of the Carolingian empire. The eighth century also saw the renascence of the Byzantine empire following the grand Arab onslaught, while farther east the Abbasid dynasty established its capital in Baghdad, inaugurating what would become the Islamic golden age. Charlemagne, who would later be considered "Europae pater," saw himself as continuing and reviving the Roman world, but a series of decisive new changes occurred in the Western world during the eighth and ninth centuries. From the eighth century significant amounts of new land were being brought under cultivation, and by 900 an agricultural transformation was under way that eventually would make the northern lands of western Europe more productive than the Mediterranean for the first time. The cultural revival of the Carolingian era, building on assistance from Ireland, England, Italy, and also the Visigoths would create the very first phase of the new Western culture. The first Western empire was established by Charlemagne, creating a new sense of the unity of Latin Christendom, while by the end of the ninth century Alfred the Great had built the institutions of Anglo-Saxon monarchy with strong government, the beginning of a major system of royal law, efficient new administration, and the use of vernacular language. During the same period, the primacy of Rome was reestablished in the West, with the full "Latinization" of the papacy (excluding Greek candidates). The founding of the kingdom of Asturias thus took place during a time of important change and innovation in western Europe and the broader Mediterranean, so that the first historically continuous Spanish institutions roughly coincided with the first phase of the new Western civilization itself.

The eighth century established the permanent southwestern frontier of Western civilization in the Iberian Peninsula, for the limits of Islam would mark the boundary of the West, even though Muslim assaults and depredation would continue in one form or another for an entire millennium. They would cease only when the European powers became strong enough not merely to crush the depredation but also increasingly to dominate the Islamic world. As soon as that domination receded, depredation was resumed in the form of Islamist terrorism. Spain would remain the direct cynosure of the "polemical dialogue" between Europe and the Islamic world for a thousand years, a hinge on which Europe depended.

The nascent kingdom of Asturias soon looked beyond the Pyrenees to the Frankish monarchy for support and was not disappointed, Charlemagne intervening in the peninsula in the latter part of the century, ending the Muslim threat to Septimania and securing Christian society in the eastern Pyrenees and as far south as Barcelona. The "Marca Hispánica" then developed as the most European part of the peninsula, the part most closely connected to French and Italian culture, but this was a matter of degree as much as of kind, for in early Catalonia the conscious sense of continuity was as strong as in Asturias and sometimes emphatically expressed, the early Catalan elite often calling themselves *gothi*.

Even the apparent retrocession of Spanish strength during the height of the caliphate's power in the tenth century—the so-called iron century—paralleled similar developments in the same period in other parts of the West. During the eighth and ninth centuries the west European world was under assault from Vikings and Danes from the north, Magyars from the east and Muslims from the south, as Sicily was conquered and a Muslim toehold established in south Italy.

New consolidation then began to take place in the core areas of the West during the second half of the tenth century, crystallization of new institutions and further economic development starting only a generation or two before the balance of power started to shift decisively in the peninsula. Both the weakening under foreign assault and the strengthening near the beginning of the eleventh century roughly coincided with the broader experience of western lands.

The Reconquest also proceeded in parallel with other aspects of Western expansion, both internally and externally. The eleventh century was generally a time of decisive growth in the West. Beyond the Iberian Peninsula the southern Normans carried out the reconquest of Sicily, and the Genoese republic cleared the Muslims from Sardinia. Islamic naval dominance in the west Mediterranean was broken, making the western states stronger at sea than on land, a process that contributed to the First Crusade. The halt to the Spanish Reconquest imposed by the Moroccan invasions would then more or less coincide with the weak assistance provided to Crusader Palestine and its reconquest by the Muslims late in the twelfth century. Though subsequent crusades to regain the Holy Land failed, the Spanish Great Reconquest of the thirteenth century similarly paralleled another major phase of European expansion and of the growth of Christendom in northeast Europe, and of the expansion of the English monarchy in the northwest.[4] By that point the general "medieval expansion of Europe" was under way and would never entirely cease.[5] The Spanish Reconquest represented the peninsular phase of a broad process that would eventually prove decisive not merely in the history of the West but also in the history of the world.

From the second half of the eighth century, the Asturian leadership was in contact with both France and Italy, drawing a small number of specialized craftsmen from each area. Though initially papal influence was not great, Asturias strongly emphasized its Catholic orthodoxy against both Islam and Mozarab Christian accommodationism. During these early medieval centuries, all the Spanish Christian principalities structured public institutions similar to those of France and other European kingdoms. There was no Spanish "third way" equidistant between Islam and Christianity, and the same may be said for architecture, culture, and municipal development. During the course of the medieval centuries, every single key western institution would be found in the Spanish principalities, from the typical institution of monarchy to feudalism (though not equally in every principality), the structure of aristocracy, seigneurial domain, the institutionalization and structure of municipalities, legal organization, and the universities. The Spanish principalities participated in all the major movements and trends of the era, even helping to initiate one or two of them, and were leaders in religious endeavors ranging from major new orders to the crusades, and in the extension and structure of legal rights and of the first formal representative assemblies. Some of these institutions did not become as well developed in the peninsula as in the most advanced European states, but much the same might be said of a number of other regions. From the eleventh century, particularly, there was considerable immigration from France, as well as a limited amount from Italy, and foreign specialists were common, ranging from prelates of the Church to military crusaders, from merchants and skilled artisans of all types to the architects of cathedrals. Medieval Spanish society was arguably the most open of all the large areas in Europe, and very receptive to immigrants, as well as to foreign elites and specialists, from whom a good deal more "acculturation" was absorbed than from the Andalusis. This was a normal experience for the major semiperipheral lands of western and central Europe. The Normans introduced a good many new continental influences into England, helping to "Europeanize" it, and German-speaking people did the same in Hungary.

The key institution of Latin Christendom, the papacy, developed a special relationship with the Spanish principalities, as, in a different way, it did with France and Germany. This was highly complex, involving the papacy's zeal to promote the Spanish Reconquest, the concern of the newer monarchies (such as Aragon and Portugal) to obtain papal recognition and support, and the papacy's own ambition to gain special political power within the Spanish principalities, which it tended to see as "crusader states"—ones that should become politically subordinated to it. On the one hand, it promoted the unity of the Spanish principalities to expedite the Reconquest, but just as frequently it incited disunity in order to advance its own political influence.

The Catholic Church was the key institution in the development of Latin Christendom and hence of Western civilization. Not merely did it provide the religious and moral content of the culture, but it decisively influenced a broad range of developments. The Church's focus on the person was a basic element in the formation of Western individualism, even though that was not its original goal. The distinction between the spheres or swords of church and state, and the insistence on the autonomy of the Church, though not intended to free the state from the Church, was equally fundamental to the slowly evolving but ultimately decisive distinction between church and state, especially since one church had to deal with such a multiplicity of states. Catholic education helped to found the university system, the rise of Western rational thought and the medieval origins of modern science.[6] The papacy provided the first example in the Western world of rational bureaucracy, stimulating the development of administration and the state. Church law, particularly canon law, demonstrated the ways in which different legal principles and approaches might be synthesized, and was fundamental to stimulating the medieval legal revolution, on which modern Western law is ultimately based.[7] Catholicism also encouraged the doctrine of natural rights and of more responsible government, as the application of the later medieval doctrine of the "king's two bodies" promoted greater respect for law, morality, and the well-being of the realm, as distinct from the caesaropapist despotisms common to earlier history.[8] All these influences were felt in Spain, although some aspects were more attenuated in the peninsula than in certain other parts of western Europe.

To use the language of Immanuel Wallerstein, Spain formed what should be termed "the semi-periphery of the core" of Latin Christendom.[9] It was a part of that core but not at its center, and also not a periphery external to that core. A true periphery partly extraneous to the core would only develop during the overseas expansion, primarily in central and southern America, and also to some extent in Russia, where it formed a related yet distinct civilization, based on Eastern Orthodoxy rather Roman Catholicism.

Geography, the legacy of Reconquest particularism and also the extraneous political interests of the papacy, all combined to retard political unity equivalent to that of France or England. Italy and Germany, however, were just as divided as Spain, if not more so, while the institutions of Catholic Poland-Lithuania would later prove weak in the extreme, however progressive part of their content may have been.[10]

One feature of the last phase of the Middle Ages was the growth of ethnic (and to a certain extent of racial) discrimination in the West during the fourteenth and fifteenth centuries. The two most striking innovations associated with the united monarchy of the Catholic Monarchs—the Inquisition and the expulsion of the Jews—constituted the extreme Spanish version of a broader trend. They represented attempts to remedy existing anomalies of Spanish life and achieve a political and religious unity approximately equal to that of France and England. These two core Western countries had never had a Jewish population at all proportionately equivalent to that of Spain, and both had ended up expelling all their Jews by the beginning of the fourteenth century. Thus what made the Spanish monarchy seem so "different" stemmed from the efforts of its leaders to be "the same."

Spain arrived at the center of European power, politics, culture, and religion in the sixteenth century, for the first time functioning as part of the west European core. While historians nowadays distinguish carefully between the activities and priorities of the Spanish Habsburg crown and those of Spain proper, the strengths and achievements of Spain would always remain the key basis of the crown's power. Not merely was the latter for a century the strongest state and military power in western Europe, but Spain was also a major player in the European economy and for the only time in its history a major influence in European culture, religion, and even in such things as clothing styles. Moreover, that influence was not exerted on behalf of some exotic "Mozarabic" set of cultural values but was fully within the traditional framework of European Catholicism and culture. This influence was not at first carried out merely in the name of rigid traditionalism, for it also featured an effort to create a more liberal Catholicism under Carlos V. After that had failed, Spain became the single most important force in the Catholic Reformation, the most crucial transformation of the Church for centuries. All these matters have been extensively studied by historians. The key point is that Spain's role in the sixteenth and early seventeenth centuries was not that of a semi-oriental periphery, but was intrinsic to the core culture of Europe at that time.

The Second Cycle of Western History

At this juncture there began to emerge the greatest paradox, or singularity, of the history of Western civilization—the rise of a second cycle of a related but in some respects crucially different cultural era within Western civilization itself, what we generally call the modern era or the modern West, as distinct from medieval and traditional culture, sometimes termed the old West. Of all the civilizations in world history, the West is the only one to have generated two different cycles of culture, the second bearing novel characteristics sometimes profoundly at odds with the former. The old West was traditionalist, monarchist, and Catholic, not primarily dominated by material values. The modern West has become increasingly antitraditional, egalitarian, subjectivist, and materialist, and for centuries was largely led by Protestants, even though most of the germs of its culture might already have been found in the old West.

It is not possible to divide simply and neatly the two different epochs of Western culture, since the roots of the modern West lie deep in the old West, and the latter has continued in certain key ways to influence the former. The role of Spain with regard to the two cultural eras has been the most unique of all the major European lands, for in no other has the relationship to the two eras been so sharp and distinct, even though Spanish culture participated in both cultural epochs as well as in the transition between the two. What was special about Spain was that its Golden Age had by the middle of the seventeenth century achieved the highest development of most, though not all, major features of the traditional Western culture to be found in any land, but it found itself poorly positioned for the transition to the modern era. The only other country in which the culture of the "Old Regime" was more highly developed than that of Spain was the France of Louis XIV, but that in turn had relied on Spanish culture, and conversely also possessed more initial features of the new modern epoch.[11]

It would be a mistake, however, to see the Spanish culture and society of the Habsburg era as merely high-level traditionalism bereft of modernizing tendencies. The latter were in fact fairly numerous, though distinctly weaker than in the

French society of the same period. In the late sixteenth century Spanish society generated a high level of urbanization and also of educational development, with the first glimmering of mass society and urban mass culture.[12] There was an aston- ishing volume of cultural creativity in literature, the fine arts, religious thought, in philosophy, and in law.[13] Nothing was more potentially transitional than Spanish Late Scholastic economic theory of the sixteenth and seventeenth centuries, with its market-oriented calculations on value, price, wages, justice, profits, and banking—in some respects more sophisticated than what was then found in the economically more dynamic north European (mainly Protestant) societies.[14] In general, however, Spanish culture, despite its multifaceted creativity during this era, still fit within the traditionalist framework, something perhaps most easily demonstrated by comparing one of its major new forms, the theater of the Golden Age, with the other major theater of the period, in Elizabethan-Jacobean England. Both theaters developed significant new techniques and styles, and examined many different facets of human behavior. Spanish drama and theater, however, never stepped very far beyond the orthodox cultural framework, whereas that of Marlowe, Shakespeare, and their English successors much more broadly inhabited a new and uncertain, often agnostic, potentially amoralist landscape, definitely nearer the modern sensibility.[15]

Moreover, as a result of the Reformation and the conflicts that ensued, there took place in Spain a partial cultural withdrawal from Europe, symbolized by the crown's decree of 1569 forbidding study abroad in most European universities. Similarly, the Inquisition placed boundaries on new thought and inquiry, al- though it did not block the flourishing of high culture.

The Seventeenth-Century Decline

The gulf between Spain and "modern Europe" did not de- velop as a result of the Muslim conquest, as some essentialists would have it, and was not the inevitable cultural product of any abyss between the fatalistic, abulic "oriental" Spanish and their more enterprising northern neighbors. It was above all the result of key structural, political, and more broadly historical developments of the seventeenth century. The deep variation that developed at that time was not a mere cleavage between a backward, fanatical Spain and the Protestant world, but rather a gap that began to develop between the more dynamic and en- terprising areas of northwestern Europe (mainly Protestant) and most of the rest of Europe, whether Catholic, Protestant, or Eastern Orthodox. It was not a reli- gious divide alone, for the Catholic society of the Low Countries was just as well prepared to take advantage of new opportunities as their Protestant counterparts, and the extent to which they were not quite able to do so was due primarily to political and military developments, not directly to religion. The majority of the features that fueled new enterprise, wealth creation, and discoveries in England and Holland were also present to some extent in Spanish society, but to a distinctly lesser degree. They were also increasingly choked off by the specific policies of the Habsburg state, whose priorities were oriented toward endless dynastic wars and crushing taxes. The disastrous effects of these policies were compounded in Spain by the effects of the plague and even of climate change, as the relatively warm climate of most of the Middle Ages, which had encouraged the growth of the West, had given way to a colder natural environment. The peninsula was struck by a series of afflictions during the seventeenth centuries, with great floods, rains, and droughts, while the Ebro River is said to have frozen seven times between 1505 and 1789. What occurred in Spain was, in general, not so different, mutatis mutandis, from what happened in most of the rest of Europe, only a minor share of Western society participating fully in the precocious early modernization of the northwestern countries during that era.

There is no question that a country like England, the leader in modernization, was better positioned than Spain to develop new forms and techniques in commerce, economics, technology, and politics in the seventeenth century. It was more united in law and institutions (though not always in politics), had a more open and individualistic society, much greater entrepreneurial initiative, and more concerted state support for new enterprise.[16] In Spain—with the partial exception of Catalonia—status won out over enterprise, and the result of all the negative tendencies that came to fruition by the 1650s and 1660s was a profound decline, which affected nearly all avenues of Spanish life.

During the first part of the Franco regime historians reacted against the understanding of a "Spanish decadence" that had largely informed thinking about this phenomenon for the two preceding centuries. They advanced instead the interpretation of "exhaustion," which was certainly true enough, concluding that the grueling and continued effort to meet the titanic challenges of the seventeenth century had simply worn Spain out. This was clearly the case, but along with the prostration of the third quarter of the century there was also a general retrocession in nearly all the key features of Spanish activity—absolute and extensive demographic decline, a significant reduction in economic production, absence of new initiatives, radical decline in what only recently had been a flourishing cultural activity, and a retreat and a diminution in religious affairs as well. The Spanish had ceased to innovate in administration and in military and maritime activity, and even their religious thought was becoming primarily defensive. For six generations, since the 1480s, the Spanish had been engaged in a series of massive enterprises, and that exhaustion began to sink in increasingly following the breaking point of 1640, when the Portuguese and Catalans abandoned the project of the Spanish monarchy. If this was not decadence, it was certainly a remarkable decline.

Some distinctions should be made. Artistic and cultural creativity continued to some extent into the 1670s, and, although the Spanish crown could do little for the Spanish territories in the Americas, they were strong enough to fend largely for themselves, which speaks well for the accomplishments of the earlier era. Moreover, by the 1680s definite symptoms of reform and recovery were apparent in Spain, Catalonia at that point initiating the start of the "modern pattern" by which economic growth in that region would precede progress in the rest of Spain.

Spanish decadence was not a matter of loss of cultural and religious values, all of which remained intact, and there was no danger that the decline would produce a new culture antagonistic to its predecessor, as in some historical declines elsewhere, but there was a drastic falling away. It also occurred at a time when northwestern Europe, including much of France, was advancing more rapidly than ever before. The result was the opening of the "modernization gap," which would bedevil all subsequent Spanish development until the gap was finally closed after more than three hundred years, late in the twentieth century. From 1659 to 1985 key aspects of the history of Spain could be treated under the theme of the struggle for modernization.

The decline also meant the abandonment of the special Spanish project that had begun to form in the late Middle Ages on the basis of a sort of "Spanish ideology" (see chap. 3). The Spanish project intended to expand the frontiers of Christendom while leading Europe in the struggle to maintain creative tradition and religious orthodoxy. By the end of the seventeenth century both aspects of this project had largely been abandoned. The goals of Spanish institutions, rather than projecting outward into Europe and into unknown territory, had become primarily defensive. Spanish affairs would become increasingly divided between the defensive traditionalists and the reformers who sought not only to introduce productive changes in economics and institutions but also to encourage the country to adopt some of the new doctrines and practices present in northwestern Europe.

This meant that from the end of the seventeenth century the country was becoming more peripheral to the core of the modern West than had been the case earlier, but it did not mean that culturally it was in the process of becoming an "orientalized" North African land not part of Europe or the West. That said, the Spanish drama was played out in most other European countries, in quite different ways, for example, in Germany and Ireland, and even more in Italy, Austria, and Poland. The struggle to achieve a new modern framework would nonetheless be especially difficult and bitter in Spain, more than in any of the other larger countries issuing from Latin Christendom. Spain had momentarily risen to the height of European and world power under the traditionalist Old Regime, with the result that traditionalism had become more firmly entrenched in some respects than in almost any other part of Western Europe, while the reformist and innovative tendencies were proportionately weaker.

In this struggle, Spanish government applied nearly all the standard policies of European enlightened despotism and of European liberalism, the latter at a precocious phase of historical development. Some of these policies were successful, but many failed in whole or in part. Reform and innovation would follow each new phase of Western modernization, and, in fact, Spanish political innovation by the nineteenth century preceded that of most European countries, even those that surpassed it in economic and social modernization. Between 1833 and 1923 Spain lived for more years under parliamentary government than did one of the great "modernizing mentors," France. In 1812, 1820, and even during the 1830s, Spanish liberalism (however premature and sometimes even destructive) served as an inspiration to many other countries in Europe and in Latin America. This was in itself an extraordinary record. No other country more thoroughly experienced the entire gamut of European political and social practices during the nineteenth and early twentieth centuries. All the modern European trends were present in Spain, sometimes in exaggerated or extreme form, often locked in mortal conflict.

5   Identity, Monarchy, Empire

The crisis of identity that overtook the Western world in the late twentieth century had a particularly severe impact on Spain. The long dictatorship of Franco had stressed unity, centralism, and Spanish nationalism, but its consequence was to discredit the very idea of Spanish nationalism, and to some extent even of the Spanish nation, in the succeeding generation of democracy, individualism, and hedonism. During the final decades of the century the country was filled with more claims for new kinds of "fractional" nationalism—which may variously be termed micro, peripheral, or deconstructive—than in any other Western land, the great contrast being that there were few spokesmen for a Spanish nationalism.

Many commentators then opined that a single or united "Spain" had been little more than a figment of the imagination, that the country had never been more than a loose community of regions governed normally by a monarchy, and later on occasion by artificial despots in Madrid. This was an extraordinary climate of opinion that could not be equaled in any other European country, with the alarming exception of Yugoslavia in the 1990s. As deconstructive discourse mounted, it pro-voked a reaction in a series of works that affirmed a common historical identity of the diverse regions of Spain, even prior to the united monarchy, and insisted that from the sixteenth century on the country had constituted an increasingly united nation.[1] The internationally famous *Historikerstreit*—the controversy among the historians—in Germany was in some ways surpassed by the broad controversies about Spanish history, both with regard to earlier eras and also to the twentieth century.

It seems clear that despite the political fragmentation of the peninsula under the impact of the Islamic conquest and the following long struggle, a common cultural, religious, and juridical heritage from the Visigothic era remained. There was some sense of common identity at least among the elites of the medieval Span-ish principalities, but the question is the extent to which this went beyond the religious and the geographical. The problem was first extensively examined in José Antonio Maravall's *El concepto de España en la Edad Media* (1950), though some historians conclude that he exaggerated the conscious sense of common identity, particularly with regard to political issues.

The philosopher Gustavo Bueno argues that the elites of the Hispano-Christian states thought of themselves as forming something analogous to a sepa-rate peninsular political community or "empire," as something absolutely inde-pendent from trans-Pyrenean rulers.[2] This was certainly the case among some of the elites in certain periods, but probably posits more of an "ideal type" than an empirical historical description.

There is no question that medieval elites often referred to their principalities as forming part of "España," the term that in its several spellings and versions (Es-panha, Espanya, etc.) developed with the rise of the new vernaculars. On various occasions the medieval chronicles referred to the Spanish rulers collectively as *reges Hispaniae*, but this can be read as a merely geographical reference. Medieval writ-ings also refer to Spain as a collective entity in other ways, using expressions such as "toda España," which may be found with some frequency in Latin, Castilian, Catalan, and Portuguese texts. The new word for its inhabitants—"español" and "españoles"—developed during the twelfth century, expanding from Pyrenean Aragon, though the conclusion of some that it was originally a Provençal word from beyond the Pyrenees has not been substantiated.[3] From that time the term was recorded as the family name of a certain number of individuals, as well. Medie-val writing also frequently referred to "las Españas" in the plural, something that would continue to be found until the eighteenth century; in the Middle Ages, though, it was common to refer in the plural to any number of European coun-tries, which in modern times would be known only in the singular.

The sense of community or special relationship that existed among some of the elites of the Spanish Christian kingdoms was also reflected in the ambition of the rulers of Asturias-León-Castile to claim or establish a broader hegemony over them all.[4] The extent of these claims varied, sometimes being merely rhetorical, at other times referring only to the present kingdom itself, at still other times more vaguely to the entire peninsula. Alfonso II, with the expansion of Asturias, was the first to call himself *Imperator*. Alfonso III later used the title of *Rex Magnus* as ruler of the only true Hispano-Christian kingdom and as claimant to the entire inheritance of the Visigoths. After defeating the Muslims at the battle of Simancas in 939, Ramiro II termed himself *Imperator* and *Rex Magnus*. The next step was taken by Sancho el Mayor, who created the concept (though not the full reality) of the *regnum Hispaniae*, as he termed himself *Rex Dei gratia Hispaniarum* and *Princeps diversarum gentium*.[5] A kingdom, or regnum in medieval parlance, was just a distinct principality and not necessarily even a fully sovereign state. Sancho's usage affirmed a completely independent entity, what in traditional parlance was termed an empire, though he made no specific claim to empire itself. Even before, Alfonso II had introduced the title of emperor as a means of defining the total independence of Asturias among Christian kingdoms, not beholden to the more genuine empire of Charlemagne, a usage briefly revived by Ramiro II more than a century later.

Alfonso VI used the titles of both king and emperor—*Princeps diversarum gentium* and *Imperator super omnes Hispaniae nationes*. These formulae implied recognition of the plurality and diversity of Hispanic states but did not define it. The title of emperor was used most extensively of all by his grandson Alfonso VII, ruler of the self-styled *regnum-imperium* of León and "emperor of Spain," whereas earlier, during the reigns of Alfonso II and III, the title of emperor was used in official documents primarily to refer to the kingdom of León itself, and not primarily to its claims over other territories. Invocation of empire by Alfonso VII was not merely a matter of grandiosity, since his primacy was to some degree accepted by other rulers who were temporarily subinfeudated to him.[6] In the traditional usage only an empire could be considered totally independent and totally sovereign, and the claim of imperial status for the Hispanic states was an affirmation of their uniqueness, referring to their independence and full sovereignty, as an entity or entities not inferior to the claims of the French crown or the Holy Roman Empire in Germany-Italy. Hispanic empire, however, was never fully established juridically, depending for whatever effectiveness it might have on the temporary power of individual rulers, and hence the tendency to be used more frequently by chroniclers and by descendants of the kings of León than by these rulers themselves.[7] Alfonso VII ended by dividing his kingdom among his sons.

A further step was taken with the thirteenth-century Reconquest, which made of Castile a major European territorial state. Fernando III termed himself *rex in omni Spania* and Alfonso el Sabio *Imperator totius Hispaniae.*

Elements of a common Hispano-Christian identity were clearly present throughout the Middle Ages, but they were essentially nonpolitical in nature. They involved a common continuity with Hispano-Visigothic culture (stronger in some areas than others), including the common use of Visigothic law (the Fuero Juzgo), the Visigothic script, and common forms of art and architecture. Religion was the most important unifying factor, with common use of the Visigothic or Mozarabic rite for three centuries.[8]

The emergence of the separate kingdoms was, however, not due exclusively to geographic differences and the Reconquest wars, but also to specifically political factors as well. The strengthening of independent Christian societies in the north only increased political particularism. Much the same might be said of papal influence, which encouraged concentration on the Reconquest but otherwise stimulated division and rivalry between the Spanish states to strengthen the papacy's influence in each one individually. Thus the mounting influence of European Catholicism had something of a centrifugal effect, partly because of papal policy and partly because it severed the connection with the traditional common Hispanic expression of Catholicism. In the process, the most specific common point of reference—the Mozarabic community of Al-Andalus with its traditional Hispano-Christian culture—had disappeared with the advance of the Reconquest and the Moroccan invasions.

The legal/institutional revolution of the High Middle Ages (eleventh through thirteenth centuries) had differing effects in various parts of Europe and also in the peninsula. Ironically, one of the philosophical inspirations for the new concepts of sovereignty that developed in the French and Norman states (including England) from about 1100 on was the doctrines of San Isidoro, but the new changes did not take root to the same extent in the peninsula. The medieval legal/political revolution raised the status of a kingdom to that of total independence, subordinate to no external empire, for, as the Norman kings of England would subsequently say, "We are an empire."[9] The new policy emphasized the power of the king as complete head of his realm and of the kingdom as a complete unit.

It brought a new, more sophisticated concept of law, administration, and responsibilities, with the doctrine of the king's two bodies or natures, both human and divine, an idea perhaps derived from the distinction between the bishop and his episcopal function in the Church, and certainly from the theological doctrine of the two natures of Christ. This program would introduce the first new European and Christian concept of government and the state, basing the legitimacy of royal law not simply on inheritance, will, or power—factors long present in pre-Christian history—but on law and legal jurisdiction, and on the crown's responsibility to establish both justice and peace under the rule of codified law. This would be administered by a "modern" rational royal bureaucracy, somewhat modeled on that of the Church. It declared the king ruler of all the people, denying completely independent privileges to the aristocracy, now enjoined from swearing any political oath in opposition to the crown.

During this era none of the Hispanic states formed completely closed and internally unified entities, equivalent to the English and Norman states (or, to some extent, the kingdom of France). They remained subject both to royal patrimonialism (which might divide the principality) and to centrifugal seigneurialism. Despite the revival of the Visigothic divine unction in royal consecrations, no sacralization of Hispanic princes equivalent to that of their northern counterparts took place, and thus they lacked the symbolic reinforcement enjoyed by the latter.

By the eleventh century Catalonia became in some respects the most organized and had the most fully developed legal structure (crowned by the Usatges), as well as the strongest institutional basis for the development of new law, with its territory fully defined by the beginning of the thirteenth century. Similarly, only in Catalan cities would one encounter civic development somewhat approximating cities in other parts of Europe.

At the same time, the Catalan elite shared in the common sense of the cultural, religious, and geographical community of the Spanish states. The Catalans had earlier categorically affirmed their own neo-Gothicism, and in the immediate aftermath of the Muslim conquest their ancestors may have had a stronger sense of identity and continuity with Visigothic institutions than did the Asturians. There are many references in the Catalan chronicles to the Catalans being "de Espanya" or "d'Espanya" and occasionally even declarations of Espanya as the "patria" of the Catalans. By comparison, neo-Gothicism was much later in entering Navarre and Aragon. This concept was not merely peninsular in scope, but for the Catalans for some time included the right of sovereignty over Visigothic Septimania northeast of the Pyrenees.

The Rise of Castile

Castile became by far the largest Christian principality and hence also the most powerful militarily, but did not develop a political, legal, or institutional structure of equivalent solidity, at least prior to the fourteenth and fifteenth centuries. As a separate kingdom in the earlier period, León was equally or even more prone to elite dissidence. The attempt to maintain a completely independent León ended in failure, due to the absence of internal unity and coherence, though initially León had enjoyed more juridical and institutional development than Castile, and had convened pre-parliaments (*concilios*) and parliaments (*curias/Cortes*) before any other in Europe. The disappearance of León as a discrete entity on one level might be considered the first major Spanish political failure, even though the final union with Castile ultimately constituted a step forward. Though it early achieved some of the first forms of medieval development, such as local autonomies in some districts and an initial convocation of Cortes, Castile was slow to develop effective institutions equivalent to those of France and England. Its society was strongly dominated by aristocratic seigneurialism, like that of most of Europe, but it never experienced fully organized feudalism, with the tightly binding reciprocal relationships between lord and vassals found in France, England, or Aragon-Catalonia. Thus in the first centuries the potentially strong monarchy of Castile was effective only when there was a strong monarch ruling; in other periods it might be quite weak. This was the general tendency in all medieval kingdoms, but it was particularly noticeable in Castile. For several centuries the Castilian aristocracy remained quite independent, at first rather more so than that of the Aragonese principalities. Rather than resting on a developed and institutionalized juridical basis, as in the best organized medieval kingdoms, elite relations in Castile rested on loose pacts or agreements between crown and aristocracy, eventually called "costumbre de España," that did not recognize the fully overriding authority of the crown. The kingdom was based on a loosely defined territory, with only rudimentary institutional structure, and little political or constitutional sense of the king as "king of the Castilians." Royal power tended to be conceived primarily as willpower and superior military strength. Compared with a kingdom such as England, royal law was much more limited. Thus the semi-autonomous cities and concejos were somewhat stunted in their development and, despite the relative freedom of early Castilian society, in the long run never developed the same political status as did cities elsewhere. Autonomous local institutions were structured especially to expedite local military strength, not political or economic development.

The most positive feature of medieval Castilian institutions was the limitation of serfdom. Castile had fewer serfs than most parts of medieval Europe, a consequence often judged to have been a result of its more open status as a frontier region. Despite the growing dominance of the aristocracy, Castilian peasants were thus juridically, at least, freer than elsewhere, even though probably poorer in economic terms, and may have imbibed the aristocratic ethos to a greater degree than peasants anywhere else in medieval Europe. One consequence of this increasingly aristocratic ethos was the pronounced tendency toward pride, arrogance, and touchiness—something remarked upon by Catalan writers even in the Middle Ages. Later, foreign commentators would come to consider these some of the defining characteristics of the Spanish in the sixteenth and seventeenth centuries, constitutive factors, in fact, of the Black Legend.

The downside of weak political development in medieval Castile was that the powerful monarchy frequently broke down under weak rulers. Civil strife was distressingly common, and occurred even more often than in some other medieval principalities, sometimes even leading to temporary collaboration by factions, or by the crown, with Muslim potentates against their Castilian rivals.

The "model" European medieval kingdom was France, where by the thirteenth century the crown had been sacralized according to the new doctrines and fulfilled a sacramental role for the mystical body of the kingdom (a concept derived from the Church as mystical body of Christ). The king's function was partly theocratic, but at the same time limited by law, for he was in charge of justice and supervised development of the legal structure. He had a special role as leader of the Church and possessed great authority in dealing with the papacy. As supreme military leader and king, he always fulfilled caesarist functions, but to some degree he governed with parliament and with the courts and legal system. Thus the crown enjoyed a special charisma as leader of France and of the French. By comparison the English system would become yet more united and representative, even achieving proto-republicanism by the seventeenth century, while the crown of Aragon enjoyed the difficult distinction of ruling over the most complex royal system in Europe, but one that in the final medieval centuries tilted heavily in the direction of a rigid re-feudalization, increasingly weakening royal government.

The reign of Fernando III "el Santo" was one of the most extraordinary in the history of medieval Europe, as the territory comprising the kingdom of Castile-León doubled in size within twenty years. By the middle of the thirteenth century, there was a sense that the reconquest of the peninsula had been essentially completed, since the main remaining taifa emirate, Granada, was comparatively small and reduced to being a vassal of the crown of Castile. The "Great Reconquest," as it is sometimes called, came at a price, for Castile could not immediately absorb so vast a territory, and the movement of population had the effect of weakening the economy, while the Muslim level of production could not be sustained in the southern territories. The experience was extenuating and, curiously, did not strengthen the crown politically, although it added greatly to the territory under royal domain. The crown's authority during this reign derived from crusading, nominally a religious function and little accompanied by political development. The crusader king left, at the time of his death, a relatively discontented and autonomous nobility, willing to use the "costumbre de España" to rebel against the crown; he had, however, failed to identify the Church leadership fully with the crown, as in France.

His son Alfonso X, who would be known as "el Sabio" (the Wise, or the Learned), was the most ambitious and also by comparison one of the least successful of all Spanish kings. He sought to equal and even exceed the achievements of his father by extending the crusade to Africa, reestablishing and expanding the tenuous political hegemony in the peninsula briefly enjoyed by Alfonso VII, and helping to guarantee the latter by winning election as ruler of the Holy Roman Empire (a candidacy to which he had only the most dubious title). He created a systematic new legal code for Castile, all the while stimulating a remarkable cultural program that would translate and distill in Castilian the learning and literature of the Muslims and Jews.[10] These were breathtaking ambitions which could not possibly have all been realized at once, and which in fact conflicted with and contradicted each other.

Don Alfonso has become best known as a dynamic cultural figure, thanks to the work of literature professors. The cultural enterprise of Alfonso X was uniquely cosmopolitan, but also prized vernacular language more than did any other contemporary monarchy. It represented a combination of the oriental and occidental, reflecting the unique cultural situation of thirteenth-century Castile.[11] It failed altogether to deal with the impressive new achievements of the European universities in philosophy, theology, and jurisprudence, which at that moment were largely beyond the Castilian ken. In some ways it resembled the work of San Isidoro in attempting to record a comprehensive approach to knowledge, and in its typically Western "eccentric" attempt to incorporate the learning of a different civilization reflected a special Castilian focus of what was already coming to be a characteristic of advanced Western culture.[12] The attempted new philosophical-cosmological synthesis could not be achieved, for it lacked objectivity, rigor, and true political and intellectual sophistication. The main accomplishment was to complete a stunning variety of translations of Muslim and Jewish materials and also to produce new writings in the vernacular, especially much important work in history. It produced no completely new knowledge or intellectual analysis to speak of, and failed to spark any cultural renascence in Castile, but it certainly constituted a unique enterprise. The *Estoria de España* was not merely the first vernacular history of Spain but also the first attempt at a broader history of the peninsula, even though its primary purpose was narrow, presenting Alfonso's version of the history of the Asturian-Leonese-Castilian monarchy as its legitimate ruler.

Everything else about the reign was a disaster, ending finally in the deposition of the king himself. The crusading and imperial ambitions were completely frustrated, wasted great amounts of money, and sparked much internal discontent. The attempt to generate systematic new legal statutes for the realm trampled much of historical law and custom, and was strongly resisted. The effort to regulate by law a controlled commercial economy through what would later be called mercantilist regulations backfired badly. Finally the effort to deport a portion of the Mudejar population of the south to make room for Castilian settlers boomeranged even more badly, leading to a formidable Mudejar revolt that could only be put down thanks to extensive assistance from Aragon and Portugal. The attempt to impose a new *Fuero Real*, or code of royal law, taking precedence over the rights of the cities and the aristocracy, led to generalized revolt and breakdown of the kingdom, an opportunity seized by the emir of Granada and the sultan of Morocco to invade the south once more, a disaster from which Castile was again saved by assistance from the Aragonese and Portuguese. Royal policies of steeply increased taxation, fixation on politics in Italy and Germany to win the imperial crown, and a destructive economic program brought Castile ever closer to ruin and produced a general agreement to depose its conflictive ruler in 1282. In reply Alfonso formed an alliance with the Moroccans, producing yet another invasion of the south and eventually a political compromise in the melancholy final years of his reign.

Alfonso was the very opposite of "sabio" in terms of vision, objectivity, prudence, understanding of problems, or astuteness. It would, however, be fair to term him "el iluminado" or "el alumbrado" (visionary), as Villacañas Berlanga suggests. His political approach was sheer disaster. The famous *Siete Partidas*, more than a system of practical legal reform, was an exposition of Alfonso's politico-juridical ideology, in which the crown was all-powerful and potentially all-controlling. There was no understanding of the role and character of a Western city as a potentially autonomous and self-governing *universitas*, and no sense of the kingdom as a corporative or organic entity, with objective laws and self-limiting justice that recognized rights, representation, and autonomy. Alfonso was indeed a unique figure in Spanish and in all of European history. He saw himself as endowed with a special towering charisma, a sort of messianic genius with the unique ability to establish a new order. In part, at least, by reaching too far he squandered the opportunities achieved by Castile through the Great Reconquest and left his kingdom unable to realize its full potential, wracked by internal disputes for the next two centuries.[13] He did, however, set a new norm for a juridically strengthened monarchy and the potential expansion of royal law, and to that extent charted the direction followed, however uncertainly, by the Castilian crown during the next two centuries, until it eventually developed impressive power.

In his imperial designs Alfonso el Sabio had not proposed to deprive the other principalities of their autonomy, for he had clearly recognized in the "Partidas" that the ruler of an empire held only a second category of rule over imperial domains and could not rule them directly like a king over his own kingdom or like the rulers of a republic. Empire was an hegemony, above all for purposes of external defense and a coordination of mutual problems. As it was, the only Hispanic empire developed during the late thirteenth and fourteenth centuries was that of the crown of Aragon in the western Mediterranean, the most complex European system of its time. Given the political failure of Castile, the leading role in peninsular affairs for the next century or so passed to the Aragonese rulers.

Pacts of cooperation and marriage alliances among the Hispanic states continued, and conflicts were somewhat reduced, but still persisted. Within Castile, ambitions were expressed from time to time of making its king "emperor of Spain." The last major Moroccan invasion was thoroughly smashed in 1340 by Alfonso XI, the only strong Castilian ruler of the fourteenth century, and by that time the habit, which had hung on for half a millennium, of intermittently calling on a Muslim ruler for assistance against another Hispanic primcipality, largely came to an end. The elites of the Hispanic kingdoms, including Portugal, continued to recognize each other as belonging to a kind of geographic and even politico-cultural community, and they all continued to consider themselves Spanish, but any effective political union was lacking except within the politically sophisticated crown of Aragon.

At no time did expansionist ambitions come to an end, with the exception of landlocked Navarre. Granada lay within the Castilian sphere, and during those years in which the emirate paid tribute, a traditional relationship continued in which direct conquest was often not held to be necessary. Castile nonetheless continued to chip away at Granada's frontiers, and the dream of expansion into Africa was never forgotten. Alfonso X had conquered the Moroccan coastal city of Salé in 1260, slaughtering its inhabitants, and in 1402 Enrique III briefly entered Tetuán, while the conquest of the Canaries had already begun, if slowly and uncertainly. The ultimate goal in financing the expedition of Columbus was not to discover America—which no one dreamed of—but to outflank Islam and ultimately to hasten the Second Coming.

The fifteenth century was a time of recovery for Castile and of political, social, and economic decline for the crown of Aragon, particularly for Catalonia. The growth of the Castilian economy seems to have become notable during the second quarter of the century, beyond which it continued to climb, which helps to account for the sizable amount of impressive new construction in Castilian cities during the late fifteenth century. The factors involved in the decline of Catalonia have been well defined by Catalan historians, to which was added political and social conflict. Though the economy eventually stabilized, decisive new growth in Catalonia would not begin until the last third of the seventeenth century.

The Aragonese kingdoms had become politically static, dominated by the oligarchies enshrined in their elaborate constitutional systems, their monarchy increasingly debilitated and their oppressive social structures prone to internal convulsion and conflict. By the fifteenth century, in contrast, the Castilian monarchy had grown politically stronger, developing an increasingly formidable institutional structure that extended royal administration and royal law, making it for a time one of the most "modern" of European monarchies.

The "Hispanic Monarchy"

The remarkable marriage of the rulers (later known as the Catholic Monarchs) finally effected the combination that could bring together all but one of the peninsular states under a single dynasty (after the conquest/inheritance of peninsular Navarre in 1512). The observation that an alternative marriage with Afonso V of Portugal would have created a different dynastic alliance based on a more coherent institutional structure/logic that combined Castile and Portugal, instead, is perhaps sensible in the abstract but overlooks the fact that Afonso V of Portugal was an aging king who might not have been able to generate a new dynasty. That the new united monarchy ruled over a diversity of states was in no way unusual, for that was in fact the norm among European monarchies at that time, and the Aragonese monarchy merely had the most complex of these structures. Thus, it was the Aragonese model that was adopted by the new Spanish monarchy, with the major difference that it now included a "great power" state, Castile.

The international marriage alliance arranged by the united monarchy enabled it to inherit a European dynastic empire on the very eve of the age in which the conquistadores would carve out a vast American territorial empire. The combination of the two produced the most unique imperial structure in world history, consisting of both a discontiguous European continental empire and the first true world empire, with possessions in America, North Africa (cities on the coast of Morocco and Algeria), and later, in the western Pacific. The temporary dynastic union with Portugal added to its vast extent and heterogeneity. There has never been a European empire like that of the Spanish Habsburgs, for all the other major intra-European empires (Charlemagne, the Holy Roman Empire, Austria-Hungary, Poland-Lithuania, tsarist Russia, and the Ottomans) consisted of contiguous territorial domains. Conversely, the first European oceanic empire, that of Portugal, was a coastal thalassocracy that did not include significant territorial colonies until the development of Brazil. The complexity and geographical discontinuity of the Habsburg European crownlands would always be a major problem, leading to the severing of the eastern and western Habsburg domains after little more than a generation, a decisive act that merely reduced but did not resolve the inherent difficulties involved.

In more recent times, the main concern about the political identities of this era has to do not with the empire but with the united monarchy in the peninsula. To European opinion, the Iberian principalities of the united monarchy simply constituted "Spain," although no such single uniform political entity existed. There was a united monarchy that functioned as a single state for foreign and military policy, but internally governed on the basis of the individual autonomy of the several Hispanic principalities.

Modern Spanish patriots and nationalists for understandable reasons like to refer to the "origins of the Spanish nation," and so on. Claudio Sánchez Albornoz and other "essentialists" have posited an enduring essence of sociocultural characteristics among the native population of the peninsula since pre-Roman times, though the eminent medievalist refers to the kingdom of Asturias as the "origin of the Spanish nation," as do some others. What one clearly had in Asturias was the beginning of the state that directly evolved in a long historical process, without total interruption, into the modern Spanish state, but that is a different proposition. More commonly, Spanish patriots have seen the origin of the modern nation in the united monarchy in the late fifteenth century.

The modern concept of a nation as a single institutionally unified society with a common language and history, and common rights and restrictions for all citizens, either possessing or aspiring to possess an independent state (or at the very least complete autonomy), is a product of the era of the French Revolution. It is further accepted that the major European nations all have deep historical roots, and in no case were merely "invented" in the eighteenth or nineteenth centuries, despite the faddish and misleading language of commentators.[14] The only major nation to have developed nationhood as early or earlier than France was England, which as the United Kingdom of England, Wales, and Scotland began to develop a distinctive highly assertive nationalism in the second half of the eighteenth century that transcended the earlier English proto-nationalism.[15]

The case of Holland is interesting, for only Holland was developing a society and system that was as modern as England during the first half of the seventeenth century. Several commentators have suggested that Holland was becoming the first modern nation, which in some respects may have been the case, yet Dutch political development, though dynamic and precocious, became arrested during the course of the seventeenth century so that Holland failed to blossom fully at that time into a completely unified nation.

Prior to the era of the French Revolution, the word "nation" had several different meanings, none of them equivalent to the modern sense. The term obviously refers to the birth origins of an individual or a group, and in earlier times was used to refer variously to individual regions, ethnic groups, or principalities, or to general language groups or even to broadly identifiable areas. Any one of the Hispanic states or regions might be referred to as a nation in the traditional sense, just as groups of traders from any or all of the peninsular ports might be identified abroad as Spanish or of the Spanish nation, and as all students from the peninsula in other European universities might be lumped together as the Spanish nation, though their own native languages might vary. Conversely, in Bruges a "Vizcayan nation" was formed by the late fifteenth century, which included not merely Vizcayans but traders from other ports of northern Spain. In the traditional usage, "nation" referred essentially to a place or a territory, or even groups thereof, or to those who spoke a particular language, but not to a unified political entity. In this traditional or historical sense, Spain may have been the oldest "historical nation" but not at all the first modern political nation.

Prophetic and even apocalyptic images were not uncommon in the peninsula, as elsewhere in Europe, during the fourteenth and fifteenth centuries, and these included prophecies of the future unity of all the Hispanic states and their special role in history. After formation of the united monarchy, the term "nación de España" was used by several Castilian writers and at least one Aragonese writer,[16] but the Catholic Monarchs scarcely ever called themselves "monarchs of Spain," Fernando, for example, referring to the "crown of Spain" on only one public occasion in 1514. In such an event, the crown of Portugal was always quick to complain, because the sense of Spain as an all-peninsular term remained very strong, and would remain so into the eighteenth century.[17]

The most common term for the next two centuries would therefore be the less direct form "la Monarquía hispánica," the term introduced by Felipe II to distinguish the state later known to historians as "imperial Spain" from the central European Habsburg domains, which had been split off under the rule of his Austrian cousins. The plurality and distinct institutions of the crown's principalities were always acknowledged, and historians would later devise the term "monarquía compuesta" (compound monarchy) for the totality involved. Nonetheless, specific Spanish terminology would be applied to the crown more and more, as "crown of Spain" or "de las Españas," even though never an official title, while Felipe II sometimes termed himself *Princeps Hispaniorum* or *Hispaniorum et Indorum Rex*, which referred to the principal domains and base of, but not all the patrimony of, the monarchy.

There were a multiplicity of legal or constitutional systems to be dealt with and a wide variety of identities and sensibilities that needed to be respected, even within the peninsula. This raised the question not merely of pluralistic internal policy, accommodated through the various administrative councils ("Council of Castile," etc.), but also the question of the power of the crown itself. Political theory throughout western Europe held that authority or sovereignty was derived from the general community, but that the monarchy held "preeminent" power (including the right to make new law) and was answerable ultimately to God, although it was expected to abide by the established laws of each principality. On various occasions the Castilian Cortes of the fifteenth century had emphasized that God "made kings his vicars on earth," consistent with the medieval doctrine of the sacralization of monarchy and its functions.[18] Moreover, during the fourteenth and fifteenth centuries there had developed the concept of the crown's "poderío absoluto" (absolute authority), giving rise to the early modern doctrine of "absolute monarchy," for long exaggerated by historians. The united monarchy of Spain rarely claimed absolute power, especially during the sixteenth century, and the doctrine referred not to absolute despotic power but to the hierarchical superiority and independence or indivisibility of royal authority, which also had the power to make new laws. Even in Castile, the Cortes and the cities continued in various ways to contest legally the powers and policies of the crown.[19] Outside the peninsula, the variety of principalities and legal systems was bewildering, but in the Habsburg Italian states, the largest part of the dynastic empire outside Spain and the Low Countries, a considerable sense of loyalty and legitimacy was maintained, and even at the low point under Carlos II there was little susceptibility to French political blandishments.

The word *patria* was employed as flexibly and on as many different levels as the word "nation."[20] In his *Tesoro de la lengua castellana* of 1611, Sebastián de Covarrubias defined the term as "Patria: the land where one was born. It is a Latin term, *patria*. Compatriot, someone from the same place." In the expansive *Siete Partidas*, Alfonso X had been the first European writer to employ the term in the vernacular, without giving it any precise application. As distinct from the traditional use of nation, the word "patria" did not connote simply a fact of origin (however uncertain in application) but also a mutual relationship of duty and responsibility. The term was most commonly used for individual principalities, and even more for local regions and districts, for what would become known in colloquial Castilian as the "patria chica" (little fatherland).

The writing of history advanced rapidly during the sixteenth and early seventeenth centuries, and on all levels.[21] It culminated in the first great history of Spain, Juan de Mariana's *Historia general de España* (Latin, 1592; Castilian, 1601), which would remain the standard work for two and a half centuries. This was followed during the first half of the seventeenth century by a series of works by Castilian authors affirming Spain in the form of the policies of the monarchy and to some extent of the institutions of Castile. Fray Juan de Salazar, in his *Política española* (1619), hailed common government of the peninsula for the Spanish as a "chosen people," a not uncommon attitude at court and among part of the Castilian elite.

Integrationism culminated in the program of the Conde-Duque de Olivares for Felipe IV to govern as "king of Spain," though even this continued to respect the distinct politico-legal systems. The result was dismaying to the Conde-Duque, who continued to identify nation and national in the traditional sense as concepts limited to the separate principalities, and variously lamented "Cursed be nations, and a curse on national men!" and "I am not national, which is something for children," off-cited complaints.[22] Although Castile was the main base of the state and also contained more advocates of a more integrated system, Castile itself remained a specific nation in this traditional sense and a patria in the common usage, and a strong sense of distinct Castilian identity remained, with its own interests.[23]

By the early seventeenth century, the term "nation" was being used in the peninsula in at least three different ways. The most common usage referred to individual kingdoms or principalities. Beyond that for a small minority stood the "nation of Spain," though, contradictorily, it in turn was held to be made up of lesser nations. A very few even referred to a sort of "monarchist nation" that embraced all nations or principalities of the entire western Habsburg dynasty, but that was too complex and tenuous a usage to have much currency.

Historical works devoted to principalities and smaller areas proved yet more common, however, with the popularity of the genre known as "corografía," devoted to local histories. The affirmation of an integrated all-Spanish policy, which never went very far before Olivares, was met in turn by vigorous new affirmation of the identities and laws and constitutional systems of the several principalities, particularly in the Basque provinces and in Catalonia but also in some other regions. Catalan writers and historians developed their own myth of an absolutely separate and autonomous ethnogenesis during the ninth and tenth centuries.[24] If Mariana had set a new standard for Spanish historical writing, the new regionalist histories of the sixteenth and seventeenth often went in a diametrically opposite direction, led particularly by the Vizcayans, as they elaborated fantasies, which in some cases they knew had no basis in fact.

The Habsburg dynasty has been almost universally, and accurately, criticized for the stubbornness and destructiveness of its foreign and fiscal policies. Its domestic policy, however, was modest in the extreme, compared with the domestic policies of the French and English monarchies, which slowly but steadily worked to build broader and more united polities. The Spanish Habsburgs accepted a highly legalist interpretation of the domestic status quo, which they rarely tried to change. The kingdom of Castile had been made increasingly responsive to the crown, its Cortes after 1538 the only European parliament composed exclusively of the third estate. It had relatively effective fiscal and judicial institutions, as well as an aristocracy generally trained to cooperate with the crown. This contrasted sharply with the elaborate but ossified constitutional structures of the Aragonese principalities, intensely elitist and oppressive, unwilling to pay any new taxes or even contribute to the common defense. Felipe IV was a more astute ruler than he has usually been given credit for; he understood the desirability of achieving equal rights and responsibilities in all the Spanish principalities—even though at no time was so sweeping a reform proposed, even by Olivares.[25]

The separatist conflicts developed by Portugal and Catalonia in 1640 were in neither case united patriotic struggles, since each also involved an internal civil war, though the supporters of the separatist policy were stronger in both instances. By the second half of the seventeenth century traditionalist particularism was once more dominant, though the independence of Portugal and the reconquest of Catalonia began for the first time to draw the modern dividing line of Spain and Spanish, stopping at the Portuguese frontier but including all the rest of the peninsula. Such a definition was finally accepted by the Portuguese after the early eighteenth century.

Empire

The Asturian-Castilian crown had intermittently aspired to "empire" since the end of the ninth century, an empire that was to extend over the entire peninsula and then, in a further projection of the Reconquest, into North Africa, as well. The crown of Aragon had created a genuine Mediterranean empire that included a degree of indirect hegemony over small portions of North Africa, though it never pretended to be more than an extended "composed monarchy." The conquest of Granada revived classic Castilian aspirations that began to be realized through the subjugation of several sites on the African coast, before the attention of the crown was diverted. Interest in crusading had revived in various parts of Europe after the fall of Constantinople in 1453, but nowhere else was this so strong as in the Iberian Peninsula, for the obvious combination of historical, political, geographical, and cultural reasons.

Carlos V realized the old ambition of Alfonso el Sabio to be elected head of the central European Holy Roman Empire, being in as strong a position to do so as that of the Rey Sabio had been weak. The Holy Roman Empire—which because of its loose, secular, and essentially Germanic structure has been described as "neither holy, nor Roman, nor an empire"—was the classic historic European "empire" supposedly deriving its origins and legitimacy from Charlemagne and from Rome itself. As a central European entity, however, it represented something quite different from the historic ambitions of the crown of Castile.

Carlos V assumed the imperial title during the first phase of the Protestant Reformation and sought to restore religious unity and achieve harmony in Europe, tasks totally beyond his reach. Early in his imperial reign, his advisors posited the goal of achieving "universal empire," not in the sense that Don Carlos would achieve direct sovereignty over all European states, but that he would achieve a position of hegemonic leadership that would guarantee peace and harmony. This was not to be, but instead inaugurated the beginning of the modern era of what would much later be known as the "balance of power," as other European states allied in opposition to any one dominant force. By the middle of the century both Spanish and imperial foreign policy had become essentially defensive, but the dynastic possessions of the crown, even after the imperial title and the central European domains had been relinquished, remained so extensive that attempting to hold the status quo meant endless warfare in Italy, France, the Low Countries, central Europe, and at times against England. Further charges of seeking "universal monarchy" were hurled against the Spanish crown, after which the target for nearly two centuries would be France. Moreover, for most of the sixteenth century, the responsibility of defending the Islamic frontier cost as much as the wars in Europe and even more in loss of lives. This stood as a basic Spanish obligation, not shared to the same extent by any other state, a burden that eased only after 1585. It was a task that the representatives of Castilian taxpayers were willing to bear, while they frequently urged the crown to seek peace and reduce military obligations in Europe.

Henry Kamen has emphasized the international nature of the leadership, administration, financing, and military resources of the far-flung domains of the Spanish monarchy.[26] This is to a considerable degree correct, for the crown followed not a "Spanish" but a dynastic policy that relied considerably on non-Spanish personnel. The absence of Hispanocentrism in this policy sometimes elicited strong protests from Castilians, but Castile remained its financial and military base and, even though most of the crown's soldiers were not Spanish, the Spanish Tercios (infantry battalions) remained the hard core of its armed forces.[27]

The American empire, which eventually expanded into the first true world empire that included possessions in the Pacific, raised different problems. Dominion was nominally derived from papal authorization, which, however, pertained only to general sovereignty, not to the ownership of land or the domination and exploitation of the native population. This produced modern Europe's first moral confrontation with the issues of colonialism and imperialism. Religious and intellectual figures in Spain and Spanish America addressed the resulting dilemmas with honesty, compassion, and intellectual originality, resulting in new development of natural law and innovations in international law as well, but the humane and path-breaking definitions by part of the religious and intellectual elite were never really implemented, and the new empire mostly became domination pure and simple.[28] Ancient Rome served as a kind of conceptual model, though not as a practical model, while the conquest of exotic peoples also awakened a new consciousness in reflective Spaniards, who by the sixteenth century did not find the origins of Spain in the Visigoths but to an increasing degree in the native population of the peninsula who had resisted the Romans, just as Indians resisted Spaniards.[29] Similarly, from the very beginning in the 1580s North American Indians reminded some Englishmen of the original Britons and Picts of their own home island.

The overseas empire was never termed such by the monarchy in the sixteenth and seventeenth centuries, and was technically just the patrimony of the crown of

Castile, though contemporary Europeans considered all this simply the "Spanish empire." There was no historical precedent for this kind of empire, and its territories were never called "colonies" prior to the eighteenth century. Rather, they were to some extent considered overseas equivalents of the lands won in the peninsular reconquest, and were made new "reinos" (lit., kingdoms) of the crown of Castile.

The American empire received little attention and not that much emigration during the sixteenth and seventeenth centuries, the crown's main concern being reception of the gold and silver (primarily the latter) that became crucial to its finances. The estimates are that no more than 300,000 Spaniards went to America during the entire colonial period, while not all the survivors of the journey remained there permanently. These were just enough to establish the beginning of a new hybrid creole and mestizo society, which, largely left to its own devices, proved impressively loyal and resilient amid the trials of the seventeenth century.

A surprisingly small number of colonizers thus achieved complete success in laying down the roots of a unique new society, but in later times its development would become increasingly problematic, the very opposite of the success story of North America. The differences in many ways were the differences between early modern Spain and seventeenth-century England. Indeed, England was rapidly overtaking Holland as the most modern and innovative country in Europe, while Spain during the imperial era largely failed in the modernization struggle.[30] The Spanish empire constituted a totally unique historical precedent to which the English paid considerable attention, but the newer "commercial empires" of the seventeenth and eighteenth centuries pursued different policies and priorities. The empire was not used as a factor of integration or nation-building within the peninsula, because such a goal simply did not exist prior to the eighteenth century, leaving the empire primarily the preserve of Castilians and Basques. Similarly, the priorities of rigid state regulation of commerce (even though the economy was based on private enterprise) and emphasis on bullion extraction were narrowly conceived and precluded use of the empire to achieve economic development at home. When the priorities changed in the second half of the eighteenth century, the era of the empire was nearly over.[31]

6 Spain and Portugal

The capacity of Spain and Portugal to turn their backs on each other in modern times has been extraordinary. Given its size, Portugal has never been able to ignore Spain to the same extent that the latter ignores Portugal, but this difference is only relative. In earlier centuries, despite difficulty in communications, the Spanish kingdoms always had much more to do with Portugal, and vice versa, restricted to a large degree, to their common peninsula. After 1668 they tended more and more to go their separate ways, though with certain notable exceptions, until finally brought together again not by a peninsular entente but by the European Union in 1985.

The initial paradox is that Portugal was not institutionally, culturally, and structurally the most singular of the peninsular principalities. That distinction would have to go to Catalonia, which was considerably more different from its counterparts than was Portugal. The earlier institutions and culture of the kingdom of Portugal were basically derived from those of Galicia and León, and there was no extraordinary innovation in type or character among the earliest Portuguese institutions.

Spanish historians have often seen the origins of Portugal as stemming from a sort of politico-dynastic accident, and a considerable argument may be developed on behalf of this position. The establishment of what was to become an independent state and monarchy by Afonso I Henriques in 1128 was a typical political development of that era, as León was separated from Castile, Aragon became a kingdom, Navarre was associated with Aragon and then separated from it, and various efforts were made to establish Galicia as a distinct kingdom. Indeed, Alfonso VII did not view the new Portuguese principality as other than a vassal state of Castile, a further feature of the heterogeneous, "imperial" structure of his monarchy.

The uniqueness of the case of Portugal was not any profound difference in the culture and politics of the erstwhile new kingdom compared with these other examples, but simply that subsequent historical developments made possible the full establishment and consolidation of an independent monarchy, and ultimately of a separate country. This was due to the interplay of politics and history—contingency, in effect—and not to intrinsic and profound differences. Had the right kind of effective marriage alliance been made between the crowns of Castile and Portugal, rather than between Castile and Aragon, the resultant union would have been at least as logical and effective as that developed by the heirs of the Catholic Monarchs, if not more so. This is not to deny that Portugal over several centuries developed a very firm and distinct identity and eventually formed a more united separate nation than did Spain, but rather to stress that this was the result of a complex process of historical development. It did not lie in some predetermined essence at the roots of that process. Numerous efforts have been made by historians of Portugal to identify and define unique differences in early history, and even to advance a geographical argument for Portuguese singularity, but none of these is especially convincing.[1] A unique original Portuguese "essentialism" prior to the twelfth century has yet to be discovered. This is not to deny that certain specific individual traits might be identified in nascent Portugal, but only to emphasize that these do not appear to have been any greater than equally specific and individual traits, which might have been found in the other Hispanic states, as indeed in all small medieval principalities.

During the eleventh and twelfth centuries, León and Castile had failed to develop the levels of political and institutional coherence that were being achieved in the smaller principalities of Catalonia and Aragon, and the arrogation of independence in the southwestern territories of the crown of León by Afonso Henriques, a grandson of Alfonso VI, was only one of a series of centrifugal political actions in that era. The people of his territories mostly spoke their own form of Romance, different from the vernacular of greater León, but the same was true of the people of Galicia. Moreover, the latter possessed a much older, more distinctive, and more complex and sophisticated culture and set of institutions than could be found in the southwest. About this time Galician became the principal vernacular form for "high culture" and poetry in most of the peninsula, and Galicia was more of a distinctly organized entity than were the somewhat amorphous territories of Afonso Henriques. Initially, the lands of the new monarchy were somewhat divided from the rest of León by mountains, but mountain barriers are common in the peninsula, and just as present in the case of Galicia. Later, as the kingdom of Portugal advanced southward, they would be completely absent in the newly reconquered territories. The crown of Portugal, like that of Aragon, looked to the papacy for legitimation of its independent status. The latter granted this in return for recognition of papal suzerainty, since Rome's diplomacy was as interested in maintaining the internal political disunity of the peninsula, to further papal influence, as it was conversely, and sometimes a bit contradictorily, to encourage a countervailing military unity against the Muslims. At the same time, the first king of Portugal, like his Aragonese counterpart, felt compelled to recognize a loose form of homage to his cousin Alfonso VII as Hispanic "emperor," limited though this acknowledgement was.

Of the multiple new marriage alliances among Hispanic rulers between the twelfth and fourteenth centuries, the only ones to achieve any new enduring unions were the two that reunited Castile and León and that created the "composed monarchy" of the greater crown of Aragon, while conversely Navarre broke completely free of its temporary association with Aragon.

With each passing generation the independent kingdom of Portugal developed an increasing sense of unity and identity, forging effective institutions of its own, however much they may have formally resembled those of Castile. As a typical Hispanic frontier kingdom, Portugal had the opportunity to extend its frontiers southward, strengthening its crown and providing an independent sphere of action for its own elites, thus completing its own reconquest by the middle of the thirteenth century. This closed its peninsular frontier and further assisted the distinct process of ethno-formation that was under way, until a unique and fully structured separate kingdom had been formed no later than the fourteenth century.[2] Portugal had begun to assume its full historical form, though at that time no European territory constituted a modern nation.

After Portugal successfully asserted its independence from Castile in the succession crisis of 1383–85, the kingdom soon set forth on its course of overseas expansion. Although expansion beyond Hispanic home waters had been begun by the crown of Aragon at the end of the thirteenth century, the remarkable growth of overseas Aragonese territories took place within the classic Mediterranean world. The first extrapeninsular conquest of the Portuguese—Ceuta in 1415—established a foothold in North Africa (something that Aragon and Castile had also briefly attempted), but this extension of typical Hispanic Reconquest policy was soon expanded into the program of Atlantic exploration and expansion, which became the unique enterprise of Portugal in world history.

The Portuguese would later speak of their Atlantic vocation, but this failed to transform domestic Portugal, which in the sixteenth century remained much more like Castile than was, for example, Catalonia. The Portugal of the expansion was a society of dual elites, the lesser elite of merchants, royal agents, and a portion of the aristocracy favoring oceanic projects, and the opening of enterprise beyond the Atlantic islands, all the way down the African coast and, eventually, to India itself. The main interest group of the military aristocracy, however, remained true to the classic (medieval) crusading ideal, the Reconquest now projected into the Maghrib, aimed at conquering as much territory as possible in Morocco for purposes of booty and the creation of new landed domains.

Both enterprises derived inspiration from the fifteenth-century religious revival, which affected Portugal about as much as Spain, and in the entire peninsular context (including also Valencia, so that it was not merely a matter of Castilian and Portuguese speakers) this assumed a pronounced apocalyptic tone, aimed at the crusade and ultimately the liberation of Jerusalem. It was also a major incentive for the Atlantic voyages. The famous Prince Henry was not a scientist but saw himself as a crusader; later, the court of King Manoel (who would be called "The Fortunate") lived in a kind of apocalyptic fervor, so that the dispatch of the expedition of Vasco da Gama represented not merely an opportunity to cut into the south Asian spice trade but also an effort strategically to flank the Islamic world, establish new geopolitical conditions, help to regain Jerusalem, and expedite the Second Coming.[3] Much the same set of motivations as in the case of Columbus.

Until the development of Brazil in the later sixteenth century, the original Portuguese empire was not a land empire but what historians have termed a "thalassocracy," that is, an ocean-going empire built around the possession of a long string of ports and coastal fortresses, rather than extensive territories. For most of the fifteenth and sixteenth centuries it remained a kind of schizophrenic empire, the Afro-Asian thalassocracy having to compete with the military crusade and territorial conquest in Morocco. For that matter, the thalassocracy itself was never a "commercial empire" of the kind later developed by the Dutch and English. Though commerce was important to it, this functioned within the broader "conquistador" ethos of early Portuguese expansion that emphasized force. By the mid-sixteenth century the cost was becoming greater than the benefits: although some income continued to be earned from the south Asian and African spice trade, the Portuguese crown was increasingly hard pressed for resources.

Once the romantic and crusade-minded Sebastian came of age and assumed power in 1568, the stage was set for complete domination of policy by the crusaders, leading to the large-scale invasion of Morocco ten years later and the dynastic and national disaster of Alcazarquivir.[4] During its final generations, crusading was supposed to help achieve apocalypse, and it certainly did for the Portuguese monarchy. There could have been no greater demonstration of the ubiquity of the crusade in the general Luso-Hispanic culture. In this the Portuguese proved the most "typically Spanish" of all the peninsular kingdoms. In no other European state was both a dynasty extinguished and independence lost as a result of an aggressive military crusade abroad. In Portugal the "guerra divinal" produced the most extreme consequences.

The claim of Felipe II to the Portuguese crown was contested, but no other claimant could boast clearly superior legitimacy. Even though temporary military occupation by the troops of the Duque de Alba enforced that claim, the accession of the Spanish ruler was generally accepted within Portugal. In 1580–81 the peninsula was at least reunited for the first time since 711, even if historians have difficulty defining exactly what kind of union it was.

It has sometimes been said that Portugal accepted the leadership of the Spanish crown when that was to its advantage, and rejected it in 1640 when this was no longer so. There is much to be said for such an interpretation. Portuguese attitudes were always somewhat divided. This was the case in the independence conflict of the 1380s, in 1580, and also in 1640, as in all these crises sectors of the Portuguese elites supported the Spanish crown. In general, however, a Spain in decline was no longer a useful associate. Instead of offering support to Portugal, the embattled Spanish monarchy was itself requesting assistance. Instead of providing protection to the Portuguese possessions overseas, Spanish policy exposed the Portuguese thalassocracy to endless conflict with the Dutch republic, at that moment becoming the most efficient sea power in the world.

Portugal was able to cut free partly because of its geography, which made reconquest less of an absolute priority for the Spanish crown than was regaining Catalonia. Extrapeninsular factors helped as well. English assistance was important in the decisive phase of the 1660s, when Spain had ended the war with France and could concentrate dwindling resources against Portugal. And in the long run, the "second empire" (meaning Brazil, not the original Afro-Asian thalassocracy) would prove a significant source of economic strength.

A Change of "National Character"?

In the twenty-first century, many of the Portuguese look back with some amazement at the worldwide accomplishments of their ancestors. This in turn raises the question as to exactly how much of a break the seventeenth century meant in Portuguese affairs, which is just as important as in the case of Spain, although the answers may be somewhat different. Broad generalizations about "national character" are dangerous, but the general impression is that the modern Portuguese have been a prudent, relatively subdued, and unambitious people, often characterized by the sadness associated with *saudade*, melancholic nostalgia. Any such generalization is doubtless exaggerated, but has been advanced by many observers and offers a portrait at considerable odds with what we know of the Portuguese elite during the fifteenth and sixteenth centuries.

Portuguese society and institutions, like those of any country, eventually came to have its own distinctive characteristics, medieval Portugal being even more agricultural than Castile, which featured greater cattle production. Yet in general, Portuguese institutions and culture paralleled those of Castile and León. The development of the kingdom largely resembled that of its eastern neighbors, so that the expansion of Portugal in the fifteenth century did not necessarily reflect any unique "Atlantic" or "mercantile" society any more than it did a somewhat archaic, typically Iberian crusade-and-reconquest mentality. The Portuguese did indeed introduce some new interests and techniques, the subsequent thalassocracy developing maritime and commercial concerns of a new kind, but throughout this period the Portuguese elite continued to be dominated by the most traditional of religious, aristocratic, and traditional values, honored and emphasized to the point of self-destruction in 1578.

The Portuguese of the expansion revealed an extraordinary degree of self-confidence, an almost infinite daring and courage very similar to that of Spanish conquistadores, and a profound sense that they were the most warlike and proficient of all the Latin Christians. They scoffed at any notion of military dependency, but this had changed by the seventeenth century. The Portuguese mentality altered from the offensive to the defensive, from the audacious to the prudent. Whereas they had fought off the crown of Castile all by themselves in the fourteenth century, by the seventeenth century they looked to outside assistance to a degree unknown before, and by the eighteenth century would, when in trouble, sometimes call upon the English to send a general to organize their forces. Portugal would not again expand overseas until the nineteenth century.

When one talks of "national character" in this regard, the reference is primarily to the psycho-emotional ethos of the elite sectors. The Portuguese aristocracy never fully recovered from the trauma of 1578, which destroyed some of its leading elements. Though the domestic social structure would remain much the same for three centuries, the fire and drive was gone from the old military nobility, which preferred to live off its rents. It might be asked whether this reflected a subjective change on the part of the elite, or rather an objective adjustment to a world of increased competition in which the Portuguese could inevitably expect to achieve less. The answer probably is that it reflected a certain amount of both.

It may be objected that the concept "change of character" creates a caricature. Ordinary Portuguese behaved much the same before and after 1578. In both eras the most typical subject of the Portuguese crown was a peaceful peasant who worked the land. Moreover, there was never a monolithic Portugal. The fifteenth-century elite had been sharply divided about the wisdom of crusading in Morocco, and also about the Atlantic voyages. There had always existed more prudent and practical elite sectors, whose point of view imposed a more pragmatic and "modern" policy after 1640. Rather than a change of character, this might be interpreted as a natural evolution, even though crucially precipitated by trauma.

A certain militancy and expansionism was regained under modern nationalism in the nineteenth and twentieth centuries, and Portugal was much more successful in this regard than was Spain, amassing the second largest empire of any of the smaller European countries, a situation that greatly stimulated German cupidity on the eve of World War I. Given the relative poverty of modern Portugal, this was a considerable achievement, but of course at no time had the country been wealthy, in comparative terms, and the "third empire" (Angola, Mozambique, and Guinea-Bissau), though noteworthy, did not reflect an originality and a daring equivalent to the fifteenth century. Portuguese society to some extent lost its atavistic military ethos without developing the full structure and values of a modern society. This also paralleled the experience of Spain, but in the case of Portugal the disaster of 1578 and the temporary loss of full sovereignty marked a before and an after. Though later exceeded in character and extent by the radical transformation of Germany after 1945, it constituted a more marked change than was to be found in the early modern history of any other European country.

The positive side of the decline in militancy in modern Portuguese culture has been the absence of civil war and prolonged civil violence, except for the conflict of 1832–34. The perpetual instability of the "Primeira República" (1910–26) produced intermittent violence that was nonetheless low in volume. Even the long Portuguese dictatorship of 1926–74 was comparatively gentle, the only one in Europe referred to as "uma catedocracia" (a professorocracy) because of the prominent role of university personnel.

The "Precocity" of Portugal

Portugal has never been a particularly modern or advanced country, and did not hold such status even at the time of its expansion in 1415. Nevertheless, it has exhibited certain symptoms of precocity to the extent that it carried out new achievements or introduced new institutions earlier than did Spain or other parts of southern and eastern Europe, or even, in some cases, northwestern Europe. The "advantages of backwardness," as it is sometimes called, offer no explanation, for this refers more to the possibility of making unusually rapid advances by taking advantage of institutions or policies already pioneered by more developed countries.[5] The only advantages that Portugal possessed were a militant ethos, a compact geography and privileged strategic location.

Among the many Portuguese "firsts" may be found:

1. The first Hispanic kingdom to complete its full southern reconquest;
2. The first western kingdom to initiate major expansion in Africa and Asia;
3. Establishment of the first maritime constellation to span much of the globe;
4. Introduction of a new program of administered monarchist capitalism, though in the long run this proved a failure;
5. Beginning the transatlantic slave trade;
6. Initiating the development of the plantation economy of the Atlantic islands and of the Western Hemisphere;
7. Carrying out the first peaceful decolonization in the Western Hemisphere;
8. Becoming the first Iberian country to resolve the liberalism/traditionalism conflict in the nineteenth century;
9. Becoming the first Iberian country to stabilize nineteenth-century liberalism;
10. Introducing the first permanent new republic of the twentieth century in Europe (1910);
11. Establishing the first new-style twentieth-century authoritarian regime in Europe (1917–18), though it did not last;
12. Introducing Europe's first corporative constitution in 1933;
13. Initiating the first overthrow of an authoritarian regime in southern and eastern Europe during the late twentieth century (1974).

Some of the internal political achievements or innovations were no doubt facilitated by the small size of the country, and one or two of them possibly encouraged more by weakness than by strength. Moreover, several of these innovations were destructive, as has been the case in the history of most human societies. In general, however, they indicate a degree of initiative that has been overshadowed in foreign perceptions by Portugal's social and economic backwardness. These more precocious features of change, however, reveal a not inconsiderable degree of continuing activism, despite the limitations of the socioeconomic context.

Land of the "Negative Superlative"

At the first meeting of the International Conference Group on Portugal, held at the University of New Hampshire in October 1973, the sociologist Herminio Martins referred to his native country as the land of the "negative superlative." By this he meant that while some countries are referred to in terms of positive superlatives such as the most, the biggest, and the like, comparative references to Portugal in modern times have been in the negative superlative as the most backward, most underdeveloped, poorest, most illiterate of the west European countries. So long as one is looking at the main part of Europe north and west of the Balkans, such negative comparisons have usually been statistically justified.

At no time has Portugal been an economic or a technological leader (except for certain aspects of maritime science in the fifteenth and sixteenth centuries) and, from the seventeenth century on, it has been a relatively underdeveloped country that in comparative terms lost rather than gained ground during the nineteenth century. This is a story somewhat reminiscent of Spain, save that the comparative Portuguese statistics in modern times have been rather lower than those for Spain as a whole. Only in a few other parts of southern and eastern Europe has economic development been slower.

During the Middle Ages Portugal experienced the relative economic marginality common to most of the Christian kingdoms in the peninsula, though, as we have seen, in a time of generally slow economic change this did not result in a situation of profound underdevelopment. In the fifteenth century, Portugal, like Castile, probably ranked not much lower than a "low medium" on the general comparative scale of western economic development. Moreover, it momentarily took the lead in several specific areas of maritime technology and of long-range commercial organization, though these advantages would not long endure.

A fundamental question in Portuguese history is why the income generated by the thalassocracy for several generations was not used to stimulate positive economic growth. Several factors seem to have been important. One was that the maritime enterprise of the "first empire" was not as profitable as might have been thought. Certain voyages and initiatives did return a considerable profit, but conversely the overall expenses were very great, and remained extremely high even as profits declined. Militarization of the process in some respects increased rather than diminished. The Portuguese expansion was not based on a highly productive hinterland, but moved fairly rapidly from a modest domestic base to a large-scale enterprise without any significant development of that domestic base. It may be argued that almost all major enterprises spring initially from modest origins. In the Portuguese case, however, no positive balance was achieved, partly because the motivations and priorities were not primarily economic in the first place. Though Portugal did briefly pioneer certain forms of royal and long-range commercial organization, it did not constitute a capitalist society to the extent that Venice and Genoa already had during the Middle Ages or that Holland and England would become in the seventeenth century. Portuguese society and priorities remained more traditional, the crusade eventually trumping commerce, even though the two were supposed to be intertwined. This may be considered typically "Luso-Hispanic" but not very modern. Moreover, the maritime breakthrough did not in the long run provide the country with the kind of commercial advantages that briefly appeared to be the case at the beginning of the sixteenth century. International competition soon increased, while Portugal did not possess—and proved incapable of developing—the kind of financial basis and commercial network to take full advantage of these opportunities. At least as important was the contradiction/competition between the crusade of conquest in Morocco and the long-range thalassocracy. They had begun as different parts of the same enterprise, but the former came to overshadow the latter. Already by the middle of the sixteenth century the crown encountered severe financial trouble; the twentieth-century historian Garrett Mattingly has described João III as "the proprietor of a bankrupt wholesale grocery business."[6]

In the case of Portugal as in that of Spain, much of whatever profit derived from empire was skimmed off by the crown and invested in nonproductive military exercises. What little profit entered Portuguese society was largely absorbed nonproductively by the aristocracy. Not much was invested in productive enterprise within the country. The modest extent of the domestic market made it unpromising, and a relative absence of creative economic undertakings guaranteed that that would continue to be the case.

The "second empire" in Brazil became quite profitable by the late seventeenth century, yet it seems that very much the same story repeated itself. The crown and a small elite prospered, and by the early eighteenth century it had become possible to reconstruct the Portuguese navy, at least in part; yet again the proportion of money invested in stimulating domestic enterprise was comparatively slight, even though from the late seventeenth century on the Portuguese government was at least cognizant of the problem. It was not until the repatriation of capital from Brazil after the latter's independence that empire-generated capital began to be invested more directly in domestic activities, and even then much was sunk into the disamortization of landed estates, though this also made possible enough investment in the national debt to maintain to some extent the financial stability of the government. Moreover, by the nineteenth century it had become necessary to run much faster merely to stand still and not lose more ground, as far as the international competition was concerned, a problem equally challenging in the case of Spain.

An aristocrat-dominated traditional social structure was common in one way or another to nearly all of Europe, but Portuguese society was unusually emphatic in its absence of internal economic enterprise. Given the small market and very limited purchasing power, together with the absence of natural resources or prior domestic accumulation, the possibility of becoming a second Belgium was never a genuine possibility. At the same time, terrain and agricultural conditions meant that it could scarcely become a second Denmark.[7] A more feasible model might have been something like a second seafaring Norway, but for this constituent factors were also lacking.

A Comparative Contemporary History?

Spanish historians consistently ignore the history of Portugal as much as they possibly can, with the primary and laudable exception of Hipólito de la Torre Gómez, despite the fact that the history of Portugal much more closely parallels that of Spain than does the history of any other country. Though the preceding generalization is undoubtedly correct, the disparity in size of the two countries renders a less useful parallel or heuristic field than might be the case for countries of more nearly equivalent dimensions. On that level, of course, the appropriate comparison for Spain is with the contemporary history of Italy, and it is certainly true that of the larger European countries no two have as many similarities as do Spain and Italy. The main differences in comparability between Spain and Italy have to do first with politics and second with economics. Prior to 1860 Italy was never a united country, and for nearly four centuries before that time comparability could be achieved in political terms only at a high level of abstraction. Second, the spurt of industrialization that Italy experienced in the 1890s continued for some time, so that by the end of World War I Italy—which in the early nineteenth century overall had a per capita income scarcely superior to that of Spain—was for the time being at least twenty years ahead of Spain in economic development and modernization. Spain did not generally catch up until the last years of the twentieth century.

Despite the difference in size, comparability with Portugal is greater in every period and in almost every dimension. After the final separation between 1640 and 1668, the two countries continued to follow closely parallel courses. Their Old Regimes overall were remarkably similar, prone to the same problems and even to some extent the same reforms. The loss of colonies took place at approximately the same time, though neither lost all their colonies. The relatively peaceful Portuguese decolonization obeyed the generally more moderate and, if not less conflictive, then at least less violent tone of Portuguese affairs since the mid-seventeenth century. In both countries the effects of the French invasion and—to a much lesser extent—the loss of most of the overseas territories made possible the imposition of political liberalism, which was equally weak and prone to conflict in both countries. Because of Portugal's smaller size, relatively stronger leadership, and lack of regional institutional particularism, it ended the liberalism/traditionalism conflict endemic in early nineteenth-century liberalism in 1834, long before Spain. For somewhat the same reasons, a two-party liberal "turno" (*rotativismo* in Portuguese) was largely achieved two decades before this took place in Spain. The basic problems of weak cultural, social, and economic preparation were present in both countries, together with the restrictive, elitist, somewhat artificial character of the liberal regimes.

During the 1850s, when both countries seemed peacefully embarked on parallel paths, the Iberian federalist movement enjoyed greater support in both Spain and Portugal than would be the case later on.[8] At the time of the abortive Spanish dynastic change in 1868–69, some of the more liberal sectors of Spanish politics might have preferred to introduce a Portuguese prince, since during the preceding two decades the Portuguese monarchy was generally viewed as more sincerely liberal than that of Spain, but a Portuguese candidacy was discouraged in Lisbon.

During the central part of the nineteenth century both countries struggled with economic development with limited success, and largely sought to avoid foreign involvement, though with certain exceptions and differences. After 1807 it seemed as though the center of the Portuguese-speaking world had been displaced to Río de Janeiro, something that never occurred in Spain. For approximately a decade the de facto governor of Portugal was a British general, and the British connection remained fundamental to the country's foreign relations. In both countries there was a certain surge of nationalism and expansionism during the middle part of the century. In Portugal, though, where certain fundamental political issues seemed to have been resolved earlier, this took the form of a new concentration on Africa as the "third empire," a goal on which Portuguese policy finally began to make good with substantial occupation of Angola and Mozambique by the last years of the century. Both countries then in turn experienced the imperial frustrations common to the south European states during the 1890s. Once more Portugal was first, receiving an "Ultimatum," as the Portuguese always called it, from its British ally in 1891, which forever ended dreams of "the rose-colored map"—the goal of a broad empire of Portuguese-controlled territory across south Africa from Angola to Mozambique.

What can be called "liberal nationalism" enjoyed significant support in both Spain and Portugal during the nineteenth century, the difference being that it was developed more strongly in Portugal. The reaction to the Ultimatum—"Portugal's 1898"—was also different. In Spain, as similarly in Italy and even to some extent France, such an experience produced a kind of national soul-searching, but also stimulated a "regenerationism," which mostly functioned within the existing political system. The result in Portugal was to stimulate the republican movement, which—generally unlike republicanism in Spain—developed as a strongly nationalist and even imperialist enterprise.

Since the pace of cultural, social, and economic modernization was even slower in Portugal, at the beginning of the twentieth century the working-class movements were very weak, distinctly more so than even in the case of Spain. The pressure from the worker Left was so slight that in this regard Portugal was more like a Latin American than a European country, though it was also distinguished from nearly all Latin American countries by the existence of a relatively stronger middle class and stronger political nationalism. In some ways the best comparison in Europe at that time was Greece, which had somewhat similar characteristics.

The result was another Portuguese "first"—the easy overthrow of the monarchy in 1910 and the introduction of the first new republic in twentieth-century Europe. There were notable differences between Portugal in 1910 and Spain in 1931: Portugal was a much smaller, weaker, and more underdeveloped country, but in possession of a large African empire. Portuguese politics made only a pretense of being democratic and were still dominated by a restrictive nineteenth-century middle-class liberalism, though now radically anticlerical. The idea that the Portuguese republic introduced twentieth-century democracy—as did its later Spanish counterpart—is totally false. The Portuguese republicans in power restricted the electoral franchise to literate males, enabling only a large minority of males to vote, in some respects narrowing the suffrage over what existed in the last decades of the monarchy.

The goal of the dominant faction of Portuguese republicans was a kind of civic "progressivism" that would eliminate conservative influence, especially that of the Church, so that the denial of the vote to the Catholic peasantry was one of its most fundamental features. The falsely titled Democratic Party, the main republican group, developed the most formidable electoral machine seen in the Iberian Peninsula during the early twentieth century, and could never be defeated in normal elections under the restricted suffrage, which was never significantly reformed.

The Democrat electoral machine may have been stable, but the "First Republic" of 1910–26 enjoyed the dismal distinction of being the most unstable regime in Europe. Since this was also a time of considerable instability in some other countries, such an achievement may be considered another Portuguese "negative superlative." It had little to do with pressure from the worker movements, a common source of instability elsewhere. Rather, the notorious political instability of the Republic stemmed from middle-class and elite dissidence, faced with a typical nineteenth-century problem—the lack of access to government due to the domination of the Democrats. The history of the republic was thus filled not merely with severe dissidence but also with armed revolts and attempted revolts, so that even historians have difficulty keeping it all straight. Although there was much conflict and disorder, the total number of victims of violence was limited, which some would think of as typically Portuguese. The limited political mobilization in a nondemocratic system and the small size of both the country and the partici-pating political elites guaranteed that none of these conflicts metastasized into a genuine civil war, something that has happened only once in modern Portuguese history.

Dissatisfaction with the narrow system of republican domination inevitably led to a search for alternatives, and thus to another Portuguese "first"—a new kind of moderate authoritarian system in the form of the "República Nova" of Sidónio Pais in 1917–18, which also introduced the phenomenon of a new kind of mass charisma projected by its leader. Though it was soon overthrown, the República Nova was a harbinger of things to come after the military finally put an end to the parliamentary republic in 1926. The military coup in Portugal resembled that of Primo de Rivera in 1923, not the counterrevolutionary insurrection of 1936 in Spain, and, like the former, was initially supported by some sectors of liberal opin-ion. The leaders of the new military government, like their contemporary Primo de Rivera, were soon bewildered by the problem of how to operate the state coher-ently, or how to begin to build an alternative system. In a more underdeveloped, politically only partially mobilized, society, however, they never had to face as much pressure as did Primo de Rivera during his final months in office and by 1930 had found the man capable of building that alternative, the Coimbra eco-nomics professor Dr. António de Oliveira Salazar.

In later years Franco and Salazar would often be lumped together as twin Iber-ian dictators, yet the difference between them and between their two regimes was very great. Salazar was a professor and an intellectual, not a military man, and throughout the long history of his regime had to face intermittent dissidence from the military, something that scarcely bothered Franco. Salazar's "Estado Novo" (New State) evolved from the original military dictatorship, which itself had been the result of a virtually bloodless coup, so that the politically undermobilized Por-tugal of the era between the wars experienced no trauma even remotely similar to that of the Spanish Civil War.

In 1933 Salazar introduced another Portuguese "first"—the first new corpora-tive constitution in contemporary Europe. At that time there was much talk of corporatism because one statist authoritarian form of it was propagandized by Italian Fascism while nonstatist economic corporatism had become a semi-official doctrine of the Catholic Church. The Estado Novo in fact featured a dual system: a corporative economic chamber and economic system flanked by a restrictively elected parliament. It preserved aspects of the republican system and maintained the nominal separation of church and state, though in fact the Estado Novo strongly supported Catholicism in almost every way. It was less repressive than the Franco regime, partly because in Portugal there was less opposition to repress; Sa-lazar, in fact, never fully overcame internal dissidence and intermittently had to face political challenges and abortive military revolts. Whereas the initial Franco regime was at least semi-fascist, with a fascist state party, the Estado Novo did not have a full-fledged state party, its União Nacional more nearly resembling the Unión Patriótica of Primo de Rivera. Salazar drew a sharp distinction between the highly conservative and moderate authoritarianism of his regime and the radical style, doctrines, and practice of Fascism and National Socialism. Unlike that of Franco, his government's policy in World War II was genuinely neutral, tilting toward Great Britain. Indeed, the papacy had some tendency to think of the Estado Novo as the most appropriate "third way" between fascism and Communism, while for years it held the more radical and bloody Franco regime at arm's length.

Though there was one limited Spanish military intervention in Portugal in 1847 to uphold the existing order, relations between the two countries during the nineteenth century were generally peaceful and cooperative. There was greater tension during the first decades of the twentieth century, when the radicalism of the Portuguese Republic aroused the apprehension of monarchists in Madrid and even prompted Alfonso XIII, during the summer of 1913, to float inquiries with the major European states testing the possible reaction to a Spanish military intervention that would restore the monarchy.[9] Later, when both countries were governed by rightist military regimes in the late 1920s, relations became more harmonious.

After 1931 it was Spain that introduced a left-wing republic, the Azaña government demonstrating sharp hostility to Salazar and abetting armed efforts of the Portuguese opposition to overthrow him. Once more the accession to power of more conservative forces in Madrid restored better relations at the close of 1933, only to see those relations deteriorate again with the triumph of the Popular Front.

By the beginning of the Civil War, Salazar concluded that his regime could scarcely survive the triumph of a revolutionary Republic in Spain and aligned it completely with Franco, even though Portugal lacked the strength to intervene militarily. This record of loyal collaboration was not altogether reciprocated afterward, for the victory of the Nacionales, followed by those of Hitler in 1939–40, touched off a powerful current of imperial ambition in Madrid, which, particularly among Falangists, sought to extend Spanish hegemony over the entire peninsula. After Franco's meeting with Hitler at Hendaye, the Spanish dictator ordered his general staff to draw up a plan for a rapid invasion of Portugal, but this ambition, whatever its dimensions, was swiftly overtaken by events. Would Franco really have invaded Portugal? The answer probably is that he would have done so *only* under conditions of a broader Axis victory, which would have, at least indirectly, helped to underwrite the enterprise, and such a situation never developed.[10]

Once more a swing in a more moderate direction in Madrid restored fully harmonious relations. Once Franco had dismissed his Falangist brother-in-law, Ramón Serrano Suñer, the latter's successor as foreign minister, Gen. Francisco

Gómez Jordana, made neutrality and cooperation with Portugal cornerstones of his policy, leading to formation in 1942 of the "Bloque Ibérico" to maintain peninsular independence. For the remainder of their long lives, the two dictatorships enjoyed good relations, seeking to reinforce each other. The Salazar regime endeavored, though without success, to bring Spain into NATO.[11] Conversely, an aged Franco prudently resisted pressures for a Spanish military intervention at the time of the Portuguese revolution of 1974.

The Estado Novo had in the interim even managed to survive the demise of Salazar in 1968, becoming one of the few non-Communist authoritarian regimes to outlive its founder. It would also have survived the demise of Franco as well, at least for a few years, had not the colonial war against African liberation movements exacted a price that by the early 1970s could not be sustained—not because the physical means were lacking, but because the cadres of the military in metropolitan Portugal themselves began to lose heart and turn against the war. Consequently the Estado Novo, Europe's longest-lasting non-Communist authoritarian regime (an entire decade older than that of Franco) came to an end as all its European predecessors had—as a result of military action, in this case the military revolution of April 1974—the "revolution of the carnations." In typical Portuguese fashion, this was a bloodless coup, much like the one that had introduced dictatorship in 1926.

The Portuguese revolution remained faithful to Portuguese history in that the overthrow of a restrictive regime once more failed to introduce genuine democracy, just as in 1910. The revolutionary regime introduced a new kind of left-wing pretorianism, in which the military held the deciding voice. It also represented a new kind of political reaction, which some might call "postmodern," as rebellious military for the first time fully identified psychologically with leftist aggressors and antagonists. This resulted in another peculiar kind of Portuguese "first": the first time that the victors in a European military coup attempted to establish a leftist-collectivist regime, a form of Portuguese "socialism," as enshrined in a new constitution. This outcome seemed much more like the politics of a Latin American or Afro-Asian country than a European one.

Yet Portuguese society was indeed European, not Latin American or African, and the military regime itself was even less representative than the Estado Novo had been. Though much of society in poor and agrarian southern Portugal rallied to a Portuguese Communist Party (miraculously resurrected by the military and handed a significant share of power), lower-middle class and Catholic northern Portugal manifested complete opposition. The military were in fact divided, some of them supportive of more genuine democracy, so that elections were finally permitted after a year, and that outcome clearly did not favor the extreme Left. Moderate elements in the military came to the fore, and during 1975–76 the new regime moved toward democracy. It remained semi-pretorian, however, and the last vestiges of special state and political power for the military were not removed for a decade. The transition to democracy was thus entirely different in Spain and in Portugal, initially less democratic and much more conflictive in the case of the latter. This was the only instance in all contemporary history in which political affairs were more conflictive in Portugal than in Spain. And even then, there was less violence in Portugal, because of the virtual absence of terrorism.

Conversely, the political party system normalized more rapidly during the 1980s in Portugal, where the absence of a heritage of civil war or a harshly repressive dictatorship was a factor in making possible the early emergence of a new center-right party, which moved to a position of leadership in a more moderate Portugal more than a decade before its counterpart would do so in Spain. Democratic Portugal has experienced nothing remotely comparable to the political tensions or the center-periphery conflict of democratic Spain, and in a referendum of 1998 even rejected proposals for federalization, the government then opting simply for some degree of decentralization within a unified structure. Thus Portugal has as usual remained less conflictive than Spain, though also less dynamic economically.

7 Decline and Recovery

Spain is the only western European country for whom "decline" became an obsessive theme, first for foreign writers and then for Spanish historians and commentators. It is sometimes observed that the seventeenth century was a time of crisis and decline for the greater part of Europe—most of the south and east, and also much of the center. This is true enough, but the case of Spain has seemed more extensive and spectacular than those elsewhere, even though internal decline and destruction was probably in proportionate terms equally severe in the case of Germany, due to the Thirty Years' War. To take a different example, the tsardom of Muscovy suffered a profound political and military crisis early in the century, but after some years recovered to become stronger than ever.

More recently, Henry Kamen has challenged the idea that Spain declined, maintaining that Spain itself (as distinct from the Habsburg empire) had never risen very far in the first place. It is certainly correct that the literature on the "rise of Spain" is smaller than that treating the "decline of Spain." Thus before considering decline, it seems legitimate first to ask the question—to what extent was there a "rise of Spain"? Skeptics point out that creation of what foreigners called the "Spanish

Habsburg empire" was simply a product of contingency, a marriage alliance that yielded extensive dynastic crownlands.

This was obviously the case, yet a closer reading indicates that there was indeed a "rise" of peninsular Spain itself (see chap. 5). From the fifteenth to the late sixteenth century, population increased to about 8.5 million and the economy expanded. This made possible increased military and overseas activity, the taxes of Castile providing for much of the cost of an enormous military program, as a tiny proportion of that kingdom's population conquered the largest empire in world history. This was accompanied by the most extensive cultural flowering in any European country of that era. Thus there is no question that a major "rise of Spain" indeed took place, and the issue of decline is a fully relevant one, just as most historians have contended.

Antonio Cánovas del Castillo, who became one of the first modern historical specialists on the seventeenth century, at first concluded that the decline constituted a genuine decadence, though with further research, he retreated from that position. Later nationalist writers and historians insisted that it merely constituted a case of natural exhaustion following a protracted titanic enterprise. The two interpretations are not mutually exclusive. Virtually all historians agree that the principal sources of decline were the enormous strains of the endless dynastic wars, after 1640 further extended by the two major rebellions in the peninsula, whose great tax burden exhausted an already deteriorating economy, especially in Castile. The Spanish case was simply the most dramatic and extensive of what would later be called examples of "imperial over-reach" in European history.

Many societies have been ground down by long and costly wars, but by the middle of the seventeenth century Spain seemed to reveal a deeper malaise than temporary fatigue. While it is true that the country would have had to have run faster than it had in the sixteenth century merely in order not to lose ground during the seventeenth century—a period of greater competition and development among the "modernizing" northwest European countries—it was unable to maintain even the pace of 1600. By the second half of the century the society and culture, not just the economy or the military, showed signs of decadence in the stricter sense of the term. The society of 1670–80 was weaker in every respect than that of a century earlier.

Population loss was not relative but, for Castile, absolute, dropping by approximately a million people before beginning to recover in the last part of the seventeenth century. This was the worst period of epidemic disease in the country's history, except for the Black Death of the fourteenth century, to which were added the effects of war, heavy taxation, economic decline, and extensive malnutrition. The accompanying economic decline began in a few regions as early as the 1580s, but had become generalized by the mid-seventeenth century. Reduction in the Atlantic trade was equally steep, and the shipment of silver bullion diminished in much the same proportion. Similarly troublesome was the sharp rise in foreign competition, with which an enfeebled Spanish economy could not compete either at home or in America. Fundamental throughout was the weakness of state policy, unable to cut its losses in foreign wars and unable to protect or stimulate domestic production, its program being extractive and inflationary, which only made things worse. The government (and the aristocracy) soaked up available capital, which was not spent on new investment but almost exclusively on consumption, often for goods produced abroad. Moreover, the climate also deteriorated, with prolonged colder weather and greater, often destructive, precipitation.

Nearly all societies, of course, undergo longer or shorter periods of economic decline; what was remarkable about the Spanish economic decline was that it continued, with intermittent breaks, for decades, and was accompanied by social and cultural changes, which only accentuated it. Most notable here was the increasing withdrawal from new activity and creative enterprise, and the fixation on social status as an alternative to work and having to pay taxes. Under Felipe IV there was a considerable increase in the number of new aristocratic titles, and then a much greater expansion under Carlos II, during whose reign nearly three hundred new titles of nobility were created. Even worse was the fact that the mania for "endonamiento," or being made an aristocrat, consumed much of the middle classes. This was a Europewide phenomenon during the seventeenth century, but its effects were more extensive and destructive than elsewhere, a manifestation of the Spanish tendency in modern times to carry things to an extreme.

A counterpart was the declining interest in work or achievement. In an interesting study of the number of "achievement images" per thousand words of representative Spanish literature over a five-hundred-year period, Juan B. Cortés, S.J., found that in samples from the years 1200–1492 the mean was 10.74, declining for the years 1492–1610 to 6.07, and for 1610–1730 to only 2.67. It was not atypical that Felipe III would give his personal tailor two different patents of hidalguía (aristocratic status) but fail to pay him for four years of extended service. This eventually had deleterious effects on what had historically been perhaps the most important of Spanish professions—the military—as the elite increasingly shunned military service, while naval crewmen were even more looked down upon.[1]

Not merely did urban production decline, but the basis of the economy, agriculture, shrank both in terms of overall output and perhaps for a time in terms of per capita production as well, a result not merely of external pressures but also of internal structural changes, which handicapped and discouraged peasant production. After about 1580 there would be no real growth in agricultural production until the second quarter of the eighteenth century.[2]

The problem was not that the Spanish had never had any drive for achievement or completely lacked entrepreneurial skills. All these had existed to some extent in the fifteenth and sixteenth centuries, but such talents declined significantly. There developed a perverse situation in which the price of urban labor was high, due to inflation and taxation, yet there was also considerable unemployment. Even a seeming positive, such as the strong Spanish emphasis on charity, may have had the effect of discouraging work. Foreign merchants, artisans, and entrepreneurs had played a role in Spanish society since the eleventh century, if not before, but their presence was much greater by the second half of the seventeenth century, when they partly compensated for the atrophy of Spanish enterprise, the total number of foreigners reaching perhaps 150,000, some of them in middle-class roles, amounting to more than 2 percent of the entire population.

What José Antonio Maravall and others call "baroque society" was a society turning in on itself. Through the reign of Felipe IV surprising amounts of money were spent on ostentation and conspicuous consumption, but from the 1660s even esthetic culture began to atrophy. By that point secular and religious culture had become largely defensive, and had lost nearly all its creativity. The case of higher education was symptomatic. In 1590 there were some twenty-seven thousand students in Spanish universities and other institutes of higher education, for a brief time proportionately the largest student body in advanced studies in Europe. However, the dynamics of higher education belied the notion that this was a precondition for societal progress, since the Spanish system was increasingly oriented toward the attainment and maintenance of status in the bureaucracy and clergy. Then, with accelerating economic decline, the number of students in higher education also dropped greatly, while curricula stagnated.

Militant Tridentine Catholicism—in which to a considerable extent Spain had shown the way—was fully dominant, but religion also had lost much of its creative spark by the second half of the seventeenth century. The ranks of the clergy swelled, less due to spiritual zeal than to a kind of clerical bureaucratization. Older estimates that the clergy amounted to 3–4 percent of the total population were nonetheless exaggerated; the increase may have been more like a growth from 1.3 to 2.5 percent of the total society, but the most significant factor was that the expansion of the clergy accompanied a certain decline in spiritual creativity. Though the Church in Spain had helped to lead the way in the new reforms of the sixteenth century, by the seventeenth century travelers wrote that they found Spanish Catholicism "different" and in some ways more archaic. What they particularly noted was the apparent power of the monastic orders, a perceived tendency to mix the profane and the religious, as well as the emphasis on a kind of religious theatricality and a stress on the extremes.

The cultural accomplishment of the Siglo de Oro from the mid-sixteenth to the mid-seventeenth century was indeed monumental, concentrated in literature, painting, and religious thought. Of science there was much less, though some new activity was carried on in science and even in mathematics. The flowering of the arts was due above all to the patronage of the Church and of a wealthy aristocracy. This became a kind of transition culture, opening new dimensions for tradition, but without being able to achieve a total breakthrough into more modern forms. On one level *Don Quijote* can be read as an elegy to an age that was passing much more than as a window to a new era. Spanish baroque culture raised the culture of traditional European civilization to the highest level that that culture had ever experienced, but for the most part it was not part of the new, more modern culture that began to develop in seventeenth-century Europe, and by the 1670s its creative spark had largely expired.

The distinction can perhaps be seen most clearly in the difference between the dramatic literature of the Spanish theater and that of Elizabethan-Jacobean England. For several generations Spanish drama, headed by Lope de Vega and Calderón, was the most diverse and creative in continental Europe, yet it lacked the full range and depth of its English counterparts.[3] Elizabethan theater was much more daring and innovative in treating morality, personality, and the range of human behavior, and a more direct precursor of modernity, with all its virtues and vices.

Here the vexed issue of Reform and Counter-Reform in religion remains important. The Protestant revolt destroyed much of traditional religious culture in northern Europe, and intensified internal and external conflict. It also stimulated new energies of individual enterprise, political reform, and critical and scientific thinking that opened the way, for better or worse, to modern culture, politics, and capitalist prosperity. The point is not that much of this could not develop under Catholicism, for indeed the roots of all of it developed in traditional Catholic culture, and, later, Catholic Belgium would modernize and industrialize almost as rapidly as England. In the face of the Reformation, however, Catholic society and culture became increasingly reactive and defensive, and were slower to adapt and adjust, so that from the seventeenth century it was the Protestant countries who would lead the way.[4]

It must be recognized that the standard view of the Spanish decline—shared in varying degrees by the classic Black Legend and by many modern Spanish historians and Hispanists—is a kind of caricature that posits an ideal type and is suggestive only of fundamental tendencies. Spanish moralists themselves began to present what seemed to them negative features of the "Spanish type" even before the close of the sixteenth century. The best recent summary of this approach has been presented in Bartolomé Bennassar, *L'homme espagnol: Attitudes et mentalités du XVIe au XIXme siècle* (1975), a book about "national character."[5] It revolved around such issues as the mania for conspicuous consumption (particularly on clothing and spectacle, not on food, drink, and housing), the attitudes toward work, social status, and lineage, the exaggerated stress on honor to the exclusion of morality, and less and less concern for education and intellectual activity. Such issues would be commented on ad infinitum during the three centuries that followed. These were serious problems and not merely inventions of the enemies of Spain, but they do not constitute a fully accurate picture of Spanish society in the seventeenth century.

Even at the trough of the decline, as Ruth MacKay has recently reminded us, most Spaniards continued to work normally at their professions.[6] She and others have pointed out that it is a mistake to read the novel *Lazarillo de Tormes* as if it were an empirical sociological study. Amid the scramble for status and conspicuous consumption, ordinary artisans managed to preserve a different sense of honor of their own, even as it attached to humble work, and sometimes in written statements stressed the importance of their contribution to "la república," not at all in the sense of a new political system but in the original meaning of *res publica*—the common weal. Moreover, that Spanish society did not merely constitute some sort of "pathological" Counter-Reformation society compared with northwest Europe is further indicated by the recent research on crime by Tomás Mantecón, which shows that, despite the importance of crime and banditry in the images of Spain in decline, the two largest cities, Madrid and Seville, seem to have produced no more or even slightly less violence than their northwest European counterparts, while indices of violence further declined in the late seventeenth and eighteenth centuries in a manner congruent with the data from northwestern Europe.[7]

Some aspects of society and culture may be described in conventional terms as "decadent" by the later seventeenth century, but if one employs such terminology it is important to stress that Spanish society never experienced the full form of decadence in which it lost faith in or subverted its own values. The basic culture, religion, and system of values persisted throughout the entire seventeenth-century decline and remained fully intact at the time of the transition to the new dynasty. The main "arbitrista" (reformist) literature covered the half-century 1590–1640, when it was assumed that the ills analyzed could be corrected. From about 1640 the critical literature began to die away, perhaps because by that time the decline was pronounced and obvious, and the main question now seemed to be self-affirmation and self-confidence. During the trough of the decline, Spanish writing about Spain remained remarkably positive. Comparisons with the decline of Rome were almost universally rejected, though on the grounds that the Spanish monarchy was more legitimate and less tyrannical than Rome, and could not be made subject to comparison, for there had been none other so thoroughly dedicated to and identified with Catholicism, so that it would never be merely abandoned by God.[8] Providentialism is of course not the best basis for political and economic analysis.

Though economic conditions deteriorated greatly, at no time was there any question of a social or psychological implosion. Not even the humblest sector of society, whether those labeled as "pobres de solemnidad" or mere beggars, was cowed and cringing, or lost a sense of self-worth. Throughout the century foreign visitors continued to complain that ordinary Spaniards violated the class-based sumptuary laws more than in any other country, and continued to dress as they pleased, while the same visitors also denounced what they called the insolence and rudeness of the lower classes. Even beggars, when receiving alms, might insist that the almsgiver remove his hat, and also address them as "señor." To visitors, of course, this represented a Spanish grotesquerie, further examples of the dysfunctional. In some sense that might be the case, but it was not indicative of any decline in social norms.

Finally, Spain must be compared with Europe as a whole, not just with England and Holland. The historian finds that during the seventeenth century, eastern Europe not merely suffered a decline somewhat equivalent to that of Spain but underwent much worse social regression with the expansion of serfdom. There was not remotely any equivalent to that in Spain. Military hegemony disappeared forever, but Spanish society itself did not regress so much as did that of much of eastern Europe. If it began to lose ground decisively to the dynamic, modernizing northwest, it should be seen as part of a category of relatively stagnant southern Europe during that era, a category more of declining intermediacy than of the worst regression.

The recovery in fact began in the 1680s, in the midst of the reign of Carlos II "el Hechizado" (Charles II the Bewitched) and in Catalonia even earlier, during the 1660s. Population decline began to level off, though full demographic recovery did not occur until the 1720s and 1730s. The reformers who referred to themselves as "renovatores" were active from the beginning of the reign of Carlos II.[9] The Real y General Junta de Comercio was created in 1679 to stimulate new enterprise and enjoyed at least a limited success. A small number of noblemen had never ceased to engage in a variety of practical enterprises, and a decree of 1682 specifically authorized their involvement with textile factories so long as they did not work with their hands.

Eighteenth-Century Reformism

The Bourbon dynasty of the eighteenth century then undertook the project of reform that its predecessor had been unable to carry out. There is no question concerning the reformist bent of the "Siglo de las Luces" (Century of the Enlightened), but it probably amounted to a difference in degree rather than a difference in principle. Reevaluation of the eighteenth century began with Richard Herr's *The Eighteenth-Century Revolution in Spain* (1958), but what actually took place was more a positive evolution than a revolution.

With the rise of peripheral nationalism in democratic Spain, much attention has been given to the unification and centralization of law and institutions, as the separate constitutional structures of the Corona de Aragon (with the exception of certain law codes) were eliminated by the new dynasty.[10] This, however, was obviously not the beginning of a broader government of Spain, although it marked a major step forward toward unification. There has been a tendency, particularly on the part of Catalan historians, to exaggerate the degree of change. At the beginning of his reign, Felipe V had ratified all the particularist institutions and fueros of the northeastern regions. The elimination of Aragonese institutions was a result of the subsequent struggle by dominant sectors of the latter against the new dynasty. Only in Valencia were all the regional structures abrogated completely, while Mallorca retained most of its institutions. Catalonia and Aragon lost their abusive criminal law but kept a portion of their legal systems. Save for the loss of criminal jurisdiction, seigneurial domain remained unaltered. Most notably, the new dynasty failed to unify the Spanish systems of taxation and military recruitment, which remained quite compartmentalized. Though tax quotas were at first raised for the former Aragonese principalities, they subsequently remained flat, and by the end of the century these regions were once more paying extremely low taxes, as did the Basques and Navarrese throughout history. Similarly, equal terms of military recruitment were never instituted, so that the Spanish army of the period was raised almost exclusively in Castile.

Bourbon reformism was always a halfway house. The various Spanish Academies were created and by 1785 there would be a common Spanish flag for the first time, while the king of Prussia gave as a gift the music for what became the "Marcha Real Granadera," later looked on as Spain's first national anthem. The social and economic effects of the legal, commercial, and fiscal reforms of the new dynasty were beneficial, for they ended certain residues of feudalism and more often than not improved the situation of the peasantry. Trade was much freer across the country, and Spanish America was later opened directly to the entire Spanish economy for the first time. Catalonia, which lost most of its separate institutions, was also the region to benefit most in economic terms.

The eighteenth century was more a time of continuity than of change, though there was more than a little change. Some transformation took place, but it was not drastic. The introduction of a new dynasty, the loss of the European dynastic empire, and the change in Spain's international relations opened the country a good deal more than before, and the new leadership introduced pronounced government reforms as well as new ideas. Spanish history had always lived under the burden of major projects: Reconquest and expansion, defense and propagation of the faith, the integrity of the dynastic empire and of Europe. The big difference in the eighteenth century, as J. Marías says, was that Spain then became "a project of herself," the beginning of what much later would be termed "España como problema."[11] For the first time, the maladies of Spain—something that seventeenth-century government had never been willing fully to recognize—became a central issue, sometimes the key issue, though this approach also implied that there was something wrong about the way Spanish culture, society, and institutions had developed.

Well before the close of the seventeenth century, the primary foreign stereotype of the Black Legend—the Spaniard as violent and sadistic fiend, a creature of moral monstrosity—had given way to Stereotype 2, the Spaniard as proud, pompous, vainglorious, and invincibly indolent, incapable of working or studying. The second stereotype continued its triumphant advance through the eighteenth century, reaching its climax in the famous denunciation of Spain's total lack of modern accomplishment by Nicolas Masson de Morvillers in the *Encyclopédie méthodique* of 1782.

That raised the question of Spain's participation in the Enlightenment, answered in the affirmative by Herr and by Jean Sarrailh.[12] The main foreign influences were from France and Italy (Carlos III having been king of Naples for twenty-five years before coming to the Spanish throne). Spanish writers added little to the philosophy of the Enlightenment, the main Spanish thinkers dedicating themselves in pragmatic terms more to application than to doctrine. One advantage of this approach was that the Enlightenment in Spain was much less prone to radicalism and exaggeration than, for example, in France. Though, as elsewhere, it may have sometimes gone to excess in stereotyping and rejecting some aspects of traditional society, in general in Spain it made more sense and was more practical. Spain's leading philosopher of reform, the long-lived Fray Benito Jerónimo Feijóo, stood as one of the most reasonable and constructive figures of Catholic Enlightenment in Europe.[13] Major aspects of the Enlightenment in Spain seemed almost closer to the "empirical" Enlightenment in England, Scotland, and the United States than to the abstract/radical "ideological" Enlightenment in France, though from the 1790s on small sectors of the intelligentsia began to veer sharply toward the latter, leading to manifold pathologies in nineteenth and twentieth-century Spain.[14]

The "short eighteenth century" was, at least in relative terms, Spain's most peaceful century, if it is dated from the end of the Succession War in 1714 to the beginning of the wars of the French Revolution in 1793, which effectively put an end to its relative progress and prosperity. Peace did not arrive immediately, for the first years after 1714 were devoted to further military enterprises to regain dynastic possessions in Italy, but after that military action became infrequent, at least until the reign of Carlos III. The navy was rebuilt, becoming by the latter part of the century the third largest in the world. The army was reorganized on the French model, but by comparison never developed much strength, for much of the conflict during this era was maritime. During the greater part of the century, Spain's most consequential military action was the assistance provided to the North American colonists in the first modern "national liberation war." This support was more extensive both militarily and financially than has been appreciated, and came at a militarily and psychologically decisive moment when Great Britain could not afford to face further enemies, particularly one with a large fleet.[15] The ministers of Carlos III were sufficiently astute to realize that in helping the dynamic North American colonies gain independence, they ran a major risk of creating a serious competitor for the Spanish world in the Western Hemisphere, but they could not resist the temptation to weaken a Britain that only a few years earlier had become hegemonic.[16]

With the expansion into California and a few other border areas, the American empire reached its greatest extension, and by that time was being treated as a "Spanish empire" for the first time, all parts of the country enjoying equal commercial rights and a concerted effort being made, also for the first time, to exploit the broader range of the American economy for Spanish interests. Taxes were rationalized and made more efficient at home, but also extended more broadly into America, and certain aspects of administration more centralized, provoking in turn a natural reaction that stimulated growth of a kind of political consciousness in creole society.

Though the Spanish empire was not at all the kind of economic powerhouse that the British empire was becoming, the imperial reforms of the ministers of Carlos III seemed, in some respects, more effective than those of his contemporary George III. The Spanish imperial domains had never been considered "colonies" in the British sense, but neither had the American "kingdoms" ever been permitted the full constitutional systems of the peninsular principalities, and were thus easier to deal with than the thirteen British colonies, each of which possessed autonomous parliaments. Moreover, an absolute monarchy in Madrid theoretically ruling over multiple "kingdoms" possessed greater flexibility for maneuver than did a parliamentary government in London, which insisted on its own complete and undivided sovereignty but, as a result, enjoyed increasingly less room for compromise.

Since 1603 Great Britain had had a "composite monarchy" that bore comparison with the "monarquía compuesta" of Habsburg Spain (discounting the continental Habsburg dynastic domains). After the Act of Union with Scotland in 1707, the "progressive" British system moved to extend the sovereignty of a single parliament over all these territories. By contrast, in Madrid parliament had been largely reduced to a "Diputación" of the traditional Cortes, and the crown itself was politically and administratively absolute. This, however, gave it power to attempt sweeping reform and redefinition, something that by 1775 was no longer possible in British North America.

For the first time in Spanish history, by the later eighteenth century "patria" and "nación" began to be used in ways approaching their modern sense, and the Caroline imperial reforms sought to create what one minister termed "un solo cuerpo de nación," a single Spanish-speaking nation spanning the Atlantic. The largest empire in the world was to be replaced by the largest nation in the world, as for the first time a more comprehensive Spanish administrative system was directly introduced into the Americas. A basic problem that the crown could not resolve, however, was that it proposed a two-tier system, largely administered by Spaniards. Creoles received new rights and opportunities, but not fully equivalent ones. Pan-Hispanic representation was to be achieved merely through the appointment by the senior Spanish administrators of a handful of American representatives to the Diputación de las Cortes in Madrid—the standing committee, which was nearly all that was left of the traditional Cortes under eighteenth-century absolutism. This idea was carried over by Spain's first constitutional liberals in 1810–12 and 1820–23, maintaining the notion of an immense Spanish-speaking nation, but at no time would the liberals be willing to grant equal, as distinct from highly limited, representation, ultimately dooming the project. The Spanish American revolts of 1780–82 in Peru and Nueva Granada (Colombia) were suppressed, but the problem of American participation and representation would slowly, but steadily, grow more acute.

For Spanish society it was the mellow autumn of the traditional culture, a time of reform and relative enlightenment without drastic transformation. Traditional society remained largely intact, having lost some of the more pathological characteristics of the seventeenth century. This golden autumn was not a very creative time in high culture and the arts, at least until Goya appeared at the very end, but it was a period of a curious fusing of high culture with some of that of the lower classes. Popular culture reacted against foreign models, producing the first expressions of modern "casticismo" (Spanishness) in the new "majeza" (lower-class elegance) of the urban lower classes. In time "art" became more "popular," an indication of a partial change and transformation, as the aristocracy sometimes aped popular styles, a fashion unthinkable in the preceding century. The theater in Madrid and other cities was the principal medium that brought these strands together, at least by the late eighteenth century, and to some extent reflected the rejection of sophisticated "afrancesamiento" (Frenchification) by lower-class majeza.[17] It was the last century of traditional Spanish culture, a time in which Spanish society was generally calm and to a considerable degree at peace with itself.

This was obviously not a drastically new, transformed, and "modern" society. There were many reform projects, and considerable growth and expansion, particularly during the reign of Carlos III, but it still remained a traditional society.[18] Many things improved, commerce expanded greatly, industry increased in Catalonia and several smaller zones, and cities on the periphery became the major new centers of growth, but this was expansion with only limited transformation. As John Lynch said of Spanish agriculture during the eighteenth century, "agriculture grew but did not develop."[19] Food production increased as agriculture expanded into marginal land, becoming more extensive rather than more intensive. Population growth required regular food imports, living standards for the ordinary population in Madrid began to decline once more, and infant mortality apparently increased slightly during the second half of the century, indicating that no decisive new breakthrough had been made. Similarly, "enlightened despotism" did not by any means signify the beginning of a new kind of Anglo-American-style political system. Nearly all the truly decisive reforms were resolutely rejected.[20] By the 1780s, however, small educated minorities were calling for much more advanced and decisive changes.[21]

Popular cultural change has been much less studied than the writings of the elite. By the latter part of the eighteenth century, the rejection of traditional Castilian elite culture was accompanied by the growing acceptance of critical Enlightenment norms on the one hand, accompanied on a different level by the growing plebeanization of culture and attitudes, which among the common people was becoming xenophobic, emphatic, and shrill. Jesús Torrecilla has pointed out that traditional culture was largely Castilian and featured seriousness, sobriety, austerity, dark colors, a rather cold realism, and objectivity, emphasizing certain standards of work well done, characterized by slowness, reflection, a certain astuteness, and calculation. Hallmarks were gravity, decorum and dignity. This was increasingly replaced by a modern "Andalusian" popular culture that emphasized rhetoric, bright colors, frivolity, "la bullanga jaranera" (merry uproar), cheerful irresponsibility, and new marginal forms of behavior and indulgence, a general style trend, some aspects of which would continue for about one hundred fifty years and beyond, into the middle of the twentieth century. This would become the culture in evidence of "romantic Spain," forming the third major stereotype of Spanish culture and character. The keynote was no longer aristocracy but lower-class majeza. In its own way this would quickly assume more modern form, as the traditional "corrida de toros" (bullfighting) crystallized in its classic style, dressing its bullfighters in what would be an unvarying eighteenth-century costume (even in the twenty-first century), the first modern "plazas de toros" being constructed in Andalucía during the 1770s and quickly moving northward. Interestingly, they can be considered the first modern mass public sports facilities in any country, inaugurating for an archaic spectacle a trend that would slowly but inexorably accelerate around the world for more modern sports during the next two centuries. Other aspects of "popular style" also crystallized, the various regional traditional costumes and popular dances assuming their full form during the second half of the eighteenth century. Similarly, at the very end of the century the new Andalusian musical style known as flamenco would begin to emerge, finally assuming its modern form in the third quarter of the nineteenth century. In the shadow of the rationalist Enlightenment, the ingredients of romantic Spain were already being assembled. Later, much of this would be the delight of tourist and Spaniard alike, though far from the tone and quality of the elitist culture of the Golden Age.

Impact of the French Revolution

In Spain as in France, the Old Regime was overthrown by the great revolution of the 1790s, in France directly and in Spain by the French military invasion that subjugated much of the country and introduced a Napoleonic regime of radical reform, based on some of the more moderate aspects of the revolution. Whereas the English revolution of republicanism and Puritanism of the 1640s had few international repercussions, the French Revolution was a world-historical event, because France at that time was the leading continental European power and because French radical ideas led what to some extent had become an international movement.

The French Revolution had a profound effect abroad, not so much in the creation of radical regimes elsewhere (all of which were overthrown) as in stimulating nationalism and also the long-term diffusion of liberal, as distinct from radical, ideas. Nowhere, however, did the revolutionary and Napoleonic era have so great an impact as in the Iberian Peninsula. For Spain it produced the greatest upheaval of modern times prior to the Civil War of 1936–39.

The reign of Carlos IV exhibited political confusion and weak leadership, slackening the pace of the reformism notable under Carlos III, though, after an initially sharply conservative reaction to the revolution, some reformism was resumed. Spanish government steadily lost initiative, however, until the royal family allowed itself to be carried away into French captivity—the Portuguese royal family, by comparison, having the perspicacity to flee to Brazil, a far preferable option.

The result of the French takeover was the Spanish War of Independence, universally recognized as by far the broadest and most intense popular and national reaction to Napoleonic domination found anywhere in Europe. It gave rise to a great mythology both inside and outside Spain. Within the country it produced the myth of the great national resistance of patriotic self-sacrifice, the "guerrillero" as representative of the traditional and patriotic people. In western Europe it helped to establish Stereotype 3 about the Spanish—the vision of "romantic Spain," which partially reversed the preceding stereotypes. This would achieve full canonic formulation by the second quarter of the nineteenth century, holding that when Spaniards took to violence they were not sadistic monsters but unusually brave and death-defying heroes willing to sacrifice themselves to preserve their independence and way of life. Rather than being mindless religious fanatics, Spaniards preserved a spiritual approach to life and culture that defied the gross materialism of the modern world. Rather than being lazy good-for-nothings, the Spanish represented human and social values that they refused to sacrifice on the altar of industrialization and profit. Rather than being closed to science and enlightenment, the Spanish sustained a common popular culture that prized song and dance, expressing an artistic and esthetic vitality lost to bourgeois society beyond the Pyrenees. Whereas Stereotype 1 was a product of the sixteenth and early seventeenth centuries, and Stereotype 2 a product of the late seventeenth century and the Enlightenment, Stereotype 3 would dominate much of the thinking about Spain in other western countries during the nineteenth and twentieth centuries—at least until the 1970s—though often also mixed with aspects of Stereotypes 1 and 2.

Within Spain itself the myth of the idealistic and self-sacrificing resistance of the Spanish people has generally prevailed on both the Left and the Right, although most recently aspects of it have been called into question by historians such as José Álvarez Junco.[22] Scholars have usually recognized that part of the elite supported the reformism of the monarchy of Joseph Bonaparte, and that the resistance was fundamentally divided between majoritarian traditionalists and minoritarian middle- and upper-class liberals, the latter better organized and politically more active, or at least geographically better situated. In general, however, the clergy were more important than political liberals in mobilizing large sectors of the population, who fought for religion and their traditional way of life more than for any modern concept of "Spain." Most had no perception of the modern idea of nation, but the liberals certainly did. Localism and regionalism were important in the resistance, as they have been throughout the history of the country. In some areas certain aspects of the guerrilla shaded off into banditry.[23] The War of Independence was indeed a titanic struggle but also politically and ideologically more complicated than it has often been presented.[24] It produced the two new political and military terms that Spain provided the modern world: guerrilla and liberal.

It marked the beginning of the "two Spains" of modern times: one Catholic and traditionalist, the other liberal and anticlerical (though at first also largely

Catholic, in a more moderate sense), which within another century would evolve into a division between Catholic conservatives and anti-Catholic social and political radicals. It also meant the end of most of the Spanish American empire. Whereas the North American colonists won their independence in the face of the dominant new imperial power of that generation, the Spanish Americans faced the opposite—a complete breakdown of Spanish government in the face of foreign invasion and occupation. At that time the various regions of Spanish America would never have initiated a process of self-government, soon to affirm independence, had it not been for the vacuum of power in Spain. The independence of the Latin American countries would eventually have taken place, but not so soon or in the same way.

The War of Independence was a remarkable disaster. For the past century France had been considered a friend and sometimes an ally, only to subject Spain to a brutal assault. Though the Spanish resisted bravely and ultimately successfully, the cost was enormous. The country had been spared desperate military conflict for nearly a hundred years, and was hardly prepared—no country would have been prepared—for the massive atrocities, suffering, death, and destruction that ensued. A significant aspect often passed over is the enormous amount of looting of valuables and art treasures by the French, the better part of which was never returned. Of the three great "lootings of Spain"—that by the Arabs, the French, and the revolutionaries of 1936, this was arguably the worst. The war cost Spain an entire generation of cultural and economic development, so that in the 1820s it had scarcely regained the level of 1800. In proportionate terms, Spain would thus begin the nineteenth century in worse comparative condition than it had the eighteenth century, so that whatever progress had been made in the "Siglo de las Luces" was seemingly placed in doubt. The war would inaugurate a new "long century" (1814–1923) marked by frequent and extensive conflict, both political and military, internal and external, that would continue even beyond, until the middle of the twentieth century. It initiated an attempt at political modernization and liberalization under some of the worst conditions, which helped to guarantee that it would for long not be very successful.

8 The Problem of Spanish Liberalism

Historic Spanish liberalism has not enjoyed a good press, and among Left and Right alike has often been judged a failure. Yet it dominated Spanish affairs and governed for approximately a century, so that, if a failure, it was certainly a long surviving failure, implying that the standard caricature, like so many of the caricatures and stereotypes in Spanish history, may be something of an exaggeration.

It would be excessive to say that liberalism truly governed Spain between 1810 and 1814, given the chaos of those years, while the second liberal regime of 1820–23 was overthrown by foreign invasion, albeit in this case a foreign invasion that was accepted by much of Spanish opinion. From the death of Fernando VII in 1833 until 1923 some form of liberalism governed the country, usually fairly conservative, though occasionally quite radical. By 1923 Spain had lived under liberal parliamentary government for more years than had any other large continental European country, including France—no mean achievement for a "historical failure."

The liberal breakthrough resulted from the complete breakdown of government as a result of the French invasion, but this did not mean that the seizure of leadership by the liberals was the result of a conspiracy by a tiny minority, as some interpretations have had it. During the second half of the eighteenth century the slow but steady evolution of Spain's society, culture, and economy had encouraged the emergence of a small middle class and had also transformed the attitudes of part of the nobility. Something, at least, of the basis for a more modern economy had been laid, even if the general structure remained traditional. The new more liberal and capitalist interests were not hegemonic, but they were expanding, even if politically inarticulated. Most potential liberals would probably have been willing to continue to accept government by an evolutionary reformist monarchy, had such a regime continued to exist. In 1809–10, by contrast, they responded to a new vacuum of power, though they themselves continued to represent no more than a limited minority of Spanish society.

The Constitution of 1812 was, in fact, the great European liberal constitution of the early nineteenth century, more judicious and reasonable than anything found in revolutionary France, and stood as the most influential charter of liberalism to be found in Europe during the next two decades. This new "Spanish national model" inspired liberals in Italy, Germany, Russia, Latin America, and elsewhere, representing an attempt to reconcile the differing ideas of the French Enlightenment, the Anglo-Scottish and Spanish Enlightenments, and the Scholastic tradition with its doctrines of natural law.[1] It was a unique achievement for its time, offering a broad, semidemocratic but nonetheless "organic" suffrage, taking care not to offend most aspects of traditional culture. This was a special achievement of the original Spanish moderate liberal elite, before passions had become inflamed by partisan conflict and the influence of more radical doctrines.

Though early Spanish liberalism originally had considerable influence in Spanish America, it was later virtually forgotten by American historiography, which preferred a manichean portrait of "liberal Latin America" versus "absolutist Spain."[2] The Cortes of Cádiz included a tiny minority of representatives from Spanish America, and its constitution provided for direct American representation in the future Spanish parliament, even though on a very limited basis.[3] Neither the Cádiz liberals nor most of the "exaltados" (radicals) of the second liberal regime were willing to grant greater proportionality for a transatlantic Hispanic nation, nor the complete equality and freedom of commerce demanded by Spanish Americans, so that any prospect of maintaining a transatlantic state proved completely illusory.[4]

The restoration of absolute monarchy by Fernando VII was in some respects a caricature of the kind of absolutism practiced by Carlos III. Most of the "enlightened" aspects of absolutism disappeared, to be replaced by extremes of authoritarianism and repression. The Constitution of 1812 offered a reasonable basis on which to initiate a moderate and Catholic form of liberalism, but this was never attempted, first being overthrown by Fernando and then, in its second incarnation, bypassed by the exaltados, the second generation of radical liberals, who inaugurated what might be subsequently termed the "exaltado tradition" in Spanish affairs, according to which periodically the axis of politics was shifted so far to the Left as to tip over into armed conflict. By 1823 both of the polarities of modern Spanish politics had been established, and would remain in place for the next century and a half, until consensus was finally achieved.

Undoubtedly the introduction of direct liberalism in Spain was somewhat premature, and would never have had the strength or opportunity to impose itself at that time had it not been for the destruction of regular government by the French invasion. In Spain there existed a liberal intelligentsia, as well as certain middle- and upper-class social and economic interests that could be mobilized on behalf of liberalism, but an adequate civil society on which to build a liberal system did not exist. The result was the emergence of the "Spanish contradiction" for much of the period between 1810 and 1939—the persistent efforts of small liberal or radical elites to introduce "advanced" systems, which lacked an adequate social, cultural, or economic base. The Spanish contradiction finally ended in the later years of the Franco regime, when it was replaced for a time by the "Franco contradiction"—a political system more retrograde and backward than the society and culture over which it presided.

Traditionalism was strong in all parts of Europe during the early nineteenth century. Nowhere did traditionalism enjoy such militant popular support as in Spain, however, not because traditionalism was absolutely that much stronger than elsewhere, but rather because only in Spain had liberalism been forced on a society and culture that was still so traditionalist. In most other European states more traditional monarchies prevailed, in most cases—at least in the middle of the century—avoiding liberalism and popular mobilization almost altogether.

Carlism has been called the largest, virtually the only, political mass movement of nineteenth-century Spain, which is probably correct. It has often been seen as a sort of Spanish peculiarity, another Spanish exceptionalism, but, as in the case of other perceived Spanish exceptionalisms, this has led to exaggeration. Traditionalism existed in nearly all continental countries. In France during the 1790s, massive military action and wholesale violence, bordering on genocide, was required to crush French traditionalism. The difference in Spain was that traditionalism endured longer, to a minor degree persisting at least until the mid-twentieth century.

The dimensions of the traditionalist reaction after 1833 were due above all to the fact that in Spain liberalism was introduced at an earlier phase of the country's overall modernization than was the case elsewhere, making the Spanish contradiction particularly acute during the early nineteenth century. The strength of Carlism seems to have been correlated especially with two factors: first the force of religious and ultraroyalist sentiment, and second the vigor of traditional institutions. Thus Carlism was weakest in the south, enjoyed intermediate strength in the north-central part of the country, and was strongest in the Basque provinces, Navarre, Aragon, and Catalonia.[5]

In such conditions, with a weak liberal monarchy, a relatively fragile elite liberalism, and a generally traditionalist society, civil war was not surprising. The liberals won not because they would have been able to carry a national plebiscite, which is doubtful, but because of their control of the state and the military, and because of foreign support. Whereas in 1823 foreign intervention had favored the Right (and would do so again in 1936–39), foreign assistance during the First Carlist War favored the liberals. Most of the upper classes, who might have been thought to support traditionalism, in fact backed the liberals, partly because Carlism seemed to a large extent a menacing popular movement of poor peasants, the Carlist bands often showing "hatred of the rich."

The conflict between liberalism and traditionalism, between revolution and counterrevolution, was not a morbid peculiarity of the Spanish but to a greater or lesser degree was characteristic of the politics of most of western continental Europe during the six decades that followed the Napoleonic wars, roughly through the 1870s.[6] That there was much less civil war in France, Italy, Austria, or Germany than in Spain during that period was due primarily to the strength of the state in those countries. The German, Austrian, and Italian states simply held liberalism at bay almost altogether, until limited and nondemocratic forms of liberalism were finally adopted by the 1870s, somewhat the same as in Spain. France experienced more advanced liberalism, only to succumb to a modern form of new authoritarian state from 1851 to 1870, and thus counted fewer years under parliamentary government than Spain, with a convulsive history that had passed through three more revolutionary experiences by 1871. Spanish liberalism was in power proportionately longer than the parliamentary forces in any of these countries, but by comparison could only build a weaker state prone to convulsion. The frequency of convulsion was due not merely to that weakness but also to the narrowness and exclusiveness of the dominant liberal elites, the limited basis of civil society, and the loss of legitimacy in the system. The first sixty years of the new Spanish American republics were equally convulsive, until their political systems also began to stabilize somewhat by the 1880s.

Much better for Spain during the first half of the nineteenth century would probably have been a more advanced form of the reformist monarchy of Carlos III. It would have spared much conflict, bloodshed, and destruction, though such an alternative presents a quasi-utopian counterfactual that at no time existed as a genuine possibility. As it was, the reintroduction of liberalism in 1833–34, like its original eruption in 1810, was due to a unique contingency, in this case the dynastic dispute.

The third phase of liberalism began modestly with the Royal Statute of 1834, a very limited charter that sought to reconcile the Old Regime with a circumscribed liberalism, but was overtaken by radicalization within no more than two years, following a seeming iron law of Spanish politics. In this case, the *Wechselwirkung* or "reciprocal influences" of civil war radicalized both Left and Right, heightening the Spanish contradiction. Moreover, the mid-1830s first revealed sociopolitical fragmentation as a consequence of limited modernization, at least in Spain, though the slow pace of that modernization would make it possible, most of the time, to hold the fragmentation in check for another century. The next constitution (1837) was more liberal but not democratic, for even the more "progressive" liberals feared democracy, as was almost universally the case in European liberalism at that time. Nearly a decade would be required before the moderate liberals finally gained control of the situation.[7]

These struggles and conflicts were only enhanced by the intensity with which much of the Spanish elite lived the Romantic era in European culture. Though romantic literature was not as distinguished in Spain as in some other countries, romanticism reflected well the Spanish mood in the first half of the nineteenth century, a time of heroes and caudillos and dramatic, if often destructive, public events. As J. Marías says, in some ways during that era Spain was the romantic country par excellence, one of the reasons why it appealed so greatly to visiting romantics from other lands. The romantic ethos continued through the 1860s, giving way afterward to weariness and a more pragmatic attitude.

During the following generation, Carlism declined yet maintained much of its base in the northeast. The advance of those combined processes generally grouped under the rubric of "modernization" would inevitably weaken traditionalism, yet the pace of traditionalism's decline was slow, due to several factors. One was simply the rhythm of nineteenth-century economic development, which had long left some of the basis of traditionalism intact. A second was the concentration of the traditionalist base in the northeast, where it became increasingly identified with the defense and survival of local and regional institutions, even among certain social sectors that elsewhere might have come to support liberalism.

Even after Carlism weakened, it could still be resuscitated by radical new challenges, when combined with the weakening of the political system. Such a situation developed immediately under the First Republic, and later under the Second Republic. Had Spain been able to sustain an orderly parliamentary evolution, the last two Carlist uprisings (1873, 1936) would presumably not have occurred, dependent as they were not upon opposition to liberalism itself (though that opposition always remained) but upon the breakdown of liberalism.

The First Carlist War was an exhausting and debilitating struggle, which further retarded Spain's development, but the liberals won a complete victory, even though they continued to recognize Basque fueros and Navarrese rights, as well. The international and domestic politics of violence in Spain between 1808 and 1840 had produced a more decisive and liberal outcome than would have existed had the country continued the peaceful evolution of the eighteenth century. The result was a political and social rupture that produced a series of weak liberal governments. The liberals had won both politically and militarily, but lacked the strength to govern with consensus and to sustain a rapid pace of development, even though they forced decisive legal, institutional, social, and economic changes. Though leftist critics later charged that the liberals had compromised excessively with the aristocracy and the Church, the liberals dominated so thoroughly in political terms that the main challenges were social, economic, and cultural.[8] Under a more traditional monarchy willing to confront practical issues, government would have been less liberal but stronger and more unified, and the pace of modernization possibly somewhat more rapid, but that is a counterfactual speculation.

The only kind of liberalism that nineteenth-century Spain could sustain was a highly elitist and restrictive liberalism, which precluded democratization, but this was typical of most parliamentary systems of the mid-nineteenth century. Historical and political commentary in the twentieth century often held that this was because of the tyrannical and oppressive character of the "bourgeoisie," or whatever the ruling elites were to be called. Only recently have some historians come to realize that the real obstacle was more nearly the nature of society and culture, which could not generate a broader civil society until well into the twentieth century. Moreover, in recent years historians have concluded that Spanish liberalism was more genuinely middle class, and less allied to the traditional aristocracy (which survived as a social and sometimes economic group rather than as a political force) than was in fact the case in most European countries. Bereft of most of the traditional elites as well as of the ordinary population, Spanish liberalism was politically dominant but socially restricted, a fact that for some time weakened its stability.

The effects of the great disamortization of Church and common lands that took place in the middle decades of the century received much criticism for the country's limited development. The disamortization, however, did not so much introduce new evils as to ratify the new scheme of things that was already emerging. Given the economic weakness of small landowners and sharecroppers, the political and economic conditions of that age scarcely permitted any other outcome, and agricultural development would not have accelerated had the disamortization never taken place. To conceive of a utopian land reform by censitary or restrictive liberalism is an idle enterprise. One major effect, however, was to consolidate the new liberal elite politically and economically, guaranteeing the collaboration of the landowners with the liberal system.

As it was, the censitary form of Moderado liberalism governed the country for most of the eight decades after 1843, first under the convulsive reign of Isabel II, and then in a more enlightened, tolerant, and comprehensive form under the evolutionary and reformist Restoration system initiated in 1875 by Antonio Cánovas del Castillo, arguably Spain's leading modern parliamentary statesman. Cánovas's reputation has fluctuated a good deal, like that of nineteenth-century liberalism in general, but in recent years more historians have come to recognize his system as the civic achievement that it was—one that provided a generally tolerant framework for reformism and improvement, overcoming the failures of its predecessors and providing a means of moving more confidently into the twentieth century.[9]

The successful compromises of the Restoration were possible in considerable measure due to the disillusionment with earlier failures and the multiple disasters of the democratic sexennium of 1868–74. Practical experience is often of great benefit in public affairs, and a mood chastened by experience was something that the Restoration had in common with the democratization of the country, which began almost exactly a century later.

Spanish Nationalism

The concept of the Spanish nation was clearly affirmed for the first time by the Cortes de Cádiz. Nationalism declares the sovereignty of the citizenry, as affirmed in the Constitution of 1812. It also declares the formation of a national community of equal rights, with all citizens equal before the law. A basic difference between modern nationalism and traditional patriotism is that the latter is largely defensive, while nationalism is proactive, future-oriented, and tends to take the form of a project, or a series of new claims.

Nineteenth-century Spanish liberalism assumed the project of affirming and developing the modern Spanish nation. This involved constructing a new liberal interpretation of Spanish history based on the medieval liberties of parliaments, rights, and fueros, with a special place for the failed rebellion of the Castilian Comunidades in 1520–21. It reached its highest expression in the massive multivolume *Historia de España* of Modesto Lafuente, which would continue to be reprinted well into the twentieth century. This presented a classic "liberal interpretation" of Spanish history, focused on the historical process of the development of the Spanish nation.[10] Such a discourse would subsequently be modified in a more conservative direction, on the one hand, while radical liberals, on the other hand, would later change it in a more radical direction.

The doctrine of the nation was nevertheless not as fully and firmly developed and accepted in Spain as in France or even in Italy, though during the nineteenth century it seemed to make impressive progress, as revealed in the Moroccan war of 1859 and even to some extent in the final Cuban conflict of 1895–98. Nonetheless, the twentieth century would demonstrate the fragility of the nineteenth-century unified nation.

During the first half of the nineteenth century Catholicism was an obstacle to this process. Religion had provided one of the most important sources of Spanish identity throughout history but inevitably possessed a more universal and trans-Hispanic dimension, whereas to Catholic leaders nationalism seemed a radical and secular doctrine stemming from the French Revolution, which to a considerable extent it was. It has often been observed that the clergy were the most active and effective elite in fomenting armed resistance against the French; their appeal was religious, universalist, and also patriotic, but not truly nationalist. Carlists, for example, resisted the project of a modern Spanish nationalism, which they associated with liberalism and revolution, in favor of maintaining tradition. Only in the 1850s, with the nation seemingly firmly established, did Catholic writers and ideologues begin to develop their own interpretation of the historically Catholic nation, defining a kind of right-wing Catholic nationalism, more in line with the reading of nationalism by many Catholics in Poland.[11] The traditional "Spanish ideology" was thus updated to embrace a form of modern nationalism, its leading avatar being Marcelino Menéndez Pelayo and its vision of Spain expressed in a variety of textbooks.[12] Moreover, by the end of the century, with liberalism more firmly established than ever, Carlism developed its own project of building a traditionalist Catholic nationalism.[13]

The nineteenth-century project of the Spanish nation was never effectively completed. Slow development of the national economy and of a national education system were two factors that impeded fuller integration and the formation of a national consciousness. The absence of universal military service may have been another. Moreover, the tenacious resistance to national uniformity by traditionalists and regionalists, particularly in the Basque Country and Navarre, proved intimidating to a weak liberal nationalism, which won on the battlefield but continued to respect special fiscal privileges that would never be overcome. Related to this and perhaps more important was the sense of national failure by the end of the century, combined with the absence of any foreign threat or major new national project, which might have served as motivating and unifying influences. The consequence was the growth of Catalan, then Basque, nationalism, as well as other regional movements, so that both in the early and later parts of the twentieth century the term "nationalism" more often than not would refer to the micronational and peripheral movements, not to Spanish nationalism, which, despite its victory in the Civil War of 1936–39, had faded by the last years of the Franco regime, along with all the major western nationalisms, and would subsequently seem almost nonexistent.

War and Underdevelopment

Even though Spain faced no challenges from other European countries after the defeat of Napoleonic France, the liberal state was involved in military operations on many occasions during the nineteenth century. The Spanish army became notorious for its political pretorianism (see chapter 15), but in fact was never truly militaristic, despite the fact that it was involved in significant military campaigns for more years than any other European army during the nineteenth century.

Rather than facing international conflicts, under liberalism Spain became the classic land of civil war, beginning with the limited struggle of 1822–23, followed by the insurrection of the Catalan peasantry in 1827 (Guerra dels agraviats), the First Carlist War (1833–40), a minor Carlist revolt in Catalonia between 1846 and 1849 (Guerra dels matiners), and the Second Carlist War (1873–76), to which must be added the republican cantonalist rebellion of 1873–74 and many civil and military "pronunciamientos" (attempted coups d'état) of shorter duration, some of which involved serious armed confrontation. The First Carlist War lasted seven years, during which nearly 150,000 men died, a very high figure for the population of those years. In addition, there were large-scale campaigns to suppress Hispano-American independence movements (which might also be considered civil wars), first during the decade 1815–25 and later during the Ten Years' War in Cuba (1868–78), followed by the brief "Guerra Chiquita" or Little War (1879–80) and the disastrous final Cuban war of 1895–98, climaxed by the conflict with the United States.

Spain was the only country for whom the nineteenth century began and ended with major international conflicts, with France and United States, respectively. During the intervening years occurred a war with Morocco (1859–60), a naval conflict off the western coast of South America, and a lesser military conflict with Morocco in 1894. The two main Cuban campaigns cost the army more than 100,000 deaths, and altogether, the Spanish colonial conflicts of the nineteenth century were by far the most costly in human and economic terms of those waged by any European state—at least in comparative terms—ending in absolute failure. The only country that might even begin to equal Spain in terms of the number of civil conflicts through the early twentieth century was Colombia.

The economic cost of all this was very great. Not merely did it retard development and modernization, but required that most of the state budget be devoted to the military, which remained backward and completely second rate. This also helped to guarantee miserably inadequate funding for education, arguably the greatest of the failures of nineteenth-century liberalism.

The Failure Debate

For much of the nineteenth century Spanish nationalism was relatively optimistic. It affirmed Spain's grand national past and looked to modern development to lift the country to an important place in the future. Pessimism first began to set in during and after the sexennium of 1868–74, when the nation seemed almost to dissolve amid major colonial war, civil conflict, and cantonalist insurrection. When all this was combined with lagging social, cultural, and economic development, the present and future looked dark. As early as 1876 the novelist Juan Valera expressed gratitude for the existence of Turkey, whose abysmal circumstances guaranteed that Spain would not quite be at the lowest rank of European and Mediterranean countries.

The Restoration provided stability and restored some degree of competence, but by the 1880s a persistent sense of failure could be perceived in some quarters, for it was obvious that liberalism, modernization, and success had obviously not followed together. The "regenerationist" societies did not begin after 1898, but were foreshadowed by a number of new groups formed in Castile during the 1880s, seeking to regenerate the Castilian economy and strengthen the nation.[14]

A more adequate perspective on the "failure debate," replete with empirical data and rigorous analysis, would be provided by the flowering of Spanish historiography one hundred years later. Considerable expansion of economic history took place during the last part of the twentieth century, and one of the main questions addressed by the new scholars in this field was that of *El fracaso de la revolución industrial en España* (The Failure of the Industrial Revolution in Spain), as the title of a well-known earlier book by Jordi Nadal put it.[15] The futility of direct comparison between Spain and England began to be appreciated. Comparative study of Italy, for example, was more fruitful, but this also revealed shortcomings in Spanish performance, at least by the end of the nineteenth century.[16] The historians tended to single out state protectionism as the most deleterious government policy, even though that was not always entirely convincing.

The reasons for slow development were numerous, to the extent that the absence of protectivism might simply have encouraged an almost exclusive concentration on the production of agriculture and raw materials. The persistent price of war was certainly a factor, to which might be added the litany associated with underdevelopment: infertile soil, low agricultural productivity, slow formation of capital, inadequate transportation and finance systems, poorly educated labor, and an absence of entrepreneurship. The critics are nonetheless correct that concentration on the internal market for industrial growth was inadequate for rapid advance.

It is important to place Spain's economic record in broader perspective. Although no major transformation had taken place during the eighteenth century, there had been steady growth, with the beginning of changes in commerce and production that helped provide a basis for later advances. The expansion of commerce in all of western Europe, including Spain, had been dramatic during the second half of the eighteenth century, and the most important part was the growth of Spanish commerce with other European countries. Comparatively little of Spain's domestic production, as distinct from its commerce, was connected with the American empire, so that the economy was affected surprisingly little by the latter's loss. Trade had remained strong with Europe until 1805, and soon began to expand once more after the end of the Napoleonic war.

The fashion once was to regard Spain's economic performance in the nineteenth century as a complete failure, a wasted opportunity, but it was, in fact, a period of fairly constant change and expansion, the main exception being the first third of the century from 1805 to 1840. Those years were a time of decisive change and growth in the more advanced parts of the Western world, but Spain was held back by the destruction wrought by the French invasion, followed by the country's own internecine struggles. All this proved a great handicap in the beginning of the dynamic nineteenth century, even though a significant recovery was soon made.

In general Spanish economic growth moved pari passu with that of Europe, but started at a distinctly lower level than in the more advanced countries, so that, in an era of rapid growth, it had to run fairly fast not to lose proportionate ground, and at the close of the nineteenth century seemed nearly as far behind the most advanced countries as in 1800. Thus, despite steady growth, as of 1900 certain statistics might be read to make it appear that Spain was relatively more backward than it had been a century earlier. The Spanish economy would not really begin to make up ground with northwestern Europe until the era of World War I and the 1920s.

The third quarter was generally the most expansive time of the nineteenth century, the economy growing rapidly in the 1850s and from 1866 to 1873, until the disaster of the First Republic. In general, the total growth rate, according to Prados de la Escosura, averaged 1.84 percent per year between 1850 and 1883, slowing somewhat in the latter part of the century. By the 1880s certain conservative compromises in policy had been made, foreign investment dropped, and there was some closure of the economy. After 1900, however, the rate increased once more to 1.34 percent until 1913, and then to 1.49 percent for the years 1913–20, the economy reaching its first phase of modern "take-off" during the 1920s, when it averaged

3.54 percent growth per year. Another way to put it is that total domestic production tripled between 1830 and 1910, after which it accelerated considerably further. Altogether, per capita income nearly doubled during the nineteenth century, even though it remained far below that of the most advanced countries. This was in general a steady and creditable performance, which by the 1920s was finally achieving rapid growth.

Throughout the nineteenth century economic growth surpassed the expansion of the population. Foreign trade grew steadily in volume and also expanded its place within the domestic economy, as the changes in the terms of trade for most of the century favored Spain, minerals and food exports maintaining their price level while the cost of major manufactured imports proportionately declined. During the middle decades of the century, the liberal regime began to build the infrastructure for a modern economy, with the creation of the rail networks, financial and institution reforms, and the expansion of mining. The Catalan textile industry gained strength, and minor industrial nuclei also developed elsewhere, sustained growth of Basque metallurgy beginning after the last Carlist war. In the late nineteenth century, per capita income was about the same as that of the united Italy, until the latter began a takeoff in the 1890s, which Spain would not equal for nearly twenty-five years.

Agriculture expanded more slowly during the nineteenth century, continuing the eighteenth-century pattern of growing extensively but not intensively. In Roman times the peninsula had been famous for its production of wheat, wine, and olives, and this focus had not substantially changed. Food production rose slightly more than the growth in population, but the "first agricultural revolution," which had taken place in northern Europe and relied on greatly increased uses of fertilizer and new plowing techniques, simply could not be applied in the Mediterranean environment. The "second agricultural revolution," emphasizing the beginning of mechanization and artificial fertilizers, began to appear in Spain only after 1900. During the first decades of the twentieth century, modernization and increased productivity advanced, albeit rather slowly, only to be interrupted in the 1930s.

An alternative perspective is that, with the primary exception of the two great international wars, the economy had been growing steadily, if slowly, since the 1680s. By the late nineteenth century agricultural productivity was clearly rising, though also slowly. This slow transformation had finally reached a point by the early years of the twentieth century that two major modern industrial zones had been consolidated, and a basis had been created for further industrialization and the introduction of more modern technology. Accelerated growth that began to make up ground, starting to close the gap with the advanced economies, finally occurred in the early part of the new century, climaxing with the prosperity and growth spurt of the 1920s, after which worldwide depression, civil war, world war, and restrictive state policies combined to end growth for two decades. The "disaster" of 1898 paradoxically played a role, because it produced a repatriation of capital that helped fuel domestic expansion, shortage of capital being a prime factor in limiting growth during the nineteenth century.[17] During the late nineteenth and early twentieth centuries there was a significant increase in life expectancy, which, according to one computation, had reached fifty-one years by 1910.[18] This figure, if correct, would indicate that for the first time in several centuries a key index of well-being was beginning to approach that of the advanced countries. The population had doubled since the late eighteenth century, reaching approximating 20 million, with a significantly higher standard of living, something apparent since about the middle of the nineteenth century. The liberal regime could not be considered an economic failure, though neither was it a spectacular success.[19]

Disaster and Regenerationism

Spain's loss of most of its empire partially paralleled the experiences of Great Britain, France, and Portugal. Like its European counterparts, after 1825 Spain had retained a portion of its overseas possessions (initially more than France, for example). During the rest of the century, the remaining parts, especially Cuba, enjoyed great saliency in Spanish policy and in official discourse. Despite the enormous drain of the Ten Years' War, the Restoration regime continued to stress the importance of empire, necessary not so much to Spain's economy, though that was of some significance, as to its self-image and its place in the world. Cuba held a special place in the nation-building discourse of the period.[20] Official policy deemed it to be a direct extension of Spain itself, with representation in Madrid but hence not eligible for self-government. This foreshadowed the policies of France and Portugal in the mid-twentieth century. It constituted the major political error of Cánovas's career, but one that was relatively commonplace in the history of European imperialism. Only Britain, after the experience of 1775–83, learned to avoid such mistakes in the future, particularly in dealing with the English-speaking dominions. The change in British policy developed during the nineteenth century and formed the basis for the eventual Commonwealth, which in turn did not fully emerge until the century that followed.

Even in the late eighteenth century, trade with Spanish America amounted to scarcely more than half the country's total foreign trade, and though trade with the Antilles increased threefold between 1850 and 1900, it in fact increased less rapidly than did Spanish commerce with the rest of the world, declining to only 12 percent of the total by 1890. Spanish exports to the Antilles may have increased in volume, but as a percentage of total exports they dropped to 17 percent by 1894. By that time Spain provided 35 percent of Cuba's total imports, but received only 10 percent of its exports. The economic importance of the imperial market and its resources to Spain was persistently exaggerated. As it would turn out, much of that limited market would be retained by the Spanish economy after 1898.

The Restoration system was consistently reformist, and its reformism by 1890, when the regime was firmly established, might have included autonomy for Cuba, even with the realization that this was likely to lead eventually to independence. Evolution was of the nature of the regime, but four centuries of history, together with the apparent failures of modern times, deprived the leadership of self-confidence in national well-being without the empire, though its loss might, with foresight, have been phased in by degrees. To have done so, however, would have gone against the grain, not merely of Spanish policy, but of the entire culture of European imperialism at the height of its expansion in the late nineteenth century. British leaders could reconcile themselves to the almost complete autonomy of the English-speaking dominions first because ties remained very close, and second because the "new" British empire of the nineteenth century was in no danger and had become the grandest in the world. Even Portugal had a large new empire in Africa, but for Spain remnants of the old empire made up the only empire there was. For Spanish leaders to have adopted a different policy would have required a kind of superhuman vision, courage, and self-confidence, which they simply did not possess.

Although the Spanish empire was clearly the weakest of the European empires, with the possible exception of Portugal's, its destruction at the hands of the United States is also correctly seen as merely the Spanish instance in a series of defeats for weaker, less developed Catholic and Orthodox (and also Muslim) states, usually at the hands of Protestant countries. The first example was the defeat of France by newly united Germany, touching off a considerable discussion in France about French failure and inadequacy, which was nonetheless greatly palliated by the enormous expansion of the French African empire during the decades that followed, something that Spain had neither the desire nor the means to emulate or to contest. It would be the vortex of the new French imperialism, not any independent Spanish initiative, that would finally draw Spain into Morocco during the years 1906–13.[21]

The disaster years for the peripheral European states began with the veto by Britain of further Portuguese expansion in southern Africa in 1891, followed by the humiliating defeat of Italian forces by a black Ethiopian army five years later, which, for the time being, halted all further Italian expansion. The Greek irredentist invasion of Thessaly was thoroughly defeated by Turkey in 1897, while the same year that witnessed Spain's defeat saw Britain block further French expansion in Africa. Nine years after Italy was defeated by an African army, the Tsarist Empire was defeated by an Asian army and navy. In 1912 the Ottoman Empire was almost eliminated from Europe altogether. There is no absolute common denominator to these experiences, for France retained a gigantic empire and was one of the most modern countries in the world, while the Tsarist Empire remained a great power that had simply lost a strategically awkward war. All five of the south European countries, however, could see themselves as laggards in modernization who either had further lost status or, in the case of Italy, could not attain it.

It has been observed that there was a much greater reaction in Spain to the loss of the remnants of empire than to the loss of most of the original empire in 1825. The reasons for this difference had to do with the greater increase in literacy and political self-consciousness, together with the expansion of the intelligentsia by the end of the century, and the fact that the defeat occurred at the height of worldwide European imperialism, whereas 1825 had been a relative low-point in general European empire. In fact, "disaster literature" began by the mid-1890s at the latest, well before the so-called disaster, as an expression of the mood of self-criticism and regenerationism that had already set in during the last quarter of the nineteenth century.

What is extraordinary is that the authors of the disaster literature and the writers of the "Generation of Ninety-Eight" had such a skewed perspective on their country. There was great preoccupation with failure and stagnation, partly because of the humiliation in military affairs, when in fact modernization was finally beginning slowly to accelerate, and for the first time the country was beginning to improve even in comparison with the more advanced economies. "Europeanization" was seen as both a problem and a goal, but at the beginning of the twentieth century Spain was in closer consonance with western Europe than at any time in the past hundred years or, possibly, the past three centuries. Part of the problem was that most of this writing was done by journalists and literary men with an uncertain relationship to empirical reality.

Regenerationism, in a great variety of guises, became the watchword well into the 1930s, and even after. This took three forms: political, socioeconomic, and cultural. Both cultural and socioeconomic regenerationism were quite successful. Building on some already significant achievements of the late nineteenth century, the writers and artists of what later would be known as the Silver Age raised Spanish culture to its highest comparative level since the third quarter of the seventeenth century. Economic development and social transformation continued to accelerate until 1930. Political regenerationism was the least successful.[22]

The process of political democratization was difficult throughout central, southern, and eastern Europe, and, for that matter, had been enormously conflictive in nineteenth-century France. There was no reason to expect that it would be anything other than difficult in Spain, as well. As in much of southern and eastern Europe, the foundation in terms of literacy and social and economic development had not been laid prior to World War I, and in Spain would only begin partially to emerge during the dramatic transformation of the 1920s. The older restrictive, elitist systems encountered increasing stress in every European country either before or immediately after the war, though in almost every case the upheaval led to the introduction of nominal universal male suffrage, except in Portugal. Yet by the 1930s, the new democratic parliamentary systems had given way to authoritarian regimes almost everywhere save Czechoslovakia. Thus it was in no way surprising that Spain and Portugal encountered severe difficulties.

World War I and the Russian revolution initiated a generation of political and social conflict absolutely without precedent in European history, what has sometimes been called the era of international civil war. The interwar generation presented Spain with a grave political dilemma analogous to that of a century earlier, yet more extreme and more complex, due to the consequences of modernization. In both cases, the old order was clearly inadequate, while sufficient conditions for a new order were not yet at hand. To cite the words of the Italian Marxist theorist Antonio Gramsci, "The old is dying and the new cannot be born. In the interregnum, a great variety of morbid symptoms appear." Spain simply had no easy or simple way out of this predicament. As it was, several other European countries did even worse.

The Restoration regime had been the most appropriate for Spain in the late nineteenth century. As David Ringrose has written, "Rather than reading the topic teleologically, as Spain's failure to be as democratic as it should have been, we should view Spain's combination of parliament, elections, and traditional patronage as a phase in the evolution of political culture that appeared all over Europe" (and, indeed, in parts of the United States, as well).[23] It was based on what Carlos Dardé has fittingly called "the acceptance of the adversary," involving what the Italians called "trasformismo," with continuing reform and the co-optation and inclusion of new adversarial elites.

Reformism began to falter with the failure of the Maura and Canalejas governments between 1909 and 1912, after which the system began to fragment and enter crisis, reaching a low point in 1917 with the impact of the war and major new social and political mobilization.[24] Salvador de Madariaga, the Spanish writer and diplomat, has considered the failure of the diverse reform movements of 1917 the turning point in the history of the constitutional monarchy.

The old elitist, pre-democratic political parties had outlived their usefulness, and were fragmented and ineffective, while the final effort to reunify the Liberal Party in 1923 was not very successful.[25] The alternative in 1923 was to encourage greater reform and democratization or to attempt reform differently under an authoritarian government. Choice of the latter would fail to provide any lasting solution, or to achieve genuine reform, since Spanish society had long been predominantly liberal, while workers and farm laborers were becoming increasingly politically conscious and leftist.

Spain did not possess all the qualities needed for a successful civil society of democracy, yet a counterfactual case can be made that democratization might have stood a better chance after 1923 than after 1931.[26] Despite the growth of the revolutionary worker movements, in 1923 Spanish civil society had been trained to live under an evolutionary, reformist constitutional monarchy and might have responded positively, not with radicalization, to democratic reforms. During the preceding generation the main republican forces had taken increasingly moderate positions, and were in considerable measure disposed to cooperate with a reformist parliamentary monarchy. As it was, the sequence of events between 1923 and 1931 was destructive in the extreme. It must always be kept in mind, however, that democracy failed everywhere in central, southern, and eastern Europe except for Switzerland and Czechoslovakia. Modernization produces fragmentation, and the fragmentation had become so extreme in Spain that the country was not likely to have become an exception to the failure of democracy.

If democratization was not possible, then continuation of a moderate authoritarian system for another fifteen years, until the end of 1945, would probably have been the second-best solution. For example, the Pilsudski regime in Poland was, compared with other dictatorships, only moderately repressive and would have lasted for some time into the future had it not been for the sudden German invasion in 1939. Catholic, internally diverse, and still in large measure agrarian, Poland was the east European country most similar to Spain. Yet a "Pilsudski solution" was not possible in Spain, for several reasons: Since nationalism was weak in Spain, it could not serve as a unifying, stabilizing force as in Poland. Second, Primo de Rivera was no Pilsudski. Both were moderate, semiliberal authoritarians, but Primo de Rivera had no real political vision and no idea how to build a viable alternative regime. Franco was more brutal, but also more astute. At the end, Primo de Rivera could think of no way to prolong his system other than to try to copy Italian Fascism more directly, something not likely to work in Spain. Finally, the liberal tradition in Spain was so strong that Spanish opinion, even within the military, was simply not willing to tolerate authoritarian government for very long, despite unprecedented prosperity, once the initial problems that elicited authoritarianism seemed to have disappeared.

Collapse of the monarchy in 1931 was a grave blow. This was not because of anything magical about parliamentary monarchy, for most democracies do well enough without it. Rather, it was because Spain had experienced grave problems of stability in the preceding century and by 1930 was living amid a European political culture that was fragmenting and entering crisis conditions, which would inevitably have grave repercussions in Spain. For half a century the monarchy had been able to serve as a reasonably successful moderating power, both a symbol and a force for unity and continuity, qualities whose absence in Spain would soon lead to disaster.

It is a commonplace that Alfonso XIII was discredited by having consented to the dictatorship. Of this there is no question, and here the principal counterfactual issue would be whether an immediate return to general elections within six months of the downfall of the dictator might have permitted the return to a functional, reformist, and democratizing parliamentary monarchy. There is no guarantee that this would have been the case. The old monarchist parties had virtually disappeared, and their leaders were terrified of a new leap in the dark. But that leap eventually took place in April 1931, with a disastrous long-term outcome. In retrospect, new parliamentary elections in April or May 1930 would have been preferable. Even had this initiative failed, it is hard to see how the eventual outcome would have been worse.

Finally, what should be history's verdict on the political role of Alfonso XIII?[27] Under the constitution of 1876, the king's role in the political system had been reduced, but he remained the crucial arbiter of access and the rotation between the two established parties. He was accused of interference and arbitrariness, and there were occasional instances of such action, but in general he strove to recognize and cooperate with the political forces generated by the system. To think that the king was personally responsible for the division, factionalism, blockage of reform, and growing pressure on the system is preposterous. Nor did he conspire with the dictator in 1923 but accepted the results of a pronunciamiento that no political or military force seemed willing to contest.[28] Eventually, after it became more than clear that the dictator had lost support, the king asked for his resignation. This is not to say that the king's actions between September 1923 and December 1929 were wise or judicious. At various times he should doubtless have acted differently, but it should be recognized that he was called upon to deal with an increasingly complex and difficult situation, and that whatever happened was not primarily the result of any unique initiative taken or not taken by the king himself. At the end, he chose to vacate his throne rather than to encourage civil conflict. It was a tragedy that his successors on both the Left and the Right did not follow his example five years later.

Part III

Dilemmas of
Contemporary History

Provincial divisions of modern Spain

9   A Republic . . . without Democrats?

Had anyone reading this book been in Madrid or Barcelona on the evening of April 14, 1931, or the day following, the scenes of jubilation, accompanied by the general absence of violence, would have convinced him that the new Republic was welcomed by the vast majority of Spanish society. A logical corollary might be that the latter possessed the civic maturity and responsibility to enable a twentieth-century democracy to function successfully. But, as everyone knows, this did not prove to be the case.

There remain certain standard explanations for the failure of the Republic. For the Left, this stemmed from the unremitting hostility of the Right, which refused to accept "reforms." For the Right, it resulted from the violence and extremism of the Left, aided and abetted by Moscow, which never intended to practice democracy. For more than a few professional scholars, it stemmed from the civic immaturity and polarization of Spanish society, influenced by the European conjuncture. In fact, these various explanations should not be seen as mutually exclusive, for there are elements of truth in all of them. The factors involved will be taken up in the succeeding chapters, but any reexamination of the problems of the Republic must begin with the republicans themselves.

There is no doubt that by 1931 a large part, probably the majority, of Spanish political opinion wished to see the inauguration of political democracy, even though such an interest was not shared by at least a large minority of political opinion. This was partly the result of the six and a half years of direct dictatorship—something never seen before in Spanish affairs—which "inoculated" a sizable part of political opinion against authoritarian solutions. Another fundamental factor was the revolution of rising expectations wrought by the transformation of Spanish society in the 1920s. During those years the rhythm of economic growth, social and cultural transformation, and expansion of education was the most rapid in all of Spanish history to that time. This resulted in greatly heightened expectations of change and improvement, both among the lower classes and among much of the middle classes as well. The experience of the Republic cannot be understood without keeping in mind this background of rapid and sweeping transformation. The standard image of "backward Spain" is not incorrect, for the country remained underdeveloped in comparison with northwestern Europe, but it altogether fails to capture the pace of change and the sociocultural dynamism at work from the late 1920s on. The most important conditioning factor was not the influence of "underdevelopment" but rather the profound psychological effects of rapid change and the ways in which the country was ceasing to be merely underdeveloped. All this led to greatly increased expectations, not merely in the political realm but also in social and economic affairs.

A basic problem was that political society had not naturally evolved through reformism into democratic practice, but had lost contact with its own parliamentary traditions—thanks to the hiatus of the dictatorship. A new democratic republic was being attempted ab ovo with new leaders and mostly new political organizations, all something of a leap in the dark.

With the exception of the Radical Republican Party of Alejandro Lerroux, the republican parties of 1931 were of comparatively recent creation, as indeed some of the leaders themselves were recent converts to republicanism. Several of the key moderate figures, such as Niceto Alcalá Zamora and Miguel Maura, became republicans only in 1930, and most of the other republican parties had been formed only in recent years. Moreover, most of the new leaders had little political experience, so the depth of their commitment to democracy could only be demonstrated under the new regime.

The first test occurred with the elections of June 28, 1931, which were swept by the new republican coalition. Monarchists and conservatives found themselves in disarray, ill-prepared to contest the elections. Even so, the new republican forces were determined to dominate, and in cities and provinces where the opposition made a serious effort, it was harassed and in some cases shut down altogether. Because of the confusion and disarray of the right, the republican coalition was bound to win these elections even under scrupulously democratic conditions, but the degree of electoral control and harassment of the opposition demonstrated that "republicanism" did not by any means indicate a clear break with the electoral practices of the monarchist regime.

The new system introduced a series of rapid changes, and in the early twentieth century change tended to fragment. The variety of new political parties and movements was extraordinary, one of the most varied and diverse to be found in any country in the world. These groups represented quite varied agendas, making it difficult to achieve unity behind a single democratic, parliamentary program, all of which has been commented on ad infinitum in the historical studies of the period.

A brief tour d'horizon of the political scene reveals this diversity and how little agreement existed in support of any specific project. The initial republican coalition was composed of three distinct elements: the Left republicans, the centrist liberal or moderate republicans, and the Socialists. Each had a different political agenda, which only with the greatest difficulty could be combined and coordinated into a common and coordinated republicanism.

The group that led the government during the first biennium, setting the tempo and much of the agenda, were the Left republicans, at first composed of several different parties, several of which eventually collapsed, until by 1934 the main Left republican force was the party of Izquierda Republicana (Republican Left), led by Manuel Azaña. The only other major and enduring Left republican group was the Esquerra Catalana (Catalan Left). Though the Left republicans frequently gestured toward democracy, they were not as interested in constitutional democracy, free elections, and the rule of law as they were in a new kind of radically reformist regime. It was this regime of radical middle-class reformism that they referred to as "la República" and "el republicanismo," compared with which procedural democracy was secondary. In their concept, republicanism stood for a vigorously anti-Catholic program, separating church and state, eliminating Catholic education, and strictly controlling Catholic interests and activities. This was to be accompanied by other major institutional reforms dealing with education, culture, Catalan autonomy, and the reorganization and subordination of the military. In 1933–34 it was broadened to include extensive intervention in the economy as well, but remained primarily a program of cultural, educational, religious, and institutional reforms oriented toward the secularized sectors of the middle classes.[1]

The problem was that this program was never supported by more than about 20 percent of the electorate. Even if this figure were slightly increased, it would be nowhere near a majority, so that Azaña always recognized that the Left republicans had no hope of maintaining themselves in power without the support of the Socialists.

The Socialists, however, accepted the Left republican program only as an initial minimum program, their own goal being the construction of an economically collectivist socialist regime. The Socialists were no more than "semiloyal," at best, to a democratic nonsocialist Republic, so their alliance with the Left republicans was inevitably limited and circumstantial. Whenever the development of the Republic took a path that would not lead to socialism, the Socialists would cease to support the Republic. But since the popular vote of the Socialists also never amounted to much more than 20 percent—scarcely more than the Left republicans—it was not clear how a socialist regime could be established by democratic republican politics alone.

Did Azaña's concept of an exclusively leftist, radically reformist republic therefore make any sense if it was not going to lead to a socialist regime? Azaña seems initially to have believed that full Socialist support would be needed for no more than a few years, after which a united coalition of middle-class republican parties in a radically reformed Spain might have the strength to govern. The other main republican force, the parties of the moderate liberal democratic center, soon refused to maintain the alliance with the Socialists—who did not accept the democratic regime as an ultimate goal—nor did they agree with the extent or radicalism of the reforms imposed by a government led by Left republicans and Socialists. To maintain the strictly leftist option, the Left republicans were thus dependent on the Socialists, who nonetheless refused simply to settle for the Left republican program. Though for the moment disunited, Left republicans and Socialists rejected the results of the second republican elections of 1933, which returned a majority for the moderate republicans and the Catholic Right. Left Republicans and Socialists immediately launched a series of attempts to cancel the results of the most honest and democratic elections in Spanish history. Much more than the contest of 1931, the elections of 1933 reflected the competition of a fully mobilized electorate, and would constitute the freest and fairest contest known to Spain until 1977.[2] If even the Left republicans would not accept the results of democratic elections, the question of the future of a democratic republic lay in grave doubt.

The only large party to support a democratic republic *tout court* were the Radicals, whose share of the vote was, mutatis mutandis, no greater than that of the Left republicans. At one point the Radicals had sought to form an all-republican government (that is, a coalition of all the republican parties), but the virtual disappearance of the Left republicans in the new elections made that impossible. The Radicals were therefore willing to work with the moderate Right, in this case the new Catholic party, the CEDA (Confederación Española de Derechas Autónomas—Spanish Confederation of Autonomous Rightist Groups), which had suddenly emerged as the largest party in Spain; with only about 30 percent of the vote, however, it was far from having a majority.

From June 1933 the key figure in Spanish politics was not any of the major party leaders but the president of the Republic, Niceto Alcalá Zamora, who, because of the extreme political fragmentation, assumed a dominant role. The Republican constitution required that each parliamentary government face a "double responsibility"—responsible not merely to a majority of the Cortes but also to the approval of the president of the Republic, who had the power to force the resignation of any cabinet of ministers. Alcalá Zamora used this prerogative with a vengeance, further destabilizing Republican politics.

He was a veteran of the Old Regime, a former leader of one of the more progressive wings of the old monarchist Liberal Party. A practicing Catholic, scrupulously honest in his personal affairs, Alcalá Zamora in theory supported the Republic as a liberal democratic system. He opposed both radical anti-Catholic reformism and any form of rightist authoritarianism, believing that he had a special responsibility to "center the Republic," as he put it. To that end he constantly interfered in parliamentary affairs, making and unmaking governments according to his own will, to the extent that he himself became one of the Republic's chief political problems.

As Alcalá Zamora saw it, the main problem facing the Republic was the resurgence of the Right in the form of the CEDA. José María Gil Robles and the other leaders of the CEDA did not propose monarchist restoration but affirmed drastic reform of the constitution and the establishment of a system of Catholic corporatism. As the chief representative of the Catholic middle classes, the CEDA stood for law and order, and carefully obeyed the law, but despite this "legalist" posture, Alcalá Zamora refused to allow the largest parliamentary party to form a government. First he engineered a minority government of the Radicals, supported by CEDA votes, and—when the latter finally demanded a share of power, Cedo-Radical coalition governments, always led by the Radicals—which governed from October 1934 to September 1935. The Socialists used the entry of three CEDA ministers into the government in 1934 as an excuse to launch a revolutionary insurrection, the fourth revolutionary insurrection in less than three years (following three smaller ones by the anarchosyndicalists of the CNT-FAI). From that point the country was increasingly polarized between Left and Right, between revolution and counterrevolution.

Alcalá Zamora seized the initiative once more in September 1935 and soon thereafter manipulated certain corruption charges to discredit the Radicals. He then dissolved parliament prematurely and unnecessarily, calling new elections for February 1936. He suffered from the illusion that his government could invent a new centrist party to replace the Radicals, but this attempt at government control and coercion failed altogether, leading to a victory of the Left in the new elections. Alcalá Zamora had failed completely in his attempt to "center the Republic."

The only political sector that supported a liberal democratic government, with honest elections and fair rules of the game, was the republican center. The only large center party, the Radicals, had expanded rapidly and then completely lost all cohesion amid the corruption charges of 1935. Of the large parties, only the Radicals believed in "a Republic for all Spaniards," as Lerroux put it, abandoning most of their old anticlericalism and rejecting extreme changes either by the right or left. Yet this newly expanded Radical Party was a weak coalition of liberals, pragmatists, and opportunists, sound and constructive in its basic orientation but novel, rootless, and centrifugal in its membership, too weak internally to face a major challenge.[3] Beyond the Radicals, the other centrist parties were small and weak, with the partial exception of the Lliga Catalana. President Alcalá Zamora, who proposed to lead the center and a liberal democratic Republic, undermined both with his egotism and manipulations, which made genuine parliamentary government impossible.[4]

The two largest parties of Left and Right, the Socialists and the CEDA, in some respects mirrored each other as semiloyal parties. The Socialists supported the Republican government from 1931 to 1933, with the stipulation that it must soon move into socialism. The CEDA supported the Republican government during 1933–35, expecting that it would lead to drastic constitutional changes and eventually a corporative system. The key difference was that the CEDA rejected violence and followed a strict policy of legalism (with the possible exception of the administration of a few electoral districts in Granada province in February 1936).[5]

The extreme Right (monarchists, Carlists, Falangists) all firmly rejected the Republic but were too weak to have any political effect, all their conspiracies coming to naught. The same might be said of the revolutionary extreme Left. Down to 1934–35 the anarchosyndicalists of the CNT-FAI, Communists, and the independent Communist BOC/POUM all sought to overthrow the Republic by violent revolutionary means, but were too weak to achieve anything, the three anarchist insurrections failing completely.[6]

The key elements in republican affairs were the republican parties themselves, even though all combined they could scarcely have achieved a majority of the vote in fully competitive elections. Their mutual enmity cast doubt on the future of the regime. From 1934 on, Azaña and the Left republicans chose to ally themselves with the worker revolutionaries, abandoning any pretense of merely supporting a liberal democratic Republic of equal rights for all, in favor of a leftist exclusionary Republic. Due to the disastrous leadership of Alcalá Zamora, the centrist liberals managed the astonishing feat of self-destruction, so that after February 1936 supporters of a liberal democratic Republic with equal rights for all had shrunk to a tiny minority in the Cortes.

10 Who Was Responsible?

Origins of the Civil War of 1936

Historians can agree that the Spanish Civil War began on the weekend of July 17–20, 1936, when in a variety of poorly coordinated actions various garrisons and units of the Spanish army rebelled against the Republican regime. Ever since that time, supporters of the Left have held that the cause and origin of the Civil War are perfectly clear—it was the military revolt. No military revolt, no civil war. In the most immediate sense, this is an obvious and logical argument.

Supporters of the military rebels, however, from the very beginning argued that this was a gross oversimplification. They contended—and their supporters still contend—that the civil breakdown had already taken place in the unprecedented decline of the rule of law in Spain during the spring and early summer of 1936. Some have even contended that the Civil War began initially in October 1934, with the revolutionary insurrection of the Socialists. The military revolt was held to have taken place not against the legal order, but to restore a legal order and to put an end to widespread civil conflict that long predated July 1936.

The contention is also made that the military revolt per se did not necessarily begin a civil war, since it was intended to be more like a pronunciamiento or coup d'etat. According to this argument, the war began not on July 17–18 with the start of the military revolt but on July 19 , when the Left Republican government began to "arm the people," that is, to give weapons en masse to the leftist worker organizations. This sought to create a second armed force with which to combat the insurgent sector of the army, opening the way to widespread civil war. According to this interpretation, the Republican government, when faced with a massive challenge like Alfonso XIII on April 14, 1931, should also have responded like Don Alfonso—who said he wanted to avoid civil war—by handing over power. That would certainly have been a means by which the Republican government could have avoided civil war, but the weakness in this argument, at least by analogy with the collapse of the monarchy, was that in 1931 there were not two potentially large and polarized forces—Left and Right—as in 1936.

During the course of the Civil War, many different explanations of the causes and character of the conflict were presented at home and abroad. The Left always preferred to define it as a struggle between democracy and fascism. For the Right, it was a crusade by Christian civilization to overcome godless revolution and barbarism. For both sides, it was soon touted as a national liberation war. The Left was freeing Spain from Nazi Germany and Fascist Italy, the Right was liberating the patria from the clutches of Stalin, the Soviet Union, and international Communism. These in turn became claims concerning the causes of the Civil War, which were often held to be exogenous, and located in Moscow, Rome, or Berlin.

Altogether, a series of arguments and allegations have been presented concerning the causes and responsibilities for the war, which are worth examining: (1) the argument that civil war began in 1934; (2) the "breakdown thesis": the constitutional Republic had already ceased to exist; (3) efforts to avert civil war; (4) the "provocation" thesis; (5) the initial plan of the rebels; (6) the "exogenous" thesis (role of foreign powers); and (7) the contention that the final crisis alone was decisive.

The Civil War Began in 1934

Revolutionary insurrection was common in Spain between 1930 and 1934. The Republicans launched a military revolt against the monarchy in December 1930, and the CNT-FAI, or sectors thereof, launched three insurrections against the Republic during 1932–33, while a small band of military rebels did the same in August 1932. The Socialist insurrection of October 1934 was by far the most serious and extensive of these outbursts, affecting many different provinces and seizing control of much of Asturias. Revolution was proclaimed in Asturias, with the execution of political prisoners, priests, and seminary students, much destruction of property, and large-scale looting of money. Major military action was required to put down the insurrection, which in all Spain cost 1,500 lives and led to more than 15,000 arrests.[1] To conservatives this was what they had always feared: revolution on the march. It produced intense polarization and an enormous propaganda campaign during 1935–36 in which the Left ignored their own atrocities while accusing the authorities of crimes and excesses during the repression, which in turn might be interpreted as a classic case of the perpetrators blaming the victims.[2]

The insurrection had many of the features of civil war, but was this really the beginning of the war of 1936–39? That seems quite doubtful, since for sixteen months after the insurrection the country was governed by moderate coalition governments that upheld law and order, followed by democratic elections in February 1936. What would be more accurate would be to say that this was the beginning of the rhetoric and propaganda of civil war by Left and Right. During the two years that followed, Spain was inundated with atrocity stories about Asturias and the repression by both sides, which began to create a psychological climate of civil war in the country. From October 1934 the Left stood for increasingly radical, even revolutionary, changes, and polarization was greatly intensified.

Yet there still remained nearly two years, and many good and reasonable opportunities, to avert the civil war that eventually erupted.

The "Breakdown" Thesis

The military rebels who began the conflict at first declared almost unanimously that they were taking violent action not to overthrow the Republic but to save the Republic, since the constitution had become a dead letter, and law and order had broken down. Certainly the breakdown of law and constitutional order that had occurred in Spain was unprecedented in any modern European country in peacetime. Unpunished violation of the law took place in at least fourteen areas.

1. The electoral victory of the Left was later followed by the greatest strike wave in Spanish history, featuring many labor stoppages, in some cases without practical economic goals but rather seeking direct domination of labor relations and of private property, often accompanied by violence and destruction of property.

2. Illegal seizures of property, especially in the southern provinces, sometimes legalized ex post facto by the government under the pressure of the revolutionary movements. Manuel Tuñón de Lara has calculated that, between illegal seizures and the acceleration of the agrarian reform, approximately 5 percent of all agrarian property in the country changed hands within five months—not a revolution, but a precipitous change.[3]

3. A wave of arson and property destruction, particularly in the south.

4. In addition to the destruction, numerous seizures of churches and church properties in the south and east and in some other parts of the country.

5. Closure of Catholic schools, provoking a crisis in education, and in a number of localities forcible suppression of Catholic religious activities as well, accompanied by the expulsion of priests.

6. Broad extension of censorship, with severe limitation of freedom of expression and of assembly.

7. Major economic deterioration, which has never been studied in detail, with a severe stock market decline, the flight of capital, and in some southern provinces abandonment of cultivation, since the costs of the harvest would be greater than its market value. Hence several southern Socialist mayors proposed the "penalty of remaining" for proprietors, rather than the penalty of exile.

8. Many hundreds—indeed several thousand—arbitrary political arrests of members of rightist parties.

9. Impunity of criminal action for members of Popular Front organizations, who were rarely arrested. Occasionally anarchosyndicalists were detained, since they were not members of the Popular Front.

10. The politicization of justice through new legislation and policies, in order to facilitate arbitrary political arrests and prosecution, and to place the rightist parties outside the law. In spite of the four violent insurrections of leftist parties against the Republic—which had scant counterpart among the rightist parties—none of their members were charged with illegal action in this regard, since justice had become completely politicized, in keeping with the Popular Front program.

11. Forcible dissolution of rightist groups, beginning with the Falange in March and the Catholic trade unions in May, and moving toward the CEDA and Renovación Española in July. Illegalizing the rightist organizations was designed to create a virtual political monopoly for the leftist parties, first achieved in the trade union groups.

12. Falsification of electoral procedures and results, which, according to Alcalá Zamora, passed through four phases. The first was produced by the series of disorders in various provinces on February 16–19, which destroyed a certain number of ballots, produced repeat voting of dubious legality in several locales, and distorted final registration of the votes. The second phase occurred during the run-off elections two weeks later, when, in the face of physical intimidation, the conservative parties withdrew. The third phase was the

arbitrary and partisan actions of the Electoral Comission of the Cortes in the second half of March, almost universally condemned by historians, which arbitrarily reassigned a sizable number of seats from the Right to the Left. The fourth phase was the extreme coercion exerted in the new Cortes elections in Cuenca and Granada at the beginning of May, with the arbitrary detention of rightist candidates and activists and severe restriction of rightist activity, producing completely unilateral elections, taken by the opposition to the government as a signal of the end of democratic voting in Spain.[4]

13. Subversion of the security forces through reappointment of revolutionary officers and personnel earlier prosecuted for violent and subversive actions. One of these commanded the illegal police squad that kidnapped Calvo Sotelo. Equally notable was the addition of special "delegados de policía," normally activists of the Socialist and Communist parties named ad hoc as deputy police, though not regular members of the security forces. This followed the precedent of the Hitler government in appointing violent and subversive SA and SS activists as *Hilfspolizei* in Germany in 1933, and one of these fired the bullet that killed Calvo Sotelo. It should be noted, however, that this procedure was not followed on a massive and systematic scale, as in Germany.

14. The growth of political violence, although its extension was very unequal in different parts of the country. Some provinces experienced relative calm, while in others there was widespread violence, especially in some of the capital cities. Estimates by researchers of those killed by political violence within five and a half months range from a low of 300 to a high of 444.[5]

Even historians sympathetic to the Left have called this a "pre-revolutionary situation," and it was certainly one that would have elicited a sharp and probably violent reaction in any other country. But did this mean that the constitutional Republic had ceased to exist, as the rebels claimed? A simple yes-or-no answer would probably be ingenuous, since the situation was complicated in the extreme. The Republican government had not become a dictatorship (in which case there probably could not have been a major military revolt) but neither did it maintain constitutional order. Spain lived under a limited but capricious and decentralized tyranny of the leftist Republican government and the Popular Front parties, in which life continued with relative normalcy in much of the country but was severely disturbed in some key dimensions and especially in certain provinces. Spain had entered a kind of gray zone in which the extent to which the established law would apply was becoming increasingly uncertain.

Whereas the worker parties looked to a completely new revolutionary regime, the government of Manuel Azaña and Santiago Casares Quiroga planned to develop an exclusionary all-Left (but not socialist) Republic which would extend radical reform but preserve most private property. It gambled that if concessions were made to the revolutionaries, the latter would eventually be willing to support such a regime. It also gambled that the forces of the Right were weak and would be unable to contest the capricious tyranny through which the country would have to pass to achieve the new radical Republic. The gamble was lost.

Efforts to Avert Civil War

From October 1934 commentators began to warn of the danger of civil war. Such a prospect was welcomed and preached only by the more extreme sectors of the revolutionary Left, on the grounds that a successful revolution always involved at least a brief civil war, though in 1935 the Communists changed their policy in this regard. The extreme Right attempted to formulate its own plans for armed insurrection, which were perhaps not so different from those of the revolutionaries, since all groups envisioned only a brief period of fighting.

As violence, disorder, and the various forms of pre-revolutionary activity mounted, warnings of civil war began to take on a new urgency by May 1936. It was clear to most rational observers that the danger of breakdown or serious civil conflict could only be averted by a stronger, probably more broadly based, government. There were at least three different proposals to achieve this.

The first began when Azaña was invested with the powers of the presidency of the Republic on May 10 (following the destitution of Alcalá Zamora). For three months he had as prime minister presided over a weak, minority all-Left Republican government and now would have to authorize a replacement. The prime candidate was Indalecio Prieto, leader of the semimoderate sector of the Socialists. Prieto sought to form a strong majority government of Socialists and Left Republicans, hopefully with the participation of other leftist parties as well. He proposed to govern vigorously, pressing social and economic reforms, repressing disorder, and purging the military. Such a government could probably have averted civil war, but it was vetoed by Largo Caballero and the revolutionary Socialists, who rejected any further Socialist participation in a "bourgeois" government. Since a strong majoritarian leftist government was impossible, Azaña adopted the alternative of another weak minoritarian Left Republican government led by his crony Casares Quiroga, an uncertain administration that was capable of many arbitrary deeds but refused to adopt the measures that could have averted civil war.

Soon afterward, at a meeting of the leaders of his tiny Left-center National Republican Party on May 25, the eminent jurist Felipe Sánchez Román presented his own proposal to "save the Republic." Azaña was a personal friend of Sánchez Román, for whom he felt great admiration, but after helping to write much of the original Popular Front program, Sánchez Román had withdrawn from the leftist alliance before the elections, concluding that it was wrong for republicans to ally themselves with violent revolutionaries. He now proposed a "national republican government" of all the republican parties, Left and center, with strong powers from the presidency to enforce the constitution fully and strictly, repressing disorder from any source, and disbanding all the party militias. The Socialists would be allowed to join the government if they endorsed this program. Despite his great respect for Sánchez Román, Azaña rejected his proposal because it would have required allying with the moderate center and breaking altogether with Socialist radicalism, disrupting the Popular Front. Azaña continued to reject the moderates and insist on an all-leftist policy, despite the risk of civil war.

The third kind of proposal came from several centrist liberals and a few of the most moderate members of Azaña's own Izquierda Republicana. This called for a temporary "national Republican dictatorship," given plenary powers of martial law by the president, to repress disorder and enforce the constitution. Its most public presentation was made by the centrist liberal Miguel Maura, one of the founders of the Republic, in a series of articles in the Madrid daily *El Sol* late in June. This too was rejected by Azaña and most of the Left Republicans as excessive, unnecessary, and requiring a complete split with the worker Left, the voting support of the Socialists being fundamental to Azaña's program.

Once the war had actually begun, Azaña finally reversed course and accepted Sánchez Román's proposal on the night of July 18–19, authorizing formation of a broader all-republican government under Diego Martínez Barrio, who led the most moderate of the Popular Front parties. The task of Martínez Barrio was to reach a new compromise and preserve law and order. Coming even a single week earlier, it might have been successful, but after the conflict began, it was too late.

The "Provocation" Thesis

It has sometimes been observed that neither the Left Republican leaders nor the revolutionary Socialists should have complained about the military revolt, since their policy was based on expecting and waiting for such a revolt, even trying to provoke it, in order to take advantage of suppressing it. Such a thesis offers a correct reading of the policy of Largo Caballero and the revolutionary Socialists, who had no program for seizing power directly but were relying on the spread of pre-revolutionary activity to provoke a revolt, which would destabilize the situation to the point where the moderate Left would have to make way for the revolutionaries to lead the government, in effect beginning the revolution. This was a correct prediction of exactly what happened, but reflects the policy only of the revolutionary wing of the Socialist movement.

Indalecio Prieto and the semimoderate Socialist sector had no such blithe confidence in provoking and overcoming an armed rebellion, which they preferred to avoid, realizing that such a situation could lead to a major civil war. Prieto called both for greater moderation, for law and order, and for a stronger Republican government that would purge the military. At the same time, however, the prietista Socialists themselves could not resist exploiting the weakness of the Left Republican government to violate the constitution and advance the program of the Socialists, so that in practice it was sometimes difficult to find much difference between the deeds of the followers of Prieto and of Largo Caballero.

The provocation thesis raises complex issues when applied to the government of Casares Quiroga. Certainly there is no evidence that any of the Left Republican leaders wanted a civil war, and late in June the Ministry of the Interior even sent a circular to provincial governors instructing them to avoid actions that might provoke the military.

It would seem that Casares Quiroga himself was of two minds on this issue. He was determined not to be a mere "Kerensky," a sort of puppet who would end up giving in to the revolutionaries. He was also aware that a conspiracy existed in the army, and expressed some confidence that it would never amount to more than a repetition of the "sanjurjada," that futile rebellion of August 1932. Some of those who spoke with Casares Quiroga got the idea that he even welcomed what he believed would be a feeble revolt, calculating that its suppression would not be difficult and, rather than weakening the state to the point where the moderate left would have to cede powers to the revolutionaries (as Largo Caballero calculated), would actually strengthen the government, enabling it to control the revolutionaries more easily. This may explain why no stronger measures were taken on July 13–14, after the murder of Calvo Sotelo, to conciliate the opposition or to apprehend those responsible, even though the state security forces had been involved.

The Planning of the Rebels

The military conspiracy began in multiple strands of confusion and uncertainty soon after the electoral victory of the Popular Front. It did not achieve any focus until a significant sector of the officers supporting rebellion began to recognize Brig. Gen. Emilio Mola, commander of the garrison in Pamplona, as the overall leader at the close of April. Mola once had a reputation as a moderate liberal, and the plan that he developed for the revolt envisaged replacing the existing leftist government with an all-military directory, which would supervise the drastic reform of the Republic in a rightist direction. This envisaged a kind of "Portuguese solution," creating a corporative, more restrictive, and authoritarian republic similar to Salazar's Estado Novo in Portugal.

Developing broad support for the conspiracy was difficult, for many key sectors of the military were reluctant to commit themselves. Though the monarchists and the CEDA leaders eventually pledged support, José Antonio Primo de Rivera only finally committed the Falange at the end of June, while the Carlists refused to come on board until July 15. Just before the latter date, an embittered Mola was prepared to throw in the towel, which would mean accepting the fact that an effective revolt could not be organized and possibly having to flee abroad.

The plan for military action also accepted that a direct coup d'état in Madrid would probably not be successful. Other units would have to be concentrated against the capital, and all this would require a week or two of military operations. The plan thus conceived of a "mini"-civil war, but not a long conflict, rather similar to the thinking of the revolutionaries.

The "Exogenous" Thesis

Soon after the conflict began, both sides began to develop the idea that the real cause of the conflict lay abroad. The rebel Nacionales advanced the thesis that Soviet policy and the Comintern were to blame, targeting Spain for a Soviet-style revolution by the end of August. This charge was false, and will be dealt with in chapter 11.

Since Hitler and Mussolini began to provide limited military assistance to the rebels before the end of July, the Republicans soon charged that the military revolt had been conceived in Rome and Berlin to allow the fascists to take over Spain indirectly. This charge was equally false, since Berlin had refused to have anything to do with the conspirators before the revolt. Mussolini had signed an agreement with the monarchists in May 1934 to assist a rightist overthrow of the Republic, but that plan soon fell through and became a dead letter. In the spring of 1936 the Italian leader refused to deal any further with Spanish conspirators, judging their activities to be futile. Limited military assistance for the rebels was only decided in Berlin and Rome between July 25 and 27, when Hitler and Mussolini—both initially surprised by the revolt—judged that the rebels were strong enough to be worth supporting. Stalin, in turn, only decided to provide military assistance to the Republic in mid-September.

The Final Crisis

In retrospect, it seems clear that the final opportunity to avoid civil war came after the murder of Calvo Sotelo on July 13. This magnicide had a traumatic and catalyzing effect on rightist opinion, not merely because of the identity of the victim but even more because of the identity of the murderers and the way in which it was done, which seemed to demonstrate either collusion by the authorities or state security forces completely out of control. Only then did Franco, for example, firmly commit himself to the revolt.

Had Azaña taken the action on July 13 or 14 that he took late on the night of the eighteenth, replacing the Casares Quiroga government with a more moderate and conciliatory administration, the conflict might yet have been avoided. According to the Left Republican Mariano Ansó, Mola even sent an officer to meet with the minister of the interior to learn if the government was now going to change its policy, but such a meeting was denied.

Azaña was urged by some advisors to dismiss Casares Quiroga, but he refused, alleging that any such action would be tantamount to an admission of the government's guilt. But that was the point exactly at issue. Though the government had not authorized the murder, it was responsible for tolerating and even encouraging the climate in the security forces that made so subversive an action possible, and its officials had indeed connived in illegal activities on the night of July 12–13 (as they had many times before), but not in the murder itself. If this culpability could not be recognized and rectified, then it was unlikely that civil war could be avoided.

The government promised an investigation and punishment of the authors of the crime, but that was soon short-circuited. Instead, the government immediately resumed its customary policy of "blaming the victim," the only action taken being to close various rightist centers and carry out arbitrary arrests of some two hundred more rightists, as though they had been responsible for the killing. The government's totally counterproductive response—one of the worst imaginable—only intensified polarization and convinced halfhearted conspirators like Franco that armed revolt was the only alternative. The time had come when it seemed more dangerous not to rebel than to rebel.

After the war began, one of the Left's most bitter criticisms of Casares Quiroga concerned his failure to purge the military and eliminate the danger of revolt. Both Azaña and Casares, however, were following a high-risk strategy of trying to maintain the unity of all the Left (except the anarchists) without falling prey to the revolutionaries. To make this work, it seemed important not to weaken the security forces or the military, who in a crisis might be needed to counterbalance the revolutionaries. Casares was convinced that any military rebellion would be comparatively weak and isolated, and could be crushed by the government. Similarly, he issued strict orders not to "arm the people," even after the military revolt began, for that probably meant handing power to the revolutionaries, something that he was determined to avoid.

Azaña at first agreed. Once it became clear by the night of July 18 that the rebellion was stronger and more widespread than had been anticipated, he did not turn to the revolutionaries but authorized the moderate Left Republican leader Martínez Barrio to form a broader and more moderate Left-center government and also try to conciliate the military, even at the cost of certain concessions to them.

This was the best available solution, but was tried several days too late. The rebel leaders had pledged not to retreat once the revolt began, and rejected the compromise. They believed that Azaña and his colleagues could not be trusted and that the Martínez Barrio government would be too weak to cope with the revolutionaries. Indeed, by the early morning of July 19 there was a vehement demonstration against the compromise government led by the Socialists and also by some of the more radical Left Republicans. Martínez Barrio resigned and almost immediately Azaña appointed a new Left Republican government that began to "arm the people." The final responsibilities thus were those of Azaña for not changing policy immediately after July 13, the determination of the rebels to accept no compromise once the rebellion had begun, and finally the Republican authorities' decision to "arm the people," guaranteeing full-scale civil war.[6]

11 | Moscow and Madrid

A Controversial Relationship

When Hitler invaded the Soviet Union in 1941, Franco's brother-in-law and foreign minister, Ramón Serrano Suñer, delivered a dramatic speech from the balcony of the Falangist headquarters in Madrid: "Russia is guilty! Guilty of having caused our Civil War! Guilty of the death of José Antonio, our founder, and of the deaths of so many comrades and soldiers fallen in that war provoked by Russian Communist aggression! . . . The extermination of Russia is a necessity of history and for the future of Europe!"[1] This expressed graphically the stance of the Movimiento Nacional and the Franco regime, whose official position was that the Soviet Union and its Comintern had instigated the Civil War, and had engaged in military aggression against Spain. The truth, however, was different and much more complex.

In fact, the Communist International, or Comintern, bore comparatively little responsibility for instigating the Civil War. In the final weeks before the conflict its leaders had sought to discipline and in certain ways to moderate the revolutionary Left in order to avoid a cataclysm, even though they encouraged an aggressive Communist policy in parliament. More broadly, Communism had a certain indirect responsibility only to the extent that the era of the Russian Revolution had opened a generation of "European civil war," launching the menace of revolution and counterrevolution that would last through the 1940s.

The Partido Comunista de España (PCE—Communist Party of Spain) was founded by two agents of the Comintern in 1920, with the assistance of young radicals who had broken away from the Socialist Party. For the next sixteen years it was distinguished primarily by its insignificance, failing to establish a significant base. Until 1935 the policy of the Comintern was nonetheless to foment immediate revolution in almost every country in which there was a Communist Party, and to move immediately to "form Soviets." In Spain the Second Republic was rejected as "bourgeois reaction," but the emphasis on immediate revolution proved entirely fruitless.[2]

The policy of the Comintern, and therefore of its underling the PCE, changed drastically in August 1935 with adoption of the tactic of the Popular Front. Communist insistence on immediate violent revolution had isolated the movement and led to a variety of disasters, above all the triumph of Hitler in Germany. Comintern leaders defined the Popular Front as a change in tactics rather than a change in strategy, abandoning the isolationist insistence on immediate revolution in favor of forming electoral alliances with other leftist and even liberal democratic parties, not to install Communism but rather first to "defeat fascism." They declared that the new tactics would ultimately hasten rather than delay revolution.[3]

In Spain this coincided with the new priority of the Left Republicans and the semimoderate sector of the Socialists for an all-Left alliance to win the next elections. Azaña had little desire to include the small revolutionary parties, however, and it was only at the insistence of Largo Caballero and the revolutionary Socialists that the Communists, with their small numbers, were brought in, although the alliance did eventually adopt the Comintern terminology of "Popular Front," somewhat to the distaste of Azaña and the Left Republicans. It was thanks primarily to the assistance of these new allies that the Communists gained seventeen seats in the Cortes elections of 1936. By this time the PCE was growing rapidly for the first time, while the revolutionary sector of the Socialists declared their own goal to be what they called "bolshevization," though their aim was to absorb the Communists rather than vice versa.

In the spring of 1936 the leaders of the Comintern encountered a situation in Spain without any precedent. For fifteen years, down to 1935, the Comintern had preached immediate revolution and had gone from defeat to defeat, usually in isolation. In 1936, after adoption of the electoral alliance of the Popular Front, the Left found itself in power in Spain, and the Communists, though not in the government, were allied with a leftist administration, something that had never happened before. As Hitler's rearmament continued, Stalin sought to reduce the fear of Communist revolution in Europe so as to gain allies against Germany. The first victory of this new tactic had occurred in Spain (even though Spain had not been the primary objective), and for the first time allies of the revolutionary Left were in power in a large European country. If the latter played their cards right, the new tactic might make it possible to achieve the preliminary goals of revolution by legal and parliamentary means, a totally unprecedented situation. Thus the Comintern sent instructions to the PCE between April and July 1936 to work to moderate the more extreme and violent actions of the revolutionaries, whether anarchist or Socialist. Whereas for fifteen years the Comintern had done virtually nothing but preach revolutionary civil war, in Spain it sought to avert the civil war that was looming, for the latter could open a Pandora's box that might ruin what was suddenly, for the Comintern, the most promising political process in any country in the world.

Nonetheless, the program, propaganda, and activities of the PCE in Spain during the months before the Civil War were far from being either "moderate" or "counterrevolutionary," as the extreme revolutionary Left and some historians would later claim. Comintern policy directed the PCE to champion a policy of "legal radicalization," making use of the Left's complete domination of parliament to go much farther than the program of Azaña and Casares Quiroga. Communist tactics sought to avoid unnecessary violence and extremist strikes but encouraged widespread legal confiscation of property, strong state censorship, falsification of new elections, and making illegal all the conservative and rightist political organizations, all this in order to create a complete monopoly for the Left. Through semilegal means this would transform the Spanish system into a new all-Left Republic, a "people's republic," which would for a time remain semipluralist, but only for leftist groups. In the Comintern scheme of things, at some future date the all-Leftist Republic was to give way to a "Worker-Peasant Government," which in turn would then create conditions, in the final phase of a three-step process, for a Communist regime. That, of course, would lie at some undetermined point in the future. Whether or not such a scheme would ever be workable, the Spanish Communists, thanks to Comintern tutelage, had the only coherent strategy of any of the revolutionary movements in Spain, though in immediate tactics they were not the most extreme. Nothing so clear-cut would be found in the planning (if one can call it that) of the two large movements, the anarchosyndicalists of the CNT and the revolutionary Socialists.

The Communists concentrated their activity and propaganda especially in the capital, as Lenin had earlier done in Russia, and the sight of thousands of uniformed Socialists and Communists marching in Madrid with banners hailing the Soviet Union—the young women chanting the scandalous slogan "Children yes, husbands no!"—gave frightened conservatives a greatly exaggerated notion of the power and numbers of the Communists. In April they had managed to take control of a merged Juventudes Socialistas Unificadas (JSU—United Socialist Youth) and by the end of June 1936 claimed to have 100,000 party members in Spain, but that was probably an exaggeration. Even so, if the real figure was only half that, it was equivalent in proportionate terms to the numbers of the Bolshevik Party in Russia in November 1917. The difference, of course, was that Spanish society was politically much more diverse and more mobilized than that of Russia.

Comintern leaders in Moscow feared outbreak of civil war in Spain, which they thought might come either from a military revolt or another premature anarchist insurrection that would play into the hands of the Right. After the military insurrection began, they were appalled by the violent outbreak of revolution that followed the "arming of the people" in the Republican zone, and immediately outlined a program that insisted on complete unity of the Left, moderation of the revolution, and total priority for the military effort, abandoning the multiparty revolutionary militia in favor of a disciplined new "Ejército Popular" (People's Army), modeled on the Red Army that had won the Russian civil war of 1918–20.[4]

Stalin decided on direct military intervention in the Spanish conflict after only two months, in mid-September. He had first to determine whether the Spanish Left was capable of sufficient unity to make a realistic effort at winning, and the formation of an all-Popular Front government under Largo Caballero apparently convinced him of that. Soviet intervention advanced incrementally, through a series of steps. Economic assistance was provided by the Soviet trade unions early in August, and formal diplomatic relations were then established with the Republic for the first time, Soviet diplomats arriving late in the month. Next, a small number of Soviet aviators came as "volunteers" to fly in the Republican air force, and the decision to send major Soviet military support was finally taken in mid-September, the first Soviet arms arriving at the close of the month, with major shipments arriving before the end of October.

Altogether, Soviet military assistance was substantial, amounting to 5,000 trucks, 800 warplanes, 330 tanks, and sizable numbers of artillery, machine guns, and rifles. In addition, nearly 250 fighter planes were manufactured according to Soviet specifications in the Republican zone. Conversely, the number of Soviet military personnel sent to Spain was very limited, somewhere between 2,000 and 3,000, of whom few more than 200 were killed. None of them were simply soldiers, since all the Soviet personnel consisted either of airplane or tank crews, technicians, or higher-level advisors. In addition, the Soviet and Comintern network assisted in large-scale acquisition of arms and other supplies on the international market.[5]

All this was paid for after the Republican government shipped most of the gold reserve of the Bank of Spain (fourth largest in the world), amounting to more than $600 million, to Moscow at the close of October 1936. Leaders of the Republican government contended that the Non-Intervention Policy of the Western powers left them with no major source of military supply other than the Soviet Union, and the latter in turn periodically converted varying amounts of the Spanish reserve into rubles or other foreign exchange to pay for shipments, until by 1938 it declared that the entire gold supply had been exhausted. During the final year of the war some $200 million in credits were extended to the Republican government to cover the last shipments of arms.

In addition, the Comintern organized in the autumn of 1936 the famous "International Brigades" of volunteers to assist the Republican army. Most of the volunteers were Communists, and until September 1937 the Brigades were not formally integrated into the structure of the Republican forces. Though their numbers were relatively limited (amounting to no more than 42,000 men, compared with the more than a million men mobilized by the Republican forces in Spain), they played an important role in key battles between the autumn of 1936 and the summer of 1938.

The Comintern was also extremely active in the propaganda war, but the Communist line was carefully differentiated according to three different levels of discourse. On the international level, it completely denied the existence of any revolution in Spain, insisting that the struggle was simply one of fascism versus democracy, the Republic merely representing parliamentary democracy, as in "France, England, or the United States." Within the Republican zone, the Communist line championed the wartime Republic as the first European "people's republic," not a Communist regime, which needed to discipline and channel the extremism of the anarchists and others. In Catalonia the line was slightly different, as the new Partit Socialist Unificat de Catalunya (PSUC—United Socialist Party of Catalonia) had to contest the hegemony of the CNT and declared itself the "partit únic bolxevic revolucionari de Catalunya" (sole Bolshevik revolutionary party of Catalonia), the only force capable of leading a victorious revolution, carefully disciplined and channeled.

Within the Soviet Union, no effort was made to conceal the revolutionary character of the Spanish conflict, officially defined as the "Spanish national-revolutionary war." This Soviet definition held that it was simultaneously a Spanish war of national liberation from Germany and Italy, and a revolutionary struggle of emancipation and dominance for the popular classes of Spain. This formula subsequently became official in Soviet historiography, and to some extent is repeated in historical accounts in Russian to this day. It was also officially adopted by the writers and propagandists of the PCE, who continued to employ the same formula until the final years of the Franco regime.

During the Civil War, the PCE became a mass organization for the first time, by early 1937 swelling to more than a quarter million members. More than any other group, the Communists preached the priority of military strength and winning the war, and soon gained a disproportionate number of command positions in the Ejército Popular, which adopted the Soviet red star as insignia, the German Communist clenched fist as military salute, and the Soviet system of political commissars to maintain loyalty and morale.

Even before the war began, the Comintern had specified that the goal of the Popular Front would be, depending on possibilities, the establishment of a new-style "people's republic," the first regime of this kind having been introduced by the Soviets in conquered Mongolia in 1924. The people's republic was not a Communist regime but an "advanced middle-class parliamentary republic" that, in the theory of the Comintern, would prepare a later transition to Communism as the conclusion of a three-step process. Communist spokesmen officially designated the new revolutionary republic of the war years as people's republic in March 1937, but this concept was never accepted by the other leftist parties. The type of economic structure appropriate for such a regime, the Communists said, was not the sweeping revolutionary collectivism inaugurated by the anarchists and the rest of the extreme revolutionary Left in Spain, but the New Economic Policy (NEP) established in the Soviet Union in 1921, which stipulated a mixed economy based mostly on private property, with only major industry nationalized by the state. According to the Communists, another priority was to win the lower-middle classes to the support of the Republic, possible only under their policy but not under the policy of the extreme revolutionary Left. Communist spokesmen vehemently denied that this involved "counterrevolution," as the latter constantly charged, insisting that only a carefully channeled and limited revolution was possible so long as the war lasted. Within the Republican zone, Communists stressed that a people's republic was completely different from a bourgeois, capitalist republic, since decisive political, military, and economic power was no longer in the hands of the bourgeoisie.[6]

Communist military and political influence increased steadily during the first year of the war, and then expanded further after Largo Caballero was replaced by the Socialist Juan Negrín as prime minister in May 1937. Contrary to what was later charged by many critics, Negrín had not been handpicked by the Communists, but was chosen by the semimoderate sector of the Socialists (to which he belonged) and by Manuel Azaña, president of the Republic. He was more a pragmatist than a revolutionary but believed strongly in a Socialist Spain that must at all costs win the war. Negrín seems to have been convinced that if Franco won the war, Hitler and Mussolini would take over Spain. He never became a mere stooge or puppet of the Communists, but he cooperated very broadly with them, especially in military affairs, because they provided the strongest military support and because he considered continued Soviet assistance indispensable to winning the war.[7] Communist influence reached its height in 1938, achieving a position of partial hegemony in Republican affairs, but at no time did it completely control the Republican government or army. By the last months of 1938, this partial hegemony produced ever greater resentment among the non-Communist forces, until by the first part of 1939 the Communists, though still powerful, found themselves with few allies outside the prime minister and part of the army.

Stalin, in turn, began to lose hope for Republican victory, and during the late spring and summer of 1938 Soviet diplomats signaled to their counterparts in Germany and other countries that the Soviet Union might be willing to terminate support for the Republic so long as Hitler and Mussolini ended their support for Franco. The Axis leaders, however, were not interested in such a deal, and Stalin therefore could find no "exit strategy" from Spain.

Non-Communist Republicans would later charge for many years that in the end Stalin simply "abandoned" the Republic, while trying to leave the non-Communists stigmatized with responsibility for the defeat. Available evidence suggests the contrary. A final large shipment of Soviet arms began to enter Catalonia in the last days of 1938, though Franco overran the region before the deliveries were complete. Hours before the coup d'état against Negrín led by Col. Segismundo Casado in Madrid on March 6, the last words from Moscow urged the Communists and other Republicans to resist to the last. Soviet policy only changed in August 1939, when Stalin signed his pact with Hitler, opening the way for the start of the Second World War in Europe.

Subsequently one of the few things on which the spokesmen of the extreme revolutionary left and the Franco regime could agree was that the Communists had controlled the Negrín government, creating the first example of the kind of people's republics imposed by the Soviets after 1945 on the lands that they occupied in eastern Europe. Leading figures of the Spanish Communist Party in exile, such as Dolores Ibárruri ("Pasionaria"), claimed the same thing. Such rare unanimity might be thought evidence of accuracy in this assertion, but was that really the case?

In fact, the revolutionary wartime Republic in Spain might be called a people's republic of sorts, in so far as it was an all-leftist regime from which democratic liberals and conservatives had been excluded, but it was not the same sort of regime as the ones established in eastern Europe. In Republican Spain, Communist influence became partially hegemonic, but it was by no means completely dominant. Important areas of the government, the armed forces, and the economy always lay outside Communist control. The east European people's republics languished under total Soviet military occupation for many years, and Communists completely controlled their governments, armed forces, security forces and economies. This went well beyond the situation in Republican Spain.

The Communist influence that existed in Spain was extensive enough that it aroused mounting resentment and opposition among the other leftist parties, all the more since by the end of 1938 there seemed little chance of winning the war. Thus, paradoxically, the Spanish Civil War ended the way it had begun, with a revolt by sectors of the Republican army against the existing Republican government, alleging that the latter had succumbed to Communist domination.

Whereas thousands of Communists around the world were shocked by the Hitler-Stalin Pact, this seems to have offended Spanish Communists considerably less, angry as they were with the Western democracies for having failed to support the anti-Fascists in Spain. For the next two years, Soviet and Comintern policy was oriented against Britain and France, the enemies of Stalin's associate Hitler, who were condemned as capitalist, imperialist, and militarist. London and Paris, rather than Berlin and Moscow, were blamed for the war in Europe. This abruptly changed in June 1941, when Germany invaded the Soviet Union. Spanish Communists were then instructed to create a broad national front, even including conservatives, against Franco. This proved impossible, because the other leftist and republican parties remained hostile to the Communists, to the extent that during the first years after the Civil War, the Spanish Left in general were more anticommunist than leftist forces in any other Western country. Only toward the end of World War II was it possible to rebuild a general alliance against Franco in which the Communists were included.

In general, Stalin and Franco followed curiously symmetrical policies during the first half of the world war. Each began the war as technically neutral, but both were strongly tilted toward Berlin, even though Hitler's relationship with Stalin made Franco nervous and was not approved of in Madrid. What was similar was that both Stalin and Franco hoped to achieve territorial expansion in the shadow of Hitler with only limited military activities of their own. During 1939–40 Stalin occupied large areas in eastern Europe, in only one case with hard fighting, while Franco later hoped to do much the same in northwest Africa and southwestern Europe. Hitler's subsequent invasion of the Soviet Union generated intense enthusiasm in Madrid, though Franco was careful not to accompany the dispatch of the Blue Division ("División Azul," after the blue shirts of the Falangists' uniform) to the Russian front with an official declaration of war. Stalin took much the same approach. A full Spanish division fought for two years against the Red Army (while 3,000 Spanish Communists fought with the Red Army), but Stalin chose not to complicate natters further by officially declaring war on Spain. Given the enormous dimensions of combat on the eastern front, one single Spanish division was not that important.

This did not mean, however, that Stalin intended to ignore Franco. During 1936–37 he had paid close attention to events in Spain and to the Soviet intervention, though subsequently it became less of a priority for him. At Potsdam in 1945 he denounced five neutral or non-belligerent governments, which he claimed had aided Hitler—those of Spain, Turkey, Sweden, Switzerland, and Argentina—and urged the Allies to take action against them. Although the Western powers rejected military intervention, Spanish Communists initiated a guerrilla war against the Franco regime in October 1944, with an invasion from France through the Vall d'Aran. Anarchosyndicalists later participated in their own smaller insurgency, while the Communists persisted in armed action until 1952, though after 1949 this amounted to very little. The attempted insurgency, raising the specter of violent revolution once more, probably strengthened rather than weakened the Spanish regime, and at no time threatened its stability.

Stalin's animosity did not lessen during the later years of his life. Soviet contingency plans for a major war in Europe envisioned a sizable amphibious invasion of the Iberian Peninsula, but in fact the Soviet armed forces probably never had the means for such an ambitious undertaking. Relations between Madrid and Moscow only began slowly to normalize in 1956, three years after Stalin's death, when the Spanish regime was admitted to the United Nations as part of a broad international compromise. Six years later, the most intense phase of the Cold War came to an end, and relations gradually improved during the 1960s, full diplomatic relations being restored after the death of Franco.

In the 1970s the Spanish Communists, by that time largely independent of Moscow, moved toward a kind of democratic reformism. They were never able to restore an effective alliance with the Socialists beyond the municipal level, but the two main leftist parties of Spain's democratic transition agreed for a number of years on a more neutral position in the Cold War and on opposition to joining NATO, reflecting much of Spanish public opinion, seeking to avoid commitment in the international affairs of the day. At one point this brought Moscow's special commendation of Felipe González and the Socialist policy, but that also marked the final phase of the classic Spanish Left, as the Socialists soon moved toward a more pragmatic stance.

That Spain was undergoing a definitive move toward the Left-center (and Right-center) was nonetheless not so clear to the Soviet leadership during the very last years of Soviet expansionism. Following the disastrous defeat of Carrillo in the decisive Spanish elections of 1982, the Soviet government, counseled by its "Iberian specialist," Vladimir Pertsov, invested more than a little money in Spain in a vain effort to revive an orthodox Soviet-style Communist Party.[8] This effort was unsuccessful, and by the end of the decade it was the Soviet Union, not capitalism or democratic Spain, that was collapsing, ending the long political relationship with Spanish Communism initiated seven decades earlier.

12 | The Spanish Civil War

Last Episode of World War I or
Opening Round of World War II?

D uring the Civil War the Republicans developed a discourse that identified Italy and Germany as the real source of the conflict, which they often called an international struggle against fascism. The Nacionales, in turn, called their effort part of an international struggle against Communism. In 1938 the negrinista slogan "Resistir es vencer" (To resist is to win) was predicated on continuing the war in Spain until it became part of a larger conflict in which Britain and France, once they were at war with Germany, would supposedly help the Republic to achieve victory. As soon as the Second World War began in Europe, Republicans in exile declared that their own war had constituted the "opening round," "first shot," or "prelude" to the greater European war. This later became the theme of several scholarly studies, such as Patricia van der Esch's *Prelude to War: The International Repercussions of the Spanish Civil War* (1951).

Franco, conversely (and much to the disgust of Hitler), officially announced the neutrality of his government in any broader European war at the time of the Munich crisis in September 1938. Though he remained close to the Axis dictators and signed agreements with them in the months between the Spanish war and the European conflict, as soon as the latter began he once more proclaimed Spain's neutrality. This changed with the imminent fall of France in June 1940, when Franco announced his regime's status of "non-belligerence," something not recognized by international law but invented less than a year earlier by Mussolini to indicate a policy in which his country would not enter the fighting yet in its sympathies and actions tilted toward Germany. "Non-belligerence" was thus a kind of pre-belligerence. From June 1940 through the spring of 1941, at least, Franco indicated that he was willing to enter the war against Great Britain on the side of Germany so long as Hitler guaranteed major economic and military assistance, and large territorial concessions—all of which Hitler refused to do. In the meantime, Franco and his associates declared on various public occasions, and also in their private conversations with Axis leaders and diplomats, that they considered the Spanish conflict the first part of the greater European war, which was its continuation. Even though Franco stopped saying such things in 1942, for a time he seemed to agree with the Republicans. Was, therefore, their common contention not correct?

In one obvious sense, the answer has to be no. The Spanish war was a clear-cut revolutionary-counterrevolutionary contest between Left and Right, with the fascist totalitarian powers supporting the Right and the Soviet totalitarian power supporting the Left. World War II, on the other hand, only began in Europe when a pan-totalitarian entente was formed by the Nazi-Soviet Pact with the aim of allowing the Soviet Union to conquer a sizable swathe of eastern Europe while Germany was left free to conquer as much of the rest of the Continent as it could. This was a complete reversal of the terms of the Spanish war.

The formula might be reversed, with the conclusion that the Spanish Revolution and the Civil War constituted the last of the revolutionary crises stemming from World War I. Just as the military characteristics and weaponry of the Spanish war sometimes resembled those of World War I as much as those of World War II, so the Spanish situation had more characteristics of a post–World War I revolutionary crisis than of a domestic crisis of the World War II era. Among these characteristics were (1) the complete breakdown of institutions, as distinct from the direct coup d'états and legalitarian impositions of authoritarianism more typical of the era of World War II; (2) the development of a full-scale revolutionary/ counterrevolutionary civil war, a relatively broad phenomenon after World War I, but elsewhere unheard of during the 1930s and appearing only in Greece and Yugoslavia during and after World War II; (3) development of a typical post–World War I Red Army in the form of the Republican People's Army; (4) an extreme exacerbation of nationalism in the National zone (and in two regions of the Republican zone), again more typical of World War I and its aftermath than of World

War II; (5) frequent use of World War I–style military matériel and concepts; and (6) the fact that it was not the product of any plan or initiative by the major powers, and in that sense resembled post–World War I crises more than those of World War II. Similarly, the extreme revolutionary Left both inside and outside Spain hailed the Spanish revolution as the latest and one of the greatest, if not indeed, the greatest, of the revolutionary upsurges of the post–World War I era.

It was negotiation of the Hitler-Stalin Pact, rather than the Soviet intervention in Spain, that obeyed the Soviet doctrine of promoting and profiting from the "second imperialist war," the Soviet term since the mid-1920s for the next great European war, an orientation that long antedated the rise of Hitler. According to this doctrine, the Soviet Union should not discourage war among imperialist capitalist powers so long as it could avoid involvement, for war would weaken the major capitalist states. The Soviet Union was to strengthen itself as much as possible and then be prepared to enter the war at the decisive moment to determine its final outcome in order to advance Communism. To a degree, that was the way that the Second World War worked out in the long run, but in 1935 Stalin had been so alarmed and frustrated by the threat of German aggression targeting the Soviet Union that he had turned instead to a policy of collective security, which sought cooperation between the Soviet Union and the Western democracies against Nazi Germany, reversing the Soviet position. Intervention in Spain was supposed to complement collective security, but in fact it failed to do so. Only after the failure of both that policy and of intervention was Stalin able subsequently to establish through the Nazi-Soviet Pact, the terms which were supposed to guide Soviet policy toward the next great European war.

In September 1939 the Comintern Executive Committee then dutifully launched the slogan that the new war between Germany and the Western democracies was an "imperialist war" in which Communists should not be involved (though, like Franco, to some extent they should tilt toward Germany). The new war would benefit them by hastening the day of revolution. Members of the PCE were less disturbed by the Nazi-Soviet Pact than were those in most Communist parties, for the Spanish war left them with a great sense of bitterness toward Britain and France, which they were now happy to leave to fight Germany alone. The diary of Georgi Dimitrov, the Comintern secretary, for September 7, 1939, quotes Stalin as saying to him: "It wouldn't be bad if the position of the wealthier capitalist states (especially England) were undermined at Germany's hands. Hitler, not understanding and not wishing this himself, is weakening and undermining the capitalist system. . . . We can maneuver, support one side against the other so they can tear each other up all the better." With regard to Hitler's first victim, Poland, it was just another "fascist state," whose destruction by Germany was welcome. "The destruction of this state in the present circumstances would mean one less bourgeois fascist state! It wouldn't be bad if, as a result of the crushing of Poland, we extended the socialist system to new territories and populations."[1] Later in the month a Comintern circular went out explaining that "all efforts to kindle a world revolution have so far been unsuccessful. What are the natural prerequisites of a revolution? A prolonged war, as expounded in the writings of Marx, Engels, and Lenin. What, therefore, must the attitude of the USSR be to hasten a world revolution? To assist Germany in a sufficient degree so that she will begin a war and to take measures to insure that this war will drag on."[2]

Meanwhile Franco never formally entered World War II. Some historians have therefore denied the Spanish conflict any significant effect on broader international affairs. Pierre Renouvin judged its consequences to be merely "modest," saying that "it would be an exaggeration to see in this war a 'prelude to a European war.'"[3] In his *Origins of the Second World War* (1961), A. J. P. Taylor calculated that the Spanish conflict had no "significant effect" on the great powers. The author of *The Origins of the Second World War in Europe* (1986), P. M. H. Bell, concluded that the Spanish war was simply "mucho ado about nothing" as far as broader events were concerned.[4]

This conclusion, however, is too simple and reductionist. For Hitler, the Spanish war in fact served several purposes, of which the two most important were the strategic and the diversionary. He intervened to avoid the development of a leftist Spanish regime that would be friendly to France and the Soviet Union, while weakening the strategic position of Italy. Victory by Franco would neatly reverse that situation, potentially catching France between two fires, while strengthening the position of Italy. Equally or more important, the Spanish war served as a major diversion or distraction, shifting the attention of the Western powers away from German rearmament and expansion. Thus by the end of 1936 Hitler was particularly concerned that the Spanish war continue for some time, serving this purpose of diversion through 1937 and even into 1938. In addition, it had the added advantage of dividing the French internally, and for a while Hitler even hoped that civil war might break out north of the Pyrenees. Finally, it brought Italy and Germany closer together, while worsening Italian relations with Britain and France.

Of the three dictators, the one most concerned with the Spanish conflict was not Hitler or Stalin but Mussolini. Of the three governments that intervened, only Italy was a Mediterranean power, so that the outcome in Spain vitally affected its strategic position. Only for Mussolini was victory in the Spanish war an absolutely vital interest. Thus Italy contributed significantly more than Germany to arming and assisting Franco's forces, and invested a much higher proportion of Italy's limited military resources in this endeavor than did either Germany or the Soviet Union on opposing sides. This continued to such an extent that it left Italy in a slightly weakened position militarily by 1939, even though that probably was not a major factor in the continuous military defeats it later suffered. Moreover, Mussolini's large-scale intervention began to bind him closer and closer to Hitler and generated increasing hostility with Britain and France (all of which benefited Germany more than Italy).[5]

After the fall of France, Franco was quite interested in entering the war on Hitler's side, provided that the latter was willing to concede the rather steep terms that Franco wished to exact. Moreover, in the following year Germany's invasion of the Soviet Union aroused great enthusiasm in Madrid. Whereas Franco had been taken aback by Hitler's destruction of a Catholic authoritarian regime in Warsaw, which had been somewhat similar to and also sympathetic to the new Spanish state, Hitler's war seemed to make perfect sense by mid-1941, since the Franco regime considered the Soviet Union its prime enemy. Franco agreed fully with his Republican foes, publicly declaring that the broader European war was simply a continuation of the counterrevolutionary, anti-Soviet struggle begun by the revolt of the Nacionales in Spain. From June 1940 to October 1943—that is, for the greater part of the entire European war—the Franco regime was officially "non-belligerent," not "neutral," with an official tilt toward the Axis.

All of Hitler's major associates during the war in Europe sought to create their own "parallel empires" in the shadow of Hitler's conquests. The first was Stalin, who used the Nazi-Soviet Pact to conquer sizable new territories in eastern Europe during 1939–40. Next was Mussolini, who endeavored to wage his own "guerra parallela" to carve out a great new Italian empire in Africa, the Middle East, and Greece. Hitler then awarded Hungary a major expansion of its territory in 1940, and Romania sought compensation by conquering the southwest Ukraine as Germany's ally in 1941.

Ironically, Franco sought to emulate Stalin more than Mussolini or the rulers of Hungary and Romania, for he hoped to achieve significant territorial expansion with comparatively little fighting, as the Soviet Union had attempted to do in eastern Europe. He nonetheless insisted on stiff terms before Spain would formally enter the war, requiring massive military and economic assistance, and the cession to Spain of all Morocco, northwest Algeria, and a large chunk of French West Africa. For roughly two years, from August 1940 to the summer of 1942, Hitler sought to obtain Spain's entry into the war, but he always refused to grant Franco's terms, which would have had the effect of alienating the satellite Vichy regime in France, whose cooperation was very important to Germany, both strategically and economically. The Spanish Blue Division fought for two full years with the Wehrmacht on the eastern front, subsequently generating by far the most extensive literature of any division in any army in the entire Second World War.[6] Franco, however, was never willing to run the risk of entering the war directly. From the middle of 1942, especially, he grew increasingly reluctant and apprehensive, though his return to neutrality came much too late to avoid tarring his regime with the "Axis stigma," leading to international ostracism for a number of years once the war was over.[7]

All the while Stalin had been too Machiavellian for his own good. By assisting Hitler during his war against France and Britain, he facilitated Germany's stunning victory over France, which then placed Hitler in a position the following year to launch a devastating one-front war that came very close to destroying the Soviet Union.

Stalin was saved by Hitler's gratuitous and self-destructive act of joining Japan's assault against the United States. By doing so, Hitler encouraged the conditions that enabled the Soviet Union eventually to achieve a complete victory in eastern Europe. This created a large new Soviet empire of "people's republics," which were much more totalitarian than anything that had existed in semipluralist Republican Spain of the war years, transforming the Soviet Union into a superpower. The war worked out almost as well for the USSR as Stalin had ever hoped, even though it was the most destructive in history, costing the lives of nearly 30 million Soviet citizens.

In December 1941 an international alliance was created, primarily through the recklessness of Japan and Germany, one that was politically much broader than the Popular Front in Spain, since it also included conservative capitalist society in the United States, Great Britain, and other countries. Did not the Spanish war foreshadow this development? Not really, for the Spanish Republic represented only the forces of the Left, whereas the broad alliance of 1941–45 included the equivalent of many of the forces on Franco's side during the Spanish war. If Hitler had only had to fight the forces of the Left, he would have won his war decisively. Neither the European war of 1939–41 nor the truly world war of 1941–45 merely replicated the Spanish conflict.

Even though the Spanish war was no mere "prelude" or "opening round" of World War II in Europe, it contributed significantly to the terms in which the European war developed. Without directly linking the Spanish war and World War II, historians often advance the argument that the Spanish conflict contributed significantly to the perceptions and psychology that precipitated the greater combat. Thus it has not infrequently been contended that the behavior of Britain and France vis-à-vis the Spanish war stimulated the false perception by Hitler and Mussolini that the Western democracies lacked the will to fight, and therefore would not respond to much bolder military actions by the fascist powers. In this interpretation, the Spanish war would not be a unique prelude but simply the longest in a series of crises in which those powers acted aggressively and the democracies passively: Ethiopia (1935), the Rhineland (1936), Spain (1936–39), Austria (1938), the Sudetenland (1938).

Hitler's policy of using and prolonging the Spanish conflict as a grand international distraction to deflect attention from his own rearmament and expansion was generally successful. On the one hand, he exploited the complications arising from the Spanish war as an excuse to avoid any broader understanding with Britain and France. On the other, he calculated successfully that the continuation of this war would serve to divide France internally and distract it from focusing exclusively on Germany during the period (1936–38) when German rearmament had still not proceeded far enough to achieve parity.

The Spanish war also provided immediate incentive for the beginning of the Italo-German entente that Hitler had always sought. Mussolini became primarily committed to the Spanish struggle, which deprived Italian policy of freedom of maneuver and tied it increasingly to a Germany that became the dominant partner and exercised the major new initiatives, all the time progressively burning Italy's bridges to Britain and France. It was this Italian realignment that made it possible for Hitler to incorporate Austria as early as March 1938, while also making it more feasible for Hitler to move rapidly against Czechoslovakia.

From this perspective it was not that Britain and France ignored the Spanish war but indeed sometimes dedicated almost as much attention to it as to Austria and Czechoslovakia. As Willard Frank has observed, "Even in 1938, the year of Munich, British MPs asked almost half again as many parliamentary questions about Spain and the Mediterranean as about Germany and central Europe. . . . The French Chamber of Deputies had to suspend its deliberations twice in one day for fear of a free-for-all fight over the Spanish question."[8]

The Spanish issue significantly divided France internally, while complicating and disorienting broader policy. One result was to bring France to defer more and more to British decision-making, so that British initiatives became dominant in the alliance of the two democracies.

The Italian and German intervention in Spain elicited a Soviet counterintervention that Stalin would not expand sufficiently to achieve Republican victory, partly for fear of the international consequences of too strong an intervention. For Germany this had the benefit of intensifying the democracies' suspicion of and alienation from the revolutionary Soviet Union. To the French general staff, this only confirmed its conviction that the goal of Soviet policy was to provoke war among the Western powers. The more Stalin intervened in Spain and the more active the role of the Soviet Union in the Non-Intervention Committee, the less likely was any rapprochement between Paris and Moscow against Berlin. Soviet policy proved counterproductive, except for the gains in espionage made by the NKVD. The Soviet Union was more isolated in April 1939 than in July 1936. Hitler largely outsmarted Stalin, as he would do the second time during 1939–41, until he made the absurdly fatal mistake of trying to make war on the two largest powers in the world at the same time.

The outbreak of the European war in no way depended on the Spanish conflict and would undoubtedly have taken place even if there had been no war in Spain, but the ramifications of the latter helped to determine the pace and timing of broader European affairs. Without the complications arising from Spain, the Western democracies might have taken a stronger stand against Hitler, and conceivably Mussolini might have delayed or even avoided an entente with the latter. Similarly, without these complications and distractions, Hitler would not have been able to move as rapidly as he did in 1938.

Yet this scenario can also to some extent be reversed. A Republic without civil war and dominated exclusively by the Left, functioning as the most leftist regime in western Europe, would also have been a complicating factor, but not to the same extent as the Civil War was.

Later, after the conclusion of World War II, the myth of the "Spanish national-revolutionary war" was sometimes invoked in the establishment of the new Soviet people's republics in Eastern Europe. It served as a beacon for the possibilities of revolution in the West, and Communist veterans of the International Brigades played important roles in the development of the new totalitarian regimes, particularly in military and security affairs. This myth achieved special importance in the German Democratic Republic, serving as a major reference for a Western revolutionary antifascism.[9]

The counterfactual question may be raised of the historical consequences had the Republic somehow won the Civil War. Such an outcome would not absolutely have been guaranteed by continuation of the war into September 1939, because French strategy had become so defensive that war with Germany might rather have dissuaded it from, rather than encouraging, any intervention in Spain. The outcome might simply have depended on the intrapeninsular balance of power at that time, presumably still quite unfavorable to the Republic.

On the one hand, had the Negrín government won the Civil War, it would have been strongly allied with the Soviet Union, as Negrín had promised Stalin. But on the other, Republican victory would also have posed the question of the future of the Republic itself, and that might have lessened dependency on the Soviet Union. Furthermore, the broader European war would have reduced Soviet assistance, thus limiting Communist influence. The same confrontation as in March 1939, though in a somewhat different form, might then have taken place following a Republican victory. A victorious Republic might have been crippled by its internal contradictions and its severe economic problems, which would have been as bad as those of the early Franco regime, or even worse. Its policy during the European war might have mirrored that of Franco in reverse: neutrality, though with a tilt toward Hitler's enemies.

Another possibility to be considered is that a victorious leftist Spain would have continued to play a role as a distraction and limitation on French policy. This might so have preoccupied the Western democracies in their concern about the expansion of Soviet influence that they would even have acquiesced in Hitler's conquest of Poland as a check on that influence. That in turn might have hastened conflict between Hitler and Stalin.[10]

If, conversely, the European war had proceeded as it did, would a victorious Hitler and Mussolini in 1940 then have felt the need to invade a Republican Spain? This might have been Mussolini's preference, but two alternative scenarios have to be considered. Hitler might have preferred to avoid further entanglement, leaving Italy to neutralize Spain, trying to force a leftist Republic to subordinate its policy to that of the Axis.

Or Hitler might have judged an independent leftist Spain as something intolerable, proceeding to its destruction before turning on the Soviet Union. Yet the latter alternative would have involved Hitler in the "Southern Strategy" urged by his naval commanders in the autumn of 1940, a fuller commitment to developing Germany's strategic position in the Mediterranean. This would have violated Hitler's own priorities, delaying any attack on the Soviet Union, but, if pressed to its ultimate potential, with a German conquest of North Africa and the Middle East, this might have built for Germany a very powerful strategic base, with incalculable consequences for the future.

Yet another hypothetical scenario might be constructed in which a Republican Spain might have survived the European war as a neutral, though with a foreign policy quite different from that of the Franco regime, even if potentially adopting a "Swedish" policy of accommodating a dominant Germany, just as the Social Democratic government did in Stockholm. This would have made reasonable geopolitical sense in the short term, since it is difficult to define any scenario in which it would have been practical for Spain to intervene in the broader war unless directly invaded.

Spain would always have functioned as part of a peripheral rather than a core strategy by any of the great powers, potentially important only to the extent that its own engagement, or engagement with it by others, would contribute to much broader designs, and to the extent that its geographical location held the key to a larger strategic breakthrough. Its logical position in both world wars was neutrality, whatever importance it had being broadly strategic much more than narrowly economic or military. Stalin was temporarily interested in Spain as part of a complex, multidimensioned grand strategy, which turned out to be too complex and contradictory to carry out.

Hitler's interest in Spain was also strategic, but equally secondary, until the problem of exerting greater strategic pressure against Great Britain acquired significance in the summer of 1940. Even then, it never became such a prime objective that he was ever willing to meet Franco's price. After that, Hitler grew increasingly disgusted with Franco, whom he came to view as a cynical and unprincipled opportunist, calling him a "Latin charlatan" who was shockingly ungrateful for Germany's military assistance and hopelessly shortsighted in thinking that his regime could possibly survive a German defeat. He later opined that "during the civil war, the idealism was not on Franco's side; it was to be found among the Reds." Like many other observers, he thought Franco politically incompetent. Hitler believed that Franco's "reactionary" government would inevitably fail, leading to another civil war, and when that came, the Führer said, the next time he would support the Spanish "Reds."

During 1943 both sides asked the same thing of the Spanish government: that it stay out of the war and not favor the other side.[11] By 1944, when the Allies had gained the upper hand, Washington began to pressure the Spanish regime more than Berlin ever had. Franco reluctantly made most of the concessions required, but he never went farther than he was forced to. By the time the war ended, he had formulated a new political strategy that would enable his regime to survive, and for some time to prosper, in a postfascist world.

13 | Spanish Fascism . . . a Strange Case?

In 1997, when I published a new history of the fascist movement in Spain, I added to the Spanish edition the subtitle "The Strange Case of Spanish Fascism." At the presentation of the book, one journalist asked, "Why strange?"—a perfectly reasonable question. In history, of course, every case is in some sense unique. Moreover, fascist movements were more "national" and idiosyncratic in almost every instance than were the different national Communist parties. There was no fascist international equivalent to the Comintern, no single international center and orthodoxy such as that provided by the Soviet Union, no single bible of fascism equivalent to the writings of Marx and Lenin. The writings of Mussolini and Hitler were less systematic and did not serve the same function.

The Spanish case was "strange" first because it was one of the latest and weakest of all the national fascist movements, for five years even weaker than fascist movements in north European democracies. It was also peculiar in that it achieved power of a very limited sort as the state party in 1937. This was unusual, because fascist movements overwhelmingly failed; the only other fascist movements to reach power were those of Italy, Germany, and Romania (the latter briefly in a kind of diarchy with the military dictator Antonescu in 1940–41).[1] Moreover, in a purely formal sense it retained its limited share of state power long after the end of the fascist era, until the death of Franco. This was totally without precedent, even though the survival of the Falangist movement was predicated on a long, slow process of defascistization—another paradox. It was also the only fascist movement to undergo ideological defascistization, the original "official" Twenty-Six Points being replaced by the defascistized Principles of the Movement (1958), another change without precedent or parallel.

Prior to 1936 Spain was an unlikely candidate for fascism, as was recognized by, for example, the country's two leading revolutionary Marxist intellectuals, Luis Araquistain of the Socialists and Joaquín Maurín of the POUM, in publications of 1934 and 1935, respectively. Since they represented two of the most paranoid sectors of Spanish politics, on the one hand, but were perfectively objective and lucid in their analysis of the prospects for fascism, on the other, their examination bears some weight, and in fact was perfectly accurate.

It is also important to examine the situation in terms of a retrodictive theory of fascism.[2] Without repeating all the details of the retrodictive theory, suffice it to say that such factors were comparatively weak in Spain. The cultural crisis of the fin de siècle, despite all the discussion of "the disaster" of 1898, had less impact than in many other parts of Europe. A strong preexisting nationalism, one of the key variables, was simply not present in Spain. As Araquistain and Maurín pointed out, the Great War had impacted Spain less than it had other countries—there was only a limited sense of frustrated nationalism, no mass of returning war veterans, and even at the height of the depression crisis proportionately fewer unemployed—a noteworthy feature of the normally much-maligned Spanish economy.[3]

Even the more "fascistogenic" factors that were present had little effect in Spain. There was an unconsolidated new democratic system—a prime type of breeding ground for fascism—but nonetheless the political system was already fully mobilized, most political space firmly occupied by established forces of the Left and Right, leaving little room for a new radicalism. The country experienced the twentieth-century crisis of European culture, as well as the challenge of secularization, but in Spain the responses to this crisis polarized between the traditional Left and Right. A major challenge from the Left encouraged fascism in other countries but had no such effect in Spain, where the response was more moderate and to a large extent defined by religion, until the spring of 1936. Successful fascist movements required flexible and effective, preferably charismatic, leadership, as well as allies at crucial moments, but these factors were lacking prior to the Civil War. The Left was not monolithic, but it was fully mobilized, permitting no "national socialist" defections, and there was no sense of a failed revolution, as in Germany and Italy, since the revolutionary Left became stronger and stronger. The middle classes were not as secularized or as nationalist as in central Europe and did not seek alternative radical political representation. Each sector of the middle classes— Left-liberal, centrist liberal, and rightist—held relatively firmly to their positions, and there were no major defections, as in central Europe. There was no note-worthy Jewish minority, and no international pressures or humiliations that might have elicited a broader patriotic reaction. Though economic problems were severe, they were correctly not perceived as somehow imposed from abroad. Paradoxi-cally, fascist movements developed primarily in European countries with parlia-mentary systems and, as mass political movements, required freedom to mobilize and develop. From approximately March 1936 the political and legal systems of Spain became progressively less free, leaving a radical opposition movement with no political prospects whatsoever. Finally, successful fascist movements required a sufficiently developed or stabilized political system that would neutralize the mil-itary as rival, but the Spanish system became so skewed and disorderly that the military suddenly became major actors. The extreme weakness of nationalist sen-timent was perhaps the greatest limitation of all.

Given the weakness of the liberal center in Spain, the challenge to the Left came not from fascism but, in normal political terms, from the Catholic Right, or, in a time of crisis, from the military. When the hour arrived, these would propose to establish their own alternative systems that would be more authoritarian, but this would not be fascism. The Popular Front generated massive propaganda about "fascism," but by that term the Left simply meant their political enemies on the Right, a standard trope in Spanish leftist discourse that has continued into the twenty-first century, long after the total demise of fascism. In 1935 a revolutionary Marxist analyst like Maurín admitted that the key rightist leader Gil Robles, for example, was no fascist, but in fact "feared fascism."

The Spain of the Second Republic was not a mature north European democ-racy, but neither was it subject to the strong nationalist pressures generated in Ger-many and Italy. In some respects it was politically more similar to Austria and to certain east-central European countries. In the former the Catholic Right imposed a relatively moderate anti-Nazi authoritarian system, and in the latter the military or moderate rightist authoritarian forces predominated. Wherever the latter were in control they simply excluded fascists by force, as the Left did in Spain in March 1936. The only exception was the diarchy established in Romania in September 1940, but that lasted only a few months.

The Romanian case was the only one even remotely similar to Spain, the differ-ence being that under the diarchy the Legion of the Archangel Michael held more power than did the Falange Española Tradicionalista (FET) under Franco. That situation tempted the legionnaires to bid for absolute power, prompting a three-day civil war in January 1941 that ended in their defeat and total suppression. In Spain Falangists occasionally talked of something similar but wisely chose not to follow the Romanian example.

Given the weakness of the movement in Spain, combined with the incipient breakdown of Republican democracy, there was not the slightest chance of achieving power. Communists sometimes attempted to seize power through insurrection and civil war; fascists very rarely did. Reduced to the Communist modus operandi, the Falangists had little hope of success. In Spain, as emphasized in chapter 11, it was the Communists who, thanks to the Popular Front, reversed their course, and formed a very effective alliance that, for the first time in western Europe, associated them with a government in power.

The extensive historical commentary on the insignificant early history of Falangism is focused to a large degree on its leader and key founder, José Antonio Primo de Rivera. I once wrote that José Antonio was "everybody's favorite fascist," even on the part of antifascists. There is almost universal testimony that on the personal level he was courteous, charming, intelligent, and entirely engaging. In the tumultuous Republican parliament of 1933–36, he may have won the popularity contest. No other deputy was so well liked even by his opponents, and this in the case of one ideologically dedicated to antiparliamentary politics. Prior to the advent of Felipe González, he was the first political leader known to friend and foe primarily by his first name. With the possible exception of the continuing Mussolini cult in Italy, in no other case can such continuing fervor be found on behalf of a national fascist leader in the twenty-first century.[4]

His admirers generally claim that he was not a genuine fascist at all but the architect of an attempted political "third force" cut short by his early death.[5] There is almost universal testimony that José Antonio did not have the personal style, manner, or temperament of a typical fascist leader. He stepped into politics, at first only temporarily, after the collapse of his father's dictatorship in 1930. His primary concern at first was to defend and by some means continue the work of his father, which, as the eldest son, he felt was his particular responsibility, though initial efforts were completely unsuccessful.

Political ambition began to crystallize at the time of the initial crisis of the Republic in 1933. As his thinking evolved, he concluded that only a new kind of movement, with a modern social program, was required to achieve such national goals. José Antonio's thinking to a large extent anticipated the later calculations of Franco during 1936–37.

The year 1933 marked the "second wave" in the expansion of fascism's influence in Europe, with Hitler's triumph in Germany. Hitler, however, was only in the first stages of building his National Social regime, while Benito Mussolini enjoyed great prestige as the senior fascist dictator, given credit for already having transformed and modernized Italy and, in the eyes of some, at least, of having made it into a great power. At that moment he stood as the supremely successful "regenerator" of a major underdeveloped south European country. José Antonio was strongly and naively attracted to Mussolini and the Italian Fascist example, which seemed to provide ideology, program, and system to triumph where his father had failed. Within two more years he would begin to grasp both the dangers of imitation and the limitations of Italian Fascism, and to strive, without very much success, to differentiate his Falangist movement.

The initial political and intellectual leader of a fascist enterprise in Spain was not José Antonio but Ramiro Ledesma Ramos, the young postal functionary who provided perhaps the most clear-cut example of the radical political intellectual in early twentieth-century Spain. Ledesma originally defined national syndicalism, the basic doctrine of Falangism, as well as coining some of the major Falangist slogans. In 1933–34 he understood the essence of fascism better than José Antonio, but lacked charisma and the capacity for leadership, though he and his thinking were too aggressive to be satisfied with second place, leading almost inevitably to the breakdown of the relationship between the two and Ledesma's expulsion from the movement at the beginning of 1935.[6]

Political rivalry was important in this split, but the role of ideas and political strategy even more central. This had to do with avoiding the imitation of Italian Fascism, adopting a more revolutionary program and strategy, and forming broader alliances aimed at seizing power. On these points, Ledesma may be said to have lost the battle but won the war, for after his expulsion José Antonio sought to move the Falange to the "left," and to formally disassociate it from Italian Fascism, though he was never able to form effective alliances (which had been fundamental in Mussolini's and Hitler's rise to power). Leaders of the Comintern took this last point more to mind than José Antonio, switching a few months later from revolutionary isolation (the tactic of Falangism) to the more common fascist tactic of alliance formation when they officially adopted the tactic of the Popular Front in August 1935.

José Antonio sought a more independent path for the Falange, even while arranging a subsidy from the Italian government and appearing informally at a meeting of Mussolini's abortive "fascist international" to explain that the difficulties facing this sort of movement were more severe in Spain than in some other countries. If the Falange was becoming somewhat less "Italian," it became in some ways even more generically fascist in 1935, emphasizing a sort of "left-fascist economics" of national syndicalism, though the corporatism of the latter was supposed to give it a partial independence from the state, in terms that were never convincingly explained. The attempted de-Italianization led José Antonio to condemn briefly the idea of the monolithic "corporative state" and of "totalitarianism," but all without the slightest indication of any kind of political goals and structure that would be other than rigidly authoritarian. His attempt to separate Falangism from Italian Fascism was never completed, and probably impossible. He was more successful, however, in differentiating both Falangism and "fascism" from what he termed "Hitlerism," which he declared to be racist, mystical, and romantic, lacking the clarity of principles and doctrines of Italian Fascism.

José Antonio's attempt to lead what he termed "a poetic movement" led to tactical and ideological confusion. One of the standard descriptions of fascism is that it represented an attempt to "estheticize politics," and this was amply reflected in the Falangist emphasis on "style," but the movement soon had to face a grimmer reality. A doctrine of violence could not be avoided, though never defined with the theoretical sophistication of the Italians. Both Ledesma and Onésimo Redondo, the number three leader, endorsed violence, while José Antonio held that it was worthwhile in a "just cause," for the "patria," which somewhat paralleled the position of the Left on that issue. Because his father had been able to rule as dictator with relatively minimal violence in the quieter 1920s, José Antonio at first naively assumed that a new authoritarian system could also be imposed with relatively limited violence, but soon found himself caught up in a spiral of killing that he could not control.

One thing different about Spain, compared with other western European countries, was the strong emphasis on violence by the revolutionary Left. It was true that in Germany and Italy political violence in 1918–19 had been initiated by the Left, but in those countries they generally rejected violence, which was practiced only by a minority of the extreme Left and soon became the preferred tactic of the extreme Right. In Spain, all the principal worker parties preached and practiced violence, whereas the parties of the Right, whatever their long-term goals, pursued legal tactics. Thus Ledesma would accurately write in 1935 that "*In Spain the right is apparently fascist, but in many respect antifascist*" (italics his), for, though nationalist and in varying degrees tending toward authoritarianism, it eschewed violence and generally obeyed the law. Conversely, "*the left is apparently antifascist, but, in many respects, essentially fascist*" because of its propensity for violence and revolutionary authoritarianism.[7] This explained why the emergence of a fascist movement in Spain had been met by a wave of violence not initiated by the Falangists themselves, but which served only to elicit further the strain of violence that was at least partially implicit in José Antonio's "poetic movement." This does not mean that the Left was to blame for Falangist violence, but simply that leftist violence and Falangist violence soon became locked in a self-reenforcing dialectic that José Antonio, naively, had not foreseen.

All fascist-type movements were, however, singular, differentiated by national characteristics even more than was the case among Communist movements. In that of the Falange, revolutionary nationalism was mediated, often uneasily and contradictorily, by an attempted symbiosis with cultural and religious traditionalism. The "new man" sought by nearly all revolutionary movements, fascist or otherwise, was in the Spanish case less novel and more characterized by traditional values, a tendency that placed Falangism on a kind of cusp between revolutionary fascism and national tradition as affirmed by the radical Right. But whereas the Catholic CEDA expressed its Catholic values by adhering to republican legality, the partial espousal of Catholic values by the violent and revolutionary Falange created cognitive dissonance.

José Antonio only added to such ambiguity by defining the goals of his movement in binary or antinomic terms. He suggested several times that if key objectives of firm leadership, national unity, cultural identity, and a dynamic new national economic policy were fully assumed by other groups, such as patriotic Socialists, he would be prepared to retire from politics. Immediately after the Popular Front elections in 1936, he suggested a momentary truce to see if the new Azaña government might lead to a national political breakthrough. No other party leader expressed so binary an approach.

During 1935 José Antonio was seeking a more distinctly national revolutionary doctrine. Some of his ideas were in flux, and where these might have led in another ten years cannot be known. Ironically, just as the Communists were, after fifteen years, abandoning the tactic of revolutionary insurrectionism in favor of political alliance, José Antonio and the Falangist leaders began to embrace insurrectionism. This was a different example of the reverse radicalization to which Ledesma referred. Through the Popular Front, the Communists were adopting the fascist tactic of seeking power legally through alliance and elections. José Antonio, unable to form an alliance, was thrown back on the Communist tactic of insurrection on which the Comintern had relied for fifteen years, always without success.

The turn toward revolutionary isolationism proved disastrous. There was no hope of gaining military support for armed revolt in 1935, and when the CEDA offered the Falange a realistic electoral alliance in 1936—one seat for José Antonio, all that the party's scant numbers merited—it was rejected by party leaders in favor of continued isolationism. Loss of a seat in the Cortes may have proven fatal to José Antonio, leaving him to an arrest of dubious legality and prosecution on a series of (sometimes artificial) charges that kept him in prison until events were overtaken by the Civil War.

Like most leaders of national fascist parties, José Antonio was a failure. He failed either to win many supporters or gain allies. On their own, fascist movements managed to seize power in only two countries, though one of them was potentially the most powerful in Europe. Even so, scarcely any other principal national party did so poorly as the Falange in the elections of 1936, with only

0.7 percent of the vote. Fascist parties did proportionately better in Holland and Sweden, two consolidated democracies. Young volunteers finally began to flock to the party during the national crisis of the spring of 1936, but fascism in Spain had no alternative to the Communist tactic of insurrection and civil war, though in every instance where a fascist movement attempted it (Germany 1923, Austria 1934, Portugal 1935, Romania 1941), it failed. Success in any insurrection would depend on the army, and the cost of this was complete subordination of the movement.

José Antonio tried to bargain with General Mola for political terms, but these were limited to freedom of action for propaganda and party organization, not a share of power, and that only for so long as the Falangists fully committed themselves to the military insurgency. The terms in which the Falangists cooperated with the revolt of July 18 recognized the complete political and military leadership, indeed domination, of the military.

By the time that the Civil War began, José Antonio was totally marginalized. The scope and ferocity of the conflict genuinely horrified him, for, like the extremists on both sides, he had thought exclusively in terms of an insurrection that would involve no more than a "mini"-civil war of no more than a week or two. José Antonio was not a total fanatic and, faced with the danger of national self-destruction, preferred national reconciliation, even under a democratic republic. Hence his proposal of August 10, 1936, to travel to the Nationalist zone to try to negotiate a compromise. This would have meant indefinite postponement of his own political goals, but there is no reason to consider him insincere. This was another expression of his radical binary approach, which he had revealed before. In his final writings in prison before his execution, fascism became remote. He could be said to have entered a post-political phase of thinking, as he turned toward spiritual perspectives and a kind of metahistorical outlook.[8]

The Civil War nonetheless created a certain "fascist situation" in the Nationalist zone. Although the Falangists held no state power, they suddenly became the largest single political group, expanding numerically even more rapidly than the Communists in the Republican zone. They constituted a political presence that could not be ignored—though it could readily have been held at arm's length.

Franco chose not to do that, but to take control of the movement for his own purposes. In the next chapter I draw attention to the fact that, so far as can be determined, he had no such plan at the beginning of the revolt and very probably not as late as October 1, 1936, when he formally assumed power. He was responding to the radicalized conditions of the Civil War and the "fascist situation" in the Nationalist zone. Once Franco and Serrano Suñer decided to take over the movement, this was easy to do. The Falange had always been weak in leadership, and after the elimination of José Antonio, leadership was weaker than ever and also seriously divided. The fascistic cult of "The Absent One" made it temporarily impossible to select a new national chief and news of the death of José Antonio was long suppressed, with no strong and capable replacement available. If the expansion of the Falange and the terms of the Civil War created a "fascist situation," the rigorous new dictatorship in turn foreclosed the possibilities of anything other than an official state party under Franco, a certainty more or less recognized by the internally divided Falangist leaders as they sought to negotiate with the Carlists—the only other significant paramilitary force supporting the war effort—to achieve some sort of unity, or at least common understanding. This proved impossible, however, as a party initiative alone.

By the spring of 1937 Franco was ready to begin the structuring of an alternative regime, the notion of the authoritarian reorganization of the Republic having been abandoned. Yet he took only minimal steps in elaborating a complete new political system so long as the war lasted. The question may be asked: What exactly did he intend by the creation of the Falange Española Tradicionalista as state party in April of that year?

Some of Franco's partisans would later emphasize the ad hoc and open-ended aspects of this move, pointing out his willingness to accept members from all the non-Left parties and his announcement that formation of the new entity and official adoption of the Falangist Twenty-Six Points were a point of departure and not a final definition of the new regime. Franco was certainly not prepared to construct a complete system and obviously wanted to keep many of his options open, but he made it abundantly clear that the new state would be a radically authoritarian regime drawing considerable inspiration from its fascist allies.

Since the "Reds" normally called their enemies simply "fascists," was this not then the beginning of Europe's third fascist regime? The Franco regime had quickly become a rigid dictatorship and a one-party state, was engaged in a desperate war, and had just adopted a fascist-type program as its official ideology. This looked very much like a fascist regime, and yet subsequently most historians would tend to agree that it was not strictly fascist per se, though it certainly underwent major fascist influence and exhibited certain fascist characteristics, so that, as Ismael Saz puts it, if not "fascist" it was at least "fascistized."[9] That may be as good a way of saying it as any.

The veteran "old shirts" of the party accepted the new arrangement for lack of anything better and still hoped for the triumph of the "national syndicalist revolution," but it is doubtful that Franco even altogether understood what the latter was supposed to mean. At that time, the FET was only the third fascist-type party in power and, save for the interlude in Romania, there would be no other, except for the Independent State of Croatia, part of Hitler's imperium from 1941 to 1944. By point of comparison one might observe that the only party truly in power was Hitler's National Socialists, for Mussolini had invented the term "totalitarian" without fully carrying out a Totalitarian Party revolution in Italy, though the Fascist Party was certainly larger, more important and influential than the FET ever was.

Since the rebel regime in Spain had begun as a rightist military regime, the Falangists were in fact fortunate that Franco had become semi-"fascistized" and decided to incorporate them rather than to suppress them. Spain was unique in providing the only instance, aside from Romania, in which a rightist nonfascist regime incorporated a large fascist movement. In every other case—Salazar (Portugal), Dollfuss (Austria), Horthy (Hungary), Smetona (Lithuania), King Alexander (Yugoslavia)—the rightist regime eventually suppressed the principal fascist movement altogether. Nonetheless, it took the Falangists five years and more before they began to understand their good fortune. The decisive factor had simply been the Civil War, which so radicalized the situation in Spain.

As it was, there existed a kind of crude pecking order in the attitude of fascists in various countries toward each other. Nazis looked down on Fascist Italy as not being truly "revolutionary" in the way Hitler's Germany was, while both Nazis and Italian Fascists regarded Franco's Spain as alarmingly "reactionary" and not fully fascist. Spanish Falangists, in turn, looked down on Salazar's Portugal, Vichy France, and other rightist authoritarian systems as "hollow" rightist regimes, lacking positive fascist political content.

The Franco regime, like that of Mussolini, called itself "totalitarian," though the limitations of the system were hinted at by the Franco himself on various occasions when he likened it to the united monarchy of the Catholic Monarchs—a monarchy in fact severely limited by multiple legal jurisdictions. Franco was much more "absolute" than so-called absolute monarchy in Spain (or anywhere else) ever was, but his concept of the counterrevolution also contained limits. He obviously had no intention of handing any significant degree of power to the party or anyone else, but, rather than constructing a truly totalitarian system, he respected private property and provided limited recognition to the diverse sectors of the original National Movement of 1936—what would later be termed the various politico-ideological "families" of the regime.

Even though in the immediate aftermath of the Civil War the FET had distinctly more politico-administrative influence than any other "family" except the military, the limitations of this situation quickly became evident to some of the most radical Falangists. Hence the idea that began to develop from the autumn of 1939 that Franco had betrayed the ideals of José Antonio, a conviction that would only grow in the future among hard-core Falangists. The history of the FET-Movimiento Nacional would become the history, among other things, of semi-constant dissidence, even though the dissidence was of limited importance and always confined to small minorities.[10] It became a permanent feature of the movement, tolerated by Franco because it was not normally threatening and because the nontotalitarian character of the regime did not require complete destruction of all dissidence. The most menacing single aspect of the dissidence developed in the first year after the Civil War, when some of the ultras formed a secret junta to plan the possible assassination of Franco. So far as we know, this junta had no counterpart in any other fascist movement participating in power, but after some months it decided to cancel its activities. The major problem was that there was no one to replace Franco, and given the special place of the military, combined with the latter's anti-Falangist attitude, it seemed clear that the military would ruthlessly suppress independent violence by the Falangists, something that the latter grasped even before the abortive revolt of the Iron Guard in Romania in January 1941.

The abortive plans to convert Spain into a major military power, to follow a curiously "Soviet" strategy of intervening in a European war only at the decisive moment, were a strictly military enterprise. There was no major input by any part of the party, as in Italy and Germany, and in fact the party's very limited paramilitary resources were fully terminated by the army command in 1941.

Franco had great ambitions by the close of the Civil War, suffering from a certain megalomaniac vertigo of victory, and wanted to keep both his domestic and diplomatic options open. Leaders of the FET hoped that the course of events would favor them, and for two years after the end of the Civil War that seemed to be the case. The increasing power and influence of the Axis encouraged further fascistization in Spain and, if Hitler had scored such decisive victories in 1941 as in 1940, that indeed might have been the way that it worked out.

The most important leader of the FET was not any of its secretary generals, but Ramón Serrano Suñer. He has claimed that he sincerely sought to develop a system that would carry out the doctrine of José Antonio and also to develop a firmly structured regime with a system of law to ratify this outcome. Serrano was the first president of the FET's Junta Política, but he also understood that in Franco's regime the state was more important than the party, so that his most important roles were first as minister of the interior and then as foreign minister.

His most important attempt to transform the structure of the state was the initiative of the Junta Política in the summer of 1940 to prepare a draft for a new institutional system, though care was taken not to reduce the personal power of Franco. The text of this Law for the Organization of the State was composed of five sections: Article 1 echoed the Falangist program, declaring the state "a totalitarian instrument in the service of the integrity of the Fatherland. All its power and institutions are dedicated to this service and are bound by law and by the political and moral principles of the National Movement." Twenty of the thirty-seven articles of this project were devoted to defining the authority and structure of a new corporative Cortes that would be quite similar to the Chamber of Fasces and Corporations of the Italian regime. The most controversial aspect was Article 28: "The Junta Política is the supreme political council of the regime and the collegial organ of coordination between the state and the Movement." Article 31 continued: "The Junta Política must be heard in full session on matters that affect the constitutive power and the Fundamental Laws of the State, on international treaties and concordats, on the declaration of war and the conclusion of peace. The competence of the Junta Política in those matters defined by the statutes of the Movement remains unaltered."[11]

This alarmed non-Falangists because it proposed to give the highest organ of the party a constitutive role at the highest level of the state structure. Esteban Bilbao, one of the few representatives of Carlism in the government, wrote a letter of protest against the "systematic interference of the party" in the highest organs of state.[12] This was not the first plan or draft for a set of laws for his regime that Franco had received, for more than a year earlier both the regular monarchists and the Carlists had presented their own proposals. During those years, however, Franco sought to avoid any political structure that might tie his hands, and the project of the Junta Política, like the earlier proposals of the monarchist movements, was simply filed away.

The initial point of inflection in Spain came early, however, scarcely more than two years after the close of the Civil War. Throughout the second half of 1940 and the initial months of 1941, both Serrano Suñer and the FET hoped and believed that the tide of events was carrying the Spanish regime to decisive changes in international and domestic affairs. Indeed, had Hitler met Franco's demands at Hendaye, that is the way it might have worked out. As it was, the increasing complexity of the international situation and the disastrous decline of the domestic economy dissuaded Franco from changes; his main concern was foreign and military policy more than domestic politics. What he found after the fall of France was that the FET leaders and militants had become even more rabidly Germanophile than before, and in fact any major concessions to them would have had the effect of forcing his hand in foreign policy, as well. Therefore the high tide of Axis power in 1940–41 did not produce any decisive fascistization of the Spanish regime, as the Falangists hoped, but encouraged Franco simply to manipulate the status quo, without a decisive internal change one way or another. A second key factor was the intense hostility of the military, very critical of any further gesture of fascistization, not so much for ideological reasons but because they considered the Falangists parvenu rivals who lacked competence, integrity, or coherence.

This produced the most serious crisis in the history of the regime when the Falangist leaders challenged Franco for the first and last time by a sort of "sit-down strike" that involved the resignation of a number of party leaders. Their bitterness was expressed in the letter of resignation that Miguel Primo de Rivera (the only surviving Primo de Rivera brother), party provincial chief of Madrid, sent to Franco on May 1, 1941. It insisted that

> the politics of Spain differ notably from the thought of the person who inspired all the men of the Falange to ardent service.
>
> . . . Though it is true that the complete fulfillment of the doctrine of José Antonio would be hard to carry out in the present circumstances, . . . it is also true that the instrument created to make that doctrine effective some day, that is, the Party Falange Española Tradicionalista y de las JONS, absolutely lacks the means and minimal possibilities of carrying out its difficult mission.[13]

This was a serious challenge, for in the climate of those days Franco could not simply abandon or suppress the Falangists (even though he had all the power to do that), nor did he want to, for at that point he had no interest in any major alternative model for his regime. Moreover, this was the first and only domestic political crisis in the history of the regime that Franco could not initially control, his first response only seeming to increase the opposition. Nonetheless, in the final phase his maneuvering was masterful, reorganizing political appointments in such a way as to keep the military under control and gain the cooperation of a new set of Falangist leaders such as José Luis de Arrese, who, though they maintained the party's fascist orientation, accepted the inevitability of its permanent marriage to Franco. When this was soon followed by the elimination of the syndical boss Gerardo Salvador Merino, some of the most radical and fully Naziphile had been eliminated, and the party was on its way to final domestication, though this would always depend on the outcome of foreign affairs.

What the Falangist dissidents had sought at the beginning of the crisis was a "compact," primarily Falangist, government, and the only figure who could have led it would probably have been Serrano Suñer. The latter has declared in his memoirs that, with the final outcome, he realized that Franco had managed to divide the Falangists more than ever and to triumph in every respect. As Serrano put it, "The important thing about these developments was that I had ceased to be the mediator between the Chief of State and the authentic leaders of the Falange. . . . From that moment the FET de las JONS was above all the party of Franco. After the crisis of May 1941 the Falangists who had fought by my side lost faith in our political enterprise."[14] This, however, may be an exaggeration made on the basis of hindsight, for the group associated with Serrano may not have fully grasped the extent of their defeat for some time. In fact, Serrano still hoped to retain indirect leadership of the FET, restricting the new secretary general to technical administration, while he remained political leader. Probably neither he nor Franco initially grasped the degree of enmity and rivalry felt by Arrese, but the latter proved more adroit than Serrano anticipated. Franco found that Arrese suited him just fine, and within a few months gave his approval to the new secretary general's full control of the party. Only then did Serrano understand the extent of his defeat.

Moreover, Arrese also sought the role of maximal interpreter of the orthodox doctrine of José Antonio. He had his own intellectual and ideological pretensions, beginning with the book on the Falangist program that he had written in 1936, which was published only after the war. Originally he had sought to emphasize the social program of Falangism, but in his era as secretary general he also stressed more and more its Catholic identity and the neotraditionalist roots of the doctrine of José Antonio. Whereas for the latter neotraditionalism was above all a matter of culture and religion, combined in political matters with at least a limited anticlericalism, it achieved ever greater prominence in the FET of Arrese.

Meanwhile Serrano Suñer—rather like José Antonio before him—failed to develop significant allies, ultimately relying too much on his personal relationship with Franco. After May 1941 he no longer even had the support of most of the Falange, for Arrese and the new party leaders strongly resented him and moved to undercut his power, something which Franco did not oppose. Moreover, Serrano's political personality and deportment were very nearly the opposite of those of José Antonio. Whereas the latter succeeded in charming many of his enemies, the overweening arrogance of Serrano, as leading minister and brother-in-law of the dictator, made him "the most hated man in Spain," as the German ambassador accurately described him in reports to Berlin.

During his final year as foreign minister, Serrano became increasingly frustrated. He saw clearly that the more structured and more fascist regime of which he hoped to be a special leader (possibly the key leader) was not emerging in Spain, and that Franco had once more frozen the domestic political situation, as he had done so successfully during the Civil War. As Serrano said to the representatives of Hitler and Mussolini, only Spain's entry into the war would break open the domestic situation and produce decisive changes in the regime. As much as he wished for both these alternatives to come to pass, most of the time he had to agree with Franco that current circumstances simply made entry into the war impossible. At times he toyed with the idea of resigning to take up the post of ambassador in Rome, by far the most comfortable place for him outside of Spain, indeed leaving the post vacant for a while, probably for that eventuality.

The ensuing political crisis of August–September 1942 was not as important as that of the preceding year. Stemming from unresolved domestic conflicts, it completed the rebalancing that Franco had begun in 1941. In neither case, however, were Franco's new political appointments intended to be part of any process of defascistization. Even in September 1942 he was not ready for that, but maintained the posture that he had assumed in 1937 of leading a one-party state that contained multiple political strands, while continuing to hold in abeyance any final resolution of the regime structure. In 1942 Franco still held firmly to the "fascistized" model, even though, for the aforementioned reasons, he remained reluctant to create a fully fascist regime. Thus he continued throughout 1942 to believe that the fascist-style one-party state would remain dominant in most of Europe, and he showed no interest in any alternative model.

The first indication of a change in perspective came at the very end of 1942, when apparently he abandoned the idea that Germany could win a clear-cut victory in the war and therefore that conditions could ever favor Spain's participation. Even during the first half of 1943, however, this did not lead to abandonment of the "fascistized" model, for the regime then hoped to encourage an arbitrated settlement that would still leave Germany the most important continental power, even if not fully victorious, and therefore ensure the continuation of the Axis state model.

The second and more decisive point of inflection came in July–August 1943, with the downfall of Mussolini. This created panic reactions within the FET, though at first Franco maintained his customary complacency and imperturbability. Within a month, however, he had assimilated the political and international implications, which augured a growing dominance of the Anglo-Saxon powers both in the Atlantic and in at least western Europe, and probably a new postwar power balance not at all favorable to the fascist political model.

Thus a process of defastiscization began in August 1943, above all cosmetic but also implying certain political changes, as well. The propaganda line began to change, though Spanish news reporting would always remain relatively favorable to the Reich down to the end of the war. The ideological line of the FET also began to change. No more was heard of "the totalitarian state," and a completely new emphasis was placed on "humanism," with appropriate quotations from José Antonio. All the more fascistic points and phrases from the Twenty-Six Points would henceforth be passed over, with the limited exception of a few special party occasions. The new position, as Franco himself put it to the Allied ambassadors, was that the FET was not merely a fascist party but not even a political party at all. Rather, it was simply a sort of agency for social reforms, such as syndical organization and welfare. This was an unprecedented defascistization for a fascist-type party participating in power.

All this further added to the cognitive dissonance under which the FET operated. There had always been considerable contradiction in Falangism, even more than in most fascist movements, because of the attempt to incorporate Catholicism culturally and spiritually. This had become more accentuated in 1937, though downplayed among Falangists themselves between 1939 and 1941. The cognitive dissonance began to ease with the beginning of defascistization, which meant the increasing victory of traditionalist Catholicism in the regime's doctrines, and the progressive relinquishing of those fascist features that most clashed with it.

The FET was further downgraded when Franco undertook the metamorphosis of the regime in 1945, beginning its conversion into a Catholic and corporative monarchy. The party was left without a secretary general for several years, and Serrano Suñer, accepting the political obliteration of fascism, wrote privately to Franco that the party should simply be disbanded.

Franco, however, had no such intention. The FET, now known formally as the Movimiento Nacional, would continue to the end of the regime, setting a record for longevity for this kind of movement in official institutions. The only competitor would be Salazar's União Nacional; the latter was a more limited organization, in some ways more similar to Primo de Rivera's Unión Patriótica. Efforts at political mobilization declined sharply, however, and by 1958, when I first arrived in Madrid, the Movimiento had become an object of derision among many Spanish young people. Therefore, in the postfascist era, why did Franco not take the advice of his brother-in-law and dissolve the party?

The fundamental reason would seem to be that he considered a weak, artificial, and limited state party better than no state party at all. Franco was forever concerned to avoid the "error Primo de Rivera" and to maintain a system with institutions, structure, and some sort of doctrine. The Movimiento provided a basic cadre of supporters for institutional structure and civic mobilization, however narrow, and Franco judged that the regime would be gravely weakened without it. The Movimiento enjoyed a comeback of sorts between 1948 and 1957, regaining a regular secretary general and briefly holding slightly greater prominence. When, however, during his second tour as secretary, Arrese attempted to "constitutionalize" the Movimiento by codifying for it a special and permanent tutelary role in the state, Franco found that his own hands were tied by the evolution of his regime. The Church leaders protested most directly, and Franco canceled the project. The new government of 1957 moved in a different direction, introducing the Principles of the Movement, which completed ideological defascistization. The last special moment of the party veterans had passed, and the Movimiento subsequently played a role even more exclusively bureaucratic, finally being officially abolished in 1977, two years after the death of Franco.

With the greater freedom of the last years of the regime, there would occasionally appear a book with a title such as *¿Por qué no fue posible la Falange?* The answer was that circumstances simply did not permit a more influential or powerful party. Although the Falange never governed, it survived in one form or another much longer than any other fascist-type party and, as I suggested earlier, the second characteristic partly depended on the first. It should be kept in mind that fascist-type parties have generally been extremely unsuccessful organizations. Of the very many that have existed, only two really came to power.

Though several "fascistogenic" factors existed in Spain during the 1930s, most of the factors that encouraged fascism elsewhere were lacking. Ultimately, it was the weakness of Falangism that became its strength, such as that was, the radical environment of civil war giving it a momentum it could not have acquired in peacetime. Subsequently, its hope for greater influence lay not so much with Franco as with Hitler, whose decline and fall eliminated any such possibility.

14 | Francisco Franco

Fascist Monster or
Savior of the Fatherland?

For nearly forty years Francisco Franco was, for better or worse, the most dominant figure to have appeared in the history of Spain. None of the kings of earlier centuries wielded proportionately as much power or so drastically changed the course of the country. Every preceding ruler operated to a greater or lesser degree within established laws and traditions, while Franco led a victorious counterrevolution that, to a much greater extent, established its own rules. During his lifetime he was the most successful counterrevolutionary of the twentieth century and, in terms of the positive transformation of his country, the most successful dictator.

He has been the most extravagantly praised and the most scathingly condemned figure in all Spanish history. No other has garnered such extremes of both the positive and negative. In recent years, during the era of political correctness, Franco has received little but continued vilification. Of all the figures in Spanish history, in some respects he is the most difficult to evaluate.[1]

As in the case of many others, Franco's orientation in life was strongly influenced by his family background, which included a history of two centuries of service in the Spanish navy. Franco sought to follow in the same tradition, but restrictions in the naval academy left him the sole alternative of the Military Academy in Toledo, certainly a fateful change, for a career as naval officer would have been entirely different. His immediate family background was not a happy one, for his father (who reached the rank of admiral in naval administration) was politically radical, personally libertine, and anti-Catholic, the exact opposite of Franco's pious, dutiful, and conservative mother. After his father abandoned the family altogether to live with a mistress in Madrid, the young Franco identified thoroughly with his mother and her values, a moral and psychological formation intrinsic to the development of his mature identity.

As a very young and undersized youth, Franco was only an average student in the academy, but he took advantage of combat service in Morocco, beginning in 1912, to exhibit uncommon courage and leadership ability. Most of his experience was gained as commander of elite units, first of Moroccan Regulares and then of the newly founded Legion. In the Protectorate Franco was a combat leader off and on for twelve years, from 1914 to 1926, and this was fundamental to his personal and professional development. The Moroccan years taught him courage, stoicism, and endurance, the importance of firm, determined leadership and discipline, the art of command, and the role of prudence and sound organization. He developed strength of character, combined with a certain impassivity and a sometimes pronounced harshness. This was a colonial campaign, so that he gained no very sophisticated knowledge of modern warfare, but on the other hand he obtained much practical experience, as well as a stellar reputation. Franco won five merit citations and rapid promotion, also suffering one life-threatening battle wound; in 1926 he became the youngest peacetime brigadier, so far as is known, in any European army. Ever afterward, he would personally acknowledge the importance of the Moroccan years in his personal formation and destiny.[2]

From the very beginning he started to gain a reputation for austerity and self-discipline, and firmly eschewed the standard vices of young officers—women, liquor, gambling. He had a personally romantic streak, but women played little—usually no—part in his early years, until he finally married Carmen Polo, a very young woman of good family in Oviedo, in 1923. Though it had taken a long time, his choice of wives was as well calculated as his military moves, for he enjoyed a long, happy, and harmonious marriage, and the stability of his personal life was probably not unrelated to the increasingly dominant public role that he played. Moreover, his peacetime assignments in Madrid and in Zaragoza (where he was the first director of the new General Military Academy) gave him entrée to the social elite and provided a new veneer of sophistication, limited though it may have been, to his personality.

A seeming paradox is that prior to 1936 he had not been a prototypical Spanish "political general." This is not to say that he had no political attitudes or values, though much later, after the numerous zigzags of his regime, it would become common to view him as a cynical opportunist who sought only to perpetuate his own power.

In fact, Franco's basic political attitudes and values seem to have changed little during the course of his long life. He was trained in military values and, more than merely a patriot, was a strong nationalist (as during his early years, the military probably figured as the only significant group of Spanish nationalists). His fundamental convictions were monarchist, and also basically authoritarian and hierarchical, opposed to parliamentary democracy, even though in 1931 he understood the need to accept the "evolution of the times." Franco was a traditionalist Roman Catholic—much more so than many in the military hierarchy—and believed in a traditionalist Catholic culture. His views on economics in considerable measure stemmed from those attitudes. Like most Spanish activists of his time, he was a "regenerationist" and looked to modern economic development, which he thought should be guided by a statist and nationalist, authoritarian policy, though these economic ideas may not have crystallized until the Civil War. He was also an imperialist who believed in a kind of national mission, once oriented toward the new world but in the twentieth century toward Morocco and northwest Africa. This last was the only basic part of his political credo that he had to abandon during his later years, which coincided with European decolonization.

Always suspicious of political liberalism, by the early 1930s he became convinced that Freemasonry was the driving subversive force in liberal politics, and that the consequence of its subversion of institutions was to open the door to Communism. Despite his paranoia concerning Masonry, however, Franco was not given to the kind of knee-jerk reactions typical of the Right radical minority in the army command, but in practical affairs demonstrated a more calm and pragmatic assessment.

Though he initially opposed what he saw as Primo de Rivera's "abandonismo" in Morocco, he became a supporter of the latter's dictatorship, a source of political inspiration and an alternative to the perceived weakness and fragmentation of parliamentary democracy. Yet he tried to be a political realist and did not by any overt act oppose the advent of the Second Republic. He judged Sanjurjo's revolt in 1932 to be ill advised and hopeless, and had nothing to do with it, coldly observing afterward that "General Sanjurjo has gained the right to die"—a typically mordant Franco commentary. His discipline and prudence were rewarded after the first big spin of the Republican political wheel, gaining him major promotion to major general once the center-Right assumed power. He was called in to coordinate repression of the Socialist revolutionary insurrection of 1934 and then made chief of the general staff the following year. It was characteristic of Franco that he became identified with the center and the moderate Right (much more the latter than the former), and refused to be involved in any of the conspiracies of the monarchist radical Right or the Falangists. When urged to take the initiative in military intervention as soon as it became clear that the Popular Front was winning the elections of February 1936, he refused to accept any responsibility, observing accurately that the military commanders were profoundly divided and could not assume responsibility on their own. Instead he urged the government to use its own authority and took personal initiative in trying to activate the decree of martial law that President Alcalá Zamora gave the prime minister. Since the latter refused to use the decree, Franco's initiative was quickly canceled.

Pío Moa's observation that prior to the Civil War Franco obeyed Republican legality more thoroughly than did Manuel Azaña is correct. Azaña was associated with a military insurrection in December 1930, sought to nullify arbitrarily and illegally the most honest and democratic elections in Spanish history in November 1933, maneuvered for months to thwart the majority of a democratically elected parliament and then attempt to carry off an ambivalent "legal pronunciamiento," was ambiguously associated with revolutionary insurrection in 1934, and subsequently, as prime minister and president, endorsed the latter while presiding over massive violations of constitutional law in 1936. Compared with such a record, Franco had merely tried to expedite a presidential decree in February 1936, which the prime minister refused to put in effect.

By that point Franco had gained the strongest reputation of any figure in the military hierarchy. He was not the most intelligent or best educated, the most imaginative or the most popular, but he was widely recognized as the one who most combined all the qualities of an outstanding commander in terms of experience, personal courage, discretion, determination, professional skill, and the singular quality to command. This was also apparent to the most perceptive leftist leaders, such as Indalecio Prieto, or Manuel Azaña, who privately labeled him "the only one to fear" among the Spanish generals.

He was soon in touch with the military conspirators, but played only a marginal role, refusing to commit himself firmly to armed revolt. He viewed this as a desperate undertaking not likely to work, probably prone to do more harm than good, and something to be attempted only as a last resort. In this he reflected the views of the majority of army officers. As late as the latter part of April 1936, he did not view the Republican system as immediately in danger of collapse and sought to play a new political role by election to the Cortes on the CEDA ticket in the special elections in Cuenca. Ironically, this drew vehement objection from José Antonio Primo de Rivera, who had been added to the rightist list in the province. At that point José Antonio was disgusted with the military, and he protested that the appearance of Franco gave a "militarist" and "reactionary" look to the rightist list. More pragmatically, he pointed out that the Spanish parliament placed a premium on rhetoric and rapid debate, in which Franco might not be expected to do well. Prudently, the general finally agreed to withdraw. Two months later he wrote to Casares Quiroga that the army was not disloyal (which, technically, at that moment was more or less correct), urging him to strengthen bonds with the military and affirm national unity. Amid the multiple uncertainties of the moment, this was not a dishonest presentation of his opinion.

By the spring of 1936 Franco clearly saw himself as destined for some new role of leadership, though he would have been hard put to define what exactly that might be. He spent more time reading works on contemporary politics and economics, and after assuming his new command in the Canaries began to take regular English lessons. But as late as July 12, again like most of the military, he still refused to commit himself to armed revolt, which he continued to insist was premature and might be counterproductive. The core conspirators around Mola were disgusted with Franco, deriding him as "Miss Canarias" for his "coquetry." The killing of Calvo Sotelo on the night of July 12–13 had much the same traumatic impact on Franco as it did on a great deal of moderate and conservative opinion. In effect, he joined the revolt when he judged that it had become more dangerous not to rebel than to rebel.

The political plan of the revolt had been devised by Gen. Emilio Mola, organizer of the conspiracy. It envisaged a "Portuguese solution"—that is, not restoration of the monarchy or inauguration of a fascist regime but the establishment of a rightist, corporative, more authoritarian republic rather like Salazar's "Estado Novo" in Portugal. This was the solution that divided the military least, since only a minority of them were monarchist, and some of the top generals in the revolt (Cabanellas, Goded, Queipo de Llano) had been noted Republicans. There is no reason to think this did not accord with Franco's own thinking, for that was the sort of solution for which he had been striving in his collaboration with the CEDA. The initial announcements and proclamations by the military commanders were virtually unanimous on this point.

Nonetheless, as Clausewitz observed, the dynamics of war create a *Wechselwirkung*, a process of reciprocal interaction (and sometimes of mutual radicalization) on both sides, leading to drastically new situations and decisions. This immediately took place during the Spanish war, as the Republican government empowered the only full-scale violent worker revolution in the history of western Europe, while the military rebels quickly moved to more and more extreme positions and practices.

Naming a commander in chief late in September was an important step by the rebel leaders, for had they not done so they probably would not have won the war. Once it was decided to name a generalissimo, Franco was the inevitable choice. Some of his colleagues were not happy with this outcome, for he was more respected than popular and there was some apprehension about his penchant for domination, but they accepted the fact that there was little alternative. Monarchists played key roles, though it was not due to their initiative alone, and Franco undertook no formal political obligations to them.

His political thinking underwent considerable change and also radicalization, as it began to move from a Portuguese model to an Italian model of regime, with some degree of fascistization. The fact that key military support came from Rome and Berlin was no doubt a factor in the equation: his evolving policy was strictly sui generis and one that Franco proposed to control on his own terms. So long as the Civil War lasted, he did not see his way clear to the full construction of a new system, which was postponed to the postwar period. Franco's achievement was to achieve total wartime political unity, and the state party was an important aspect of that process, accepted (but not exactly supported) by the other political forces. Beyond that, Franco simply banned all political activity for the duration of the conflict. This, especially when contrasted with the internecine strife in the Republican zone, was an important factor in his victory.[3]

Franco had carefully positioned himself militarily (and also to some extent politically) on the eve of the Civil War by bargaining for command of the elite combat forces in Morocco. So far as we know, he had no difficulty in obtaining this, for he was not too far away in the Canaries and, in strictly professional terms, had been the obvious choice. Due to the partial failure of the rebellion, the units in Morocco (even though their effective numbers were fewer than 30,000) became indispensable to the success of the insurgency, all the more since this would provide the base for recruiting more than 60,000 additional Moroccan volunteers of high combat value. Added to this was Franco's success in attracting the attention of Hitler and Mussolini and gaining significant assistance from them.

Despite the complete victory that he gained, Franco's leadership in the Civil War would later become increasingly controversial among historians. He has frequently been accused of timidity and lack of imagination in military operations, and there is truth in such accusations, although they are sometimes exaggerated.[4] The first major criticism concerned the delay in reaching Madrid, including the priority of swinging west to secure the Portuguese frontier and then to relieve the Alcázar de Toledo before attempting a frontal assault on Madrid from the southwest. For the most part, Franco had sound reasons for his decisions. The direct route to Madrid was only slightly shorter, while he lacked the effectives to advance directly without securing his flanks. Assuring logistical support through Portugal was of considerable importance, while the rebels were under so much military pressure elsewhere (including, but not limited to, the fronts of Oviedo, Aragon, Córdoba, and Granada) that Franco had to divert small but vital units to avert the danger of collapse on other fronts. Seizing Madrid might have been of little value if the Republicans had scored key victories elsewhere, though Franco might have been better advised to approach Madrid downhill from the north than uphill from the southwest.

Combat tactics during the Spanish war were generally unimaginative on both sides. It could hardly have been very different in the case of two improvised mass armies. Only in the breakthrough in Aragon during the early spring of 1938 was a battle of movement achieved, but that was also due to a temporary Republican collapse.

Franco's strategy has also been seriously questioned during the late spring and summer of 1938, when first he elected not to seize directly a weakly defended Catalonia and then, later, to respond to the Republican Ebro offensive with a set-piece counteroffensive that moved painfully slowly by direct assault over the hills southwest of the Ebro. In the case of Catalonia, international factors may have played a role. This was the only point at which there seemed to be some danger of French intervention, while Hitler also discouraged the invasion of Catalonia at that time, with the cynical goal of prolonging the Spanish war as an international diversion that would distract attention from his own initiatives. There is, however, no conclusive evidence regarding the basis for Franco's decisions.

The battle of the Ebro revealed Franco at his most unimaginative. His judgment that destruction of the Republican forces would give him a decisive advantage in the remainder of the war was correct, but the superiority of his own army in open offensive warfare offered him the opportunity for a flanking offensive that might have trapped the Republican army west of the river. This he apparently never considered.

Franco was not a brilliant strategist, but he was a competent commander who won his war, always the bottom line. It is said that amateurs do strategy, while professionals do logistics, and Franco did logistics well. He had to organize an effective mass army, sustain its morale, and lead it to victory, all the while maintaining political unity, an adequate economic base, and the continued military assistance of Italy and Germany, while preserving his own independence and freedom of action. All these things he accomplished in the most successful counterrevolutionary struggle of the twentieth century.[5]

The worst stain on Franco's record is the repression. This is not to be excused by saying that the Republicans did much the same, or that it was similar to other repressions in revolutionary/counterrevolutionary civil wars. Both these points are correct, but the repression remains atrocious and indefensible. Moreover, Franco took about two months longer during the war to moderate it than did the Republicans, and held greater central control.

Much the same can be said of the postwar repression. Military tribunals handed down approximately 50,000 death sentences during the immediate postwar period. Though many were commuted, as many as 30,000 were apparently carried out. It will not do to say, as sometimes has been done, that many of those executed had themselves been guilty of atrocious crimes during the Red Terror. This was doubtless true, but a large proportion were condemned for political responsibilities, not criminal atrocities.

Franco evidently first developed the sense that he was destined to play some higher role as the political crisis developed between 1934 and 1936. He accepted his election as Generalísimo as an action of divine providence, a conviction deepened by the eventual victory, which he considered proof that the hand of God lay upon him, that he had been called by the Almighty to be absolute ruler of Spain. This may be dismissed by critics as hysteria or megalomania, but it would remain his conviction ever after: hence the sense of self-confidence and self-righteousness that he would display. This did not mean that Franco believed that he was a magician with a crystal ball, for he had always to calculate each political and strategic move as astutely as he was able, but it produced a sense of absolute legitimacy from which he never wavered. By the end of the Civil War, this conviction had reached a level of overweening presumption, producing the sense that Franco would be the author of a completely new era in the history of Spain. Initially, this stimulated megalomaniac ambitions of making the country a great military power with a major African empire, but it was not long before the harsh realities of the European war abroad and a desperately struggling economy at home began, step by step, to cut these ambitions down to size.

Hardly had the Civil War ended than the European war began. If the great myth of the Left in contemporary Spanish affairs is that the wartime republic was a democracy, the great myth of the Right, or at least of the franquistas, is that Franco was not *really* on Hitler's side during the war. This is also false.

The terms of the Civil War inevitably oriented Franco toward the Axis powers. He had signed special agreements with them during the final phase of the Spanish conflict, and already had an agreement with Hitler to tilt Spanish policy toward Germany (while technically remaining neutral) even before the invasion of Poland. Thus the months down to June 1940 were not a time of genuine neutrality, for collaboration with Germany had already begun, while the long period of non-belligerence that followed marked a clear tilt toward Germany (copying Mussolini's policy of 1939–40), initially intended as a phase of pre-belligerence.

Javier Tusell and others have contended that the decision that Spain not enter the Second World War was made by Hitler and not by Franco, and there is some truth to this contention. Franco wanted very much to enter the war between June 1940 and April 1941, but only on his own terms. From about the end of July Hitler also began to seek Spain's entry, but soon concluded that he could not meet Franco's terms—all of Morocco, large parts of French northwest Africa, and massive economic and military assistance. Franco's position, as he wrote to Serrano

Suñer in the autumn of 1940, was that "Spain cannot enter just for fun [*por gusto*]," but must receive firm and extensive assistance and compensation.[6]

No other government not in the war engaged in such extensive collaboration with the Axis, even though much of this collaboration was entirely or partially covert. This did not mean, however, that Madrid followed an absolutely clear-cut policy. It was also necessary at least temporarily to play a double game and to placate Britain and the United States, whose fleets controlled the Atlantic and on whom the survival of the Spanish economy depended, producing the element of ambiguity that always characterized Madrid's official policy. Then, as the war became more complicated, what at one time was conceived as a short-term necessity became a long-term policy. Franco generally agreed with Hitler and the German diplomats when they told him that his regime could never survive a military defeat of Germany. He sought to avoid any such outcome to the war, and in 1943 attempted to arrange a compromise peace, an effort that failed completely and did not gain the slightest cooperation from Hitler. As late as the beginning of 1944, Franco and some of his chief associates could not imagine that the Third Reich would be totally defeated. Rather, they hoped that it would still survive the war as a power, while they demonstrated to Hitler that Spain was Germany's last major friend, and so would be positioned to enjoy German support once the war ended. Only in the summer of 1944 did Franco accept the fact that Germany would be totally defeated, and by that time he simply had to hope that the pledges from Britain and the United States not to intervene militarily in Spain were valid. Indeed they were, though both London and Washington hoped that Franco would soon disappear or be overthrown.

In 1945 Franco was almost universally denounced as "the last surviving fascist dictator," and would never entirely escape "the Axis stigma."[7] Nonetheless, most scholars conclude that the Spanish regime was not intrinsically fascist, though it included aspects of fascism.

One of Franco's fundamental goals was not to repeat "el error Primo de Rivera" of leading a "hollow" or Latin American–style dictatorship without serious political content. Hence the partial adoption of the Italian model in 1937, though Franco made it clear that this was not an attempt merely to imitate Mussolini or anyone else but to create a new kind of Spanish system. He left it open-ended so long as the Civil War lasted, and the uncertainties of World War II then further extended the interregnum process. The events of 1941 nonetheless demonstrated that he intended to keep the Falange firmly under control and not permit the development of a true party-regime. Movement toward establishment of a corporative Cortes during 1942–43 was not much of a change in one direction or another, however, and to some extent was consistent with an Italian model.

More significant was the beginning of defascistization that began in August 1943, one month after the fall of Mussolini. By then it was becoming clear that whether or not Germany would be totally defeated, the war would not be followed by the political triumph of fascism as such, and the Spanish regime began to trim its sails. Along with this the goals of major militarization, so strong in 1939–41, had been abandoned and also those of imperial expansion. Even so, Franco generally moved slowly, so that the metamorphosis of the regime—into a corporative and ultra-Catholic system that by 1947 would be nominally converted to monarchy—was not in place until the middle of 1945, very nearly but not quite too late.

The regime survived, for several reasons. One was the political metamorphosis that Franco carried out, and another the implacable determination of the Caudillo himself, impassive amid the international ostracism of 1945–48. At the end of the greatest war in history, the only major power willing to promote some sort of direct intervention in Spain was the Soviet Union, but fortunately for Franco, Moscow was too far away. The opposition remained divided and did not present a convincing alternative in 1945, seeming to many to offer only the revival of the Civil War. The polarization of the 1930s paralyzed the possibility of the development of democracy in Spain for an entire generation, and even a leftist critic of Franco such as Gerald Brenan concluded that the country would have to remain under authoritarian rule for some time, until it had outgrown the conflicts of the past.

The second phase of franquismo, from 1945 to 1959, was unique in contemporary politico-cultural history not in downplaying fascism, which was inevitable, but in striving to complete the counterrevolution begun in 1936 and to sustain the only national neotraditionalist religious revival seen on such a scale in the Western world in the twentieth century—the only national Christian equivalent, however temporary, to the revival of Islamic fundamentalism in the Muslim world. Despite the triumph of the counterrevolution, Spain nonetheless remained essentially a modern Western—that is, secularizing—country—and the forces of secularization quickly began to win out again after 1960.

In its final fifteen years the Spain of Franco ended with the most sustained burst of economic development and social prosperity in the country's history. To Franco's many critics, his only relationship to this was "dumb luck"—he happened to remain as dictator during a great phase of European prosperity to which his ministers managed to connect the Spanish economy. It is certainly true that Franco did not understand modern development economics, but not so true that his leadership had nothing to do with rapid growth. From the beginning, he had made it clear that he intended to endow Spain with modern industry and technology, and thus achieve prosperity, but he believed that this could best be accomplished through a statist, autarchist program of "military economics." That model proved disastrous in the early 1940s, although it functioned to a certain extent during the 1950s, by the end of which it was totally exhausted. Franco was sufficiently realistic, unlike many Communist and other dictators, to accept the alternatives prescribed by his ministers. He did not understand these alternatives and was in fact skeptical of them, but to his credit and to the well-being of Spain, he did not reject them.

It has been observed that the changes and achievements in Spain under Franco can be divided into three categories: (1) those that Franco deliberately set out to bring about; (2) those that resulted from his policies as unintended effects; and (3) those that he opposed but could not prevent, though it may be artificial to try to separate unintended consequences between categories 2 and 3. The long duration of the dictatorship and the depoliticization of Spanish society were fundamental goals and achievements, which also made it possible to transcend the era of civil war. Economic modernization and prosperity were also fundamental goals, though Franco's own economic ideas would have been totally inadequate for the process.

Restoration of the monarchy was also Franco's plan, though the political decisions subsequently made by Juan Carlos fall into category 2 of unintended consequences. Similarly a certain institutionalization and depoliticization of the military was a goal, though Franco would probably not have expected this to go so far as acquiescence of the military in the dismantling of his regime. Equally, Franco intended to create an institutionalized system, which to some extent was achieved, yet he would never have intended that its institutions be used as legal mechanism to carry out a new model of transition and democratization, which is what happened. The "Spanish model" then to some extent became the standard for peaceful transition and democratization in Latin America, eastern Europe, and elsewhere. The regime eventually made a major effort to expand Spanish education on every level, and in the long run accomplished much more than any of its predecessors. The unintended consequence, however, was a better informed and more critical-minded society that preferred to embrace political change. What the regime indirectly accomplished was to prepare Spanish society to make good use of the opportunity for democracy, though that was never its intention.

What Franco never wanted at all were the profound cultural and religious changes that accompanied economic modernization and social transformation. He seems to have had the idea that economic development could be combined with traditionalist culture, but that was impossible. Franco desired a certain social transformation to create larger middle-class sectors in Spanish society, but he was appalled at the social, cultural, and religious consequences. To him, the most incomprehensible change was the secularization of culture and society in the 1960s and 1970s, which seemed to deny everything that the regime stood for.

The question is sometimes raised of Franco's place among the major dictators of the twentieth century. He did not wield either the power or the radical program of a Hitler or a Stalin, nor did he follow the intrinsically fascist priorities of a Mussolini. Similarly, he cannot be compared in equivalent terms with his longtime peninsular neighbor, Dr. António de Oliveira Salazar. Salazar was a university professor, an intellectual, and a fine literary stylist. More conservative than Franco, he also directed a more moderate regime, which he firmly and clearly endowed with a corporative constitution in 1933, remaining faithful to that model, even though it involved a partial compromise with limited residues of liberalism. Salazar never enjoyed undisputed domination of the Portuguese military, which frequently conspired against him, but his genuine wartime neutrality and rejection of the fascist model made his regime much more internationally acceptable, at least until the final African wars.

Javier Tusell has suggested that in some ways Franco can be usefully compared with the Yugoslav dictator Tito. At first glance it would seem counterintuitive to compare Franco with a Communist, yet there are notable similarities and contrasts. Like Franco, Tito led a one-party state that won power in a bloody civil war, one that Tito concluded with a massive repression which, in proportion to the population, may have claimed three times as many victims as that of Franco. Spain was not a new invention like Yugoslavia: both countries faced severe problems of internal unity. Both dictators also imposed political metamorphoses a few years apart, though of differing types. While Franco had to move beyond a semifascist model, Tito had eventually to abandon Leninist orthodoxy and try to develop a more liberal and reformist mode of Communism. Both found new sources of support during the Cold War, though Tito officially followed a neutralist policy. Both dictators were harshly condemned by the Soviet Union, which encouraged the overthrow of Franco and made a number of attempts to assassinate Tito. Both dictators enjoyed a kind of international rehabilitation, though as a rightist dictator Franco never enjoyed the adulation that the Western political leadership and intelligentsia tended to lavish on Tito, primarily for ideological reasons. Both dictators ruled for very long periods, and both presided over a long period of economic development and modernization, though in this regard Franco more fully abandoned his initial ideological rigidity and enjoyed greater success. Franco left Spain at a higher level of development in every respect. Both political systems imploded after the death of the dictator, but Spain underwent a peaceful transition to democracy, and Yugoslavia once more collapsed into civil war.

Near the final phase of his regime, Franco declared publicly that he was leaving everything "tied and well-tied." Did he really relieve that? There is every indication that he was shrewd enough to appreciate that some things would have to change after his death, yet he apparently believed that the fundamental essence of the regime could survive him. According to the testimony of Adolfo Suárez, shortly before his death Franco inquired whether the Movimiento Nacional could in some form endure. Suárez replied that it could not, responding affirmatively when the aged Caudillo asked if Spain then had "an inevitably democratic future." At the very end of his life, Franco may have intuited fairly clearly what Juan Carlos was likely to do, but by that point he was far too weak and exhausted, near death's door, to contemplate any further alternative.

Franco's death marked the end of a very long historical epoch, the era of the "Spanish ideology" of the unity, continuity, Catholic identity, and mission of a traditional culture and set of institutions whose roots lay in the eighth century or earlier. This long epoch of one-and-a-quarter millennia had perhaps the broadest chronological span of any national-ideological complex in Europe, even though it underwent innumerable variations and metamorphoses during those centuries. With Franco it was laid to rest, presumably forever. He was the last great historical figure of Spanish traditionalism, who sought unsuccessfully to combine modernization and tradition. After his death, Spain entered another historical era and, with more than a little anguish, sought a new identity.

15 | In the Shadow of the Military

In the twenty-first century the Spanish army weakens steadily both as a national institution and also as a combat force, to the extent that one wonders if any longer it can be considered as either of these. From this vantage point it is instructive to survey the role played by the military during the era of modernization in the nineteenth and twentieth centuries. The Spanish army probably passed more years engaged in some form of combat during the nineteenth century than did any other European army of that period; most of this activity was dedicated to civil war or colonial campaigns, with major international conflict only at the beginning and end of the century. What seemed most prominent was not its military but its political role, to the extent that the army appeared to be one of the major problems in Spain.

Before turning to the army as a military institution, it is important to consider the reason for its political prominence, greater than in Portugal or Greece, much greater than in Italy, comparable in the nineteenth century only to Latin American countries. Was this a "thesis" or an "antithesis"? That is, was the political initiative of the military due to a primary desire by the military itself for political domination, or was it an antithetical response to the weakness of political institutions, a response to the failure of the politicians? Any careful examination of the history of the military in modern Spain is likely to conclude that the political hypertrophy of the military stemmed from the weakness of political institutions, rather than from the dreams of the military to dominate the country, though sometimes the former did indeed lead to the latter.[1]

The problem in Spain was what political scientists call "pretorianism"—that is, the political predominance of the military, rather than "militarism"—the hypertrophy of the armed forces as military institutions, or their widespread employment in military activity. Militarily, the modern Spanish army has been a weak institution, and the only plan for "militarism" was the one attempted by the Franco regime in 1939–40 and then soon abandoned, above all for financial reasons. The modern Spanish army stems from the military reforms of the eighteenth-century Bourbon dynasty that organized the army on the French regimental model and also introduced the internal captaincies-general, though it never managed to restore the military potency that had been enjoyed down to the mid-seventeenth century. After the first half of the reign of Felipe V, rulers of the new dynasty were not given to military adventures, with the partial exception of Carlos III. The military were employed relatively rarely, and then, with a few exceptions, usually did not earn distinction. During the War of Independence much of the regular army disappeared, to be replaced by guerrillero bands, paradoxically not infrequently led, certainly often inspired, by priests.

The "military problem" of modern Spain then emerged at the same time as the "praetorian problem," and indeed to some extent the former preceded the latter. The army emerged from the Napoleonic wars deficient in organization and leadership, incorporating into the officer corps some of the leaders of the guerrilleros, lacking adequate financial support or logistical base. It was not given the resources to deal effectively with the independence movement in the Americas, repression of which seeming a doomed enterprise in any event, nor did many of the military have much stomach for it, though fighting went on intermittently for a decade.

The first modern pretorian act of the military was the forcible restoration of Fernando VII as absolute monarch, abrogating the Constitution of 1812.[2] After the War of Independence the country was severely divided politically, with a new liberal government, which did not entirely correspond to the culture and structure of society, making conflict inevitable and inviting military arbitration. Nonetheless, liberalism was the new direction of Spanish affairs and slowly grew stronger with each passing decade, though without the ability to establish clear dominance or to govern with stability. Therefore, despite the reactionary character of the coup of 1814, for the next seventy years, from 1815 to approximately 1885, most acts of political intervention by the military would be carried out on behalf of the more liberal or progressive forces, in an effort to give the latter the decisive strength which in fact they lacked.[3] A specifically Spanish phenomenon was the role of the "ayacuchos," officers who were veterans of the colonial campaigns in South America, the moniker taken from the site of their final climactic defeat. Anticipating the much later experience of some French and Portuguese officers, the ayacuchos were influenced by their former enemies and came to form a core of liberal activists within the military.

Military discipline was largely reestablished after the French intervention of 1823, when absolute monarchy was restored the second time, but the long-term military problem would be revealed by the First Carlist War and its aftermath. Since the new liberal regime held control of state institutions, the great majority of army officers rallied to liberalism, yet the army proved inefficient at civil war. After finally winning victory, the army was not restored to its proper dimensions, above all because of the permanent incorporation of thousands of officers commissioned during the civil war, as well as a certain number of Carlist officers, according to the generous terms that ended the First Carlist War. Sheer hypertrophy of the officer corps would remain one of the major problems for an entire century, down to the time of the Azaña reforms of 1931–32, and would partially reemerge under Franco, as well.

The Isabeline regime (1833–68) constituted the heart of the "era of pronunciamientos," though to some extent this would continue until the full stabilization of the Restoration system in the 1880s. The new liberal regime had largely eliminated nonliberal political elites through civil war, but it was weakly established socially and also internally fragmented, unable to create much of what political scientists call a "civil society." An inexperienced, inept, and fearful young queen was unable to act coherently as a moderating force, despite the power placed in her hands, and access was routinely denied to competing liberal groups. In a nonfunctional liberal system, the pronunciamiento, in its several forms, moderated access to power. Though most army officers were not strong liberals, the effect of military intervention was to move the political system in a more and more liberal direction, climaxing in the disastrous sexennium of 1868–74. This was a sobering experience and marked the end of successful pronunciamientos on behalf of greater liberalization. The two successful interventions of 1874 each moved the situation in a more conservative direction, the second restoring the Bourbons and marking the beginning of the more stable system directed by Antonio Cánovas del Castillo.[4]

There was never any question of military dictatorship in the Latin American or twentieth-century Afro-Asian style. The political generals of the era operated within the general framework of the political system, usually as armed representatives of regular political parties or forces. When a general led the government, he did so as the nominal leader of a parliamentary group. There was no question of a complete military supersession of the regular political system. The only occasions in which a general served as quasi-head of state occurring in the regency of Espartero in 1841–43, during the minority of Isabel II, and the brief leadership of Serrano as head of the "unitary republic" in 1874. In each case a general presided over formally constitutional and parliamentary regimes.

If during the six decades between 1815 and 1874 the military had often moved politics to the Left, the following six decades (1874–1934) were not so much a time of movement toward the Right as toward greater political balance, punctuated by the temporary rightist swing of Primo de Rivera in the 1920s. Only in 1936 did the military move decisively to the Right. A case can be made that in fact their political attitudes and values never really changed that much during this entire era. Rather, the political context changed enormously, while the political stance of most of the military remained little altered. That is, army officers as a whole were never for the most part political radicals. During the early nineteenth century the politically active sector moved toward moderate liberalism. Once the country went beyond that during 1868–74, political intervention pulled back in the opposite direction. After Primo de Rivera had temporarily moved government to a moderate form of rightist authoritarianism—at that point unprecedented in contemporary Spanish history—the politically active sector of the military once more sought to move back to liberalism. The new republic was widely accepted by the military in 1931 not as any gateway to revolution, which at that point it hardly seemed to be, but as a new national community of liberal democracy, which it turned out not to be.

Throughout this period, however, most army officers were not involved in politics. Had that been the case, the army would have ceased to exist as a military institution. The lead was normally taken by individual senior commanders, maintaining a certain hierarchical function. Sometimes the initiative was seized by more junior officers: in one case in 1866 by sergeants in the Madrid garrison. These more "subversive" junior revolts, reversing the military hierarchy, almost always failed.

Naval commanders rarely participated. The naval officer corps remained more aristocratic than its largely mesocratic counterpart in the army, and usually kept aloof from politics, a partial exception taking place in 1868. Later, the newly formed Spanish air force of the early twentieth century was too small to play a political role, and when several air force officers sought to play a major role in the Republican revolt of December 1930, they failed completely.[5]

Throughout these decades the military were steadily involved in civil wars and colonial wars, though after 1814 they were spared major international conflict except for a few months in 1898. Generally, the military record of the Spanish army in these conflicts was not distinguished. Semicontinuous combat experience did not serve to forge a more efficient fighting machine, the practical effect being virtually the opposite. The army was proportionately always underfunded, underequipped, inadequately prepared and commanded, but overofficered. For more than a century a disproportionate amount of the military budget simply went to pay officers' salaries, although those salaries were low. This stemmed above all from poor leadership; the fact that the army administration enjoyed considerable autonomy was no guarantee of concentration on professional excellence, but just the contrary. Routine bureaucratization accompanied frequent conflict—the Spanish army had, therefore, the worst of both worlds. By 1895 the army command feared to assign officers routinely to combat in Cuba and asked for volunteers. Comparatively few presented themselves, so that many of the junior combat officers in the final Caribbean conflict consisted of sergeants from peninsular garrisons who had been promoted to officer rank after volunteering for service in Cuba.

The military were imbued with a strong sense of patriotism, which during the second half of the nineteenth century, in keeping with general European trends, turned increasingly into a more militant and aggressive nationalism. It is probably no exaggeration to say that in the 1890s the nearest thing to a coherent group of Spanish nationalists would be found in the military, or at least sectors of the military, yet, in a manner once more typical of their Spanish contemporaries, the military were themselves not at all united. A large part of the officer corps consisted of routine bureaucratic careerists, but a defensive and nationalist reaction was fueled by the general feeling after 1898 that the army and navy were unfairly singled out as bearing sole responsibility for "the disaster."[6]

There was an element of paradox in this, insofar as the army itself had not served as a force for national education and integration to the same extent that military institutions in France and Germany had achieved such goals during the preceding century. In Spain, the dominance of pretorianism over not merely militarism but simply any efficient attention to the development of military institutions had meant a feebly developed army that was unable to effect the universal military service introduced in certain other countries. The practice of what was called "redención a metálica," as well as other measures, exempted most of the middle and upper classes, producing what was generally a class-based army that could not serve as an inclusive school for patriotism and national pride. Added to a grossly deficient system of primary education, it was a further limitation on the development of a more self-conscious civil or national society.

During the early twentieth century the military, partially removed from politics by the stability of the Restoration system, began to resume a political role through the Law of Military Jurisdictions (1906) and the movement of the Juntas Militares, which commenced in 1916. The Juntas Militares represented first the bureaucratization and second the indiscipline of the military, aiming at a kind of political syndicalization of officers, partly in opposition to the new combat elite of "africanistas," like Franco, who fought in the Moroccan campaigns. They marked a return to politicization, if not full-scale pretorianism, as the country's political life expanded and became more conflictive.[7]

On the other hand, the militarism of the World War I era largely passed Spain by, as most of the fighting in the Protectorate was shelved for the duration of the European conflict. No significant expansion or improvement of the Spanish military took place, leaving it proportionally even more backward and antiquated than before. Renewal of the effort to pacify the Spanish zone in Morocco led to a humiliating defeat in 1921, which placed in jeopardy the future of the Protectorate and also helped to destabilize the political system. The initiative of Primo de Rivera in 1923 could have been the last of the great nineteenth-century liberal pronunciamientos, had the dictator remained faithful to his initial declaration. As it was, he reflected hesitantly and uncertainly some of the new authoritarian alternatives of the era, governing at first through the Directorio Militar of 1923–25. Beyond that, he could not resolve the issue of reform, failing ultimately to transcend liberalism, and failing also to carry most of the military with him in his confused, abortive search for a long-term authoritarian alternative.[8]

The whole experience was chastening for the military. For the time being it cured them of political ambitions, predisposing them to accept the inauguration of the democratic republic. The new regime faced many problems, but until the final crisis the military was not one of them. The Azaña reforms of 1931–33 tried to reorder military institutions, but their major achievement was at great cost to reduce the size of the officer corps by about forty percent. The army was in general neither transformed nor significantly improved. No more than a tiny handful of officers supported the attempted revolt against the Republican government by Gen. José Sanjurjo, the weakest of all the six armed rebellions of 1930–34, the other five all being carried out by the Left. When a small group of conspirators tried to rally support for a coup at the time of the Popular Front elections in February 1936, they quickly had to give up, for lack of support.[9]

Most army officers were opposed to the Left, but few wanted to be involved in armed revolt. There was a very small leftist minority and a larger rightist minority, but the bulk sought to avoid having to play a political role; hence the difficulty of organizing the rebellion of July 18, 1936. Subsequently, the Azaña–Casares Quiroga administration would be almost universally criticized for its failure to repress and purge the military, but in fact the government's calculation would probably have been proven justified had it not been for the kidnapping and murder of Calvo Sotelo, followed by the almost incredible inadequacy of the government's own response.

The Left Republican leaders perceived correctly that most of the military were not inclined to rebel. They undertook a lengthy series of measures to reassign or to remove altogether from command the senior officers suspected of strong rightist sympathies, though these efforts turned out to be inadequate. They also calculated that too rigorous an attempt to purge or to restrict the military might serve as a boomerang, stimulating greater opposition than already existed. A second consideration was the determination of Casares Quiroga not to play the "role of Kerensky" that had been openly assigned to him by some of the theorists of the revolutionary Left. Should it come to that, a reasonably strong and intact army might be needed to repress another effort at revolutionary insurrection by anarchists or Socialists. Yet a third factor was the conviction that those elements in the military strongly opposed to the government were so few and weak that they constituted a paper tiger. Thus what would presumably be no more than a feeble effort at rebellion should not necessarily be completely discouraged, but might even be desirable. It would presumably be easy to repress, and rapid victory by the government would strengthen it both against the Right and also against the revolutionary Left. Only a few days before July 18, these calculations were perhaps not so far wrong as they have always seemed in retrospect. Had the government maintained a greater semblance of constitutional order, they might have worked out as planned. Neither the government nor most of the military were eager to institute conflict. As leading revolutionaries such as Friedrich Engels and Leon Trotsky had pointed out, even the most aggressive and radical forces prefer to pretend to act defensively in response to an initiative from their adversaries, and this was very broadly the case with quite diverse sectors, politically and militarily, in the Spain of 1936.

The paradox of the military rebellion that began the Civil War is that it was probably more eagerly desired by its opponents than any other military revolt in Spanish history. The Casares Quiroga government did not seek deliberately to provoke an armed rebellion, but neither did it make a major effort to avoid one, calculating that the results would quickly redound to its benefit. As Santos Juliá has explained, military revolt also formed the basis of the calculations of the Caballeristas, the most important single sector of the revolutionary Left.[10] Having no plans of their own to seize power directly, they calculated that the effect of a revolt would be so threatening and destabilizing that a weak Left Republican government would have no alternative but to hand power peacefully to the Socialists. By analogy with Russia in 1917, Casares Quiroga would play the role of Kerensky, and the Spanish military the role of the Russian General Kornilov. The calculation of Casares Quiroga failed disastrously, though that of the Caballeristas proved partially correct, as Azaña elected on July 19 to "arm the people" (something to which Casares Quiroga and the most moderate Left Republicans were firmly opposed) and then finally appointed an all-Popular Front government led by Largo Caballero on September 4. The ultimate weakness of both calculations, of course, was the complete failure to envision the potential strength of the revolt.

In the first edition of his *Spain: 1808–1939*, Raymond Carr followed the customary language in referring to the "generals' revolt" of July 18. In fact, exactly as the government calculated, most of the generals did not revolt. Though the insurrection would be led by a small group of generals, what gave the rebellion strength was the strong support provided by junior and middle-rank officers in approximately half the garrisons of Spain. The younger officers responded much more radically and with greater commitment, which was indispensable to the partial success of the revolt. There was concern that the ordinary recruits, who rarely were volunteers but normally draftees, often from leftist worker milieu, might not obey orders. In fact, the efforts by Communists and anarchists to subvert the military politically largely failed. There were, of course, individual desertions, but the great majority of recruits obeyed orders as long as they were resolutely led, even though they did not necessarily exhibit military enthusiasm or efficiency.[11]

The Civil War transformed the majority of officers politically. Whereas most were moderate and largely apolitical conservatives in 1936, those who joined the revolt quickly came to form a new cohort. The commanders and officers of the Nationalist Army of 1939 were strongly committed to their victorious movement and its regime, and also to a strongly right-wing and authoritarian ideology. Few of them had become converts to fascism, but they saw themselves as the genuine elite of a new nationalist system. The leaders of the military under the new dictatorship were more politically and ideologically mobilized than most of their predecessors. The new regime had begun in 1936–38 as a military dictatorship, the only complete military dictatorship in Spanish history, occupying both the role of chief of state and of the government in general. Though Franco insisted on complete military discipline and subordination to his personal command and formed a regular nonmilitary government in January 1938, the military saw the new system, not incorrectly, as a military-led regime, at least in its first phases. Military members of the Spanish "victory delegation" that visited Rome in May 1939 explained to their Italian Fascist hosts that the difference between the Mussolini and Franco regimes was that the role played by the Fascist Party in the former was played by the military in the latter.

Franco never planned a military government but intended to use senior officers in key roles, trusting some of them more than he did Falangists. The initial scheme of Franco's government in 1939–41 was not pretorianism—that is, giving the military any corporate political role—but simply to make special use of senior officers in important posts and also to make it the most militaristic regime in Spanish history. During the first year of peace, plans were drawn up for a gigantic construction program that would build an enormous navy and a 5,000-plane air force. This was so preposterous compared with the grave deficiencies of the post-war Spanish economy that within little more than a year, the plans were totally shelved. Rather than developing great new armed forces, the Franco regime soon reverted to the military norm of modern Spain: an army of poorly trained draftees led by a numerically bloated but technically deficient officer corps, provided with limited third-rate equipment. As the German consul in Tetuán reported to Berlin concerning the sizable Spanish forces in the Moroccan Protectorate: "One cannot describe the Spanish military organization here in bad enough terms."[12]

This reality did not prevent the regime's leaders and some of its generals from developing delusions of grandeur. Immediately after the fall of France there was enthusiasm for Spain's entry into the war, though among most of the military commanders this quickly dwindled, once the country's disastrous economic situation became even clearer by the end of 1940. It is a moot point exactly what role was played by the program initiated by the British government in the summer of that year of paying large bribes to more than thirty senior commanders to use their influence to maintain Spain's neutrality, an issue that cannot be resolved for lack of full documentation.[13]

Franco's use and control of the military was generally astute. Especially during the 1940s and 1950s he employed many senior officers (generally colonels and generals) in a wide variety of key state and administrative positions, more of which were held by the military than by the Falange during that period. Military men, such as Franco's childhood friend Juan Antonio Suanzes and others, in the economic institutions, particularly the Instituto Nacional de Industria (INI— National Institute of Industry), implemented Franco's program of autarchy, which should be considered at first more a program of military economics than of fascist economics.[14] Franco was careful to see to it, however, that they held offices as individuals, not as institutional representatives of the military. The armed forces were allowed no independent corporate power. An officer in government served as an appointee of Franco, not as a representative of the military themselves. In 1939 Franco separated the air force from the army and navy for the first time, beginning a practice of appointing three separate military ministers (army, navy, and air force) to his governments, averting any dangerous concentration of power.

Although they found little reason to quarrel with Franco's foreign policy, the military were keenly dissatisfied with the domestic situation in the first postwar years. In one sense, they became Spain's most important antifascists, for they bitterly resented the prominence of Serrano Suñer and the Falange during 1939–42, helping to produce the only two serious government crises of Franco's regime in May 1941 and again in August–September 1942. In each case Franco was careful not to award a clear-cut victory to the military, for he still considered the Falange important to his regime, and he did not wish to see the military become so power-ful that they could dictate to him. Serrano was eliminated in 1942, but by that time this suited Franco as well. The nearest thing to a replacement for Serrano was Captain (later Admiral) Luis Carrero Blanco, much more discreet than Serrano. Moreover, as a naval officer, Carrero Blanco was not involved in the personal rival-ries of the leading generals, who found him relatively colorless and not a menacing or challenging figure. As it was, Carrero Blanco became the most influential naval officer in modern Spanish government.[15]

Altogether there was more political discontent with Franco inside the Spanish regime during the first half of World War II than at any point during his long ten-ure as military dictator. All the different "families" of the regime expressed fairly strong criticism (though from diverse viewpoints), but none was in a position to act against Franco, not even the military. Leading generals criticized many aspects of policy, including the place given to the Falange and not excluding the personal decisions of Franco himself, but they were internally disunited and the leading personalities were astutely handled by Franco. The most dangerous ones were pro-Nazi generals like Juan Yagüe and Agustín Muñoz Grandes. Franco left Yagüe without active assignment and in internal exile for two years, and after Muñoz Grandes returned from leading the Blue Division on the Russian front, Franco personally kept him directly under his own thumb and without any direct com-mand, until the danger that he might conspire on behalf of Hitler had passed.

Few of the Spanish generals were that strongly pro-Nazi, so that the only polit-ical alternative which began to gain any support was restoration of the monarchy in the person of Don Juan, the pretender to the throne. By 1942 this even began to gain the approval of some of the pro-Nazis, but conversely few of the generals were such committed monarchists that they were willing to stand up to Franco, the main exception being the air force general Alfredo Kindelán. Antonio Aranda, who seems to have been the leading individual recipient of British bribes, and sev-eral other generals were active in discussions with British diplomats, sometimes re-ferring to a shadowy "junta of generals" that was about to take action. In fact, no such junta existed. As Javier Tusell has written, "The generals did not conspire, but only talked of conspiring."[16]

Franco reached a point of potential crisis with his military hierarchy on only one occasion, early in September 1943. Italy had just been knocked out of the war six weeks earlier, and the Allies had clearly gained the upper hand on every front. For the first time the future of the regime was directly placed in doubt, and on that occasion most of the lieutenant generals signed a very respectful letter to Franco asking if he did not think that circumstances had reached the point at which it was desirable to restore the monarchy. They swore complete loyalty and discipline during any transition.[17]

Franco, however, intended only to trim his policy and had already determined that in no circumstance would he ever step down voluntarily. He spoke with the lieutenant generals—but never with more than one or two at any one time—explaining that the situation was much too delicate for any change and that Don Juan would be incapable of dealing with such critical circumstances. Several of the lieutenant generals quickly withdrew their support from the initiative, while Franco promoted a number of his "incondicionales" (loyalists) from major general to lieutenant general, until he was certain that a majority of the top military hierarchy had become totally reliable once more. Subsequently he also incorporated hundreds of former "provisional officers" from the Civil War—more diehard franquistas than many of the ordinary officers—to regular or higher officer rank, further strengthening the political complexion of his officer corps.

What most effectively rallied the military around Franco was the beginning of the guerrilla insurgency, led by the Communists and later by anarchists, in October 1944. This threatened direct revival of the Civil War and the violent overthrow of the regime by the revolutionary Left. The armed forces completely closed ranks, and maintained firm support of the regime during the period of international ostracism that followed the end of World War II.

The regime assumed its more permanent form in the years following 1945, and by this time Franco had totally abandoned his fantasy of turning Spain into a modern military power. In fact, he settled for the opposite—a weak, third-rate army designed to police and garrison the country rather than to fight external enemies. The army settled into a rather stultified routine and continued to exhibit some of the worst features of its predecessors in the nineteenth and early twentieth centuries—a bureaucratic mass of draftees led by a bloated, not very professional officer corps, which trained little and possessed antiquated equipment. Indeed, proportionate to other modern forces the Spanish army in the years 1945 to 1953 was the very opposite of what the regime had earlier planned, and by international standards had become weaker than in 1898, thoroughly failing to keep pace with military modernization.

The senior military command adjusted to this situation quite comfortably. For junior and middle-rank officers, on the other hand, pay was low and promotion very slow. Indeed, because of the excess number of officers, promotion during the 1950s and 1960s was slower than in almost any other Western army. Amid the scarcity of the 1940s, officers had access through military commissaries to goods either unavailable or very expensive on the civilian markets. As the economy improved in the 1950s, this relative advantage was lost: while officers' salaries increased little in real terms, new barracks and housing were finally being built.

The pacts signed with the United States in 1953 provided the first significant foreign military assistance since the Civil War. American arms given Spain were always older weapons that had already seen use, but they were far more advanced than anything in the Spanish arsenal. It was finally possible to begin to retire the Civil War–vintage planes (including captured Soviet aircraft) in favor of the first jet planes, even though the latter were of a design already abandoned by the American air force. More advanced facilities and military cooperation with Washington made it possible to develop a new goal, "professionalization," in place of the politicized garrison-army of the recent past. During the next two decades the most able younger sectors of the officer corps devoted themselves increasingly to this task, encouraged by the "Barroso reforms" undertaken in the army while Gen. Antonio Barroso was minister between 1957 and 1962.[18]

After 1943 the military never again presented the slightest political challenge to Franco. By about 1960 nearly all the top Civil War–era generals had retired, and the new commanders were even less likely than their predecessors to cause trouble. During the dramatic economic development of the 1960s, little of the new funding that became available was spent on the military, whose share of the national budget declined more and more, until it was proportionately less than in many west European democracies. By that point, for the first time in Spanish history, the state was spending more on education than on the armed forces.

The officers as a whole remained conservative, with increasing interest in professionalization, but during the last years of the regime three different sectors could be identified in politico-professional terms. On the Right were the "blue generals," ultra-rightist generals handpicked by Franco to hold most of the top commands and dedicated to maintaining the present system. On the Left was a small number of liberal or leftist officers who hoped to see the armed forces support modernization. Though not truly radical or subversive, a small group who had formed a "Unión Militar Democrática" was expelled from the officer corps in 1975 and not reincorporated for many years. In between was a group of moderates who emphasized professionalization and keeping the military out of politics, while the country's political evolution proceeded. They were represented especially by Lt. Gen. Manuel Díez Alegría, chief of the supreme general staff, and his principal assistant, Gen. Manuel Gutiérrez Mellado.

It was in these circumstances that only a few months prior to the death of Franco, the leaders of the Spanish Communist Party and their partners in the Junta Democrática arranged a public hearing in the chambers of the U.S. Congress. Its purpose was to air publicly the need for strong American pressure on the Spanish military to discourage them from interfering in the democratization process that would be undertaken after Franco's death. On that occasion, I could express some confidence that this would not be necessary because the conditions that had elicited military intervention in the past probably would not succeed in the future. The military had not interfered with a democratic transition in 1931–32, which was supported by society and enjoyed relatively coherent leadership. There was a good likelihood that both these factors—strong social support and solid leadership—would prevail during the prospective new democratization, which would also be likely to maintain legal continuity and to uphold law and order. Military interference in the past had always responded to situations of fragmentation, paralysis, or crisis, which would less likely be repeated in the immediate future. No one could guarantee that capable leadership and stability would predominate, but it seemed a reasonably sound calculated risk to assume that they might, and so it turned out.

The military command in 1976–78 remained franquista, but Franco himself had trained his generals to keep out of politics, and they followed his final request that they transfer their loyalty to King Juan Carlos.[19] Despite its legalization of the Communist Party, the transition government proceeded "de la ley a la ley" (from the law to the law), maintaining legal continuity and law and order, and thus enjoyed overwhelming popular support.

There was only one point at which there was danger of military intervention, immediately following the collapse of Adolfo Suárez's government in February 1981, the only major crisis of political leadership during the transition. Even then, the goal of intervention was not to restore the Franco regime or install a Greek-style military dictatorship, but to provide a military leader for an all-party national government, one that would not technically rupture parliamentary legality but would significantly reorient national policy. This was not planned as a coup d'état, but as an updated semi- or pseudo-legalitarian version of a nineteenth-century pronunciamiento. Even this, however, never happened, because of the crown's startled and resolute reaction to the crude assault on the parliamentary chamber by the Civil Guard units of Lt. Col. Antonio Tejero Molina on February 23, 1981, a poorly planned tactical maneuver that seemed out of control.[20] Not only was the action completely quashed but, in the subsequent prosecution of key ringleaders, the civil government intervened with the military tribunals to exact longer terms of imprisonment.

The abortive pronunciamiento had the effect of moderating government policy during the year or two that followed, but it proved to be the swan song of the political influence of the military. The "long government" of the Socialists that followed (1982–96), enjoying an absolute majority in its first years, provided the strong and stable administration to institute a progressive change of policy, which was simply extended by the Aznar government in power from 1996 to 2004.[21] The "blue generals" were soon retired, and the army was focused on professional reform, integration with NATO and, later, international peacekeeping.[22] Conversion to an all-volunteer force was part of a process of relentless reduction in size that was not really compensated for by improved training and weaponry. In a stable democracy, the pretorian role of the military came to a complete end, but the Spanish army has been unable to recapture a genuine military role either, and in comparison with other countries has declined even further in strength. It is to be hoped that in the future Spain has no need to call on its army for defense from foreign foes, because even less than in the recent past has it the strength for such a mission.

16 | Controversies over History in Contemporary Spain

A common complaint about contemporary Western society is that it suffers from amnesia and has little knowledge of, or interest in, history. Growing addiction to the Internet atomizes reading, so that information is obtained in snippets or packets without sustained study or broader understanding, and without criteria concerning accuracy or reliability. This results in vast amounts of information, much more so than in any preceding era, yet without many standards, organization, or sustained comprehension. Thus the young spend untold hours seated before computer screens, but do not read books. It is alleged that they learn less than preceding generations, compared with their level of formal education. They do not study but merely "retrieve" bits and pieces of information.[1]

Is such criticism accurate? To some degree this would seem to be the case, and as far as history is concerned, it is absolutely clear that the great expansion of formal education has not been accompanied by an equivalent expansion of the knowledge of history. A culture informed by the most intense narcissism and materialism in human history is oriented toward instant gratification and thus loses touch with its own cultural tradition.

There is another side to the story, insofar as there has never been so much scholarly research on history as at the present time, and never have so many books of history been written, purchased, and, presumably, read. This is due, however, in large part to the growth in population and in the economy, and the expansion of the university systems, which creates a larger base for specialized activities. In addition, it is sometimes argued that historical thinking or historical consciousness has become more common, at least among much of the intellectually informed minority of the population, than ever before.[2] Moreover, in the United States and several other countries, there are many skilled scholars and writers of history who are not university professors. They concentrate on the kind of big topics and themes of broader interest that academic historians usually spurn, and as a result often sell large numbers of books. Military history, especially, seems to flourish in all countries, even though political prejudice largely bans it from the universities.

All these signs of interest in history exist but do so amid increasing intellectual and cultural fragmentation, and are characteristic simply of certain minorities, with little or no effect on the population at large. This produces a seeming paradox: on the one hand, a minority studies and reads history more than ever before, while the great majority—despite universal literacy and basic education—has little or no awareness of history, which recedes more and more in the educational curriculum.

Moreover, among historians the study of history has been greatly broadened on the one hand, while on the other it has been weakened by politicization, contemporary cultural trends, and trivialization. Dominant among the latter are the ideology of political correctness, totally hegemonic by the 1990s, and the consequences of postmodernist theory, two different but mutually reinforcing trends. The effect is drastic deconstruction of previously dominant paradigms, replaced by a contradictory combination of new political dogmas that coexist with radical subjectivism. In the universities, this has almost completely eliminated certain fields, such as military history, and resulted in a major de-emphasis on political history, though this is somewhat less notable in Spain. Major themes are replaced by comparatively minor considerations, which emphasize small groups, deviants, and cultural oddities. Most studies are required to fit somewhere within the new sacred trinity of race, class, and gender—the new "cultural Marxism." Research that does not conform to these criteria is increasingly eliminated from the universities, where hiring practices in the humanities and social sciences have become blatantly discriminatory.

New cultural and political trends often take a little longer to arrive in Spain, but by the twenty-first century they have become increasingly characteristic of new historical work in Spain, as well. The great expansion of the university system has indeed resulted in much more research and writing than ever before, producing historical knowledge and significant publications in almost every field, but as stated earlier, the study of history in Spain is constrained by the provincialization and trivialization of history on the one hand, and the weaknesses of the university system on the other.

Production of significant historical work in the past generation has been limited by a massive emphasis on local and regional history. This field can be as significant a field as most others, but in Spain matters have been carried to the point of political and cultural hysteria, producing a massive disproportion of attention, stimulated by the quasi-federalization of the country and the increasingly large amounts of money spent by local and regional governments on cultural affairs. Young scholars know that if they concentrate on such themes, publication is virtually guaranteed, irrespective of how petty or trivial the work may be.

Spanish universities for the most part follow these trends, because of the localist and endogamic character of most of the new universities themselves. What might be called a "national market" in research and hiring is comparatively weak. Most of the universities play to local audiences and are heavily nepotistic in their personnel practices. The failure to recruit professors on a broader basis is a major limitation, as is the lack of emphasis on achievement in their professional evaluation. These same tendencies, together with a decided politicization of the universities, currently exist in almost every country, though provincialization and endogamy are especially pronounced in Spain.

What is most notable about the treatment of history in Spain in the twenty-first century is not the almost inevitable presence of certain common contemporary trends, but the degree of controversy that exists in two key areas. The first is the effort to deconstruct a common national history of Spain, replacing it with a new focus on the regions, which in turn has produced a reaction that stresses a common national history and identity.[3] The second focuses on the Civil War and the Franco regime, particularly those issues associated with the repression carried out by the latter, and has been especially promoted in terms of what is called "la memoria histórica." Since the first problematic has already been treated to some extent in several of the early chapters of this book, I shall not go back over that ground but devote the remainder of this concluding chapter to the controversy, more political than historiographical, associated with "memoria histórica."

Spain is far from unique in having suffered a severe trauma in its history during the twentieth century. The same thing may be said of most—though not quite all—the countries of Europe, and of a good many others in other continents. In such circumstances it becomes all the more difficult to achieve the kind of detachment and objectivity that is the goal of the professional scholar.

Following World War II these experiences not only stimulated an enormous amount of new historical study but also a concern with "historical justice," a settling of accounts with past history. This stemmed from two factors. One was the greater elaboration, sophistication, and democratization of juridical practices, which had become more extensive than ever before, and the other the severity of the traumas inflicted by the military conquests, occupations, civil wars, and dictatorships of the era. People had sometimes been subjected to equivalent, or even greater, affliction, in other historical periods, but the levels of consciousness and meliorism had increased by the mid-twentieth century, and the expectations and standards of justice were higher than in times past. Moreover, the new phenomenon of totalitarianism and the mega-atrocity of the Nazi Holocaust seemed to raise organized political criminality to a much higher level. When such concerns had first arisen after World War II, postmodernist theory had not yet appeared to explain that all perception is subjective and that objective standards in complex human situations do not exist. Finally, it was argued that prosecution of the new legal category (but common historical phenomenon) of "war crimes" and the punishment of those responsible for dictatorship and mass murder was a necessary part of civic reeducation in order for democracy to flourish in the future and to avoid the situation that had developed following World War I.[4]

The best example of contemporary historical justice has been the prosecution of Nazi war crimes and the serious efforts made by the citizens of the West German Federal Republic to come to terms with Germany's horrendous recent past. If the political processes of de-Nazification were not completely effective, nonetheless the development of West German democracy—together with ongoing efforts at objective historical study, serious education, prosecution of perpetrators, and efforts to compensate the victims—was generally successful and has made Germany the most commendable example of what the Germans call *Vergangenheitsbewältigung*, coming to terms with the past. This process was not instantaneous and had its own ups and downs, while before the end of the twentieth century a countermovement had begun to "normalize" that history. On the scholarly level, this took the form of the relatively well-known *Historikerstreit*—the controversy among the historians—while more broadly there has been more and more of a tendency of Germans to see their forebears of the Nazi era as victims, as well, particularly of mass bombing from the West and monstrous Soviet atrocities from the East. The existence of a society composed both of many heinous perpetrators and of numerous victims is probably not without precedent. Of course there were many different Germans—many were major perpetrators, while others were indeed victims, either of their rulers or of the rulers' foes. By comparison, defascistization in Italy was half-hearted, producing only a limited number of prosecutions and then, after only about three years and on the initiative of a Communist minister of justice, came to a complete end.[5] In the countries occupied by the Soviet Union, defascistization was to a large extent a matter of punishing those whom the Soviets considered their principal enemies. Fascists or ex-fascists deemed useful to the Soviets were not punished and even, in a few instances, rewarded.

World War II ended in much of Europe amid scenes of apocalyptic disaster. The democratization of Spain and Portugal took place under very different conditions, amid the greatest prosperity and well-being in the history of the two countries. The Portuguese dictatorship was overthrown by force of arms and more than a year of political conflict ensued, together with a series of political arrests (at first, more than under the dictatorship) and certain gestures of punishment for notables and activists of the preceding regime. This transition was nonetheless typically Portuguese in the very limited amount of violence that occurred. The political process soon developed into a genuine parliamentary democracy, and the prosecution of notables of the Old Regime quickly came to an end.[6]

The circumstances and character of the democratic transition in Spain, by contrast, were unique. If the Spanish disaster of revolutionary civil war amid relatively normal peacetime conditions during the 1930s had been unprecedented, so were the terms of the Spanish democratization. Prior to that time, all institutionalized modern European authoritarian regimes that had existed for as long as a decade or more only lost power as a result of external war.[7] The Spanish Transition presented the first example of a democratization from the inside out, in which the laws and institutions of the authoritarian regime were used to carry out a complete transformation into a democracy. At a press conference in 1974 (shortly before the death of Franco), the historian Ricardo de la Cierva, then the reformist director general of popular culture, was asked by Spanish reporters if any such case had ever existed, and La Cierva confessed, rightly enough, that he was not aware of any.

During the Transition the country moved legally and relatively peacefully from dictatorship to parliamentary democracy. None of the regularly organized political parties engaged in violence, although the Basque terrorist organization ETA, the extreme Left, and also, occasionally, the extreme Right, did so. Violence was totally extrasystemic, unlike the situation under the Second Republic, when major systemic forces, such as the Socialists, and then finally much of the army, engaged in it. By 1975 the anarchosyndicalist movement, once the source of much violence, had simply been eliminated by modernization.

Thus Spain continued to be different, but now in a completely positive way. In earlier generations the country had differed both because of a lingering traditionalism, on the one hand, and because of persistent efforts—from 1810 to 1931—to introduce advanced new modern political systems for which the country's social and cultural structure was not fully prepared. An effective synergy was achieved for the first time after 1975.

This created a new "Spanish model" of democratic transition, not the courageous but futile models of 1808–14 and 1820 (which also had been widely and almost always unsuccessfully emulated elsewhere), but an eminently productive pattern that became in effect the new model for world democratic transition. It was emulated in Latin American countries and also in nearly all the Communist countries of Eastern Europe and in central and northern Asia, though—depending on the cultural heritage and/or level of development of these countries—some of them failed to become functioning democracies, moving into a different kind of twenty-first-century authoritarianism. Everywhere, except in Yugoslavia and Romania, something equivalent to the Spanish model was pursued, in most cases achieving democratic success.

One requirement of the Spanish model was rejection of the politics of vengeance, which meant eschewing any political or judicial quest for "historical justice." At the time, this was fully accepted by all the major political actors, with the partial exception of the Basque Partido Nacionalista Vasco (PNV), still anchored in archaic habits. The Left was just as eager to embrace this policy as the Right; standard rhetoric and posturing notwithstanding, the democratic credentials of the Spanish Left were also dubious, and they were eager to start with a clean slate. A conscious decision was made to eschew any new attempt at historical justice, for there was general awareness that this had been carried out in a vindictive fashion by the Republic in 1931–32, and later with much greater brutality by the Franco regime. Leaders of the Transition appreciated the fact that another such effort could hardly be made with impartiality, and almost undoubtedly would do more harm than good.

Generally speaking, this feature of the Spanish model was also followed in other countries. Very little effort was made to indict or prosecute the personnel of the preceding authoritarian regimes during the course of the democratizations of the 1980s and 1990s. The Czechs introduced a process of "lustration," as they called it, to deal with some of the major wrongdoers of the past, especially those associated with human rights abuses, but ultimately the Czechs made little use of it. In Germany there was more of an effort to purge Communist personnel from the East German universities, but little else. In the new Baltic republics and in central Asia, the successor regimes were primarily filled with ethnic nationals in place of Russians, but criminal indictments were few and far between. Only in time did Chile and Argentina finally initiate a process of prosecuting a small number of major figures of the preceding regimes. Generally, energetic pursuit of "historical justice" was not a policy of the newly democratic and/or postcommunist regimes.

Another feature of the Spanish Transition was great attention to recent history, featuring all manner of new publicity and research, with much new scholarly publication and even more journalism. The amount of attention in Spain, however, would seem to have exceeded that found in some of the other cases. Partly this was simply due to the fact that Spain was a larger country than many, its broader market supporting a great volume and variety of publications and other publicity.

This is one aspect in which there was some analogy with Russia, for in Russia, too, during the first relatively freer, if chaotic, years under Yeltsin, a great deal of new critical publication about recent history occurred. At the opposite extreme would be found some of the Asian successor states, particularly Mongolia, where there seems to have been less interest in investigating the recent past.

One difference between the Spanish case and many of the new democratic systems was that at first, not as much developed in the way of fabrication of new national myths in Spain to gloss over or explain away the negative aspects of the recent past. In postfascist Italy and in France, after the fall of the Vichy regime, there quickly developed hegemonic new myths of the national "resistance" to Fascism and Nazism, which greatly distorted historical reality, considerably exaggerating the extent of the resistance and glossing over the widespread complicity with the preceding authoritarian regimes. In many countries, myths of national victimhood abounded. The Austrians, the majority of whom had been relatively enthusiastic in their complicity with Nazism, developed a new national historical image of Austria as simply the "first victim" of Hitler, fostering a new cult of national self-esteem. In newly democratic Japan, there was a considerable tendency to overlook the massive atrocities of the preceding military regime and portray the Japanese as little more than the innocent victims of atomic warfare. Of the postcommunist countries, Russia has arguably been the site of the most fanatical nationalism and renewed self-delusion, as various forms of victim theories abounded. Similarly, in the successors to some of the East European Soviet satellites the emphasis was almost exclusively on the undeniable victimization of these countries by the Soviets, but this was emphasized to preclude full consideration of their own past during the World War II era, of the roles of their own native dictatorships, and in some cases of extensive complicity by some of their citizens in the Holocaust. In several instances there were public tributes and memorials to members of the Waffen SS or its collaborators, or even of a major war criminal like Marshal Antonescu of Romania. Nothing has been carried to this kind of extreme in Spain.

At the same time, sectors of Spanish political life have promoted myths and interpretations of their own, in some of the regions equivalent to those in other countries. Surviving franquistas, though not great in number, have continued to promote their vision of Franco as national savior and as administrator of a benign modernizing system. Similarly, the camouflage of Republican politics initiated during the Civil War itself became part of the permanent self-image of the Left with its mythic and routinely falsified invocations of Republican "democracy," combined with the glossing over of the revolution. Catalanists, particularly the Left-leaning Catalanists, have preserved their equally distorted myth of "Catalanist democracy." Basque nationalists arguably live in the greatest denial of all, with their delirious myths of Basque history and their portrayal of Basques as perpetual victims, ignoring the historical reality that what took place in the area (which they term the greater Basque country) was in reality a civil war among Basques. They equally ignore the persistent efforts of the PNV to betray the Republican cause during the war itself and its continuing attempts during the following decade to intrigue with all and sundry among the foreign powers to bring about the partition of Spain.

Among some of these sectors there have also been limits to their own partisan view of the past. Most apologists for the Franco regime do not deny that its policies of repression were originally extreme. The more serious Socialist historians also recognize the considerable deviations from democratic practice that took place among the Socialists of the 1930s. It was also typically Spanish that there was no totally hegemonic point of view about these matters, at least until the rise of political correctness ideology at the close of the twentieth century.

It is probably no exaggeration to say that the success of the Transition led to what might be called the cult or myth of the Transition, which tended to raise it to very grand dimensions indeed. The Transition was not always quite as smooth and fully consensual as it has been made out to have been. It had more rough spots and a certain number of failures, despite an impressive level of success. And, with the passage of time, as would probably be inevitable in the contemporary age, it came to be challenged by a countermyth, by a new sort of "Black Legend of the Transition," purveyed primarily by the extreme Left. According to the countermyth, the Transition consisted in large measure of a sinister manipulation by former franquistas, seeking a means of getting the entire Old Regime off the hook. Weak leftist elites collaborated in appeasement and, in order to obtain a transition to a new democratic system, agreed to a "pact of silence," wherein all the crimes of Francoism would be completely ignored and go unpunished. Again, according to the countermyth, Spain therefore could never be completely "democratic" until all residues of Francoism had been purged, including the institution of monarchy itself.[8]

What is particularly sinister about the countermyth invoking the so-called Second Transition is its similarity to the "myth of the Republic," sedulously propagated by Azaña and the leftist Republicans during the 1930s. They have in common absolute indifference—indeed, aversion to—real democracy in so far as the latter consists of free and fair democratic elections, responsible parliamentary government, and a constitutional state, or what has been succinctly summarized as "fixed electoral rules and uncertain electoral outcomes."

One might theorize at some length about the tendency of the modern mind, at least for the past century or so, to generate ever more severe forms of paranoia, which may be considered a relatively natural phenomenon in an atomized and increasingly subjective culture. One of the great achievements of the Transition was its success in overcoming the modern tendency toward paranoia, at least for a generation or so.

"Pact of silence" is simply a propaganda slogan. No such thing ever existed. The very opposite characterized the Transition, which was grounded in a keen awareness of the failures of the past and a determination to avoid them. Indeed, as Paloma Aguilar has written, "few processes of political change have drawn such inspiration from the memory of the past, and from the lessons associated with it, as the Spanish case."[9] It is impossible to find another instance anywhere in which such awareness was any greater. What was agreed upon was not "silence" but the understanding that historical conflicts would be consigned to the labors of the historians and journalists, and that politicians would not make use of them in their parties' mutual competition, which would direct itself to present and future problems.[10] During the Transition historians and journalists were active in the extreme, flooding the country with new accounts of the years of civil war and Francoism, which did not in any way disguise the most atrocious aspects. After a number of years there began to appear a series of detailed scholarly studies, such as those by Josep María Solé Sabaté, Joan Villarroya, Vicent Gabarda Cebellán, Francisco Alía Miranda, and others, which for the first time began to place the investigation of the repressions on a precise scholarly footing.[11] All this was the very opposite of any "forgetting," and was much more careful and exact than the subsequent agitation about "la memoria histórica."

The consensus that rejected politicization of the history of civil war and dictatorship was generally maintained by all the major parties until 1993, when the Socialists were in danger of losing the national elections for the first time in more than a decade. The prime minister, Felipe González, then made a major point of warning that a vote for the conservative Partido Popular would run a major risk of restoring some of the grimmer aspects of franquismo. This was the equivalent of what in the United States in the decades after the American Civil War was called "waving the bloody shirt." In major elections the Republican Party, which in the American case had led the victors, would regularly "wave the bloody shirt," reminding its voters of the price paid in the Civil War and alleging that a vote for the rival Democrats would mean the return of the former "slave power." This was sometimes helpful to the Republicans but not always, and in Spain it did the Socialists less and less good in 1996 and 2000. There was briefly a point, after the complete failure of the Socialists two years earlier, at which José María Aznar declared in 2002 that the use of the recent past for partisan purposes had been buried.

This was premature, for once the genie was out of the bottle it became an increasingly common feature of Spanish politics. The normally sober Jordi Pujol, president of the Catalan government, had earlier made politicized references to the Spanish Civil War, and finally even the Partido Popular would do something of the same in the face of the new leftist agenda of Zapatero after 2004. For the Left, it simply became a standard tactic.

A new phase began in the first years of the twentieth century with the rise of the agitation concerning "la memoria histórica." This did not stem from a single movement but represented a variety of distinct constituencies, many motivated by political ends, others concerned for history and archaeology. The most serious sector has been represented by Emilio Silva and the Asociación para la Recuperación de la Memoria Histórica (ARMH—Association for the Recovery of Historical Memory), which began to excavate its first unmarked common grave in 2000. Concern to identify, excavate, and properly bury previously unrecognized victims of the Civil War and post–Civil War repressions—or for that matter unidentified military casualties of the Civil War itself—is an important and laudable initiative, and one that should merit public support. Other groups went beyond that, demanding special political commemoration and formal recognition that leftists who had been executed had died "for democracy," and calling for further specific condemnation of Franco and his regime and, by implication, all those who fought against the Left in the Civil War. This was accompanied by shrill and hysterical denunciations of the Francoist repression, with the implication that was the only one, even exaggerating its character and extent. A very harsh and brutal policy was made to seem even worse, the equivalent of Nazi Germany or the most atrocious Communist regimes. Vague concepts of "memoria histórica" were thrown about, as though they were equivalent to the data of professional historical research. The result was a semisystematic attempt to rewrite and to falsify, and also sometimes to use that effort as a tactical weapon against the Partido Popular, the clumsiness with which the latter dealt with such issues only adding to the problem.

Thus it is important to distinguish between the different groups who have advocated "la memoria histórica," and to keep separate the valid and laudatory efforts to recognize the often innocent victims of repression from the extensive attempts to generate political propaganda and falsify history. When the Socialist government of José Luis Rodríguez Zapatero was formed in 2004, it embraced "la memoria histórica" as part of its new leftist initiatives, but the terms of the final legislation approved in October–December 2007 were somewhat more moderate, as we shall see.

The term itself is unfortunate, constituting an oxymoron, a fundamental contradiction in terms, something that in strict logic cannot exist. Memory is strictly individual and is subjective and very frequently fallacious. Even people of good faith are constantly remembering details quite at variance with what in fact happened. Memory does not define or fully explain past events but simply provides one version or interpretation of the latter. History, on the other hand, is neither individual nor subjective, but requires the objective and professional empirical investigation of documents and other data and artifacts. It is a supra-individual process of the society of scholars, who debate and contrast results that strive to be as impersonal and objective as possible.

There is a field of study called "historical memory" or "collective memory," but it is quite different from history and is merely a small part of the data examined by historical inquiry. During the past several generations a methodology concerning "collective memory" has developed within historical study, investigating attitudes, concepts, or opinions about the past, which are formed in various ways by activists, politicians, publicists, artists, writers, and sometimes also by society at large. In most cases these are not true collective "memories" in the sense that a majority of those who hold them have participated in or experienced the events to which they refer, but rather are the product of political, social, or cultural minorities that in various ways have propagated, diffused, or imposed their views with greater or lesser degrees of success. The founding theorists of this field, Maurice Halbwachs and Pierre Nora, have recognized this, but they argue that the study of "collective memory" is important because it is one of the artifacts that constitutes the historical record, influencing politics, society, and culture, and as such forms part of the data to be examined by history. It does not reveal history itself but is simply one part of the data that historians study.

The founding work was Halbwachs's *Les cadres sociaux de la mémoire*, published in 1925, but collective memory only emerged as a significant field in the latter part of the twentieth century. This was one aspect of the broadening and diversification of the objects and subfields of historical study that took place from the 1970s on, and has led to the development of a number of new specialized journals, such as *Pasado y memoria*, published by the University of Alicante. The first major work in this field to appear in Spain was Paloma Aguilar's *Memoria y olvido de la Guerra Civil española* (1996), which remains the principal study of that theme as collective memory and is not to be confused with a considerable number of other works that record individual oral history data.

Specialists in the field have noted the particular problems and abuses that may appear. Enrique Gavilán has spoken of what he calls "the impossibility of and need for historical memory." He draws attention to the fact that in his final work, *La mémoire collective* (1950):

> Halbwachs drew attention to the verbal excess implied by the expression *historical memory*. Collective memory is not historical but in fact anti-historical. To understand something in historical terms is to be aware of its complexity, to remain at sufficient distance to be able to see different perspectives, to grasp the ambiguities in the behavior of different actors, including their moral ambiguity. Conversely, collective memory simplifies, denies the passage of time, eternalizes, essentializes. Collective memory characteristically pretends to express an eternal or essential truth about a collective process.

Moreover, Halbwachs maintained that collective memory functions in the opposite way from what may be supposed by common sense, for collective memory is not
so much the result of the action of the past on the present, as we might tend to
think, but of the present on the past. In other words, collective memory is less a discovery than a creation.

Therefore, if one accepts the ideas of Halbwachs, the expression *historical memory* should be used with care. Nor is the idea of *recovery* of collective or historical
memory defensible, since one should speak rather of the *construction* of memory. . . .
The present plays a much greater role in configuring the memory of the past than is
generally recognized.[12]

Similarly, in an essay published in *History and Theory*, Wulf Kansteiner speaks
of the difference between those whom he calls "the makers of memory" and "the
consumers of memory," and of the "abundance of initiatives of failed collective
memory on one side and of the few cases of successful construction of collective
memory on the other." He concludes that there is inadequate study of what he
terms "the problem of reception" of collective memory, for "collective memory is
not history" but rather "is as much a result of conscious manipulation and of un-
conscious absorption and is always mediated."[13] He points out that the Israeli
scholars Noa Gedi and Yigal Elam have concluded that collective or historical
memory consists of what these two specialists call "myths."[14]

The philosopher Gustavo Bueno is yet more critical, insisting that in Spain all
this merely amounts to a political maneuver, what he calls "the invention, on the
part of the Left, of the concept of 'historical memory.'"[15] He points out that the
dean of recent memory studies, Pierre Nora, distinguished between history, whose
research seeks objectivity, and memory, which is a subjective construction.[16]
Bueno insists that historical memory can never be more than a social, cultural, or
political artifact. He defines the concept of "common historical memory" as "a
metaphysical idea" that "proposes for us . . . an abstract subject (Society, or Hu-
manity, a sort of divinity that preserves everything and maintains it in the present)
capable of preserving in its breast the totality of the past which present mortals
need to discover."[17]

Yet a different enterprise is that of "oral history," which became a subdisci-
pline of history in the late twentieth century. Gavilán stresses that in this particular field "the work of historians does not presume the accuracy of memory. On the
contrary, it is fully cognizant of the *inevitable* deficiencies of memory. Historians
know that memory not merely deforms the understanding of what has occurred,
but in fact does so inevitably. There can be no other possibility. . . . The goal is not
the past, but the present."[18]

In the objective task of excavations in funerary archaeology, we find that the
contemporary European champions are not the Spaniards of the ARMH, who

have sometimes done meritorious work but have excavated only a limited number of remains, but are in fact the Russians of the late twentieth century or the Slovenes in 2009. The country that most systematically ignored the existence of mass common graves of the dead, stemming from both the Stalinist executions and World War II, was the Soviet Union, some of whose Spanish coreligionists have been very active in the agitation about the "pact of silence" and "historical memory." Since the remains of many of the millions of Soviet war dead had never been recovered, even from the battles on Russian soil, during the 1970s and 1980s thousands of Russian volunteers devoted their spare time on weekends to the recovery of the remains of many thousands of soldiers.[19] By comparison, Spanish agitators have shown very limited initiative. In Slovenia, a mass site was opened in 2009, which apparently contains the remains of literally thousands of victims of the mass executions carried out by Yugoslav Communists in 1945. The common graves uncovered in Spain in recent years are modest by comparison.

Moreover, the most elaborate use of a collective memory of the Spanish Civil War was probably not anything seen in Spain from the successors of either side, but rather the *cult* of the antifascist, revolutionary Spanish Civil War, which flourished in Communist East Germany (DDR). An important segment of the original DDR leadership had fought in the International Brigades (where their goal certainly had not been democracy for Spain) and, hand in hand with the revelation in the Soviet Union of the crimes of Stalin, the myth of the Soviet revolution was to some extent replaced by the myth of the revolution and antifascist struggle in Spain as a kind of founding myth of the East German regime. Needless to say there was no pretense that the Spanish Republic was a Western-style liberal democracy. The decline of the collective memory myth of the Spanish war during the 1980s coincided with the more general decline of the East German regime.[20]

The rise of the agitation concerning historical memory at the beginning of the twenty-first century has stemmed from three sources. One is the passing of generations and of time, not unassociated with the great development of archaeological research since the 1980s. The serious research aspect of historical memory has developed with historical distance, and with the growth of means to accomplish the work. Passage of time does not mean that there is no political dimension to this activity, but it has certainly meant less interference from countervailing political considerations.

The second factor is the shift in politics itself, with the increasing strength of the Partido Popular during 1996–2004, and the need to associate leftist political agitation with a different kind of argument. The first and second factors are interconnected, for, with the passage of time, most of the older generation of leftist leaders of the Transition has passed from the scene. These were the ones who seriously "remembered" the Civil War, not in the sense that they had participated in it but rather that they had been keenly aware of its realities and dangers, and were agreed not to use history for partisan purposes. The complete consolidation of democracy and the passage of time also meant that any remaining compensatory influences, such as potential pressure from the military, had completely disappeared.

The third factor was the change in ideology on the Left. The Left's doctrine shifted fairly rapidly during the late twentieth century, from the various radicalisms of the 1960s and early 1970s to the social democracy and "Eurocommunism" embraced by the late 1970s. The new orientation lasted for the better part of two decades, but by the 1990s was giving way to the common new ideology of the Left in the Western world, the only major modern ideology that does not have a generally agreed name. Its most technical title is political correctness, but in Spain it has often simply been called "el buenismo" (lit. "goodism"), "el pensamiento dominante" (the dominant thought), or "el pensamiento único" (uniform thought). Even more than other radical leftist doctrines of modern times, political correctness categorically rejects the past and traditional values, fetishizing cultural revolution rather than socioeconomic revolution, in this respect differing sometimes categorically from classical Marxism.[21] Rejection of the past is central, as is the emphasis on victims and victimization and the search for special categories of people to be affirmed and, conversely, to be stigmatized. "Victimism" is particularly important to this contemporary ideology, since, like its immediate predecessors, it tends to become a secular religion or religion substitute, and thus must find means of dealing with fundamental questions of human guilt. This is accomplished by projecting that guilt onto selected scapegoats, nearly all of whom are dead white males, led in Spain by Francisco Franco. The definition and identification of victims and victimizers assumes a vital cultic significance, as victims fill the roles held by heroes in traditional culture, achieving a kind of salvific status.[22]

It is characteristic that in Spain such matters are rarely debated but most commonly simply asserted. This tends to be the case whether in the controversy over national identities or over the Civil War and post–Civil War repressions. When scholarly congresses are convened, they are normally organized by one side, which stacks the program with those representing its point of view, and the opposing side does the same. The partial exceptions have been a few congresses dealing with nationalism and identity, as well as occasional rarities, such as the "curso de verano" (summer course) held at the University of Burgos in the summer of 2005.

A hopeful sign was that the final version of the "Ley de la memoria historia," as it is commonly but incorrectly called,[23] that was finally passed by the Zapatero government, was more moderate than the earlier announcements of 2004–6. As a result of a wide variety of criticisms, ranging from those of spokesmen of the Partido Popular to professional historians (including a few of the most prestigious

Socialist scholars), the term "memoria histórica" virtually disappeared, being replaced by the term "memoria democrática," which the law proposed to foster. Strictly speaking, "memoria democrática" would have to refer to the Transition, since there was never any full democracy in Spain before 1977, with the partial exception, perhaps, of the Lerroux-Samper governments of 1933–34, against which the Socialists rose in insurrection. Presumably, however, this was not precisely the intention of the leftist legislators responsible for passing such legislation. The law recognizes that "it is not the task of the legislator to implant a specific collective memory" but then contradicts itself by directing the government to carry out "public policies directed toward knowledge of our history and the development of democratic memory," so that "within the space of a year after this law takes effect, the government will establish an institutional framework to stimulate public policies for the conservation and development of democratic memory."

The principal objective of the law is to denounce "the radically unjust nature of all the condemnations, penalties, and any other form of personal violence carried out for political or ideological reasons or religious belief, during the Civil War, as well as those suffered for the same reasons during the dictatorship," and to prepare the way for supplementary measures of compensation and rehabilitation. The term "memoria histórica" appears only in the announcement of the establishment of the "Centro Documental de la Memoria Histórica y Archivo General de la Guerra Civil" (Documentary Center for Historical Memory and General Archive of the Civil War).[24] The ultimate test of the law will be determined by how fairly the supplementary measures are applied to all categories of victims.

The controversies about history in contemporary Spain will not be resolved any time soon, for they are not fueled by antiquarian or scholarly interests but by political passions. The normal path to resolving controversies about history lies through expanded research and keener analysis, but achievements of historical scholarship are likely to have limited effect.

The only other country where equivalent controversy has taken place is not Germany, but Russia during the 1990s, where the main controversy was not just about the atrocities of Sovietism but about national history and identity more broadly. In Russia the debate has largely come to an end under Vladimir Putin, with the projection of a myth of the nation that dwells on positive aspects of the Russian past, without altogether denying the atrocities committed by totalitarianism. This has been encouraged both by the broad authoritarian powers of the Putin government and by its economic prosperity. An equally important factor is that Russian culture and society preserve certain characteristics of their own, distinct from Western culture, and are little affected by political correctness. This is true to such an extent that at least a very large minority of Russians by the early twenty-first century once more embraced Stalin as a national hero. Needless to say, Russia again provides an example of the road not to follow, and there is little danger that Spain will follow such a path.

The Spanish problem is, rather, to provide national coherence for whatever path is followed, and to recognize the ambiguity and complexity of its history. The two major historical controversies—that over the nation, and the second about the Civil War and Francoism, which are not unrelated—have no immediate resolution, since the divides are not merely historiographical but even more political, and will persist for some time.

Notes

Introduction

1. The classic account of west European reactions to Spain in the early modern period is J. N. Hillgarth, *The Mirror of Spain, 1500–1700: The Formation of a Myth* (Ann Arbor, Mich., 2000).

2. J. Tazmir, *Szlachta i konkwistadorzy* (Warsaw, 1969).

3. J. Lelewel, *Parallèle historique entre l'Espagne et la Pologne au XVI, XVII, XVIIIe siècles* (Paris, 1836). This thesis has been updated and revised by M. Malowist, "Europe de l'Est et les Pays Ibériques: Analogie et Contrastes," in the University of Barcelona's *Homenaje a Jaime Vicens Vives* (Barcelona, 1965), 1:85–93.

4. For a general guide, perhaps the best place to begin is R. Núñez Florencio, *Sol y sangre: La imagen de España en el mundo* (Madrid, 2001).

5. The classic definition is that of Julián Juderías, *La Leyenda Negra: Estudios acerca del concepto de España en el extranjero* (Barcelona, 1912; repr., Salamanca, 1997). L. Español Bouché, *Leyendas negras: Vida y obra de Julián Juderías (1877–1918): La leyenda negra anti-americana* (Valladolid, 2007), presents an interesting account of Juderías and compares the anti-Spanish legend with the anti-American legend of more recent times. Further elaboration may be found in R. García Cárcel, *La Leyenda Negra: Historia y opinión* (Barcelona, 1997); W. S. Maltby, *Black Legend in England: The Development of Anti-Spanish Sentiment, 1558–1660* (Durham, N.C., 1971); M. Molina Martínez, *La Leyenda Negra* (Madrid, 1991); P. W. Powell, *Tree of Hate: Propaganda and Prejudice Affecting United Status Relations with the Hispanic World* (Berkeley, 1971); and D. Ramos, *Genocidio y conquista: Viejos mitos que siguen en pie* (Madrid, 1998). J. Pérez, *La Leyenda Negra* (Madrid, 2009), presents an excellent overview.

6. On the formation of these images, see E. Fernández Herr, *Les origines de l'Espagne romantique: Les récits de voyage (1755–1823)* (Paris, 1973); L.-F. Hoffman, *Romantique Espagne: l'Image de l'Espagne en France entre 1800 et 1850* (Paris, 1961); L. Félix Fernández, *La España de Mérimée* (Málaga, 1990); E. Echevarría Pereda, *La imagen de España en Francia: Viajeras francesas decimonónicas* (Málaga, 1994); M. Bernal Rodríguez, *La Andalucía de los libros de*

viajes del siglo XIX (Seville, 1985); A. González Troyano, *La desventura de Carmen: Una divagación sobre Andalucía* (Madrid, 1991); B. Cantizano Márquez, *Estudio del tópico de Carmen en los viajeros británicos del siglo XIX* (Granada, 1999); D. Howarth, *The Invention of Spain: Cultural Relations between Britain and Spain, 1770–1870* (Manchester, 2007), and the excellent summary in T. Mitchell, *Flamenco Deep Song* (New Haven, Conn., 1994), 111–25. A classic, if morbid, phrase was Maurice Barrès's *Du sang, de la volupté et de la mort*, though the product was a generally uninteresting book that did not live up to its title and eventually appeared in Spanish as *Sangre, voluptuosidad y muerte*, not in Spain but in Buenos Aires in 1922.

7. After 1961 the government abandoned the slogan and generally promoted a more "serious" image. See S. D. Pack, *Tourism and Dictatorship: Europe's Peaceful Invasion of Franco's Spain* (New York, 2006), 148–53.

8. William D. Phillips Jr. has pointed to the presence of such attitudes (and ignorance) in the three books most widely read in the United States on contemporary and general Spanish history: G. Brenan, *The Spanish Labyrinth: An Account of the Social and Political Background of the Civil War* (New York, 1944; repr., Cambridge, 1990); J. A. Crow, *Spain: The Root and the Flower; An Interpretation of Spain and the Spanish People* (Berkeley, 2005); and H. Thomas, *The Spanish Civil War* (New York, 1961; rev. ed., London, 2003). See W. D. Phillips, "La otra cara de la moneda: La imágen de España en los Estados Unidos," in J. M. de Bernardo Arés, ed., *El hispanismo anglonorteamericano: Aportaciones, problemas y perspectivas sobre Historia, Arte y Literatura españolas (siglos XVI–XVIII)* (Córdoba, 2001), 161–76.

9. Hillgarth, *Mirror of Spain*, 544.

The Formation of a Hispanist

1. R. Kagan, *Spain in America: The Origins of Hispanism in the United States* (Urbana, 2002), 1–2.

2. In addition to the work by Kagan, see the older summaries by M. Romera-Navarro, *El hispanismo en Norteamérica* (Madrid, 1917), and F. S. Stimson, *Orígenes del hispanismo norteamericano* (Mexico City, 1961).

3. T. E. Chávez, *Spain and the Independence of the United States: An Intrinsic Gift* (Albuquerque, 2002), is an important new work that shows that Spanish policy was active on more fronts than it has been given credit for and had more effect on the war than has generally been thought. The Spanish intervention was a logical extension of the pro-French, anti-British policy of that era, though the more astute Spanish observers and analysts pointed out the potential "boomerang effect" of fostering a strong new independent, English-speaking power in North America. See L. T. Cummins, *Spanish Observers and the American Revolution, 1775–1783* (Baton Rouge, 1991).

4. W. H. Prescott, *History of the Reign of Ferdinand and Isabella* (1837), *A History of the Conquest of Mexico* (1843), *A History of the Conquest of Peru* (1847), and *History of the Reign of Philip the Second of Spain* (1855). For a brief summary of Prescott's work in Spanish, see M. González-Arnao Conde-Luque, "William H. Prescott: Historiador de España y de las Indias," *Historia 16*, 10.117 (January 1986): 99–106.

5. Kagan, *Spain in America*, 10. See also Kagan's article, "Prescott's Paradigm: American Historical Scholarship and the Decline of Spain," *American Historical Review* 101.2 (1996): 423–46.

6. S. T. Wallis, *Glimpses of Spain* (1849) and *Spain: Her Institutions, Politics and Public Men* (1853).

7. See the remarks of Kagan on Wallis in his articles "Un país gobernado por los curas: Reflexiones en torno a la imagen de España en Estados Unidos a comienzos del siglo XIX," in J. Martínez Millán and C. Reyero, eds., *El siglo de Carlos V y Felipe II: La construcción de los mitos en el siglo XIX* (Madrid, 2000), 1:419–36, and "La imagen de España en el mundo anglonorteamericano: Reflexiones sobre su evolución histórica," in J. M. de Bernardo Arés, ed., *El hispanismo anglonorteamericano: Aportaciones, problemas y perspectivas sobre Historia, Arte y Literatura españolas (siglos XVI–XVIII)* (Córdoba, 2001), 1:141–47.

8. For the interaction of American artists with Spain during this period, see M. E. Boone, *Vistas de España: American Views of Art and Life in Spain, 1860–1914* (New Haven, Conn., 2007).

9. Phillips, "La otra cara de la moneda," 1:61–76.

10. *España Libre* continued its biweekly publication for many years, concluding its labors only in 1977, when it declared that because of the new democratization under Juan Carlos, Spain had once more become "libre."

11. Maurín's second surname was Julià, and his personal language in Catalonia was Catalan, although most of his writing and his addresses to workers were in Spanish. He hoped to attract peripheral nationalism to the revolution, and therefore when I published my book on early Basque nationalism in 1974, the year after his death, it seemed fitting to dedicate it to his memory. For fear of the lingering censorship in Spain, however, this had to be abbreviated in the Spanish edition to "A la memoria de J. M. J."

12. Archivo de la Fundación Nacional Francisco Franco, 69:23336. The report is mistaken that I had succeeded in interviewing Aranda, who always avoided contact with me. The error probably stemmed from a police observer who noted an effort of mine to call on Aranda in his home on the calle Alfonso XII. (My thanks to Félix Morales, Secretario General of the Fundación, for this document.)

13. S. G. Payne, *A History of Fascism, 1914–1945* (Madison, 1995), is co-dedicated also to my dear friend and senior colleague, George Mosse, eminent in the study of fascism as in much else; Linz is also recognized in my later full treatment of Falangism, *Fascism in Spain, 1923–1977* (Madison, 1999).

14. For an account of this enterprise from Martínez's point of view, see A. Forment, *José Martínez: La epopeya de Ruedo Ibérico* (Barcelona, 2000).

15. S. G. Payne, "Jaime Vicens Vives and the Writing of Spanish History," *Journal of Modern History* 34.2 (June 1962): 119–34.

16. Gabriel Jackson, the first chairman of the History Department at UC–San Diego (La Jolla), arranged the purchase of this collection. My UCLA colleague John Galbraith had become the first regular chancellor of the newly expanded San Diego campus, and since I knew that he was looking for a chairman to start the History Department, I recommended Jackson, who was seeking to move to a major university and so briefly served as department chairman when he moved to La Jolla in 1966.

17. S. G. Payne, "Il nazionalismo basco tra destra e sinistra," *Rivista Storica Italiana* 85.4 (1973): 984–1043.

18. S. G. Payne, *Basque Nationalism* (Reno, 1975).

19. Sebastián Auger was a wealthy Catalan businessman who aspired to play a role in both cultural affairs and public life. Soon after the death of Franco, however, he fled the country as the result of a financial scandal.

20. S. G. Payne, *El nacionalismo vasco: De sus orígenes a la ETA* (Barcelona, 1974), the subtitle being considerably inflated. It appeared in English as *Basque Nationalism*.

21. S. G. Payne, "In the Twilight of the Franco Era," *Foreign Affairs* 49.2 (January 1971): 342–54.

22. The proceedings of this seminar were published in S. Chavkin, J. Sangster, and W. Susman, eds., *Spain: Implications for United States Foreign Policy* (Stamford, Conn., 1976).

23. As soon as Suárez was appointed, National Public Radio in Washington telephoned me at my vacation site near Yellowstone National Park to inquire about the prospects of Spain's new prime minister. In fact, at that time I knew very little about Suárez but told them that he was a reasonably experienced political figure who enjoyed the confidence of the king and would have a good chance to succeed in democratizing the system. Part of this was more a guess or a conjecture, but it turned out to be the right thing to say.

1. Visigoths and Asturians

1. "Hispania" was apparently derived from a Phoenician word referring either to "land of rabbits" or "land of metals."

2. A good statement of this interpretation for the origins of Visigothic Spain is J. Arce, *Bárbaros y romanos en España (400–507 A.D.)* (Madrid, 2005).

3. This is the burden of B. Ward-Perkins, *The Fall of Rome and the End of Civilization* (Oxford, 2005).

4. See the references in M. González Jiménez, "¿Re-conquista? Un estado de la cuestión," in E. Benito Ruano, ed., *Tópicos y realidades de la Edad Media* (Madrid, 2000), 155–78.

5. A. García Gallo, "Nacionalidad y territorialidad del derecho en la época visigoda," *Anuario de la Historia del Derecho Español* 13 (1936–41): 168–264.

6. R. Collins, *Law, Culture and Regionalism in Early Medieval Spain* (Hampshire, 1992), 204–5.

7. See especially J. Fontaine, *Isidoro de Sevilla: Génesis y originalidad de la cultura hispánica en tiempos de los visigodos* (Madrid, 2002) and *Culture et spiritualité en Espagne du IVe au VIIe siècle* (London, 1986).

8. E. James, ed., *Visigothic Spain: New Approaches* (Oxford, 1980).

9. P. Brown, *The Rise of Western Christendom: Triumph and Diversity, A. D. 200–1000* (Oxford, 2003), 366; A. Besga Marroquín, *Consideraciones sobre la situación política de los pueblos del norte de España durante la época visigoda del Reino de Toledo* (Bilbao, 1983); L. R. Menéndez Bueyes, *Reflexiones críticas sobre el origen del Reino de Asturias* (Salamanca, 2001).

10. B. Schimmelpfennig, *Das Papsttum: Von der Antike bis zur Renaissance* (Darmstadt,

1996), cited in J. L. Villacañas Berlanga, *La formación de los reinos hispánicos* (Madrid, 2006), 126.

11. Cf. J. Fontaine and C. Pellistrandi, *L'Europe héritière de l'Espagne visigothique* (Madrid, 1992). The origin of early medieval popular assemblies, found in various forms in northern Spain and also throughout most of western Europe, is a different, more problematic issue. Claudio Sánchez Albornoz, like many historians who write in English, tends to attribute this to Germanic influences. See C. Sánchez Albornoz, *España, un enigma histórico* (Buenos Aires, 1971), 1:134–39. Some Spanish historians would disagree.

12. Fontaine, *Isidoro de Sevilla*, 284.

13. Fontaine, *Culture et spiritualité*, 38.

14. Ibid., 37.

15. R. Collins, *Visigothic Spain, 409–711* (Oxford, 2004), 244.

16. A. Besga Marroquín, *Orígenes hispanogodos del Reino de Asturias* (Oviedo, 2000).

17. See, for example, A. Bonet Correa, *Arte pre-románico asturiano* (Barcelona, 1987) and V. Nieto Alcalde, *Arte prerrománico asturiano* (Salinas, 1989).

18. A judicious recent summary may be found in the splendidly illustrated synthesis by J. I. Ruiz de la Peña Solar, *La monarquía asturiana* (Oviedo, 2001). Perhaps the most assiduous advocate of the new interpretation has been Besga Marroquín, who has published several more widely read articles in the popular history magazine *Historia 16*, in addition to the books cited earlier. The classic account is C. Sánchez Albornoz, *El Reino de Asturias: Orígenes de la nación española* (Oviedo, 2001), and, for a recent popularized version, see J. J. Esparza, *La gran aventura del Reino de Asturias: Así empezó la Reconquista* (Madrid, 2009).

2. Spain and Islam

1. These multiculturalists, however, also expected all those participating in "diversity" to have the same political principles, derived from the late modern, politically correct West.

2. M. R. Menocal, *The Ornament of the World: How Muslims, Jews, and Christians Created a Culture of Tolerance in Medieval Spain* (Boston, 2002).

3. E. Karsh, *Islamic Imperialism. A History* (New Haven, Conn., 2006), presents a good brief account of Muslim military expansionism across the centuries, while P. Fregosi, *Jihad in the West: Muslim Conquests from the 7th to the 21st Centuries* (Amherst, N.Y., 1998), is broader yet.

4. The literature concerning Spain and the Islamic world is enormous. P. Damián Cano, *Al-Andalus: El Islam y los pueblos ibéricos* (Madrid, 2004), offers a good short survey, while the long conflict, with special attention to the Reconquest and the twentieth century, is narrated in C. Vidal Manzanares, *España frente al Islam: De Mahoma a Ben Laden* (Madrid, 2004).

5. I. V. Gaiduk, *The Great Confrontation: Europe and Islam through the Centuries* (Chicago, 2003), presents a broad survey that includes eastern Europe.

6. See M. Bonner, *Jihad in Islamic History: Doctrines and Practice* (Princeton, N.J., 2006).

7. R. Collins, *The Arab Conquest of Spain, 710–797* (Oxford, 1989), is the second volume of the multivolume *Blackwell's History of Spain* edited by John Lynch and effectively

summarizes and analyzes the data available at the time of writing, though new studies continue to appear.

8. "Al-Andalus" means, approximately, "the West," although the etymology is not clear.

9. On the complete predominance of oriental culture and forms, see P. Guichard, *Al-Andalus: Estructura antropológica de una sociedad islámica en Occidente* (Barcelona, 1976). The key study of the initial phase is P. Chalmeta, *Invasión e islamización: La sumisión de Hispania y la formación de al-Andalus* (Jaén, 2003). T. F. Glick, *Islamic and Christian Spain in the Early Middle Ages: Comparative Perspectives on Social and Cultural Formation* (Princeton, N.J., 1979), is also useful. Guichard's *De la expansión árabe a la Reconquista: Esplendor y fragilidad de Al-Andalus* (Granada, 2002), presents one of the best general portraits of Al-Andalus.

10. A. G. Chejne, *Muslim Spain: Its History and Culture* (Minneapolis, 1974), iv.

11. It should be remembered that a subject Christian population, much of it also speaking a form of vernacular Latin or early Romance, survived in the northern Maghrib during the same time period as that of the Mozarabs of Al-Andalus. Although its territory had begun to shrink and decline as early as the fourth century, much of the Romanized area of the northern Maghrib had been firmly Christian in religion (even more so than some parts of Roman western Europe) and at times in close contact with Visigothic Hispania. Under Muslim domination it suffered the same pressures and fate as the Mozarabs, and also succumbed to the Almohads by the twelfth century.

12. On the initial achievements of Islamic culture and the place of Islamic society in history, see M. G. S. Hodgson, *The Venture of Islam: Conscience and History in a World Civilization*, 3 vols. (Chicago, 1974), and *Rethinking World History: Essays on Europe, Islam and World History* (Cambridge, 1993).

13. J. Van Ess, *The Flowering of Muslim Theology* (Cambridge, Mass., 2006), is a good introduction.

14. Though for centuries San Isidoro was probably read by proportionately more people, Juan Vernet has observed that in his influence on Western philosophy Averroes was the most influential thinker born in the Iberian Peninsula, even if he was not "Spanish" but Muslim.

15. Though there is no doubt that Averroes was widely read, in recent years there has been a growing tendency to question the importance of Muslim cultural influence on Western thought and development, and even to question the significance of its role in transmitting ancient texts. See S. Gouguenheim, *Aristóteles y el Islam: Las raíces griegas de la Europa cristiana* (Madrid, 2009).

16. According to one study, cited in J. Vernet, *El Islam y Europa* (Barcelona, 1982), 71, of the major Muslim writers and scientists studied in western Europe during the fifteenth century, eight had been born in the eleventh and eight in the twelfth centuries, but only two in the thirteenth and one in the fourteenth centuries, by which time Muslim intellectual culture was fading.

17. A brief treatment of black slavery in Al-Andalus and elsewhere in the Islamic world may be found in R. Segal, *Islam's Black Slaves: The Other Black Diaspora* (New York, 2001).

18. J. H. Sweet, "The Iberian Roots of American Racist Thought," *William and Mary Quarterly* 54.1 (January 1997): 143–65, calls attention, in my judgment correctly, to the

importance of the influence and example of Islam in the early development of slavery among the Spanish and Portuguese.

19. B. Lewis, *Race and Slavery in the Middle East: An Historical Inquiry* (Oxford, 1992).

20. J. Rodríguez Molina, *La vida de moros y cristianos en la frontera* (Alcalá la Real, 2007).

21. B. Vincent, "La cultura morisca," *Historia 16* 18 (October 1977): 78–95. The standard work on religious differences is L. Cardaillac, *Moriscos y cristianos: Un enfrentamiento polémico (1492–1640)* (Madrid, 1979).

22. E. K. Neuvonen, *Los arabismos del español en el siglo XIII* (Helsinki, 1941), found that only one-half of 1 percent of the total vocabulary of literary Castilian in the thirteenth century stemmed from Arabic, but this does not account for additional Arabisms in local vocabularies, or the addition of further Arabisms in the later Middle Ages.

23. See E. Alfonso, "La construcción de la identidad judía en al-Andalus en la Edad Media," *El Olivo* 23.49 (1999): 5–24.

24. The fate of the enormous number of Spaniards and other west Europeans seized and enslaved during the early modern period—amounting in toto to possibly as many as a million people—is treated in R. C. Davis, *Christian Slaves, Muslim Masters: White Slavery in the Mediterranean, the Barbary Coast, and Italy, 1500–1800* (New York, 2003). On the Spanish experience, see E. G. Friedman, *Spanish Captives in North Africa in the Early Modern Age* (Madison, 1983), and J. Martínez Torres, *Prisioneros de los infieles: Vida y rescate de los cautivos cristianos en el mediterráneo musulmán (siglos xvi–xvii)* (Barcelona, 2007). The most famous prisoner was Cervantes, whose captivity in Algiers has been recounted recently by M. A. Garcés, *Cervantes in Algiers: A Captive's Tale* (Nashville, 2002). This experience was formative in the career of the great writer, and he referred to it frequently, in quite negative terms, though it did not prejudice him against Muslims, as evidenced by references in his classic novel. For that matter, one of his conceits was that *Don Quijote* had been translated from the work of "Cide Hamete Benengeli, historiador arábigo." And in the Middle Ages, the Arabs had produced great historians, more than—for example—great scientists.

25. A. Torrecillas Velasco, *Dos civilizaciones en conflicto: España en el África musulmana: Historia de una guerra de 400 años (1497–1927)* (Valladolid, 2006), 345–90, and, more broadly, M. Arribas Palau, *Las relaciones hispano magrebíes en el siglo XVIII* (Madrid, 2007).

26. S. Fanjul, *Al-Andalus contra España: La forja del mito* (Madrid, 2000), 86. See also his *La quimera de al-Andalus* (Madrid, 2004).

27. For these and further examples, see chaps. five through eight of S. Payne, *Franco and Hitler: Spain, Germany and World War II* (New Haven, Conn., 2008).

3. Reconquest and Crusade

1. Significant Muslim populations did develop in Bosnia-Herzegovina and Albania, and in parts of Bulgaria.

2. In the east Mediterranean during that era, the Byzantines had succeeded in reconquering Anatolia (which had never been fully occupied and had not in that period been Islamized), holding it for two centuries before losing it to a new Muslim onslaught.

3. J. O'Callaghan, *Reconquest and Crusade in Medieval Spain* (Philadelphia, 2003), 7.

4. J. L. Villacañas Berlanga, *La formación de los reinos hispánicos* (Madrid, 2006), 29.

5. The relationship between conversion and crusading is treated in B. Z. Kedar, *Crusade and Mission: European Approaches toward the Muslims* (Princeton, N.J., 1984).

6. Whereas in earlier generations the Arabs had usually tolerated Christian pilgrims, the Seljuk Turks, the most recent conquerors of the region, greeted Christian visitors with violence. Hence the immediate motivation for the Crusade.

7. The best new history of the Crusades is C. Tyerman, *God's War: A New History of the Crusades* (Cambridge, Mass., 2007).

8. The Aragonese conquest of Barbastro, with the help of French forces, in 1063 is sometimes considered the immediate precursor of the formal crusade, which is something of an exaggeration, but it did serve as an example to the papacy in developing the concept. Similarly, the occupation of Toledo in 1085, the first direct occupation of a full taifa state (and precipitated especially by internal developments in Toledo), was considered a "holy war" but certainly not a crusade, being in fact a kind of transaction between its inhabitants and the crown of Castile.

9. Given the relative weakness of Spanish historiography in analytic synthesis, for a very long time there was no single survey of the Reconquest in one volume, the first book so titled being D. Lomax, *The Reconquest of Spain* (London, 1978), still a very useful summary and guide. J. Valdeón Baruque, *La Reconquista: El concepto de España: Unidad y diversidad* (Madrid, 2006), also presents a summary, but the best brief discussions are the works by Lomax and O'Callaghan. There is considerable literature on the idea of the crusade in Western Christendom. The most recent, and probably the best, study of its background and process of conceptualization is J. Flori, *La guerra santa: La formación de la idea de cruzada en el Occidente cristiano* (Madrid, 2003). J. T. Johnson, *The Holy War Idea in Western and Islamic Traditions* (University Park, Pa., 2001), seeks to compare crusade and jihad. The specific meaning and use of the institution of the crusade in Spain was first brought to the attention of historians in J. Goñi Gaztambide, *Historia de la bula de la cruzada en España* (Vitoria, 1958).

10. The best guide is A. D. Smith, *Chosen Peoples: Sacred Sources of National Identity* (Oxford, 2003). Smith virtually ignores Spain, though it might have provided one of his better cases.

11. B. Anzulovic, *Heavenly Serbia: From Myth to Genocide* (New York, 1999).

12. There is an extensive literature on this. See N. Berdyaev, *The Russian Idea* (New York, 1948; repr., Westport, Conn., 1979); P. J. S. Duncan, *Russian Messianism: Third Rome, Revolution, Communism and After* (London, 2000); and T. McDaniel, *The Agony of the Russian Idea* (Princeton, N.J., 1996).

13. Quoted in A. A. Sicroff, *Les controverses des statuts de "pureté de sang" en Espagne du XVe au XVIe siècles* (Paris, 1960), 291–94.

4. Spain and the West

1. For example, M. S. Anderson, *Britain's Discovery of Russia 1553–1885* (London, 1958), and, more broadly, L. Wolff, *Inventing Eastern Europe: The Map of Civilization on the Mind of the Enlightenment* (Palo Alto, 1994).

2. Early Western civilization had no name of its own for itself. "Europe" existed as a strictly geographical term, and the Crónica Mozárabe of 754 referred to the Frankish forces that turned back the Muslims as "europeenses," but this was not broadly used at that time. The world of Latin Christendom did, of course, develop a cultural self-consciousness, and by the eleventh century employed the concept of "Christianitas," or Christendom. Europe as a general term for the political and cultural world of the West became increasingly common in the sixteenth century, and the eighteenth-century Enlightenment stressed the idea of European civilization. The contemporary usage of the West and Western civilization developed during the nineteenth century. See K. Wilson and J. van der Dussen, eds., *The History of the Idea of Europe* (London, 1993); A. Pagden, ed., *The Idea of Europe: From Antiquity to the European Union* (Washington, D. C., 2002); and B. Geremek, *The Common Roots of Europe* (Cambridge, Mass., 1996).

3. J. Marías, *España inteligible: Razón histórica de las Españas* (Madrid, 1985). J. Pérez (*La Leyenda Negra*) and others have made much the same point.

4. The Anglo-Norman monarchy justified the partial conquest of Ireland as "extending Christendom."

5. For broad accounts, see J. R. S. Phillips, *The Medieval Expansion of Europe* (Oxford, 1988), and R. Bartlett, *The Making of Europe: Conquest, Colonization, and Cultural Change, 950–1350* (Princeton, N.J., 1993).

6. There is an abundant literature on this topic. See R. C. Dales, *The Scientific Achievement of the Middle Ages* (Philadelphia, 1973); L. White, Jr., *Medieval Religion and Technology* (Berkeley, 1978); and D. C. Lindberg, *The Beginnings of Western Science: The European Scientific Tradition in Philosophical, Religious, and Institutional Context, 600 B.C. to A.D. 1450* (Chicago, 1992).

7. H. J. Berman, *The Interaction of Law and Religion* (Nashville, 1974); *Law and Revolution: The Formation of the Western Legal Tradition* (Cambridge, Mass., 1983); *Faith and Order: The Reconciliation of Law and Religion* (Atlanta, 1993).

8. B. Tierney, *The Idea of Natural Rights: Studies on Natural Rights, Natural Law, and Church Law, 1150–1625* (Grand Rapids, 1997).

9. For a brief application of this concept to modern southern Europe, see I. Wallerstein, "The Relevance of the Concept of Semiperiphery to Southern Europe," in G. Arrighi, ed., *Semiperipheral Development: The Politics of Southern Europe in the Twentieth Century* (London, 1985), 31–39.

10. The leading historian of Poland in a Western language is Norman Davies. See his *God's Playground: A History of Poland*, 2 vols. (Oxford, 1981), and *Heart of Europe: A Short History of Poland* (New York, 1986).

11. As Oswald Spengler put it, "The Western Culture of maturity was through-and-through a French outgrowth of the Spanish." *The Decline of the West* (New York, 1980), 1:150.

12. Change, new conflict, and the threat of the "subversive" in this largely traditionalist society are emphasized, perhaps excessively, in J. A. Maravall, *The Culture of the Baroque: Analysis of a Historical Structure* (Minneapolis, 1986).

13. J. B. Scott, *The Spanish Origin of International Law* (Washington, D.C., 1928).

14. The best analysis and summary will be found in A. A. Chafuen, *Christians for*

Freedom: Late Scholastic Economics (San Francisco, 1986). See also M. Grice-Hutchinson, *The School of Salamanca: Readings in Spanish Monetary Theory, 1544–1605* (Oxford, 1962).

15. L. J. Hutton, *The Christian Essence of Spanish Literature: An Historical Study* (Lewiston, N.Y., 1988), stresses the essential orthodoxy of classic Spanish literature. This is fundamentally correct, though there were an infinite variety of nuances; cf. R. Ornstein, *The Moral Vision of Jacobean Tragedy* (Madison, Wis., 1965).

16. There is, of course, an extensive literature on English exceptionalism, such as the works of A. Macfarlane, *The Origins of English Individualism: The Family, Property, and Social Transition* (Oxford, 1978) and *The Culture of Capitalism* (Oxford, 1987). On some of the origins, see F. Borkenau, *End and Beginning: On the Generations of Cultures and the Origins of the West* (New York, 1981).

5. Identity, Monarchy, Empire

1. The Real Academia de la Historia published *España: Reflexiones sobre el ser de España* (Madrid, 1997) and *España como nación* (Madrid, 2000), as well as V. Palacio Atard, ed., *De Hispania a España: El nombre y el concepto a través de los siglos* (Madrid, 2005). One of the most cogent accounts was L. González Antón, *España y las Españas: Nacionalismos y falsificación en la historia*, rev. ed. (Madrid, 2007). Other notable titles in this debate are M. Hernández Sánchez-Barba, *España: Historia de una nación* (Madrid, 1995); J. M. Otero Novas, *Defensa de la Nación española* (Madrid, 1998); G. Bueno, *España no es un mito: Claves para una defensa razonada* (Madrid, 2005); and J. P. Fusi's eminently sensible *España: La evolución de la identidad nacional* (Madrid, 2000). A somewhat different perspective may be found in J. Tusell, *España, una angustia nacional* (Madrid, 1999).

2. G. Bueno, *España frente a Europa* (Barcelona, 1999).

3. In some of the first documents it was also rendered as "espagnon," arguably a more typically Aragonese or Pyrenean form. J. A. Maravall, "Sobre el origen de 'español,'" *Estudios de historia del pensamiento español* (Madrid, 1999), 1:7–23.

4. Alfonso el Batallador, king of Aragon in the early twelfth century, frequently used the title *Rex et Imperator Hispaniae*, but only in connection with his claim to be king of León.

5. In medieval usage, "prince" was a common title for a ruler, sometimes equivalent to king, sometimes used in principalities that did not claim the full status of "kingdom."

6. A. Sánchez Candeiras, *El regnum-imperium leonés hasta 1137* (Madrid, 1951).

7. A classic discussion is R. Menéndez Pidal, *El Imperio hispánico y los Cinco Reinos* (Madrid, 1950), though many historians would not entirely agree with this formulation today. A. García Gallo, *Curso de historia del Derecho español* (Madrid, 1950), insists that all this has been greatly exaggerated, and that there never really was a medieval Spanish empire. This last point is certainly correct, but there nevertheless existed a medieval discourse of empire and emperor in Asturias-León-Castile. For a recent interpretation of medieval empire in the peninsula, see G. Bueno, *España frente a Europa* (Barcelona, 1999).

8. For a reading by the Hispanists, see R. Collins, *Early Medieval Spain: Unity in Diversity, 400–1000* (New York, 1983), and B. F. Reilly, *The Medieval Spains* (Cambridge, 1993).

9. They also, of course, asserted sovereignty over Wales, Scotland, and Ireland.

10. Alfonso's attitudes and policies regarding the other religions have recently been examined in H. Salvador Martínez, *La convivencia en la España del siglo XIII: Perspectivas alfonsíes* (Madrid, 2006).

11. For a highly favorable reading, see F. Márquez Villanueva, *El concepto cultural alfonsí* (Barcelona, 2004).

12. Cf. R. Brague, *Eccentric Culture: A Theory of Western Civilization* (South Bend, Ind., 2004).

13. In my judgment, the best study of the cultural, intellectual, and political ambitions of Alfonso el Sabio will be found in J. L. Villacañas Berlanga, *La formación de los reinos hispánicos* (Madrid, 2006), 591–702. For a full biography, more favorable to the king, see H. Salvador Martínez, *Alfonso X, el Sabio: Una biografía* (Madrid, 2003).

14. See P. J. Geary, *The Myth of Nations: The Medieval Origins of Europe* (Princeton, N.J., 2001); C. Beaune, *The Birth of an Ideology: Myths and Symbols of Nation in Late-Medieval France* (Berkeley, 1991); and the studies reviewed in D. Bell, "Recent Works on Early Modern French National Identity," *Journal of Modern History* 68.1 (March 1996): 84–113.

15. L. Colley, *Britons: Forging the Nation 1707–1837* (New Haven, Conn., 1992); F. Welsh, *The Four Nations: A History of the United Kingdom* (New Haven, Conn., 2003); R. Colls, *Identity of England* (Oxford, 2002).

16. Maravall, *El concepto de España*, 488.

17. So far as I am aware, the last major occasion on which the Portuguese crown contested the terminology of "crown of Spain" or "monarchy of Spain" for the rulers in Madrid was at the time of the Peace of Utrecht in 1714.

18. H. Kamen, *Philip of Spain* (London, 1997), 227.

19. See C. Jago, "Habsburg Absolutism and the Cortes of Castile," *American Historical Review*, 86.2 (April, 1981): 307–26; R. Mackay, *The Limits of Royal Authority: Resistance and Obedience in Seventeenth-Century Castile* (Cambridge, 1999); J. B. Owens, *"By My Absolute Royal Authority": Justice and the Castilian Commonwealth at the Beginning of the First Global Age* (Rochester, N.Y., 2006); and, more broadly, N. Henshall, *The Myth of Absolutism: Change and Continuity in Early Modern European Monarchy* (London, 1992).

20. For the broader European usage, much the same as in Spain, see R. von Friedeburg, *'Patria' und 'Patrioten' vor dem Patriotismus: Pflichten, Rechte, Glauben und die Rekonfigurierung europäischer Gemeinwesen im 17: Jahrhundert* (Wolfenbüttel, 2004).

21. See R. García Cárcel, ed., *La construcción de las Historias de España* (Madrid, 2004).

22. Quoted in the excellent brief study by X. Gil Pujol, "Un rey, una fe, muchas naciones: Patria y nación en la España de los siglos XVI–XVII," in A. Alvarez-Ossorio Alvariño and B. J. García García, eds., *La Monarquía de las naciones: Patria, nación y naturaleza en la Monarquía de España* (Madrid, 2004), 39–76.

23. I. A. A. Thompson, "Castile, Spain and the Monarchy: The Political Community from *patria natural* to *patria nacional*," in R. L. Kagan and G. Parker, eds., *Spain, Europe, and the Atlantic World: Essays in Honour of John H. Elliott* (Cambridge, 1995), 125–59.

24. J. A. Pelayo and A. S. Tarrés, "Los orígenes del Estado moderno español: Ideas, hombres y estructuras," in A. Floristán, ed., *Historia de España en la edad moderna* (Barcelona,

2004), 221–43; J. Villanueva, *Política y discurso histórico en la España del siglo XVII: Las polémicas sobre los orígenes medievales de Cataluña* (Alicante, 2004).

25. R. A. Stradling, *Philip IV and the Government of Spain, 1621–1665* (Cambridge, 1988).

26. H. Kamen, *Empire: How Spain Became a World Power, 1492–1763* (New York, 2003).

27. For an attractive and careful new description, see F. Martínez Laínez and J. M. Sánchez de Toca, *Tercios de España: La infantería legendaria* (Madrid, 2006).

28. See the classic works of J. H. Parry, *The Spanish Theory of Empire in the Sixteenth Century* (Cambridge, 1940); S. Zavala, *The Political Philosophy of the Conquest of America* (Mexico, 1953); and L. Hanke, *The Spanish Struggle for Justice in the Conquest of America* (Boston, 1965); the more recent studies by A. Pagden, *The Fall of Natural Man: The American Indian and the Origins of Comparative Ethnology* (Cambridge, 1986), *Spanish Imperialism and the Political Imagination* (New Haven, Conn., 1990), *European Encounters with the New World: From Renaissance to Romanticism* (New Haven, Conn., 1993), *Uncertainties of Empire* (Aldershot, 1994), and *Lords of All the World: Ideologies of Empire in Spain, Britain, and France c. 1500–c. 1800* (New Haven, Conn., 1995); as well as D. Armitage, ed., *Theories of Empire, 1450–1800* (Aldershot, 1998), and J. Muldoon, *The Americas in the Spanish World Order: The Justification for Conquest in the Seventeenth Century* (Philadelphia, 1994). Cf. D. Armitage, *The Ideological Origins of the British Empire* (Cambridge, 2000).

29. D. A. Lupher, *Romans in a New World: Classical Models in Sixteenth-Century Spanish America* (Ann Arbor, 2003).

30. The best comparison of the two major American empires is J. H. Elliott, *Empires of the Atlantic World: Britain and Spain in America, 1492–1830* (New Haven, Conn., 2006). Cf. C. Véliz, *The New World of the Gothic Fox: Culture and Economy in English and Spanish America* (Berkeley, 1994).

31. These problems receive extended analysis in the new study of A. M. Bernal, *España, proyecto inacabado: Costes/beneficios del Imperio* (Madrid, 2005).

6. Spain and Portugal

1. E.g., D. Stanislawski, *The Individuality of Portugal: A Study in Historical-Political Geography* (Austin, 1959).

2. Probably the best account is J. Mattoso, *Identificação de um país: Ensaio sobre as origens de Portugal 1096–1325*, 2 vols. (Lisbon, 1985).

3. L. F. Thomaz, "L'Idée impériale manueline," in J. Aubin, ed., *La Découverte, le Portugal et l'Europe* (Paris, 1990), 35–103.

4. L. Valensi, *Fables de la mémoire: La glorieuse bataille des trois rois* (Paris, 1992).

5. A somewhat different situation, however, is reflected by the achievements enumerated and described by S. G. Marks, *How Russia Shaped the Modern World: From Art to Anti-Semitism, Ballet to Bolshevism* (Princeton, N.J., 2003). The case of Russia has to do with a country that was a great power from the eighteenth century on, whose population explosion in the nineteenth century generated a large intelligentsia that produced many new ideas and innovations—quite the opposite from a very small and (after the sixteenth century) weak

country like Portugal. Moreover, much of the influence of the Russian achievements was destructive, and this was true of the Portuguese innovations to a considerably lesser degree.

6. Garrett Mattingly, in lectures of his course "The Expansion of Europe" at Columbia in the 1950s.

7. Cf. J. Reis, *O atraso económico português 1850–1930* (Lisbon, 1993).

8. J. A. Rocamora, *El nacionalismo ibérico 1792–1936* (Valladolid, 1994).

9. H. de la Torre Gómez, *El imperio del Rey: Alfonso XIII, Portugal y los ingleses (1907–1916)* (Mérida, 2002).

10. See S. Payne, *Franco and Hitler* (New Haven, Conn., 2008), for a more extensive treatment.

11. A. J. Telo, *Portugal e a NATO: O reencontro da tradição atlântica* (Lisbon, 1996).

7. Decline and Recovery

1. This position had accordingly negative consequences for the numbers and morale of naval crewmen, according to D. Goodman, *Spanish Naval Power, 1589–1665: Reconstruction and Defeat* (Cambridge, 1997).

2. Enrique Llopis Agelán, in I. A. A. Thompson and B. Yun Casalilla, *The Castilian Crisis of the Seventeenth Century: New Perspectives on the Economic and Social History of Seventeenth-Century Spain* (Cambridge, 1994). The broadest treatment of the decline in one volume is A. Domínguez Ortiz et al., "La crisis del siglo XVII," in R. Menéndez Pidal and J. M. Jover, eds., *Historia de España*, vol. 23 (Madrid, 1989).

3. As Sir Raymond Carr has observed, it was "curiously indifferent to personal character and its development. The drama of the Golden Age is strong on plots, but the dramatis personae are stock types and little more." *New York Review of Books*, November 20, 1986.

4. In some ways Scotland became an even better example than England. See A. Herman, *How the Scots Invented the Modern World* (New York, 2001).

5. The English edition is titled *The Spanish Character: Attitudes and Mentalities from the Sixteenth to the Nineteenth Century* (Berkeley, 1979). To this might be added B. Bennassar, L. Domergue, J.-P. Dedieu, and J. Pérez, "Las resistencias mentales," in Bennassar's *Orígenes del atraso económico español* (Barcelona, 1985), 124–51.

6. R. MacKay, *"Lazy, Improvident People": Myth and Reality in the Writing of Spanish History* (Ithaca, N.Y., 2006).

7. T. A. Mantecón, "The Patterns of Violence in Early Modern Spain," *Journal of the Historical Society* 7.2 (June 2007): 229–64.

8. Cf. M. E. Lépori de Pithod, *La imagen de España en el siglo XVII: Percepción y decadencia* (Mendoza, Argentina, 1998).

9. See A. Mestre Sanchos, *Apología y crítica de España en el siglo XVIII* (Madrid, 2003).

10. One of the most recent treatments is R. García Cárcel, *Felipe V y los españoles: Una visión periférica del problema de España* (Barcelona, 2002). See also J. Mercader i Riba, *Felip V i Catalunya* (Barcelona, 1968).

11. J. Marías, *España inteligible*, chap. 21.

12. J. Sarrailh, *L'Espagne éclairée de la seconde moitié du XVIIIe siècle* (Paris, 1954).

13. The reformist criticism of Feijóo did not go as far, however, as the "Reform Catholicism" advocated by a minority in France and Austria. See D. Sorkin, *The Religious Enlightenment: Protestants, Jews, and Catholics from London to Vienna* (Princeton, N.J., 2008), 215–309.

14. For a clear differentiation, see G. Himmelfarb, *The Roads to Modernity: The British, French, and American Enlightenments* (New York, 2004).

15. The basic new study is T. E. Chávez, *Spain and the Independence of the United States: An Intrinsic Gift* (Albuquerque, 2002). For a broader contextualization, see the new collective work by Gonzalo Anes de Castrillón, ed., *La Ilustración española en la independencia de Estados Unidos* (Madrid, 2007).

16. L. T. Cummins, *Spanish Observers and the American Revolution, 1775–1783* (Baton Rouge, 1991).

17. Here it might be pointed out that eighteenth-century French writers produced the first glimmerings of "Hispanism," producing the principal new histories of Spain during that era, though this would not emerge as a scholarly field until the next century.

18. The best evocation of the new trends of that generation, even though somewhat idealized and exaggerated, is still J. Marías, *La España posible en tiempo de Carlos III* (Madrid, 1963).

19. J. Lynch, *Bourbon Spain, 1700–1808* (Oxford, 1989), 208.

20. This is the thesis of F. Sánchez-Blanco, *El Absolutismo y las Luces en el reinado de Carlos III* (Madrid, 2002).

21. F. Sánchez-Blanco, ed., *La Ilustración goyesca: La cultura en España durante el reinado de Carlos IV (1788–1808)* (Madrid, 2007).

22. J. Álvarez Junco, "La invención de la Guerra de la Independencia," *Studia Histórica-Historia Contemporánea* 12 (1994): 75–99.

23. C. Esdaile, *España contra Napoleón: Guerrillas, bandoleros y el mito del pueblo en armas (1808–1814)* (Barcelona, 2006).

24. The bicentenary in 2008 produced a great volume of new historical literature, as major historical anniversaries do in Spain. J. P. Fusi and F. Calvo Serraller, *Por la independencia: La crisis de 1808 y sus consecuencias* (Madrid, 2008), presents the most elegant summary and analysis. Two of the best military accounts are A. Moliner Prada, ed., *La Guerra de la Independencia en España (1808–1814)* (Barcelona, 2007), and E. de Diego, *España, el infierno de Napoleón* (Madrid, 2008).

8. The Problem of Spanish Liberalism

1. This is the term used by M. Mugnaini, "Cult of the Nation, Religion of Liberty or Reason of State? Spain in Italian Foreign Policy (1846–1868)," in J. G. Beramendi et al., eds., *Nationalism in Europe Past and Present* (Santiago de Campostela, 1994), 1:665–76.

2. C. A. Hale, "The Reconstruction of Nineteenth-Century Politics in Spanish America: A Case for the History of Ideas," *Latin American Research Review* 8.2 (Summer 1973): 53–73.

3. M.-L. Rieu-Millán, *Los diputados americanos en las Cortes de Cádiz* (Madrid, 1990); D. Martínez Torrón, *Los liberales románticos españoles ante la descolonización americana*

(Madrid, 1992); M. Chust, *La cuestión nacional americana en las Cortes de Cádiz* (Valencia, 1999); P. Cruz Villalón et al., *Los orígenes del constitucionalismo liberal en España e Iberoamérica: Un estudio comparado* (Seville, 1994); P. Pascual Martínez, *La unión con España, exigencia de los diputados americanos en las Cortes de Cádiz* (Madrid, 2001).

4. T. E. Anna, *Spain and the Loss of Latin America* (Lincoln, Neb., 1983); M. P. Costeloe, *Response to Revolution: Imperial Spain and the Spanish American Revolutions, 1810–1840* (Cambridge, 1986).

5. The bibliography treating Carlism is very extensive. Among general accounts, A. M. Moral Roncal, *Las guerras carlistas* (Madrid, 2006), emphasizes military history, while J. Canal, *El carlismo: Dos siglos de contrarrevolución en España* (Madrid, 2000), deals more with political and social aspects. The best history of the first and most important Carlist war is A. Bullón de Mendoza, *La primera guerra carlista* (Madrid, 1992).

6. This is the argument of J. V. Serrâo and A. Bullón de Mendoza, eds., *La contrarrevolución legitimista (1688–1876)* (Madrid, 1995), and of Jordi Canal in his article "Guerra civil y contrarrevolución en la Europa del sur en el siglo XIX: Reflexiones a partir del caso español," in J. Canal i Morell, ed., *Las guerras civiles en la España contemporánea* (Madrid, 2005), 23–47.

7. I. Burdiel, *La política de los notables: Moderados y avanzados durante el régimen del Estatuto Real* (Valencia, 1987); I. Castells, *La utopía insurreccional del liberalismo* (Barcelona, 1989); M. C. Romeo, *Entre el orden y la revolución: La formación de la burguesía liberal en la crisis de la monarquía absoluta* (Alicante, 1993).

8. This follows the argument of J. Varela Ortega, "La España política de fin de siglo," *Revista de Occidente* (1998): 43–77, and I. Burdiel, "Myths of Failure, Myths of Success: New Perspectives on Nineteenth-Century Spanish Liberalism," *Journal of Modern History* 70 (December 1998): 892–912.

9. For a good introduction to Cánovas and his work, see A. Bullón de Mendoza and L. E. Togores, eds., *Cánovas y su época*, 2 vols. (Madrid, 1999).

10. The fundamental study is J. Álvarez Junco, *Mater Dolorosa: La idea de España en el siglo XIX* (Madrid, 2001). See also P. Cirujano Marín et al., *Historiografía y nacionalismo español (1834–1868)* (Madrid, 1985); I. Fox, *La invención de España: Nacionalismo liberal e identidad nacional* (Madrid, 1997); and J. P. Fusi, *España: La evolución de la identidad nacional* (Madrid, 2000), 163–96.

11. J. Álvarez Junco, "La difícil nacionalización de la derecha española en la primera mitad del siglo XIX," *Hispania* 61.3 (2001): 831–58.

12. Recent controversies have elicited a new anthology of Menéndez Pelayo's writings, under the title of *La historia de España* (Madrid, 2007). See also C. Boyd, *Historia Patria: Politics, History, and National Identity in Spain, 1875–1975* (Princeton, N.J., 1997).

13. This is the thesis of M. K. Flynn, *Ideology, Mobilization, and the Nation: The Rise of the Irish, Basque and Carlist Nationalist Movements in the Nineteenth and Early Twentieth Centuries* (London, 2000).

14. Something of this perspective may be found in J. P. Fusi and A. Niño, eds., *Antes del "desastre": Orígenes y antecedentes de la crisis del 98* (Madrid, 1996), and J. Andrés-Gallego, *Un 98 distinto: Restauración, desastre, regeneracionismo* (Madrid, 1998), and, to a lesser degree, in

J. Pan-Montojo, ed., *Más se perdió en Cuba: España, 1898 y la crisis de fin de siglo* (Madrid, 1998), and in *Los 98 ibéricos y el mar*, vol. 2, *La cultura en la península ibérica* (Madrid, 1998).

15. J. Nadal, *El fracaso de la revolución industrial en España, 1814–1913*. The cluster of books toward the end of the century included P. Martín Aceña and L. Prados de la Escosura, eds., *La nueva historia económica de España* (Madrid, 1985); Prados de la Escosura, *Comercio exterior y crecimiento económico en España, 1826–1913: Tendencias a largo plazo* (Madrid, 1982), *De imperio a nación: Crecimiento y atraso económico en España (1780–1930)* (Madrid, 1988), and *El progreso económico de España (1850–2000)* (Bilbao, 2003); J. Nadal et al., eds., *La economía española en el siglo XX: Una perspectiva histórica* (Barcelona, 1987); N. Sánchez-Albornoz, ed., *The Economic Modernization of Spain, 1830–1930* (New York, 1987); A. Carreras, *Industrialización española: Estudios de historia cuantitativa* (Madrid, 1990); G. Tortella, *El desarrollo de la España contemporánea: Historia económica de los siglos XIX y XX* (Madrid, 1994); G. Anes, ed., *Historia económica de España: Siglos XIX y XX* (Barcelona, 1999), J. L. García Delgado and J. C. Jiménez, *Un siglo de España: La economía* (Madrid, 1999); and J. M. Martínez Carrión, ed., *El nivel de vida en la España rural, siglos XVIII–XX* (Salamanca, 2002).

16. L. Prados de la Escosura and V. Zamagni, eds., *El desarrollo económico en la Europa del Sur: España e Italia en perspectiva histórica* (Madrid, 1992).

17. Cf. J. Maluquer de Motes, *España en la crisis de 1898: De la Gran Depresión a la modernización económica del siglo XX* (Barcelona, 1999).

18. J. Nadal, *La población española (siglos XVI–XX)* (Barcelona, 1984), 211.

19. For a broader discussion, see D. Ringrose, *Spain, Europe, and the "Spanish Miracle," 1700–1900* (Cambridge, 1996), which is the best analytical re-examination of the economy of the nineteenth century, and, for a more general discussion of the period that "normalizes" Spanish historical evolution, see J. P. Fusi and J. Palafox, *España, 1808–1996: El desafío de la modernidad* (Madrid, 1997).

20. This has been best brought out in the work of C. Schmidt-Nowara, *Empire and Antislavery: Spain, Cuba, and Puerto Rico, 1833–1874* (Pittsburgh, 1999), and "'La España Ultramarina': Colonialism and Nation-building in Nineteenth-century Spain," *European History Quarterly* 34.2 (2004): 191–214. The best treatment of the nineteenth-century empire in a single volume is J. M. Fradera, *Colonias para después de un imperio* (Barcelona, 2005).

21. Despite the revival of interest in Africa after the Moroccan war of 1859–60, Spain's leaders generally avoided becoming very deeply involved. M. C. Lecuyer and C. Serrano, *La Guerre d'Afrique et ses repercussions en Espagne: Idéologies et colonialisme en Espagne 1859–1904* (Paris, 1976), and E. Martín Corrales, *Marruecos y el colonialismo español (1852–1912)* (Barcelona, 2002).

22. See V. L. Salavert Fabiani, ed., *El regeneracionismo en España: Política, educación, ciencia y sociedad* (Valencia, 2007).

23. Ringrose, *Spain, Europe, and the "Spanish Miracle,"* 357.

24. It has been characteristic of Spanish historians to focus on the crisis of 1917 primarily as a domestic phenomenon. The first study to place this fully within the international context and multiple influences of World War I is F. J. Romero Salvadó, *Spain, 1914–1918:*

Between War and Revolution (London, 1999). See also the extensive study by G. Meaker, "A Civil War of Words," in H. A. Schmitt, ed., *Neutral Europe Between War and Revolution, 1917–1923* (Charlottesville, N.C., 1988), 37–114.

25. This is illustrated particularly in the work of my former student Thomas G. Trice, *Spanish Liberalism in Crisis: A Study of the Liberal Party during Spain's Parliamentary Collapse, 1913–1923* (New York, 1991).

26. See the counterfactual discussion by F. del Rey Reguillo, "¿Qué habría sucedido si Alfonso XIII hubiera rechazado el golpe de Primo de Rivera en 1923?" in N. Townson, ed., *Historia virtual de España (1870–2004): ¿Qué hubiera pasado si . . . ?* (Madrid, 2004), 93–137.

27. The principal studies are J. Tusell and G. García Queipo de Llano, *Alfonso XIII: El rey polémico* (Madrid, 2001), and C. Seco Serrano, *La España de Alfonso XIII: El Estado. La política. Los movimientos sociales* (Madrid, 2002). A. Osorio and G. Cardona, *Alfonso XIII* (Barcelona, 2005), presents both sides, while J. Moreno Luzón, ed., *Alfonso XIII: Un político en el trono* (Madrid, 2003), and R. Borràs Betriu, *El rey perjuro: Don Alfonso XIII y la caída de la Monarquía* (Barcelona, 1997), are more critical.

28. J. Tusell, *Radiografía de un golpe de Estado: El ascenso al poder del general Primo de Rivera* (Madrid, 1987), remains the key analysis.

9. A Republic . . . without Democrats?

1. J. Avilés Farré, *La izquierda burguesa en la II República* (Madrid, 1985), remains the principal study. The most extensive biography of Azaña is S. Juliá, *Vida y tiempo de Manuel Azaña (1880–1940)* (Madrid, 2008).

2. R. Villa García, *La modernización de España: Las elecciones nacionales de 1933* (forthcoming), presents the definitive study.

3. The Radicals have been studied by O. Ruiz Manjón, *El Partido Republican Radical, 1908–1936* (Madrid, 1976), and N. Townson, *The Crisis of Democracy in Spain: Centrist Politics under the Second Republic, 1931–1936* (Brighton, 2000).

4. The only full study of the Republican president is A. Alcalá Galve, *Alcalá-Zamora y la agonía de la República* (Seville, 2002).

5. R. A. H. Robinson, *The Origins of Franco's Spain: The Right, the Republic, and Revolution, 1931–1936* (Pittsburgh, 1970), is still the best account of the CEDA.

6. The principal historian of Spanish anarchism is Julián Casanova, author of *Anarchism, the Republic and Civil War in Spain: 1931–1939* (London, 2004), *Anarquismo y violencia política en la España del siglo XX* (Zaragoza, 2007), and other works. See also J. Brademas, *Anarquismo y revolución en España (1930–1937)* (Barcelona, 1974), and J. Paniagua Fuentes, *La larga marcha hacia la anarquía: Pensamiento y acción del movimiento libertario* (Madrid, 2008).

10. Who Was Responsible?

1. There is a vast literature on the revolutionary insurrection of October 1934. The most extensive treatment of events in Asturias is P. I. Taibo II, *Asturias 1934*, 2 vols. (Gijón,

1984), favorable to the insurrectionists. See, more broadly, P. Moa, *Los orígenes de la Guerra Civil española* (Madrid, 1999) and *1934: Comienza la Guerra Civil: El PSOE y la Ezquerra emprenden las armas* (Madrid, 2004); F. Aguado Sánchez, *La revolución de octubre de 1934* (Madrid, 1972); B. Díaz Nosty, *La comuna asturiana* (Madrid, 1974); A. del Rosal, *1934: El movimiento revolucionario de octubre* (Madrid, 1983); and, for the analysis of Socialist policy, see J. Avilés Farré, "Los socialistas y la insurrección de octubre de 1934," in Avilés Farré, ed., "Violencia y política en España, 1875–1936," *Espacio, Tiempo y Forma*, series 5: *Historia Contemporánea*, no. 20 (2008): 129–57.

2. B. D. Bunk, *Ghosts of Passion: Martyrdom, Gender, and the Origins of the Spanish Civil War* (Durham, N. C., 2007), treats the propaganda campaigns, their images and influence.

3. M. Tuñón de Lara, *Tres claves de la Segunda República* (Madrid, 1985), 194–95.

4. R. Villa García, "The Failure of Electoral Modernization: The Elections of May 1936 in Granada," *Journal of Contemporary History* 44.3 (July 2009): 401–29.

5. R. Cibrián, "Violencia política y crisis democrática: España en 1936," *Revista de Estudios Políticos* 6 (November–December 1978): 81–115, presents the low calculation, and J. Blázquez Miguel, "Conflictividad en la España del Frente Popular (febrero–julio de 1936)," *Historia* 16.328 (August 2003): 76–86, the higher conclusion.

For broader discussion of the role and character of political violence under the Republic, see F. del Rey Reguillo, "Reflexiones sobre la violencia política en la II República española," in M. Gutiérrez Sánchez and D. Palacios Cerezales, eds., *Conflicto politico, democracia y dictadura: Portugal y España en la década de 1930* (Madrid, 2007), 19–97; G. Ranzato, "El peso de la violencia en los orígenes de la Guerra Civil de 1936–1939," in Avilés Farré, "Violencia política en España, 1875–1936," 159–82; and the most thorough statistical study, J. Blázquez Miguel, *España turbulenta: Alteraciones, violencia y sangre durante la II República* (Madrid, 2009).

6. For source references concerning the events of July 1936, see S. G. Payne, *The Collapse of the Spanish Republic, 1933–1936: Origins of the Civil War* (New Haven, Conn., 2006), 302–38.

11. Moscow and Madrid

1. These words have been reprinted various times, most recently in X. Moreno Juliá, *La División Azul: Sangre española en Rusia* (Barcelona, 2004), 75. Many years later, Serrano would express regret for such rhetorical excess.

2. A. Elorza and M. Bizcarrondo, *Queridos camaradas: La Internacional Comunista y España, 1919–1939* (Barcelona, 1999), 19–208; J. Avilés Farré, *La fe que vino de Rusia: La revolución bolchevique y los españoles (1917–1931)* (Madrid, 1999); P. Pagés, *Historia del Partido Comunista de España: Desde su fundación en abril de 1920 hasta el final de la dictadura de Primo de Rivera, enero de 1930* (Barcelona, 1978); R. Cruz, *El Partido Comunista en la Segunda República* (Madrid, 1987).

3. For references and further discussion, see S. G. Payne, *The Spanish Civil War, the Soviet Union, and Communism* (New Haven, Conn., 2004), 22–37.

4. Somewhat ironically, "People's Army" was the name of the abortive anti-Communist military organization that "Komuch," the short-lived regime of the left-liberals of the Russian Constituent Assembly, attempted to form in the Ural region in 1918.

5. Y. Rybalkin, *Stalin y España* (Madrid, 2007); D. Kowalsky, *La Unión Soviética y la guerra civil española: Una revisión crítica* (Barcelona, 2003), 195–341.

6. On Soviet policy and Communist political activities during the war, see, in addition to my *Soviet Union, Communism and the Spanish Civil War*, R. Radosh, M. Habeck, and G. Sevostianov, eds., *Spain Betrayed: the Soviet Union in the Spanish Civil War* (New Haven, Conn., 2001); F. Schauff, *La victoria frustrada: La Unión Soviética, la Internacional Comunista y la guerra civil española* (Barcelona, 2008); and the four highly detailed polemics by Angel Viñas: *La soledad de la República: El abandono de las democracias y el viraje hacia la Unión Soviética* (Barcelona, 2006), *El escudo de la República: El oro de España, la apuesta soviética y los hechos de mayo de 1937* (Barcelona, 2007), *El honor de la República: Entre el acoso fascista, la hostilidad británica y la política de Stalin* (Barcelona, 2009), and *El desplome de la República* (Barcelona, 2009).

7. The principal biography is E. Moradiellos, *Don Juan Negrín* (Barcelona, 2006), but see also G. Jackson, *Juan Negrín: Médico socialista y jefe del Gobierno de la II República española* (Barcelona, 2008).

8. The Comintern had been dissolved in 1943 to encourage the perception of the Soviet Union as an anti-imperialist power. Its functions, however, were taken over by the new International Department of the Soviet Communist Party's central committee. During the last epoch of the Soviet regime, the International Department, which employed Pertsov, was headed by the prominent functionary Boris Ponomaryov.

12. The Spanish Civil War

1. Quoted in N. S. Lebedeva and M. M. Narinski, eds., *Komintern i vtoraia mirovaia voina* (Moscow, 1998), 1:10–11.

2. Quoted in A. C. Brown and C. B. MacDonald, *On a Field of Red: The Communist International and the Coming of World War II* (New York, 1981), 508.

3. P. Renouvin, *Histoire des relations internationales* (Paris, 1965), 8:112.

4. These references are drawn from the excellent article by W. C. Frank Jr., "The Spanish Civil War and the Coming of the Second World War," *International History Review* 9.3 (August 1987): 368–409.

5. Mussolini's policy toward Spain is treated in G. Palomares Lerma, *Mussolini y Primo de Rivera: Política exterior de dos dictadores* (Madrid, 1989); I. Saz Campos, *Mussolini contra la II República: Hostilidad, conspiraciones, intervención (1931–1936)* (Valencia, 1986); J. F. Coverdale, *Italian Intervention in the Spanish Civil War* (Princeton, N.J., 1975); M. Heiberg, *Emperadores del Mediterráneo: Franco, Mussolini y la guerra civil española* (Barcelona, 2003); X. Tusell and G. G. Queipo de Llano, *Franco y Mussolini: La política española durante la segunda guerra mundial* (Barcelona, 1985); and, within the broader setting of Mussolini's policy, in R. Mallett, *Mussolini and the Origins of the Second World War, 1933–1940* (Houndmills, 2003).

6. For a guide to the early literature, see W. Haupt, "Die 'Blaue Division' in der Literatur," *Wehrwissenschaftliche Rundschau* 4 (April 1959), and C. Caballero and R. Ibáñez, *Escritores en las trincheras: La División Azul en sus libros, publicaciones periódicas y filmografía (1941–1988)* (Madrid, 1989). Publications continue to proliferate.

7. For the relations between Franco and Hitler, see R. H. Whealey, *Hitler and Spain: The Nazi Role in the Spanish Civil War* (Lexington, Ky., 1989); Payne, *Franco and Hitler*; D. W. Pike, *Franco and the Axis Stigma* (New York, 2008); X. Moreno Juliá, *Hitler y Franco: Diplomacia en tiempos de guerra (1936–1945)* (Barcelona, 2007); and M. Ros Agudo, *La guerra secreta de Franco (1939–1945)* (Barcelona, 2002), and *La gran tentación: Franco, el Imperio colonial y los planes de intervención en la Segunda Guerra Mundial* (Barcelona, 2007). The best general account of Spanish diplomacy is still J. Tusell, *Franco, España y la II Guerra Mundial: Entre el Eje y la neutralidad* (Madrid, 1995).

For accounts favorable to Franco, see L. Suárez Fernàndez, *España, Franco y la Segunda Guerra Mundial, desde 1939 hasta 1945* (Madrid, 1997), and P. Moa, *Años de hierro: España en la posguerra 1939–1945* (Madrid, 2007).

8. Frank, "The Spanish Civil War and the Coming of the Second World War."

9. J. McLellan, *Antifascism and Memory in East Germany: Remembering the International Brigades* (Oxford, 2004); A. Krammer, "The Cult of the Spanish Civil War in East Germany," *Journal of Contemporary History* 39.4 (October 2004): 531–60.

10. For a somewhat different speculation concerning the consequences of a Republican victory, see I. Saz, "La victoria de la República en la Guerra Civil y la Europa de 1939," in J. M. Thomàs, ed., *La historia de España que no pudo ser* (Barcelona, 2007), 83–106.

11. E. Sáenz-Francés, *Entre la Antorcha y la Esvástica:Franco en la encrucijada de la Segunda Guerra Mundial* (Madrid, 2009), concentrates on the events of 1942–43.

13. Spanish Fascism . . . a Strange Case?

1. In addition there was a fascist government in Hungary from December 1944 to the end of the war, and another in Croatia in the form of the Independent State of Croatia (NDH) from 1941 to 1944. These governments, however, did not achieve power by themselves but were imposed by Hitler. On the NDH, see the special issue of *Totalitarian Movements and Political Religions* 7.4 (December 2006), edited by Sabrina Ramet.

2. Payne, *A History of Fascism*, 487–95. A retrodictive theory is an attempt to postulate the conditions that were required in a certain historical era for a certain kind of development to have taken place, in other words, what would have been necessary to have made a positive prediction in the past.

3. Araquistain's remarks appeared in his article in the New York journal *Foreign Affairs* in April 1934, and those of Maurín approximately a year later in his book *Hacia la segunda revolución* (Barcelona, 1935).

4. This sentiment is most dramatically expressed by the outpouring of activities and new publications of "Plataforma 2003," an association funded by Primo de Rivera's admirers to commemorate the centenary of his birth, with all funds raised from their own pockets.

The two best books on José Antonio are J. Gil Pecharromán, *José Antonio Primo de Rivera: Retrato de un visionario* (Madrid, 1996), the best critical scholarly account; and

A. Imatz, *José Antonio: Entre odio y amor* (Madrid, 2006), also very well informed and more favorable to its subject. For a pro-and-con approach, see E. Aguinaga and S. G. Payne, *José Antonio Primo de Rivera* (Barcelona, 2003).

5. The best argument is presented in Imatz, *José Antonio*. In this regard, the definition of fascism is fundamental. Except in the case of the Italian National Fascist Party and a few extremely insignificant organizations that formally proclaimed themselves "fascist," the term was not officially adopted by other parties of similar characteristics. As used by scholars and historians, the term does not refer to a single unified or reified entity but is employed as a generic political reference in the same way as socialist, communist, and other broadly employed adjectives. The concept of generic fascism is used as a heuristic device to refer to an ideal type or construct in the social sciences that groups together a series of political movements, primarily found in interwar Europe, possessing key common characteristics. Among these are authoritarian political structure and goals, charismatic leadership, extreme nationalism, zeal for imperial expansion, the militarization of politics, creation of a "new man" based on a radical new culture of vitalism and dynamism, antimaterialism, idealization of violence and militarization, and the development of an authoritarian national economic structure, whether national socialism or corporatism. I have treated this at some length in my books *Fascism: Comparison and Definition* (Madison, 1980) and *A History of Fascism*, and will not repeat the discussion here. Nearly all these basic components of fascism are found in the doctrines of José Antonio.

6. The best studies are those of F. Gallego: *Ramiro Ledesma Ramos y el fascismo español* (Madrid, 2005) and the long study in the volume that he coedited with F. Morente, *Fascismo en España* (Madrid, 2005). L. Casali, *Società di massa, giovani, rivoluzione: Il fascismo di Ramiro Ledesma Ramos* (Turin, 2002), is also recommendable. The *Obras completas* of Ledesma were published in four volumes in 2004.

7. R. Ledesma Ramos, *¿Fascismo en España?* (Madrid, 1935), 21–22.

8. M. Primo de Rivera, ed., *Papeles póstumos de José Antonio* (Barcelona, 1996).

9. I. Saz, *Fascismo y franquismo* (Valencia, 2004).

10. Falangist dissidence would also generate its own historiography after the end of the regime.

11. The text is from L. López Rodó, *La larga marcha hacia la monarquía* (Barcelona, 1978), 30–31.

12. Cited in López Rodó, *Política y desarrollo* (Madrid, 1970), 18–19.

13. Fundación Nacional Francisco Franco, *Documentos inéditos del regimen del Generalísimo Franco* (Madrid, 1994), 2:143–44.

14. R. Serrano Suñer, *La historia como fue: Memorias* (Barcelona, 1977), 198.

14. Francisco Franco

1. The bibliography is, of course, very great. The best one is P. Preston, *Franco: A Biography* (London, 1993), and the most thorough pro-Franco treatment is R. de la Cierva, *Franco: La historia* (Madrid, 2000).

2. The best treatment of Franco's early years is B. Bennassar, *Franco: Enfance et adolescence* (Paris, 1999).

3. The best analysis of Franco's political leadership during the Civil War is J. Tusell, *Franco en la Guerra Civil* (Barcelona, 1992).

4. J. A. Vaca de Osma, *La larga guerra de Francisco Franco* (Madrid, 1991); C. Blanco Escolá, *La incompetencia militar de Franco* (Barcelona, 1999); J. Semprún, *El genio militar de Franco* (Madrid, 2000). The best evaluation, however, is J. Blázquez Miguel, *Auténtico Franco: Trayectoria militar, 1907–1939* (Madrid, 2009).

5. M. Seidman, *The Victorious Counterrevolution* (Madison, 2011), is the first complete study of Franco's eminently successful mobilization of domestic resources.

6. Fundación Nacional Francisco Franco, *Documentos inéditos para la historia del Generalísimo Franco*, 2:1, 380–81.

7. This is best rendered in D. W. Pike, *Franco and the Axis Stigma* (New York, 2008).

15. In the Shadow of the Military

1. The leading one-volume account is C. Seco Serrano, *Militarismo y civilismo en la España contemporánea* (Madrid, 1984), which updated my earlier *Politics and the Military in Modern Spain* (Stanford, 1967).

2. The role of the military in the first part of the reign of Fernando VII is examined in R. L. Blanco Valdés, *Rey, Cortes y fuerza armada en los orígenes de la España liberal, 1808–1823* (Madrid, 1988).

3. For a brief listing of all these and later initiatives, see J. Busquets, *Pronunciamientos y golpes de Estado en España* (Barcelona, 1982).

4. For the later nineteenth century, see D. R. Headrick, *Ejército y política en España (1866–1898)* (Madrid, 1981).

5. Prior to the Civil War of 1936 there was no separate air force, aerial units being formed as the army air force and the naval air force.

6. R. Núñez Florencio, *Militarismo y antimilitarismo en España (1888–1906)* (Madrid, 1990).

7. For this era, see C. P. Boyd, *Praetorian Politics in Liberal Spain* (Chapel Hill, N.C., 1979).

8. C. Navajas Zubeldia, *Ejército, Estado y sociedad en España (1923–1930)* (Logroño, 1991).

9. M. Aguilar Olivencia, *El Ejército español durante la Segunda República* (Madrid, 1986).

10. S. Juliá, "¿Qué habría pasado si Indalecio Prieto hubiera aceptado la presidencia del Gobierno en mayo de 1936? " in N. Townson, ed., *Historia virtual de España (1874–2004) ¿Qué hubiera pasado si . . . ?* (Madrid, 2004), 175–200.

11. On the military conspiracy and the insurgency that began the Civil War, see J. M. Martínez Bande, *Los años críticos: República, conspiración y alzamiento* (Madrid, 2007), 189–451.

12. Quoted in N. Goda, *Tomorrow the World: Hitler, Northwest Africa, and the Path toward America* (College Station, Tex., 1998), 59.

13. D. Smyth, "Les chevaliers de Saint-Georges: La Grande Bretagne et la corruption des généraux espagnols," *Guerres Mondiales* 162 (1991): 29–54; see also D. Stafford, *Roosevelt and Churchill: Men of Secrets* (London, 1999), 78–110.

14. E. San Román, *Ejército e industria: El nacimiento de INI* (Barcelona, 1999).

15. J. Tusell and G. G. Queipo de Llano, *Carrero: La eminencia gris del régimen de Franco* (Madrid, 1993).

16. J. Tusell, *Franco, España y la II Guerra Mundial: Entre el Eje y la neutralidad* (Madrid, 1995), 309.

17. Eugenio Vegas Latapié first provided me with the text of this document in 1963.

18. J. A. Olmeda Gómez, *Las fuerzas armadas en el Estado franquista: Participación política, influencia presupuestaria y profesionalización, 1939–1975* (Madrid, 1988), treats the institutional functioning of the military under the regime.

19. C. Fernández, *Los militares en la transición política* (Barcelona, 1982), treats the role of the military during the first five years of the Transition.

20. The literature on the "23-F" is very extensive. See especially J. Palacios, *23-F: El golpe del CESID* (Barcelona, 2001), and A. Martínez Inglés, *23-F: El golpe que nunca existió* (Madrid, 2001).

21. J. M. Comas and L. Mandeville, *Les militaires et le pouvoir dans l'Espagne contemporaine de Franco à Felipe González* (Toulouse, 1986).

22. I. Martínez Inglés, *El Ejército español: De poder fáctico a "ONG humanitaria"* (Arrigorriaga, 2004), presents a critical survey of these changes.

16. Controversies over History in Contemporary Spain

1. M. Bauerlein, *The Dumbest Generation: How the Digital Age Stupefies Young Americans and Jeopardizes Our Future* (New York, 2008), presents a sustained critique as applied to the United States, home of the digital revolution.

2. For a discussion of this, see J. Lukacs, *At the End of an Age* (New Haven, Conn., 2002), 45–83.

3. The best single account that summarizes this broad politico-historiographical controversy is S. Balfour and A. Quiroga, *España reinventada: Nación e identidad desde la Transición* (Barcelona, 2007). "To reinvent" is, of course, a standard cliché of postmodernist theory.

4. There is a very extensive literature dealing with the processes that subsequently ensued. The most recent set of studies, which contains full bibliographic references, is A. M. Khazanov and S. G. Payne, eds., "Perpetrators, Accomplices and Victims in Twentieth- and Twenty-First Century Narratives and Politics," a special double issue of *Totalitarian Movements and Political Religions* 9.2–3 (June–September 2008). This volume is also published in book form by Routledge: *Perpetrators, Accomplices and Victims in Twentieth-century Politics: Reckoning with the Past* (2009).

5. L. La Rovere, *L'eredità del fascismo: Gli intellettuali i giovani e la transizione al postfascismo, 1943–1948* (Torino, 2008).

6. See A. Costa Pinto, "The Legacy of the Authoritarian Past in Portugal's Democratisation, 1974–6," in Khazanov and Payne, *Perpetrators, Accomplices and Victims*, 265–89, and "Political Purges and State Crisis in Portugal's Transition to Democracy, 1975–76," *Journal of Contemporary History* 43.2 (April 2008): 305–32.

7. There were of course a number of short-term and noninstitutionalized authoritarian regimes during the early twentieth century that simply collapsed or were leveraged from power by political means, but all these had been in power for less than a decade.

8. The best discussion of the Transition and of these ideas as they relate to the history of the Civil War and the Transition is G. Ranzato, *El pasado de bronce: La herencia de la Guerra Civil en la España democrática* (Barcelona, 2007).

9. P. Aguilar, *Políticas de la memoria y memorias de la política: El caso español en perspectiva comparada* (Madrid, 2008), 70.

10. These points have been made by some of the country's leading figures in contemporary history, such as S. Juliá, "Echar al olvido: Memoria y amnistía en la transición," *Claves de Razón Práctica* 159 (2003): 14–24; and the late J. Tusell, "La historia y la Transición," *Clío: Journal of Literature, History, and the History of Philosophy* (November 2002): 18.

11. J. M. Solé Sabaté, *La repressió franquista a Catalunya (1938–1953)* (Barcelona, 1985); J. M. Solé Sabaté and J. Villarroya i Font, *La repressió a la reraguarda de Catalunya (1936–1939)*, 2 vols. (Barcelona, 1989–90); V. Gabarda Cebellán, *Els afusellaments al País Valencià (1938–1956)* (Valencia, 1993), and *La represión en la retaguardia republicana: País Valenciano, 1936–1939* (Valencia, 1996); F. Alía Miranda, *La guerra civil en retaguardia: Conflicto y revolución en la provincia de Ciudad Real, 1936–1939* (Ciudad Real, 1994).

12. E. Silva et al., eds., *La memoria de los olvidados: Un debate sobre el silencio de la represión franquista* (Valladolid, 2004), 55–65.

13. W. Kansteiner, "Finding Meaning in Memory: A Methodological Critique of Collective Memory Studies," *History and Theory* 41 (May 2002): 179–97.

14. N. Gedi and Y. Elam, "Collective Memory—What is It?" *History and Memory* 8 (1996): 30–50.

15. G. Bueno, *El mito de la izquierda* (Barcelona, 2002), 283.

16. This distinction is treated more broadly in P. Nora, *Realms of Memory: The Construction of the French Past*, ed. L. C. Kritzman (New York, 1996–98), 1:xv–xxiv, 3, as cited in S. J. Stern, *Remembering Pinochet's Chile: On the Eve of London, 1998* (Durham, N.C., 2004), 9.

17. Bueno, *El mito de la izquierda*, 285.

18. Silva et al., *La memoria de los olvidados*.

19. See the account in N. Tumarkin, *The Living and the Dead: The Rise and Fall of the Cult of World War II in Russia* (New York, 1994).

20. A. Krammer, "The Cult of the Spanish Civil War in East Germany," *Journal of Contemporary History* 39.4 (October 2004): 531–60, and, more extensively, J. McLellan, *Anti-Fascism and Memory in East Germany: Remembering the International Brigades* (New York, 2005).

21. The best analysis in Spanish is J. Trillo-Figueroa, *La ideología invisible: El pensamiento de la nueva izquierda radical* (Madrid, 2005).

22. C. Eliacheff and D. Soulez Larivière, *El tiempo de las víctimas* (Madrid, 2009).

23. The precise, if prolix, name of this legislation is "Law to recognize and extend rights and to establish measures to assist those who suffered persecution or violence during the Civil War and the dictatorship." It is of course impossible to implement such a measure

fully, since a sizable proportion of the population underwent some manner of persecution, directly or indirectly and in one zone or the other, during the Civil War, and similarly especially during the first years of the dictatorship, and to a lesser degree afterward, added to which is the fact that the great majority of people in these categories are dead.

24. The preceding quotations are drawn from Aguilar, *Políticas de la memoria*, 86–89, which provides an excellent discussion of the law and, more importantly, offers by far the most thorough and objective study of the several phases of collective memory and attitudes and policies toward the past since 1939. Several key aspects are treated in S. Juliá, ed., *Memoria de la guerra y del franquismo* (Madrid, 2006).

Index

Index

Index

Erving, George, 12

Esch, Patricia van der, 189

"España" (historical use of term), 94, 105

España, un enigma histórico (Sánchez Albornoz), 4

España Libre, 20, 21

"Español and españoles" (historical use of terms), 94

Espartero, Baldamero, 232

Esquerra Catalana (Spanish party), 165. *See also* Left republicans

"Estado Novo" (Salazar's program), 124–26, 176, 220

Estoria de España, 100

ETA (Euskadi Ta Askatasuna), 21–22, 32–33, 69, 247

Ethiopia, 156–57, 194

ethnicity: discrimination on basis of, in medieval Europe, 87; as division in Islamic society, 60, 62; and the Visigoths, 48–49, 51. *See also* Jews; Muslims

Etymologies (San Isidoro), 47

Europe: as a concept, 267n2; democratization in eastern, 226, 248, 249; eastern, in World War II, 193, 194, 196; immigrants from, to Spain, 85, 86, 131; modernization in northern, 89–92, 129, 132; Muslim attacks on, 56; Muslims in, 265n1; rise of, 82–83; Spain's development as consistent with trends in, 81–92, 103, 128, 133, 134, 146, 148, 150–51, 155–57, 200. *See also* Latin Christendom; *and specific countries, rulers, and institutions*

European Union, 82, 111

Euskadi Ta Askatasuna (ETA), 21–22, 32–33, 69, 247

"exaltados," 144–45

"exhaustion." *See* "decadence"

FAI (Federación Anarquista Ibérica), 30, 167, 168, 170, 172, 188. *See also* CNT (Confederación Nacional del Trabajo)

failure: of Second Republic, 163–64; Spanish sense of, in late nineteenth century, 152–55, 157

Falange Espagñola Tradicionalista (FET). *See* Falangists

Falangists, 199–215; and Catholicism, 212, 213–14; on causes of Spanish Civil War, 180;

forcible dissolution of, 172; Franco's control of, 206–7, 221, 224, 236, 237; insurrection by, 205, 206; interest of, in incorporating Portugal into Spain, 125; military resentment of, 237–38; Payne's study of, 17, 18, 21, 23–24, 27–29; Primo de Rivera as leader of, 177, 202–11, 214, 219–20; survival of, related to defascistization, 200. *See also* Movimiento Nacional

Fanjul, Serafín, 70

fascism: definition of, 279n5; in France, 193, 208, 249; German, 125, 189–204, 206–8, 210, 211, 213, 215, 246; Italian, 124, 199–204, 207–8, 210, 221, 224, 236, 246, 249, 279n5; as more idiosyncratic than Communism, 199, 204–5; Payne's study of, 17, 25–27, 37, 199, 261n13; in Poland, 191–92; in Portugal, 125, 206, 208; in Spain, 125, 191, 199–215, 224–28, 236, 240–41; Spain as unlikely place for, 200–202; Spanish Civil War claims as an attempt to prevent, 170, 177, 181, 184, 185, 189, 196, 255. *See also* corporatism; defascistization; dictatorship; Falangists

Federación Anarquista Ibérica (FAI), 30, 167, 168, 170, 172, 188. *See also* CNT (Confederación Nacional del Trabajo)

Feijóo, Benito Jerónimo, 136

Felipe II, 79, 105, 115

Felipe III, 130

Felipe IV, 106, 107, 130, 131

Felipe V, 135, 230

Fernando II, 105

Fernando III el Santo, 68, 96, 99

Fernando VII, 143, 144–45, 230, 231

FET (Falange Espagñola Tradicionalista). *See* Falangists

feudalism, 85, 98, 135

First Carlist War, 146, 151, 231

First Republic (Spain), 147

flag (Spanish), 135

flamenco dance, 66–67, 140

Fontaine, Jacques, 46, 48

Ford, Richard, 67

Foreign Affairs (journal), 34

Foreign Service Institute, 34

Forum Iudicum, 47

Index

Index

Holy Roman Empire, 100, 101, 103, 108. *See also* Habsburg dynasty

"holy wars" ("guerra divinal"), 75, 76–80, 115. *See also* Crusades; jihads

L'homme espagnol (Bennassar), 132

Horthy, Miklós, 208

"House of War," 63, 74

Hume, Martin, 11

Hungary, 86, 193, 208, 278n1

Hunter College, 19, 27

Hutton, L. J., 268n15

Ibárruri, Dolores, 186

Iberian Peninsula: Muslim invasion of, 55–56; papal interest in disunity of, 86, 113. *See also* Portugal; Spain

Ibn Khaldun, 58

ICGP (International Conference Group on Portugal), 37, 118–19

identity: Portuguese, 112; Spanish, of Spanish exiles, 21; Spanish national, as bound up with Catholicism, 72–82, 85, 133, 150, 228; Spanish national, as established by Visigoths, 44; and Spanish "national character," 14, 33–34, 38–39, 67, 81–82, 98, 104, 132–33. *See also* nationalism; stereotypes

India, 61, 67, 114, 118

indigenous peoples (in America), 109

INI (Instituto Nacional de Industria), 237

Inquisition, 4, 13, 87, 89

Institutional Institute of Social History (Amsterdam), 30

Instituto de Cultura Hispánica, 33

Instituto Internacional, 25

Instituto Nacional de Industria (INI), 237

intermarriage, 65; bans on inter-religious, 48, 57; as basis of Spanish nationality, 81; between Spaniards and indigenous Americans, 110

International Brigades, 184, 196, 255

International Conference Group on Portugal (ICGP), 37, 118–19

Internet, 243

"In the Twilight of the Franco Era" (Payne), 34

Ireland, 85, 267n4

Iribarne, Fraga, 31

Iron Guard (Romania), 209

Irving, Washington, 12

Isabel II, 149, 231, 232

Isidro (saint of Seville), 45–48, 52, 78, 96, 100, 264n14

Islam: Hispanic converts to, 58, 59–60, 62; as influence on Spanish culture and character, 14, 66–71, 85, 87, 91; and jihad, 56–57, 63; as requiring military action against unbelievers, 56; revival of fundamentalist, 225; rules of war under, 52–53, 64. *See also* jihads; Koran; Muslims

Italy: aid to Spanish Right from, 186, 190, 192–93, 195, 221, 222; as Black Legend promoter, 81; Clough's study of, 19; comparisons of Spain with, 121; defascistization in, 246; divisions in, 87, 121; empire of, 156–57; fascism in, 124, 199–204, 207–8, 210, 221, 224, 236, 246, 249, 279n5; historiography in, 249; influence of, on Spain, 76, 85, 136, 221, 224; and liberalism, 146; military in, 229; Muslims in, 84–85; Spain's influence on, 144; Spanish Civil War claims as an attempt to free Spain from Fascist, 170, 177, 184, 185, 189; Spanish trade with, 4; in World War II, 190, 192–93, 195, 223. *See also specific places in*

Izquierda Republicana (Spanish party), 21, 165, 175. *See also* Left republicans

Jackson, Gabriel, 16, 261n16

Japan, 157, 194, 249

Japanese language, 31

Jerusalem (Holy Land), 75–76, 85, 114, 266n6

Jews: in Al-Andalus, 55, 57, 58, 60, 62, 67–68; culture of, 100; expulsion of, from Spain, 87; in Spain, 4, 5, 58, 65, 201; and Spanish national identity, 81; suffering of, 80. *See also* intermarriage

jihads, 52, 56–57, 63, 76

João III, 120

"José Antonio Primo de Rivera and the Beginning of Falange Española" (Payne), 17

JSU (Juventudes Socialistas Unificadas), 182

Juan (Don), 238, 239

Juan Carlos, 33–35, 226, 228, 241. *See also* Transition (Spain's, from dictatorship to democracy)

Juderías, Julián, 4

Index

Index

World War I: attempts to avoid consequences of, 246; as initiating long-term political and social conflict in Europe, 158, 181, 190–92; in Spain, 200, 234

World War II: Blue Division ("División Azul") in, 187, 193, 238; and Hitler-Stalin Pact, 186, 187, 190, 191, 193; Portugal's neutrality in, 125, 227; question of Spanish Civil War as precursor to, 189–98; Spain's "neutrality" and "non-belligerence" in, 125, 187, 189–90, 192–94, 212–13, 223–24, 237–38; U.S. relations with Spain in, 12, 198, 224

Ximénez de Sandoval, Felipe, 17

Yagüe, Juan, 238
Yale University, 25
Yáñez, Luis, 36
Yeltsin, Boris, 249
Yugoslavia, 94, 208, 248, 255